REAL-WORLD COUPLE
COUNSELING AND THERAPY

REAL-WORLD COUPLE COUNSELING AND THERAPY

An Introductory Guide

Jerrold Lee Shapiro and Terence Patterson

Santa Clara University and University of San Francisco

cognella®

SAN DIEGO

Bassim Hamadeh, CEO and Publisher
Amy Smith, Project Editor
Alia Bales, Production Editor
Jess Estrella, Senior Graphic Designer
Stephanie Kohl, Licensing Coordinator
Natalie Piccotti, Director of Marketing
Kassie Graves, Vice President of Editorial
Jamie Giganti, Director of Academic Publishing

Cover images:
Copyright © 2015 iStockphoto LP/tereks.
Copyright © 2015 iStockphoto LP/tereks.

Printed in the United States of America.

3970 Sorrento Valley Blvd., Ste. 500, San Diego, CA 92121

Brief Contents

Detailed Contents

Preface

The genesis for this book emerged from a number of conversations between the authors and several independent discussions with colleagues. We were both teaching couple therapy graduate classes, Patterson at USF and Shapiro at Santa Clara University. We compared and shared syllabi, texts, correlated reading materials, and approaches to classroom activities. The upshot of that professional collaboration was a common perspective that neither of us was particularly pleased with recent introductory texts for our students, particularly younger students in the 21st century.

The conversation naturally led to a potential of writing such a text. The pluses were that we each had taught graduate-level couple counseling and therapy for decades, and we both also had practices, with a specialty in working with couples. We were also comfortable working together and playing together as friends.

There was one major potential challenge. Although both of our practices and teaching were informed by systems theory, there was a major difference in our core theoretical approaches. Patterson works from a CBT (cognitive behavioral therapy) perspective and Shapiro from an existential orientation.

In some ways, these theories could not be much different. Existential psychotherapy is phenomenological and subjective, and follows an inductive logic (Shapiro, 2016). CBT is more deterministic, objective, and deductive. As we discussed our approaches in greater depth and began to present together at major conferences, it became clear that although we were approaching the couple from different angles, there were several points of similarity in our interventions, timing, and outcomes. This allowed us the opportunity to appreciate the differences, see some great points of integration, and kid each other about how the other was "obviously misguided."

Most of this text focuses on a variety of issues from that common integrated perspective. Two key aspects of treatment from both perspectives coincided particularly well. We believe that the therapeutic relationship and process are more important in couple care than specific techniques. We also both believe that clients come to therapy with a wide range of beliefs and orientations toward change. In a sense, clients have theories (Shapiro & Bohart, 2014). Some clients require insight before behavioral change; others respond exactly the opposite way—with behavior change preceding understanding. Some hold to free will philosophies; others are more deterministic in their beliefs.

What is essential in this process is that therapists adapt to clients' states. We assess a couple's goals, determine the approaches that best fit the client couple, and then proceed within that very personalized framework. When members of a couple provide distinctly different ways of viewing their worlds and perspectives on change, the effective therapist adjusts to each one, serves as a "universal translator," and helps each partner learn to understand, appreciate, and use the other's strengths.

We have observed consistently that, particularly in the current environment of financial, political, and social stress, couples want change on specific issues within a relatively short time and that our approaches must be adaptable to meet their needs. In this sense, our approach is *pragmatic*, with some interventions that fit our individual models and others are adopted from alternative perspectives that are uniquely relevant to each couple.

Our casual, yet informed observation is that most successful therapists adopt this approach rather than apply their model to each couple *carte blanche* in a formulaic, rigid manner. In essence, we agree with Lebow (1997, 2014) that we are in an integrative era in psychotherapy, and that one's preferred theoretical orientation does not determine all we do. Nonetheless, we believe it is important to have a basic model from which to operate, a template that can be drawn on and adapted flexibly.

We work toward helping couples come to realistic goals and work as a team to attain them. Our own process in coming to deal with our differences paralleled that in creating the text for this work. Like most teams (and client couples) we do not always agree. Where the authors disagree in this text, we offer text boxes, identifying and highlighting those differences. In the final chapter, the two therapists address the same client couple from our dissimilar perspectives, exploring places of consensus and disagreement. As we do with our graduate students and trainees, we leave it ultimately to readers to adopt their own approach, using what we have to offer, and to go beyond. Thus, your own world view, values, and personality enter into the equation.

On Culture

Almost every textbook in psychotherapy these days notes the importance of client and therapist cultures by presenting these in a separate chapter. We believe that the cultural issues are so important and so ubiquitous that we have taken the approach we use both clinically, and in teaching. We integrate cultural considerations into the clinical framework and present cultural differences throughout the text. At several points, we point out our strong belief that all couples are to some extent, cross-cultural, that each couple client we see has a distinctive cultural background and unique values that must be joined as part of the therapy.

One exception to this overall synthesized approach is a separate chapter (11) on the current, highly conflictual culture issue of gender. We include this more in-depth perspective on this topic primarily because it is so understudied in the couple therapy literature and secondly because the issue of gender is so controversial in today's culture. Although we include gender issues as part and parcel of all therapy with couples, we also highlight several specific issues related to gender, less to set them apart, but primarily to underscore their salience. Indeed, the method for incorporating gender in psychotherapy is similar to the manner of dealing with all cultural issues and of individuality.

Just as the notion that there is no "one-size-fits-all" form of successful therapy, we believe that there is no singular answer for all couples. Despite the use of many skills and common techniques, it is an error to consider any one couple to be exactly like any other (or as representative of any cultural group). It is an easy error to make. Indeed, it is important to note that when a therapist has done several couple intake sessions in a single day, without clear contemporaneous notes, there is a tendency for our minds to blend them together—losing sight of the uniqueness of each couple. For example, two couples may have a seemingly identical communication misconnection. Yet one of them needs to learn how to communicate, and particularly listen more effectively, while the other somehow uses miscommunication, as a means to avoid addressing major structural problems in their relationship. Clearly these issues cannot be treated as equivalent.

As much as possible, our synthesis of divergent theories, systems, and multicultural and developmental perspectives is designed to conform to best practices, wide-ranging research, and evidence-based standards in the field.

A FEW CONVENTIONS FOR THIS BOOK

Vignette Format

There are several vignettes and case examples in this book. In each, the first initial of the client is used for identification and the letter T is used to identify the therapist. Thus, if the clients (identified in the first chapter) are named Frankie and Johnny, the form of the vignette looks like this:

F (for Frankie): The problem is that Johnny is irresponsible.

J (for Johnny): Look. I apologized for the soccer game mishap; why can't you ever let go of anything?

T (for Therapist): This sounds like an issue that has been going on for some time. You, Frankie, are concerned about trust, and Johnny you feel like you are constantly being evaluated.

F: Yeah. I need to talk about the soccer game, and he says he is done going over it.

In many vignettes, the therapist's thoughts are included in addition to the chosen interventions. In these cases, the thoughts are set aside with parentheses and where appropriate, italicized.

Boxes and Figures

There are several boxes in the text that (a) provide case examples, (b) highlight differences between approaches, and (c) provide some questions for the reader.

When Our Theories Differ

Several times throughout the text, we provide opposing views, based in our theoretical perspectives. Whenever those occur, we provide both perspectives, usually in adjacent text boxes.

Acknowledgments

Any project like this involves input and encouragement from many people. Many of our colleagues expressed encouragement, excitement, and amazement that we would approach a couple therapy text from existential and cognitive behavior perspectives. Their support (and often skepticism) for the project were important motivators.

Our graduate students at the University of San Francisco (Patterson) and Santa Clara University and the University of Hawaii (Shapiro) have been a source of unending support for both of us as we tried out and honed our approaches to couple therapy over the past several decades. Their responses to a wide variety of therapeutic approaches have been informative and inspirational. We delight in the fact that so many are currently working effectively with couples as professional counselors and psychotherapists.

We also wish to thank the College of Education and Counseling Psychology at Santa Clara University for the research grant that helped defray costs for our graduate student assistant. Thanks also to several colleagues who read and commented on drafts of the manuscript. A special thanks to Dr. Sherry Wang at Santa Clara University who offered considerable assistance on the gender chapter.

In particular, we wish to acknowledge the inestimable assistance of Valentina Roveri, M.A. She served as our research assistant and also as editor of each draft of the document. Ms. Roveri, a recent (2019) graduate of Santa Clara University's master's program in counseling psychology was able to help us maintain our unique perspectives, and also to focus on a synthesis that constitutes what we hope is a real-world approach to couple therapy. In short, she served as our professional "couple therapist."

Our spouses (Susan and Jody) teach us inestimable lessons and ground us and also give us the opportunity to practice (gently) what we learn. Without them, our ideas would be more hypothetical than real.

Finally, a great deal of appreciation to Kassie Graves, acquisition editor, and to the production and editorial staff at Cognella Academic Publishing. This is the third book she has done with Dr. Shapiro, and her faith in the project and support were essential in making this book a reality.

Introduction

Dear Dr. X: I know this letter will come to you out of the blue after so many years. I have been specializing in couple therapy now for almost 20 years. Although I hated you for making me try it at the beginning, I think (as I'm sure you suspected, even back then) that I am doing it well. The specific reason for my letter is that I remembered something you said to me in class once. You apologized and said, "I dropped the ball on that one." Of course as a 26-year-old, I wasn't happy that you could make a mistake. I remember that you inquired about how that was for me and I said (do you remember?) I was shaken and relieved, and you said, "That's a lot like being a therapist or a partner in a relationship."

Well, I made a real blunder with a couple last week. It was so bad, I obsessed about it and, very atypically, I called them after the session to inquire how they were doing and when they said they were "shook up" by what I said, I apologized and said I'd like to explain what I meant to say in the next session. I will conclude by telling you that session went great and my clients said, "That was a huge lesson, that anyone can make a mistake and what is important is what you do to correct the error." Thank you for still being my teacher and being willing to acknowledge your mistakes.

I hope you think of me as a success though.

1

Introduction to Couple Therapy

Beginning a book like this is somewhat akin to starting couple therapy. There is a desire to get everything right, to connect effectively, to include everything known, to show both empathy and professionalism. It is daunting. Hopefully, what will be offered is useful and demonstrates true caring along with flexibility to be of value to a wide range of clinicians. As tempting as it may be, this will not represent simply "a highlight reel" of great moments in couple therapy. In baseball terminology, there will be runs, hits, and errors as we explore the reality of very difficult work, along with best practices to approach the inevitable difficulties.

The text focuses on what beginners need to know as well as serves as a refresher for those more experienced. We have been professors teaching graduate-level introductory and advanced classes in couple therapy and practitioners working with couples in distress for over 80 years combined.

When two individuals join together as a couple, each brings her or his prior lifetime of experiences, beliefs, history, values, and culture to the mix. The couple combination requires understanding of different backgrounds, adaptations to each other, negotiation, and compromise. The resultant couple unit draws from each and takes on a blended character. In therapy we need to understand each individual and also the integration he or she creates.

Just as we approach couple therapy from each individual's viewpoint and from his or her combined perspective, looking for strengths in their combination, we approach this book from two different theoretical orientations: Patterson from a cognitive behavioral theory foundation (CBT) and Shapiro from an existential/humanistic model. Our integration synthesizes these with systems and multicultural and developmental perspectives. As much as possible, the approaches conform to best practices and evidence-based standards in the field. Where there are clear differences in comprehension, case planning, and interventions, we have provided both perspectives, side by side. We fully expect that readers will find some value in understanding both the divergences and convergences to help inform their own viewpoints and procedures.

A Few Basic Acknowledgements

It is important to state what might seem obvious but is often not heeded in real-world work with couples:

1. Although couple psychology and therapy have some correlation to individual, family, and group therapy, it is not a direct extension of these other modalities. It is a specialty area in its own right that needs to be learned through unique training and supervised experience.
2. It can seem chaotic, overwhelming, and worrisome to clinicians who are trying to track simultaneous multiple interactions. Delving into the area without the requisite competence crosses ethical and often legal standards.
3. The ethical issues are different and complex. Most basic is a clear three-way understanding of what the couple wants to accomplish in therapy. There may also be different views regarding what would be considered a successful outcome. Assessment is more multifaceted and contains a unique component of defining who is the client, a decision that requires close collaboration between therapist and clients. Is it either or both of the partners? Is it the relationship? Is it all of these?
4. Therapists and clients will inevitably make errors that can be far reaching. The critical issue is how those errors are addressed.

Complexities of Couple Therapy

Frankie and Johnny have come to see you. They've been married for 14 years after dating for 2 years. They have two children ages 12 and 8. When Frankie called, she asked for an emergency appointment. After a brief phone conversation, they agreed to come in the next morning at 8:00 a.m. When they arrived, she seemed very angry. She spread out in the middle cushion of the couch, nonverbally indicating that it would be uncomfortable for anyone to sit on either side of her. Johnny seemed nonplussed and detached. He took a seat in the swivel chair to the right of his wife. The therapist sat in the other matching swivel chair.

The therapist began by saying, "I spoke briefly with Frankie, so I'd like to begin, Johnny, by asking you what brings you here."

J: Her (indicating his wife, but not looking at her).

T: And why are *you* here?

J: She said she'd take the kids and leave if I didn't come in. I don't even know why she is so pissy the past few days.

F: (blurting almost explosively). Tell her what you forgot!

J: Well if I forgot something, I don't even know what it was.

T: Frankie. You seem very upset that Johnny forgot something. Please tell me what it is.

F: He *forgot* to go to Ian's soccer game and when he arrived late, he forgot to bring the snacks.

J: The game time was changed, and I had the snacks she bought, but then I had to take her car in for repairs and so I had the wrong car.

T: That sounds like a bad scene. I am interested in what makes it so hurtful for you (toward Frankie).

F: I don't know why I even bother. This marriage is already broken. Why should we spend any time on funerals and post-mortems? (while Johnny glares at her).

At this point, the therapist is aware of the tension in the room and each partner's desire to be "right," regardless of the cost. There are a host of questions to be considered. How to begin?

How is Frankie's view of Johnny missing a soccer game an emergency? What makes Frankie quickly conclude that the marriage is broken?

She decides to try to explore the underlying hurt or anxiety to see why this incident is so relationship threatening.

J: She is always ready to go to the "nuclear option." Either everything gets done her way or the marriage is over.

T: You (Johnny) see Frankie's reaction as extreme. Frankie, what about the situation makes this so important for you?

F: (Glaring at Johnny) He *never* comes through on his promises.

T: So, for you, the soccer incident is one small part of a bigger worry. Is it about trust or something else?

F: (calming somewhat) No. You got it. I don't feel like I can trust him.

T: Johnny, what do you hear Frankie saying? It's more than the soccer.

J: You know I am trustworthy and follow though most of the time. I just can't stand her judging whether I have done everything to her standard.

T: So, you are anxious about being criticized and Frankie is anxious about trust.

Because of the higher likelihood of escalations and couple-induced volatility, there is less time for the therapist to ease into it as in individual therapy. Nonetheless, it is time to lean in, take a deep breath, take charge of the session by beginning to comment on these issues, and ask their consent to explore the aspects of their relationship that led them to their current extreme positions. If they are open to it, some initial understanding might be possible (e.g., their mutual anxiety). It will also be essential to explore whether they are truly "at the end of their" rope as a couple and whether they want to explore options to separate or divorce. Individual sessions with each or referral to individual therapists may assist them in expressing any such desires.[1]

As an indication of the hard work required, several experts have weighed in on working with such a couple: Bader and Pearson describe this work as "piloting a helicopter in a hurricane" (Weil, 2012); Jackson referred to this type of couple as the "Gruesome Twosome;" (Watzlawick, Bavelas, & Jackson, 1967, p. 88), and Perel (2018) adds, "Couples therapy is probably the hardest type of therapy to be in and to practice; and I have been on both sides."

Components of Effective Couple Therapy

Many clinicians and authors (Rober, 2015; Weeks, Odell, & Methven, 2005: Weil, 2012) note that one of the major factors making couple therapy hard is that because it is less well understood than individual therapy, clients often delay coming in until matters are dire. It is clear, for example, that Frankie's anger and threat to end the relationship has been building for some time and includes a lengthy accrual of resentments and perceptions of Johnny as someone on whom she cannot rely.

Couples often let matters fester because each person is looking for a change in the partner rather than him- or herself, providing less motivation for the kind of self-examination that makes therapy work. They may also minimize a problem as "a phase" that will pass. These delays usually mean matters are worse when they finally do come in. Because of this, the first order of business is getting them level enough and "therapy ready."

Key Common Factors for Couple Therapy

There are several common factors for effective couple therapy. They are explored in greater detail in later chapters.

- **Building an alliance.** The first factor requires making a close connection with each member of the couple, especially the person who is less motivated for therapy. The alliance can be tricky, because either can perceive connection with the other partner as taking sides and because, unlike individual therapy, there are several alliances to consider (e.g., therapist with partner 1; therapist with partner 2; and therapist with the couple as a unit or system).
- **Finding the relational or systemic aspect.** Second, with most couples, there is a learning curve regarding what couple therapy is and what it is not. Often the first misunderstanding that needs to be disavowed is that the therapist will listen to each person's litany of complaints and "judge" who is correct. Instead, once a

---

[1] Patterson is among the couple therapists who often have individual sessions with the members of the couple. Shapiro prefers to see the couple together and to refer for separate individual work.

careful assessment has determined that there is not serious individual psycho-pathology in one or both members, the therapist often has to help the couple redefine the problem as a relational rather than personal one. By redefining the couple discomforts as a result of interpersonal chemistry and as side effects of attempts to fix things, rather than individual intrapsychic phenomena, each person can begin to evaluate how he or she is contributing to the problems rather than simply blaming the partner.

- **Assessing for strengths and weaknesses.** Third, during assessment, strengths in the relationship must be assessed along with weaknesses. Those identified strengths will later be used to address the problems. We have seen many couples in which a single disagreement colors an otherwise fairly strong connection. Once the problem area can be placed in proper perspective, the strengths can be brought to bear on the outlying experience. Highlighting strengths also minimizes clients' expectations that they will be *blamed* for the dysfunction in the relationship.

- **Developing effective communication.** Fourth, therapy begins when there is common ground on which to address problems. Almost invariably, ineffective communication impedes getting to the real underlying issues and resultant potential solutions. For many couples, effective communication can be the pathway to discovery rather than the substance of the core issues facing the couple.

  Helping a couple clear up their ineffective communication is necessary. This may involve some education about listening to each other non-defensively (not necessarily agreeing) and responding empathically. Communication may also involve each partner comprehending the other partner's process and manner of dealing with the world based on past experiences. For example, if one member of a couple understands his or her relational world primarily from a cognitive/logical framework and the other perceives it from a more affective/kinesthetic perspective, they each have to learn to respect those differences and work to communicate in the native processing language of the partner.

- **Uncover what the poor communication and/or symptoms hide.** Miscommunication often obfuscates deeper problems. Only when the communication is clear and they both understand one another do some couples discover far more serious rifts and structural problems between them. For example, when a couple is constantly bickering about the "proper" way to squeeze a toothpaste tube, in which cabinet pots and pans should go, who is responsible for taking out the garbage on the proper day, how to "properly" load the dishwasher, or whether the toilet paper should roll over or under, they may be missing the far more important question of the fear of rejection if they are found wrong about anything or resentment over feeling controlled by their partner. Effective therapy will be able to address the underlying and most important fear only when the communication turns from bickering to an attempt to understand the partner.

  The sequence of beginning with communication work underscores a basic tenet of all therapy and is especially true of couple therapy: *Always begin with where the clients are, not where the therapist wants them to go!* This means accepting and working within their values, cultural norms, history, and needs from their families of origin, style, and clear, mutual collaboration on goals. It also requires attending to the logistics and practical realities of scheduling, finances, and client expectations of a course of therapy for six, 12, or more sessions or for a brief "problem-solving" consultation. Asking clients to do at the beginning of therapy what is hoped for at the end is likely an exercise in futility. For example, if a couple is like Frankie and Johnny, telling Frankie to calm down and talk logically is akin to trying to put out a fire with an accelerant. Of course, a goal of therapy is to help remove the impediments to her feeling safe enough to address her relationship with less volatility. This also requires helping Johnny to be more receptive to her concerns far earlier in a conversation, and for her to understand what effect angry criticism has for him. Those can be achieved only after therapeutic alliances are formed, trust is established, and the couple is ready to face one another more vulnerably.

- **Empathy for process and saying the unsayable.** The therapist may need to take on two somewhat opposite roles: acceptance of the couple's behavior, showing understanding and empathy for processes that led to the current interaction, and by contrast, being willing to say the unsayable, to confront them, to bring out what the couple will not say to elicit private experiences of each.

- **Find meaning and the consequences of symptoms.** It is usually useful to help each partner find meaning in what he or she is doing or thinking and those behaviors and thoughts of his or her mate. One aspect of that meaning is for the couple to appreciate that their current behavior, as painful as it may be, is a dynamic, often characteristic, mutual attempt to resolve a more significant dilemma. Frankie and Johnny's escalating to the relationship level over a failed soccer game responsibility may represent a subconscious agreement or a systemic adaptation to avoid a larger threat. As it turned out after several sessions, they began to address a mutual terror of abandonment. By threatening to leave over what seemed a minor infraction on the surface, they didn't have to face a far more frightening prospect—that of being rejected for who they were or that their relationship was on a shaky foundation versus over a minor incident.

  As it was later discovered, Johnny had been abandoned as a child by his unwed mother and subsequently when his grandmother died when he was only 9. Frankie's history was pockmarked with physical abuse from excessively strict parents and an ejection from the family home when she was 16.

- **Problem solving.** Problem solving is common in couple work. Whether it involves guided (Socratic) questioning, recommendations of experiments in session, or homework, it is essential for couples to seek better solutions to their problems than the ones they have coming into therapy.

- **Unique termination.** Termination in couple therapy needs to focus on the couple's functioning as a team as well as on the implications of the end of the therapeutic relationship. Transfer of training is essential in all short-term therapies and especially so in couple therapy.

These criteria of couple counseling and therapy are not completely unique to this text. In their 2012 review of over 40 years of couple therapy studies, Benson, McGinn, and Christensen distilled the most successful methods of intervention. They reported that there were five principles that governed the most effective forms of couple therapy. Although their ordering and language is slightly different, they cover similar grounds. Like the ones we have laid out, all of these methods assume that serious pathology, domestic violence, anger management, or abuse have been attended to, often with referrals. Their interventions methods, based on CBT and behaviorally oriented studies include the following:

1. *Altering views of the relationship.* "[I]t is important to increase the extent to which both partners' view of the relationship is objective, dyadic, and contextualized, rather than one-sided and blaming. Most individuals have not fully considered their partners' perspectives on their conflicts or how their own behavior may contribute to relational difficulties" (Benson et al., 2012, p. 26).

   Whitbourne (2012), commenting on the Benson study, stated, "[A]s long as they focus on altering the way the relationship is understood, the couple can start to see each other, and their interactions, in more adaptive ways" (p. 2). Barlow, Allen, and Choate (2004) describing this from a CBT perspective, state, "[A]ltering emotion-based misappraisals of salient events, or helping clients recognize how many of their beliefs about their experiences, as well as their ability to cope with those experiences, may be inaccurate" (p. 222).

2. *Modifying dysfunctional interactions.* When couples engage in behavior that is clearly dysfunctional or leads to the opposite of what they claim is their goal, the therapist has to step in to do what is necessary to reduce or substitute those actions. Sometimes this involves operating as an "emotional traffic cop" halting and guiding interactions. As Snyder, Simpson, and Hughes (2006) describe it, the activation of vulnerabilities in therapy often generates emotional dysregulation that must be addressed and deescalated. It is critical to defuse escalating arguments as early as possible, particularly when violence, harsh accusations, (ad hominem) name-calling, and insulting, dismissive words are used. Jacobson, Gottman and Shortt (1995) referred to a type of domestic violence perpetrators as "vagal reactors," indicating that such escalations can have physiological as well as psychological roots.

3. *Eliciting avoided private behavior.* Getting clients to self-disclose their unspoken thoughts and, particularly, feelings can greatly enhance the possibility of greater intimacy. Benson and colleagues (2012) conclude, "While it is possible for couples to be satisfied in their relationships without a great deal of emotional disclosure, when a couple becomes distressed and enters therapy, they are likely to be experiencing emotions and anxieties about the relationship itself and intimate disclosure becomes necessary to restore satisfaction." (p. 29). Gottman and Gottman (2006) concur, arguing that avoidance/withdrawal is a key factor in relational disruption. Similarly, Goldman and Greenberg (2007), operating with an emotion-focused therapy (EFT) orientation, conclude that uniquely vulnerable emotions lead to far greater chances of intimacy.

4. *Improving communication.* Many clients require some sort of coaching or modeling of effective communication. Far more than stopping abusive or poor interactions, the best communication involves demonstrations of active non-defensive listening, empathy, and reflective responses. Partners need to inform each other what they need from each other and more significantly what they want if they desire the best responses from their mates. Some in-session role-playing with the therapist modeling better communication can enhance couples adopting these methods,

such that each partner is able to fully understand and *validate* (not necessarily agree with) the other's feelings and perceptions.

5. Promoting couple strengths. By indicating the strengths in a relationship, therapists can offer perspective and enhance resilience. Benson and colleagues (2012) argue that all successful therapies emphasize strengths at the end of therapy if not throughout the sessions. Gottman and Gottman (2015) encourage the increase of the ratio of positive to negative statements to 5:1 in the relationship. In addition, when couples are asked directly what their partner desires (e.g., Bader & Pearson, 2016), they usually know well what would be positive and they can be encouraged to emphasize those forms of interaction rather than the obstructive ones.

Goals and methods to promote strengths for couples include discovery of self and partner, assisting the couple in appreciating one another, emphasizing and expressing thankfulness for positive experiences, accepting and resolving inevitable conflicts, focusing on dreams and fantasies and making realistic ones occur, and sharing meaning.

Several models of couple therapy focus on individual differentiation (Scharff & Scharff, 2004; Schnarch, 1997/2009; Siegel, 2015) and personal development of each partner. From a very different orientation, Halford (2002) espouses *self-regulation couple therapy* (SRCT), emphasizing the ultimate objective of each person taking responsibility for his or her own happiness and roles in the relationship.

These coordinate well with Gottman and Gottman's (2015) "sound relationship house." One example of great moments in many parents' lives is during quiet times at home noticing their child do something incredibly cute and sharing knowing smiles in real time (Shapiro, 1993). This has often been referred to as "Catch 'em being good;" intimate partners can do the same.

Common Problems in Couple Therapy

We would be remiss if we did not consider the most common issues couples bring to therapy. Several studies and surveys detail the kinds of issues common in couple therapy.

Whisman, Dixon, and Johnson (1997) reported that the "big five" were lack of loving feelings, power struggles, communication, extramarital affairs, and unrealistic expectations. Gurman (2013a), using much more theoretically based language, listed "the defining characteristics of and central culprits in couple disharmony: affective dysregulation, insecure attachment, poor communication and problem-solving, projective identification, power imbalances, faulty attributions, hierarchical incongruities, thin narratives, and poor differentiation" (p. 424).

Our experience with couples provides a similar list of 11 presenting issues that bring couples in for counseling and therapy:

- Communication problems
- Inequity in sharing responsibilities
- Ineffective decision-making and problem-solving methods
- A discrepancy between what is expected and what is real
- Parenting concerns
- Power struggles
- Financial concerns
- Family-of-origin problems

- Loss of loving feelings
- (Chronic) medical issues
- Boundary issues including the following:
  - Extramarital affairs
  - Intrusions of work into the relationship
  - Cultural insensitivity and misunderstanding
  - In-law issues
  - Living conditions

These are all addressed in depth throughout the text. We are specifically excluding from the list such major issues as individual psychopathology, domestic violence, and addictions, because these characteristically require other major interventions before true couple work may begin in earnest.

Therapeutic Approaches

Almost every form of therapeutic approach has been applied to couples. In the fifth edition of their classic edited text, Gurman, Lebow, and Snyder (2015) provide 12 theoretical methodologies divided into behavioral, emotion-centered, psychodynamic, social constructionist, and systemic approaches. In the companion clinical casebook text, Gurman (2010) offers 17 different theoretical approaches. This places couple therapy not as a singular orientation, but rather a *specialty area* within other models (i.e., there can be psychodynamic, humanistic, or behavioral couple therapy with subcategories within each, and some identified with pioneering individuals or other emerging approaches). Common foundations across approaches include a systemic context, a developmental framework, and cultural competency.

As expected, the choice of a particular theoretical approach involves many factors that emerge from the assessment: client needs, nature of the presenting (and potential deeper problems), therapist training and skill set, time and financial constraints, cultural factors, and so on. The "dodo bird" factor (Wampold et al., 1997) doesn't apply solely to individual therapies. Like for all other therapy modalities, there is no one-size-fits-all approach that assures success. Two factors seem to produce better outcomes: the mix between therapist and client theories of change (Shapiro, 2016) and a focus on function (and context) over form of therapy (Gurman, 2013b). All couple problems are not identical. Client personalities are dissimilar and what constitutes success for one client maybe different than others. What does seem clear is that therapist and the couple agree on the problem to be addressed and collaborate on an amelioration. As Gurman (2013b) suggests, the most salient universal factor about approaches is what occurs in a particular context. Without understanding the context in which a couple functions or acts in the here-and-now exchange with the therapist, it is easy to make inaccurate assumptions about the needs for any couple. Follette and Callahan (2008) describe this as "functional contextualization" which Gurman (2013a) associates with the third wave of behavioral therapy and Shapiro (2010, 2016) sets as the basis for existential couple therapy.

It is axiomatic that couple therapy is one in which a significant part of the context (the partner) is present in real time, rather than as a report. One of the great advantages of working with couples is that you get to be present with the real partner. Of course, this acts as a pressure cooker in both positive and potentially volatile ways.

The bottom line here is to begin where the couple and its individual members are functioning and use their values, styles, language, and beliefs in formulating any approach. It may well be behaviorally, cognitively, emotionally, attachment, or meaning centered. The therapist may take a more or less active role, be more warm or confrontive, closer or distant, but it should all be based on the clients and the context in which they live. As Messer (2001) calls it, therapists engage in "assimilative integration," in which form is secondary to function. Indeed, when clients recognize the precedence of function, they tend to appreciate more the therapeutic endeavor.

Formats of Couple Therapy

Therapy with couples can occur in almost any format. The most typical is the weekly 50–90-minute session. One author (Patterson) regularly does 90-minute sessions, believing that in shorter sessions much is often left unaddressed, depending on the volatility and unpredictability that may occur in any session. However, there are many variations. For example, solution-focused couple therapy (Hoyt, 2015) treats each session as a "one-and-done" complete unit. Couples sign up each time for a future session. There are also intensive, "marathon" sessions of several hours at a time. Other formats include sessions separated by agreed-on weeks or months. Sometimes couple therapy is integrated with individual therapy, either with the same or different therapists.

Tillich (2016) offers a format in which each client has an individual therapist on the same team. They meet for individual sessions and all together for joint couple sessions. Other uses of multiple-therapist approaches are through one-way mirrors with a consulting team, often associated with family therapy (i.e., the MRI approach). Some treatment is in groups of three to five couples (e.g., Coche, 2011; Coche & Coche, 1990). Finally, there are manualized approaches to couple work, commonly used in university-based outcome research.

Termination in couple therapy may also be different. It is clear from longitudinal studies that the effects of positive couple therapy may deteriorate over time. Many couple therapists provide the clients with continuing plans of action to work on issues as they arise outside of therapy. These may include exercises, warnings, and even predictions of some drop off to help ease the transition. Many also leave the door open for couples to return for "refresher sessions," or what one couple liked to refer to as a "regular oil change and lube" every couple of (months or) years post therapy.

The Evidence Base of Couple Therapy

As difficult as it is to accurately and usefully measure outcomes of individual therapy, couple therapy is far more complicated. There are an increasing number of empirical tests and quantitative (some RCTs) and qualitative studies. Many have provided significant insights into both the effectiveness of couple work and of the measurement difficulties. For example, Whisman, Dixon, and Johnson (1997) reported a treatment success rate of close to two-thirds of the couples in their exploration of primarily behaviorally oriented treatments.

Hewison, Casey, and Mwamba (2016) reported that psychodynamic approaches to therapy in naturalistic settings in the United Kingdom produced significantly positive results in the same general range. Stratton and colleagues (2015) after reviewing 227 studies on couple and family therapy in the first decade of the 21st century, concluded, "[T]his body of recent research supports (previously reported) claims of effectiveness" (p. 1).

A study by Snyder and Wills (1989) reported varying results in a study of insight-oriented versus behavioral therapy, with behavioral being more effective at termination and insight oriented being superior in a longitudinal follow-up. There was some dispute, in this study and others, over which variable constituted "effectiveness." For example, the argument was made that post-therapy divorce actually constituted "success" in that issues had been clarified and the decision was made to accept irreconcilable differences and pursue separately each partner's mental health.

Johnson (2003) reported that a variety of traditional and cognitive behavior therapies and emotion-focused therapies characteristically produced success rates in the 70% range across a number of studies. She indicated that a general finding of follow-up studies have generally shown greater longer-term success when emotional and insight factors are included in the treatment. This was magnified in at least one study, when the presenting problem was relationship distress, with EFT showing recovery rates roughly double the rate of cognitive and behavioral therapies reported by Baucom, Shoham, Mueser, Daiuto, and Stickle (1998).

Special Difficulties of Evidence for Couple Therapy Research

This last two-to-one finding exemplifies a real difficulty of comparative theoretical approaches. The goal of the therapy across studies can be quite different. Whereas reduction in the *Diagnostic and Statistical Manual* (DSM-5) of the American Psychiatric Association (2013) level symptom may favor one approach, relationship distress may favor another.

There are many other concerns about research into couple therapy that must be addressed before such studies are sufficiently useful to clinicians facing a couple with specific (and somewhat unique) problems (Sexton, Weeks, & Robbins, 2003).

There is a general bias in the literature favoring RCT studies, which are often referred to as the "gold standard." Unfortunately, while such studies are welcome and quite informative, RCTs are in fact a gold standard for pharmaceutical trials and funding agencies but are generally insufficient to capture the complex contexts in which couple work occurs. They favor the notion that it is the method, rather than the relationship or an interaction between the two, that heals. In addition, therapist experience and quality are somewhat uncontrolled; outcome measures are inconsistent across studies; and attention-placebo or comparison control groups are often nonexistent—comparing couple therapy to no therapy (often called "treatment as usual"). RCT studies are by their very nature more constrained in scope and in dependent measures, making transfer to the general clinical setting more challenging. In responding to these concerns, many RCT studies are focused on reduction of specific symptom patterns such as PTSD, domestic violence, or addiction.

Additional concerns involve internal factors within the couple such as disagreement between members of a couple regarding what constitutes success and scoring problems. For example, a study might reasonably consider an amicable break-up as a failure according to the study protocol, when for the couple it could be a subjective success.

Finally, the better studies require large-scale, long-term investigations that are usually very expensive. General funding in recent years has been limited to "medical necessity" variables, described in the current version of the DSM. This also regards treatment that allows for third-party (insurance) reimbursement. Nowhere in the DSM is there a viable category for couple problems.

The Rest of the Evidence Story

When it comes to hard-core empirical data, we are still a nascent field. Advances, however, are being made with the influx of qualitative and mixed-method approaches to studying couple work. This allows for greater sensitivity to the couple context and larger external environment in which a couple exists. It also provides more of the rich color and depth of couple life.

It is easy to be cynical when all these difficulties come into awareness, but there is also some very positive news. Those consistent overall numbers that indicate that two-thirds or more of the couples that come into therapy show improvement are impressive and compelling. Most well-trained practitioners of couple counseling and therapy have innumerable examples of successes.

The overall success rate is even more impressive when we realize that roughly 70% of psychotherapists report doing at least some couple therapy. As Lebow, Chambers, Christensen, and Johnson (2012) indicate, this suggests that much of this work is carried out by untrained professionals. That could create quite a drag on positive results. Studies in which well-trained clinicians use almost any of the major approaches to couple work (e.g., Hewison et al., 2016) show consistent positive results.

Process components of successful couple therapy involve understanding of common factors in couple work. Sprenkle, Davis, and Lebow (2009) describe the importance of describing, conceptualizing, and intervening at the relationship level. Approaching the relationship as the client, and problems as *between the partners*, is incompatible with the DSM's *within client* viewpoint, yet it seems, clinically, as particularly effective. They also indicate the salience of expanding the therapeutic alliance to both members and the couple unit, per se. This last capability can be difficult at many levels; it is common for a therapist to find one partner more likable and easier to connect with and even when the alliance is objectively fair and split evenly, and one or both clients may perceive it as taking the other's side. This is especially true when in a first session the therapist must develop a close alliance with the less-interested partner or face losing the couple entirely.

Another process variable, described by Greenberg, Ford, Alden, and Johnson (1993), Gurman (2013b), and Shapiro (2016), and demonstrated by Snyder (2005) involves noticing, underscoring, exploring, and intervening as in-session shifts occur. Often this involves close attention to nonverbal behavior or subtle shifts between clients. Two crucial shifts may involve the constructs of regard and shared humor between the members of the couple. In hundreds of studies on intimacy and the differences between successful and unsuccessful relationships, these two variables occur almost universally as differentiators (Shapiro & Diamond, 1982).

As Lebow, Chambers, Christensen & Johnson (2012) indicate, one major factor that is common in distressed couples entering treatment is a sense of demoralization, including an overhanging worry that the relationship may be doomed. Awareness of the bulk of the research may allow therapists to be far more positive and hopeful, knowing that more than 70% of couples who enter therapy leave happier about their relationship.

Of course, "happier" is a nonspecific word that may denote a number of perspectives from gleeful and content to "relieved." The latter may well indicate that even though it may become clear that a couple's differences are not resolvable, they may feel that the stalemate is shifting toward resolution and their dissatisfaction with the status quo will be resolved by dissolution of the relationship and moving on to a better situation for each partner.

Happy? Maybe, but feeling dragged out of the mud and having hope for a better future is often a highly desirable outcome. We make it clear to couples that as much as we may personally like to see them walking together hand in hand into the sunset, our main goal is for each of them to be "happy" (i.e., mentally healthy). Many years ago, Frank (1974) identified instilling hope and reducing demoralization as the primary variables in all psychotherapy.

Finally, despite all the hazards, the research is becoming more sophisticated, nuanced, and comprehensive. An interesting model is the 2-year longitudinal study by Christensen and colleagues (2004) and similar later studies. Some commonalities in successful therapies involve shifting the focus away from mutual complaints and toward teamwork approaching a common task, mutual regard, respect and acceptance, sharing of vulnerable emotions, and desirable shifts in behavior.

Whether a therapist favors the primacy of emotions, thoughts, overt behavior, meaning seeking, or psycho-physiology, he or she must be able to be sufficiently flexible to work with what is relevant for understanding *a couple at a particular time*. He or she may well begin with that aspect of human functioning that fits best within the theoretical perspective of choice but must be able to include the clients' way of functioning as the therapy evolves.

Effective couple therapists cast a wide, early assessment net that does not suffer the limitations or particular viewpoint of "reality" offered by any one school or theory (Breunlin, Pinsof, Russell, & Lebow, 2011; Gurman, 2013b).

For purposes of this text, we truly believe that, conducted properly by well-trained professionals, couple therapy can be exceptionally positive, helping clients find what is best for them personally and as part of a couple. This is magnified when the therapist shows flexibility in application of forms of treatment (whether pluralistic or integrative) and plays close attention to the multiple interactions in the therapy room, the internal system of the couple, and the complexities of the external context.

BOX 1.1: A FINAL WORD ABOUT OUTCOME EVIDENCE

Several terms are typically used as the "gold standard." These include *evidence-based practice* (EBP), *empirically validated treatment* (EVT), and even the anachronistic, *empirically supported treatment* (EST). We prefer a "platinum standard," with increasing recognition of *practice-based evidence* (Green, 2008), which refers to the wisdom that comes from the actual experience of clinicians who perform successful therapy. While we hold evidence from rigorous research in high regard, we also believe that taking into account the common factors and the experience of skilled clinicians is essential to success in couple therapy.

It is essential to note that therapist self-knowledge is vital. Couple therapists in particular must have awareness of their own values and biases about relationships, especially when it comes to the primacy of staying together or divorcing. In every community, some therapists are known to work hard to keep a marriage alive and others are known to favor divorce when the problems seem intractable. Some, because of their own personal or religious convictions, discourage cohabitation and premarital sex, while others recommend cohabitation as a way to decide on marriage. Some therapists have personal discomfort with same-sex marriage, interracial or interreligious marriage, open marriage, feminist perspectives, egalitarianism, influences of extended family, cultural differences, or different kinds of commitment.

Biases such as these, or others that may remain subconscious, become significant when they are discordant with the couple's values or antithetical to working effectively with the clients. When there are such ideological discrepancies, it is imperative that a therapist refer the couple to someone who is more compatible, or if that is impossible to self-disclose the differences and give the couple a reasonable choice. To do otherwise would be equivalent to a physician who doesn't believe in preventative medicine but treats a person with diabetes.

Frankie and Johnny

Early in this chapter we provided a short vignette with a couple that is not uncommon to couple therapists. We also described that the two authors have quite different orientations with regard to the issues that arise with such a couple. Here is an example of where the approaches mesh and where they diverge.

Where the Two Approaches Converge: Assessment, Treatment Planning, and Agreement on Goals

Frankie and Johnny were assessed for both individual pathology and relational distress. This included length of time the symptoms have been ongoing and what attempts they had made to correct them.

They agreed that the issue of "responsibility" and the power struggle were long term, that they were exacerbated when the children were born, and that they both felt overloaded with life demands. Frankie also disclosed that the first pregnancy was traumatic and that she was confined to bed rest for almost 4 months.

Neither of them seemed to qualify for a DSM-5 diagnosis, although Frankie's volatility and "going to a relationship-level" threat were noted. As a beginning of goal development, they both agreed that they wanted to make things better and to save their marriage. From what they both reported, neither of the children seemed distressed, but both withdrew when the parents were bickering.

Part of the Treatment Plan Shared With Frankie and Johnny

A treatment plan was designed that began with fixing their destructive, hurtful communication patterns, and an agreement was reached to stop threatening abandonment and ending the relationship. A secondary goal, instigated by the clients, was for them both to be more mutually respectful and for them to focus more on finding ways to please and enjoy their partner.

- **Aspects of the treatment planning goals not shared directly, but carried out validating each partner's perspective.** For Frankie this meant being empathic with her fears of not being able to trust Johnny to come through as he agreed and where that left her in her community and personally.

  For Johnny, empathy would require understanding that all errors were not fatal and acknowledging that it was hard to function when he feared that abandonment was always on the table. Therapy begin with an acknowledgment of the difficult conversation they are having and of the hurt and anger each is experiencing and expressing toward the partner. Validation included acknowledgement that Johnny felt that he could not stand up to Frankie's level of emotion and that he characteristically withdrew in response.

- **Shifting from content to process.** For the couple it was indicated that the circular pattern of pursuing and withdrawing always escalated. As it was enacted in early sessions, they were both informed of the therapist's observation that her high levels of anger and his withdrawal cyclically triggered more and larger expressions of the same.

  To slow the process down temporarily, the initial approach is to begin assessment by exploring how much this is typical for them and how it's a painful aberration. There was also an exploration of each person's and the couple strengths that was approached during this first session. It was also important to explore their courtship and early days of the relationship before addressing the question of how they got to this point and what each of them desires as a goal of our meeting.

- **Instilling hope.** Another aspect of process is that the therapist's calmness and ability to understand both Frankie and Johnny without taking sides or judging, and his focus on their interactions provided them with a sense that this could be resolved and that there was hope for a better future together (based on their expressed goal).

There was also an exploration of each person's and the couple strengths that was approached during this first session. Frankie's suggestion of ending the relationship was reinterpreted as more of a demand for a response than an actual step in splitting.

- **De-escalating arguments/refocusing on individual responsibility.** Once there was sufficient enactment to allow the therapist to understand how Frankie and Johnny's arguments escalated, he began interrupting at earlier points and requested different reactions, particularly personal experiences ("I" statements) instead of descriptions of the partner's faults. For example, when the soccer argument recurred, before Frankie could enumerate Johnny's "sins" and threaten divorce, the therapist asked her, "Frankie, when you can't rely on Johnny, what happens to you inside?" He also kept her from reverting to threats. Meanwhile, she also asked Johnny if he knew what effect his lateness had on Frankie and asked if that was his intention. When Johnny said no, the therapist told him, "Tell Frankie what you were feeling when you knew you'd be late and the snacks hadn't made it into the car you were driving."

Differences in Approaches

Although there are significant similarities in approaches, there is also a fairly wide discrepancy in perspective and points of view between cognitive behavioral couple therapy and existential/experiential modalities. Like most psychotherapy theories, CBT is a deductive approach, beginning with theory, developing hypotheses, and testing them with the clients. By contrast, existential therapies are more phenomenological and inductive. They begin with the interaction, behavior, and relationship; build hypotheses for the here and now; and create theories that are useful in the moment but are not expected to be permanent.

It is valuable each therapist is able to follow either path or some other viable approach. For Frankie and Johnny, here are the differences that would be expected.

How a CBT, deductive approach would differ or add elements include the following:

- The use of couple inventories as part of assessment
- Client use of activities and emotions logs to gather data
- Structured formative evaluation of progress at key phases of treatment
- Structured in-session exercises such as the empty chair or doubling (alter-ego) to elicit emotions
- Individual sessions with each partner to establish individual rapport and obtain additional information
- The use of collateral sessions with other key figures such as family members or close friends
- Specific instructions and inquiry to stop destructive behaviors as soon as they occur
- Handouts and recommended readings as appropriate

How an existential, inductive approach would differ or add elements include the following:

- A focus on the consequences of the current fight (what it does *for* Frankie and Johnny and what it helps them avoid
- The couple's struggle between the security of the status quo and freedom (the fear of facing the unknown)
- Consistent assessment of the awareness, experience, and meaning that the ongoing here and now experience has for each
- A careful exploration of their strengths as expressed through individual and couple-level resistance
- Exploration of existential (useful) anxiety and neurotic anxiety (avoidance of existential anxiety); use of anxiety as the engine of change
- Focus on both affective and cognitive insight and change
- Awareness of how the couple and individual interactions with the therapist reproduce a parallel process with their interpersonal struggles
- The use of the therapist as a person who can share personal (process-level) reactions in real time with the couple

It is clear that each approach has merit and that the choice depends on a number of client, therapist, and situational variables. One might use an amalgam of the two or operate more pluralistically and apply the one method that is presumed best suited to this case at this time.

SUMMARY

Couple therapy and counseling are defined as a unique specialty field with its own requisite training, theoretical orientations, and ethics. Some of the complexities of the field are exemplified in a short vignette of a couple in distress. Approaches to treating Frankie and Johnny are detailed throughout the chapter. Several key components of all forms of couple counseling and therapy are described, along with common agreements across approaches. Common problems for which couple therapy is sought are described along with therapeutic approaches. Various formats for couple work are examined. The evidence for couple therapy is detailed, and a conclusion that the combination of clinical experience and empirical studies demonstrate the value of couple therapy is an effective modality is drawn. The chapter concludes with a return to the vignette of Frankie and Johnny with exploration of two alternative methods (CBT and Existential) that can be used effectively with this couple.

2

Ethical Dilemmas in Working With Couples

Are you

- a trainee in your first practicum?
- a newly licensed therapist from a professional counseling or doctoral program?
- an experienced clinician with a thriving practice?

Place yourself in this scenario in any of the positions, bearing in mind that you have had at most one or two courses in couple therapy:

After three sessions with an individual client, your assessment indicates that your client has moderate clinical anxiety and depression, which began after 2 years of a 6-year marriage. Her symptoms are exacerbated by frequent arguments that escalate over minor issues. There have been periods of separation and repeated verbal abuse, with one incident of pushing each other to the ground. Your client suggests that perhaps they should be treated as a couple. Which ethical, legal, and clinical considerations are relevant to serving this client effectively?

The many aspects of this case will be addressed from the ethical, legal, and clinical perspectives throughout this chapter, but take a moment now to reflect and write down various options you would consider in assisting this client. What individual and couple considerations come to mind?

Couple therapists are advised to be aware of boundaries in role and responsibility that exist between them and their clients. Thinking of ethics for many is like recalling the DMV code: "When can I cross the line and follow the rules, or at least get away with it?" or "How much can I press full speed ahead the way I like without getting caught?" This perception is often due to inadequate ethics training or to a more therapist-centered attitude such as "I'm good and nobody will question me," rather than "I'm here as a public trust and I'll do whatever serves the best needs of my clients." To begin questioning your own attitude, consider the question, "If I am at an intersection at 3:00 a.m. with a No U-turn sign and no one's around for miles, would I make my turn? Your answer keys into whether you may be mostly rule bound, self-directed, or merely afraid of getting into trouble. Existentially and behaviorally, both our well-considered and split-second decisions are rooted in our world views generally, and in our self-concept specifically.

Personal and Philosophical Foundations of Mental Health Ethics

Answers to such questions lie in the philosophical and personal foundations we bring to our work; we often find that the best courses of action are rarely fixed and unchangeable, but that they lie in gray areas. While that may seem disappointing to those who see therapy as pure science or a rule-governed process, discernment and discretion is the hallmark of professional practice, and our decisions rest on art as well as theory, science, and standards of care. We bring our values to our work no matter how hard we may try to be objective. The danger lies in being unaware of how our personal values and beliefs enter into our activities, sometimes without our conscious awareness.

Knapp, Handelsman, Gottlieb, and Vandecreek (2013) offer a perspective that states that various stances on ethics involve an ethics acculturation model professionals tend to follow, much as being integrated into a new culture. The authors delineate "[t]he dark side of ethics" and view therapists as either assimilating, marginalizing, integrating, or separating themselves from ethics and professional standards of care. Those who assimilate tend to be rule governed and follow the letter of the law, leaving their personal values aside. Separators do the opposite and "follow their hearts," believing that their instincts are best; they tend to have low professional boundaries. Those who marginalize have both low personal and professional standards. Those practitioners tend to be the least effective and act in perilous fashion. With *integration* the goal is to have both high personal and professional standards and to follow them to the best advantage of their clients and themselves.

Knapp, Vandecreek, Handelsman, and Gottlieb (2013) also define an "ethical rim" in which the name we use, what we wear, our language, the appearance of our office, and our advertising all come into play, both as a means of self-disclosure and as a method for integrating our personal and professional values. Basically, there is no checking our values or identity at the door; they manifest themselves intentionally or insidiously (Shapiro, 2016).

Forrest (Clay, 2015), a professor emerita at the University of Oregon, says that psychology's education and training community isn't always well equipped to help students navigate the need to achieve competency while negotiating their own identities and beliefs. To help ameliorate this, she is developing a "conscience clause" that would enable students to opt out of training that conflicts with their personal beliefs.[1]

As an additional factor in the mix of making ethical decisions, Lloyd and Hansen (2003) discuss *ethical relativism* versus *ethical absolutism*, which considers whether there

---

1   This is no easy task. Determining whose rights are salient, or whose are being violated, have reached the U.S. Supreme Court in the "Hobby Lobby" case in which an employer was found to be able to restrict certain aspects of healthcare to employees based on owners' religious beliefs. There was a similar ruling in the case of a Colorado baker refusing to make a wedding cake for a same-sex couple. Clients must be informed up front about any such therapist "conscience" issues or religious beliefs that might conflict with clients' needs and values.

exist universal, immutable standards, or whether positions depend on situational or contextual variables.

Most ethical matters in psychotherapy lie in gray areas on a spectrum between absolute and relative, which raises the question, "If we adopt the integrationist position described, how do we bring our personal values and world view into the often ambiguous guidelines that ethical codes provide us?" Most professionals would say they are "people persons" who relish social interaction and helping others, but what of ethical constraints from joining a client at a significant celebration in his or her life when he or she invites us on a cultural and personal basis? How do we refrain from discussing political, artistic, geographic, and other preferences or opinions we have in common with clients? Do we do it always, with discernment, or never? These and other issues are addressed throughout this chapter.

Ethical Issues Related to Working With Couples

When working with couples, all of the ethical standards regarding counseling or therapy with individuals remain salient. For example, fees for individual clients should be unambiguous, related to professional time expended, and within the normative range for the community and the population being served. If sliding scales are offered, clear delineation of ranges and forms of verification must be made clear before beginning therapy. With couple therapy it gets more complex. For couple therapy these standards hold, but ethical problems may arise when billing "medically necessary" treatment to third-party (insurance company) or when couple therapy is not covered at all.

Do they require for reimbursement a formal DSM-5/ICD-11 diagnosis for one or both partners? If so, is such a diagnosis appropriate? Do you use an individual or couple therapy code? Do you charge each partner for half the session or is the identified patient (IP) charged for the entire session? Does the therapist check with the insurer for their acceptable modes? If so, what permissions are needed from clients? How may confidentiality of the partner be compromised in such a conversation?

In considering serving the best interests of clients and maintaining our own sense of integrity, many issues come to mind, chiefly knowledge of one's self and sufficient competence to fulfill one's professional purpose. Just as the primary factor for therapeutic success consistently points to the quality of the relationship, the essential component of ethical practice is a fundamental knowledge of—and attention to—our abilities, limitations, and understanding of the essential components and focus of practice.

Who Is the Client in Couple Therapy?

These issues are often dramatically disputed across theories and therapists in couple therapy; for example, the question "Who is the client?" is essential:

- Is it individual therapy with an audience?
- Is it each person?
- Is it the couple per se?
- Should treatment be conjoint? Shall I refer my individual client to another therapist for conjoint treatment or refer members of my couple for individual therapy?

The determination of who the client is has significant ethical and treatment considerations, including how we determine the contribution of individual disorders to couple dysfunction and what we do about it.

Competence: Where We Begin and End

It's almost too simple to say that the essential quality of a couple therapist is *competence*. But what does it mean? The APA "Ethical Principles of Therapists and Code of Conduct" (APA, 2017) Standard 2.01(a) states the following:

> **Boundaries of Competence.** Therapists provide services, teach, and conduct research with populations and in areas only within the boundaries of their competence, based on their education, training, supervised experience, consultation, study, or professional experience. (p. 5)

The salient terms here are *supervised training* and *experience*. Before describing how that can be first accomplished, we must acknowledge that couple therapy is indeed a specialty area, as specified by the Commission on Recognized Specialties and Proficiencies in Professional Psychology and the American Board of Professional Psychology (ABPP) through its constituent American Board of Couple and Family Psychology (ABCFP). Other mental health professions, including psychiatry, professional counseling, and clinical social work all consider it a specialty as well; the only exception is marriage and family therapy, which through the American Association of Marriage and Family Therapy (AAMFT, 2015) considers MFTs to be generic mental health professionals capable of a full range of mental health practice.

A major complication in acknowledging the need for competence lies in the fact that up to 70% of practicing clinicians (Lebow, Chambers, Christensen, & Johnson, 2012) report practicing couple therapy without awareness or belief in its status as a specialty, and many assert their competence by saying, "I've been doing it for a long time with no problems." Going back to the APA code, we see that consultation, study, or professional experience can also qualify one to be competent. But what level of these activities would be sufficient? We examine some of the standards for couple therapy in a later section of this chapter. We question whether it is truly possible to become skilled without the combination of formal training and supervision. These questions are unanswered by the APA ethics code, which intentionally leaves room for various practice areas to define their own parameters.

Standards, interpretations, and flexibility aside, let us definitively state that couple counseling and couple therapy is complex, requiring greater integration of personal, professional, and multicultural expertise than most other areas of clinical practice in the following ways:

- The interactional vectors are not two-way as in individual therapy but cycle in six directions (see Chapter 7).
- The therapist is inevitably drawn to one position, yet needs to remain balanced and neutral.
- Gender, sexual orientation, culture, and overall world views frequently come into play.

- The therapist must multitask, keeping track of content, affect, process, and flow, while keeping the treatment model and couple's objectives in mind.
- Discussions can escalate rapidly, requiring the therapist to intervene appropriately and leave the couple with a sense of optimism regardless of the final outcome.

Thus, clinicians should be advised "Don't try this at home" without formal training and supervised experience by a competent couple therapy supervisor. Let us now look at standards that have been specified by the couple therapy specialty within professional psychology.

Standards for Competence in Couple Therapy

The most thorough delineation of standards for couple therapy competence are described by Stanton and Welsh (2011) in *Specialty Competencies in Couple and Family Psychology*, starting with the foundational competencies: ethical and legal, multicultural, interpersonal, and professional identity as a couple therapist. In clinical practice, there are specific competencies in assessment and intervention with couples. They propose a model training sequence and supervision progress in the following order:

1. Doctoral education in psychology with an emphasis or track in family psychology
2. Couples/family practicum
3. Predoctoral internship with child, couples, and/or family rotation
4. Postdoctoral internship with child, couples, and/or family orientation
5. Licensed practice in child, couples, family, systems therapy
6. Board certification in couple and family psychology (ABPP)

Although ideal, few therapists follow this sequence in part due to the scarcity of programs and externships available in the specialty. In fact, there are more couple therapy practitioners who hold master's-level licenses than doctoral or postdoctoral credentials. A more practical set of standards such as the following is proposed to recognize the extent of actual couple therapy practice by therapists at various levels, and the minimal level of training appropriate to their level:

Level A: Specialists who identify as couple therapists with relevant graduate coursework and supervised experience, and who have a significant amount of post-graduate training and supervision in the field that would be equivalent to specialty designation either as an ABPP, AAMFT-approved supervisor, or certification as a family or couple therapist by state licensing boards. Continuing education would include concentrated advanced training in the field.

Level B: Clinicians who regularly treat couples conjointly and in addition to graduate coursework in the field obtain at least 12 hours of continuing education courses and consultation specifically focused in this area each renewal period.

Level C: Practitioners who occasionally see couples conjointly for relatively common problems and short duration, obtain some continuing education each licensure renewal period, utilize focused consultation as needed, and have had some graduate level training in the field.

Adoption of basic standards such as these would allow for more ethical practice for clinicians. It would help clinicians avoid running afoul of licensure guidelines requiring competency and most important, it would also ensure that clients receive the best quality of care. Dissemination of these guidelines would also allow consumers to choose therapists who meet minimum qualifications to treat couples in distress and to provide effective prevention services. It is presently too optimistic to hope that all professions will acknowledge the need for standards at ABPP levels. For this reason, we encourage further advocacy to promote more widespread adoption.

Interprofessional and Legal Implications

Scrutiny of the ethics codes of allied mental health professions reveal a wide range of detailed coverage and emphasis on certain standards. Generally, psychiatrists, social workers, psychiatric nurses, professional counselors, and therapists follow similar ethical standards regarding patient relationships, confidentiality, supervision, record keeping, research, and other professional issues. Although major prohibitions do not vary widely across professional organizations' codes, one notable example is the APA code (APA, 2017), which permits (but does not advise) sexual or romantic contact with former clients after 2 years following termination. When working with a couple, the ethical considerations are truly magnified in such romantic situations. In line with these concerns, the AAMFT (2015) code prohibits sexual relationships with former clients entirely.

> These ethical violations can end up in court. An individual client of Dr. Shapiro sued his former therapist for malpractice. Apparently, the therapist was seeing the client and his ex-wife in couple therapy. He referred the husband to Dr. S. and continued seeing the wife individually. Within hours of terminating therapy, they began a romantic liaison. The affair led her to divorce her husband. Dr. Shapiro was called in as an expert witness to testify about appropriate practices.

Decision Box 2.1: During the trial, Dr. Shapiro was asked, "What is the legitimate amount of time after termination for a personal sexual relationship?" Another expert witness for the prosecution replied "never." A second one called by the defense replied, "[A] reasonable time after the therapy was concluded." What do you think is a best answer to that question?

Another confounding factor in comparing and interpreting ethics codes is legal statutes.

Licensure is governed by each state, and state regulations can vary widely. In California, for instance, the Business and Professions Code, the Health and Welfare Code, the Welfare and Institutions Code, and the Criminal Code all apply to licensed practitioners. Psychiatrists are regulated and licensed under the Board of Medical Quality Assurance, psychologists are under the Board of Psychology, and LMFT, LCSW, and LPCC licensees are governed by the Board of Behavioral Sciences. For mandated reporting, only physicians are required to report a client's HIV status and domestic in specific circumstances, while other mental health professionals are prohibited from doing so, except in specific circumstances. Such issues may pose ethical or personal dilemmas for therapists who believe that these restrictions limit their ability to protect clients.

While state licensure regulations often incorporate professional ethical standards, legal statutes often do not provide guidance at the same level as ethical standards and are viewed as "common denominators," which prescribe the necessary (if insufficient) conditions for competent entry into the profession and minimum standards for practice. Ethical standards can be both enforceable (bottom line) and aspirational (the best practice). For example, most states have rules regarding teletherapy across state boundaries but do not incorporate common clinical and ethical standards of care, such as conducting an assessment (preferably in person), providing full informed consent, and providing for confidentiality and emergencies. Similarly, state regulations may refer to the need for competence to practice but are often silent with regard to criteria for training and experience. Examples of conflicts between licensure and ethical standards will be provided throughout this text, beginning with the "Common Dilemmas" section. Due to the differences in details among the various professions and multitude of state regulations, common general standards will be referred to in discussing dilemmas and common practices.

Culture and Gender Considerations

Aside from competence, few issues are more critical to ethical effectiveness in couple therapy than gender and culture. Chapter 11 covers the issue of gender more thoroughly. From the ethical standpoint, it is important to recognize that we each are raised and socialized with gender-based expectations and that our personal perspective comes strongly into play. All therapists need to understand their personal stance and avoid imposition on others. In couple therapy this can inadvertently occur by prioritizing attention to the more verbal person, who may or may not be the same gender as the therapist. It can easily create the impression that we are allying with one partner and ignoring the other. This can potentially harm the couple relationship, violate the clinical standard of care, and bring on malpractice sanctions.

When it comes to race, culture, religion, gender, and ethnicity, various groups view intimate relationships differently, and social structures are formed accordingly (Gallardo, Johnson, Parham, & Carter, 2009). For example, there may be significant intergenerational conflict for couples from cultures where parents traditionally arrange marriages for their children. While the typical viewpoint of therapists may be that individuals should have the freedom to choose their own partner, ethical standards[2] require us to negotiate these issues and to avoid imposing our own values.

Gender perspectives require acute sensitivity on the part of the couple therapist, not only for awareness of one's own views but also how they play out between the partners, regardless of their sexual orientation. For example, surveys have consistently shown that

---

2 An assumption is made here that couple therapists in training have already taken at least one course on ethics regarding individual work and are at least minimally versed in multicultural aspects of counseling and psychotherapy.

equity, or the perceived fairness with which partners carry out joint responsibilities, has been skewed toward women in heterosexual relationships, who carry most of the burden for household tasks and child care (Hochschild, 1989). Meanwhile, same-sex partners demonstrate a more even balance in assuming joint responsibilities (Holland, 2015), at least if they do not have children (Miller, 2018). The feminist movement in psychotherapy, which began in the 1960s (Walters, Carter, Papp, & Silverstein, 1991), has had a significant influence on therapists' views toward gender, as described by Hill, Glaser, and Harden (1998). Men have been largely influenced by gender- sensitive perspectives, social movements, and guidelines promoted by the APA Division on Men and Masculinity (APA, 2018; Levant, 1995, 2011).

Various racial, cultural, religious, and ethnic groups view intimate relationships differently, and social structures are formed accordingly. Religious values regarding birth control, premarital sex, homosexuality, and gender fluidity may make it difficult for therapists to remain impartial with couples whose lifestyles and beliefs differ from theirs. Consider the issue of polyamory, which some couples are practicing today. While there is little research on this issue to date, therapists who have either moral objections or discomfort with "open marriage" or arrangements involving three or more may become compromised and fail to offer the clients culturally relevant interventions.

Counselors or therapists who have strong personal objections to homosexuality or abortion may find it difficult to assist couples who are involved with these issues. These therapists could find themselves ethically compromised or convey attitudes of disapproval, perhaps believing that they are serving the best interests of clients. Consider the following example:

CASE BOX 2.1

An Ethical Challenge

A 14-year-old girl and her 16-year-old boyfriend come to you in crisis because she fears she may be pregnant. She is afraid to tell her parents because they prohibited any discussion of birth control. You and the parents are both devout Catholics and you live in a state that does not require disclosure of pregnancy to parents. What is the best thing for you to do as a mental health professional?

- Do not counsel her because she is a minor
- Give her information on birth control and assist her with setting up an appointment for an abortion if that is her choice
- Inform her parents of the situation because they are legally liable and possess the privilege
- Counsel her therapeutically, allowing her to weigh her options; do not disclose the information to the parents

This case requires a thorough decision-making process, including awareness of your own position, knowledge of applicable ethical and legal standards, and consideration of the best interests of the couple. It is important to note that the holder of a license to practice requires no discrimination based on client status (age) and objectivity to provide the most effective treatment and to avoid harm (*nonmaleficence*).

Similarly, a systemic perspective and adherence to ethical and clinical standards of care require that we not stereotype and instead consider the interaction of multiple complex factors, which include all of those indicated at the beginning of this section. In addition, variables such as geography, immigration status, socioeconomic status, legal status, and developmental status may confound our decision making.

Common Dilemmas and Processes[3]

Appropriate training and experience in couple therapy is the first thing a clinician should consider before agreeing to treat a couple. Some issues are often minefields to negotiate and the dynamics are multifaceted, making it easy to get lost without the foundation and resources to draw on.

Relationship issues, whether a current one or lack thereof, are the primary reasons therapy is sought. For this reason, therapists are generally open to accepting couples into treatment, whether or not they are adequately trained in the specialty. Unfortunately, without the proper didactic training and supervision, treatment of couples may be ineffective or even invite malpractice suits.

Communication

Most clients seeking couple therapy will mention that their basic problem is "communication." This is of course an important tool for couples to master, and some may need guidance on active listening and speaking, such as using an *intent-impact model* (Gottman, 1998) beginning with *I messages* (Gordon, 1970). Upon further assessment, therapists will commonly discover that while these tools are necessary, they are merely a vehicle for conveying the essential dynamics of the relationship. Communication tools can be effectively used, but when a person uses them to convey contempt, basic mistrust, or an overall negative attitude toward his or her partner, the underlying issues must be fully addressed. Hawkins, Carrère, and Gottman (2002) describe one aspect of this dynamic as "negative sentiment override," which refers to negative attributions to one's partner that are global and persistent, regardless of the context, and is a useful construct to identify when recurring arguments reappear and remain unresolved. The ethical concern is that if the therapist buys into the negative characterizations, objectivity is lost and the therapist may inadvertently reinforce destructive attributions.

As is explored in Chapters 7 and 8, sometimes clarifying of obfuscating communication serves to uncover far more problematic (structural) issues in a relationship. The ethical practitioner must be able to explore these more complex issues that go beyond better communication.

---

3   The tendency to cover the broad clinical areas of couple dynamics is great here, and we will try to steer clear of matters that are not directly ethical. However, in actual practice the clinical, ethical, legal, and theoretical orientation, and broader professional aspects, inevitably intersect.

Violence

Even before basic communication and its underlying dynamics are addressed, the most destructive aspects of a couple's relationship—such as abusive and demeaning language and physical violence—must be stopped before real couple treatment can begin. Four-letter words, put-downs, and threats become like small arrows that create deep emotional wounds. Repeated name calling, demeaning interactions, and abusive labels or comparisons delivered in an angry tone (such as "You're just like your mother") result in resentment, tension, and divisiveness that can erupt over the smallest issue and escalate into interminable disputes and violence.

In such cases, a clinician who understands that emotional abuse of adults is not a matter of mandated reporting might face an ethical dilemma wondering how to protect clients who are being repeatedly abused. Clinicians should determine during initial assessment if physical violence is occurring and carefully assess its severity, frequency, and the ability of the perpetrator to self-monitor and curb violent impulses. This might require interviewing partners individually and developing a safety plan for the abused partner, keeping in mind that it is his or her decision whether to separate temporarily or remain together with clear safeguards in place.

While our best judgment may be to advise the victim to leave his or her partner, it would be an ethical breach of the client's autonomy and likely place him or her in a more dangerous situation if retribution occurs. If state law (as in California) does not require or even permit disclosure of physical abuse of an adult, we must examine our own reactions to these events and act in the best interest of clients by facilitating a safety plan for the victim and enable treatment for the abuser. This serious and complex situation highlights a potential major conflict between ethics, law, and personal moral standards and requires us to be aware of the best clinical practice in dealing with domestic violence.

Earlier systemic thinkers (Holzworth-Munroe & Stuart, 1994) discussed the concept that intimate partner violence as an interactional dynamic, in which the abuser was acknowledged to be the primary person in need of treatment, while the victim was seen to be an enabler, either by being passive or by eliciting the anger of the abuser. This was criticized by feminists and required the couple to be treated conjointly in order to modify the destructive interactional sequence, which would often further incite the offender and result in more harm to the partner. Two clinical considerations are instructive here in order to follow the ethical principle of *nonmaleficence* or "do no harm." The first is the fact that, at least initially, therapy often causes anxiety to go up, which raises the likelihood of one partner losing emotional containment and striking out, leaving the other partner increasingly vulnerable to physical or emotional abuse. In that case, referring the abuser for impulse control or other treatment is needed before couple work can begin.

The second factor to consider comes from the research. Jacobson and his colleagues (1994) argued that violent offenders may be "vagal reactors" who are neurologically stimulated to the point where they blindly attack as their rage escalates. In this situation, we may address the client's ability to monitor awareness of mood, breathing, and heart rate and implement impulse control strategies, and potentially refer to a specialist in anger management. In cases where hypertension or other conditions are indicated, a referral for a medical evaluation is warranted.

Inadvertent Negative Consequences

Sometimes, despite a clinician's trying to provide the best care for a couple, it can work out poorly. Ignoring best clinical practices and current research may open "iatrogenic effects," which are negative consequences resulting from well-intentioned interventions (Morgan, 2006). Such results could make us vulnerable not only to ethical violations, but also to sanctions by licensing boards and malpractice suits.

CASE BOX 2.2

Best Intentions Gone Awry

In one such situation a therapist was seeing a couple through a low fee clinic. When he left the clinic to begin his private practice, he agreed to continue to see the clients at a very reduced fee. However, after 3 weeks the clients said they could not afford that fee but offered him some services as barter. He agreed that they would do some minor repairs at his home in return for continued couple services. They signed a contract.

Although they began the repairs, they left them unfinished and dropped out of therapy. He tried to get them to finish the agreed-on fees based on the therapy sessions they had completed.

When he sent them a letter asking them to either pay the agreed-on fee or complete the job; they refused and made a complaint to the licensing board. The therapist was sanctioned to work under supervision for a year and to refrain from any future bartering arrangements.

Ethical practice requires us to use the best decision-making procedures, such as those described by Barnett, Behnke, Rosenthal, and Koocher (2007), and a modified one, which is summarized as follows for any situations when diverse standards may conflict:

- Provide full informed consent
- Consider the best interests of clients
- Check relevant laws, codes, and best practices
- Consult with an expert (independent, malpractice insurer, association counsel)
- Document thoroughly

Change of Format

Consider receiving a call in your independent practice in which an individual indicates he or she is feeling depressed, having trouble concentrating, and feeling alienated from their spouse.

Do you

- schedule an individual session and discuss factors contributing to his or her depression?
- inquire about his or her marriage and whether the spouse is amenable to conjoint treatment?

- see him or her individually and then attempt to bring in the spouse for couple therapy?
- proceed to treat the person individually?

The answer to these questions depends on a number of factors, including the preference of the client, availability of the spouse, scheduling, and so on, but it primarily hinges on your general theoretical approach. You may have either a psychodynamic, humanistic, or behavioral foundation, but if your lens is mainly a *systemic* one, in which you view relational dynamics as primary, you will initially emphasize the importance of involving the spouse in treatment. When we operate from a systemic perspective, we see the couple as the client, and every decision hinges on our view of serving their joint interest. From an ethical perspective, we are led to examine the research on the effectiveness of individual versus couple therapy for certain conditions and to proceed accordingly.

After proceeding with couple therapy for a number of sessions, it is common to discover that a condition such as severe substance abuse, violence, or psychopathology requires intense individual treatment. How do we decide whether to continue with one individual versus another, refer both, or make the proper referrals? In this situation the clinical literature guides us to avoid ethical pitfalls such as practicing outside the boundaries of our competence and engaging in dual relationships. Gottlieb (1995) provides excellent guidance in deciding on changes in format by considering both ethical and therapeutic implications, such as avoiding comingling of records if partners are interviewed individually.

A related issue involves the decision to have individual sessions during couple therapy to establish rapport, allow partners to speak freely, and gather assessment information. Perhaps we will invite an outside individual such as a parent or in-law into a session in order to better understand dynamics with our clients. The latter is referred to as a *collateral contact*, and these persons who join a session are not actual clients. Therapists do not have the same obligation (known as a *fiduciary relationship*) to these persons. With both collateral contacts and individual sessions during couple therapy, it is advised to keep separate records for each individual in order to protect information from being accessible by other persons (Gottlieb, 1993). Guidance on collateral sessions may be obtained by reviewing Framo's (1992) *Family of Origin sessions* in which he involves multiple generations in conjoint sessions, often for marathon sessions over a weekend or longer. Shapiro has successfully used such sessions in which the larger extended family is brought together as "consultants" to help the couple in distress. In one such case, the long-term distrust between the current wife and the husband's mother were reconciled in a moderated face-to-face interaction. Prior attempts had been hindered by the two women speaking different languages and coming from radically different cultures.

The result of the interaction with her mother-in-law helped reduce her resentment toward her husband and her jealousy toward his deceased first wife.

Patterson has used a briefer version of collateral sessions by inviting an in-law to a couple session in which the couple was arguing over one spouse's parent—whom they felt was disparaging their parenting practices—and another where an older client couple who could not accept their adult son's homosexuality. Questions regarding change of format and record keeping may seem tedious and are often not widely practiced, but they allow us to uphold proper ethical and legal standards and ultimately serve the best interests of clients.

A further issue regarding format is how often and how many sessions to schedule couple therapy. While these are basically clinical and practice issues, the ethical codes advise us to treat clients only as long as is reasonably beneficial to them. Without measures to determine whether client objectives are being met, we risk violating ethical guidelines by continuing treatment beyond a practical limit.

Confidentiality

Privacy, confidentiality, or the legal term, *privilege*, is essential to maintain integrity in all aspects of clinical practice. More subtle circumstances may present themselves in couple therapy, such as when a partner contacts us outside of therapy by e-mail, text, or phone, or draws us aside as a partner is leaving the office. Minor, innocuous comments are often not critical, but when they reveal important dynamics that have not been discussed conjointly in sessions, it can create ethical dilemmas. How do we handle them? We return to our comment that the *couple* is the client and thus remind the individual that we must share the issue with their partner, preferably together, with the client taking the initiative. This might involve a lengthy phone conversation with one partner, after which we offer an individual session to the other partner and in the subsequent conjoint session open up the shared matters to both. It is untenable to spend additional time with one partner, or to keep an issue critical to the couple therapy secret.

Secrets

As indicated, it is a disservice and in violation of the fundamental ethical principle of *do no harm* for a therapist to keep a major issue regarding couple dynamics to him- or herself and to not work with the client to divulge it. While there is considerable controversy on this issue, the argument will be made here on ethical, clinical, and risk-management bases.

Critical secrets most commonly involve affairs, money, addictions, and family relationships. One partner can covertly run up excessive amounts on a joint credit card or make a large purchase affecting their joint credit. Gambling, drug, or sex addiction may adversely impact a relationship. One partner may have a child outside of the relationship, either before or after the relationship began, without the other's knowledge. These are obvious issues the partner should divulge, and then there is the most frequent issue of affairs, either emotional or physical or both.

Affairs

The stance a therapist assumes upon learning of a clandestine affair is a critical point that sets in motion a series of actions. Is it a past or current affair? Is it ongoing? If it is past or if the client agrees to terminate it immediately, does it have the same salience as one that is ongoing? Does emotional involvement matter to the primary relationship as much as a physical one (see Moller & Vossier, 2015)? The moral and religious values of both the therapist and the clients play a role in assessing the impact of the outside relationship on the couple. To the extent possible, a careful assessment of these issues is helpful in guiding a treatment plan, though ultimately an affair that involves time, physical, logistical, emotional, and psychic energy impacts the primary couple and must be addressed lest we risk being ineffective in our treatment and harming the couple.

First Look Inward

As in all aspects of clinical practice, an ethical stance begins with awareness of one's personal worldview in relation to the clients' position. Do we take a strict religious or moral perspective that sex is only for procreation and only between married men and women, or more of an "open marriage" or polyamorous one? Do we have a *laissez faire* view on affairs within a committed relationship, so long as they are unknown to one's partner? Whatever our opinion may be, we need to understand the couple's perspective clearly and, rather than judge their morality, assess how it is working for them in terms of their implicit or explicit understanding about external sexual and emotional relationships. Imposing our view and mismanagement due to countertransference (Silverstein, 1998) or other personal issues violates the key principles of

- nonmaleficence or "do no harm,"
- respect for people's rights and dignity,
- competence (adhering to standards of care), and
- confidentiality and record-keeping (see APA, 2017).

How to Proceed?

In regard to competence, the literature indicates various paths for clinicians to take in regard to whether an affair should be revealed, to what extent, in what format, and how to maintain a balanced stance with the couple (Kaslow et al., 2007; McCarthy & Wald, 2013; Stefano & Oala, 2008). While clinical, theoretical, and moral perspectives are implicated in these issues, a main ethical point is that neither the perpetrator of the affair, nor the offended partner should be cast into a negative "one-down" position, and the pre-affair state of the relationship should be brought to light. In other words, the offended partner has every right to expect full transparency, but not to the extent where it may elicit obsessive details and rumination over the occurrence. The offending partner cannot be cast into the position of being eminently untrustworthy and have his or her sense of autonomy impeded to the extent where every subsequent move is scrutinized. Such a balanced position on the part of the therapist requires personal awareness, respect, restraint, and knowledge of ethical codes and clinical standards and procedures.

Confidentiality and Treatment

Confidentiality also plays a pivotal role in considering the ethical dimensions of treating affairs. First and foremost, what if the offending partner refuses to tell the other and your systemic lens requires that you serve the best interests of the couple as a unit? Telling the offended partner unilaterally violates the cardinal ethical principle of confidentiality, while keeping the secret appears to be untenable for continuing effective work to improve the couple's relationship. Some clinicians feel that they are obligated to do so, while most will work (briefly) to facilitate the offending person telling his or her partner while offering both partners individual sessions as needed.

Acute sensitivity to each client's reactions and a balanced perspective is required on the part of the therapist. Patterson states that in decades of practice he has never had a client refuse to tell a partner about an affair. Shapiro reports that it has occurred rarely in his practice. In those cases he has informed the offending partner that he could not continue with a secret from the partner. He did not reveal the secret directly but told the offending partner that if she or he was determined to keep it secret, he would have to withdraw from treating them. There are also situations where the therapist discerns that an affair is or has occurred, but neither member of the couple has disclosed it. It is common for a couple therapist to have a release of information to discuss the couple's case with either or both partner's individual therapist. In some very tricky situations, such a consultation with one of the client's individual counselors has provided information about an affair that has not been revealed in couple therapy.

In cases where such information about an affair is available to the therapist but not the spouse, the therapist may need to tell each, "An issue has arisen that I cover in my informed consent with couples that will not allow me to continue couple therapy, and I would offer a referral if desired."

This highlights the extreme value of tailoring one's informed consent form to cover the eventualities that may occur in specialty practice.

Secrets and Records

Records are always confidential and *privileged* by legal statute. Further, the content is essentially the property of clients. Of course, this brings up the issue of the definition of who is the client with rights to records. If there is a single record that covers both joint and individual sessions with members of a couple, a partner could become aware of a previous "secret" (Gottlieb, 1993).

For the most part, proper record keeping will maintain confidentiality. However, it is important to note that in the event of a legal case and a subpoena by a court, all records may have to be turned over to authorities. Therapists' work product does not have the same level of privilege as attorney–client interactions.

Other Secrets

Although affairs are the most common type of secret that occurs in couple therapy involving confidentiality, records, and competence, others such as money, addiction, and other types of relationships may interfere with the progress of therapy.

Finances, such as excessive spending on a joint account or one partner's holding of an unknown separate account, are often a point of contention with high-conflict couples (Fruzetti, 2006). In addition, both financial and relational issues may come to light in learning separately about addictions to gambling, drugs or alcohol, Internet gaming or porn sites, and even prior marriages or children without the partner's knowledge.

Consider the case of Mr. Z who reveals a major secret to you in a phone call and has not told any of his friends or family, including his wife.

What if Mr. Z and his wife had been your clients in couple therapy for some weeks? After one of the sessions, he calls you and reveals over the phone that he has another family, including two small children, and that he supports them and "loves them very much." Neither of his partners knows about the other, and he has not shared this secret with anyone besides you.

How would you proceed? Take a brief moment to review these guidelines to uphold the highest ethical standards.

Your personal moral standards professional (e.g., APA) code of

Confidentiality

Records

Clinical standard of care

Risk management

Responsibility to the wife, who is also your client

In similar fashion, you may discover that a husband who travels frequently engages in high-stakes gambling using cash from a secret account, while his wife has been saving a large portion of her salary in their joint account to purchase a home. Although disclosure may be challenging and undesirable for the partner keeping the secret, guidelines such as those listed will help you manage the situation in order to serve the best interests of the couple. In any case, the principles of *beneficence* and *non-maleficence* would not allow a clinician to keep this secret while continuing to treat the couple. You are facing double jeopardy if you tell the secret without the client's permission from both risk management and ethical perspectives, or if you do nothing in such situations.

Common Errors and Pitfalls

Even with years of clinical practice, it is possible to err in judgment and to be on a "slippery slope" toward violations that could elicit sanctions. The following is recommended as a way to remain on solid ground:

- Stay up to date on ethical, legal, and clinical standards
- Self-monitor by reviewing personal values and procedures regularly
- Maintain a network of resources by discussing issues with peers and consulting with experts
- When in doubt, use a decision-making process as outlined and ask, "Why *would* I take this course of action?" It is often the inadvertent slip-ups that lead to difficulty rather than the deliberate ones we consciously avoid

Without delving into the background or remedies for these matters, the following are offered as reminders of issues that require close attention:

- **Incomplete informed consent.** Although incomprehensible, we find that many clinicians neglect to provide *written informed consent*, violating many ethical and legal guidelines.
- **Ambiguity around fees.** Incorrect handling of fees can easily derail treatment and become an emotional flashpoint for both clients and therapist.
  - Explain your fee policy at the outset
  - Have an efficient means of collecting fees
  - Collect fees at each session
  - Consider not raising the fee for current clients or, although a legal matter, avoid referring to a collection agency in the event of unpaid fees
- **Inequity by favoring one partner over another.** Keep your wide-angle, systemic lenses in focus and remind yourself frequently in each session that the *couple* is your client.
- **Failure to detect violence, self-harm, and severe psychopathology.** A key to attending to major issues is to always conduct a systematic assessment that fits your practice model. Even when not required, checking symptoms using the DSM-5 can keep counselors from missing a condition requiring intensive or outside treatment.
- **Changing format** (e.g., couple to individual). Do not change format without considering clinical need or equity (described earlier).
- **Faulty record keeping.** Ethical, clinical, and legal standards exist as useful guides to maintaining proper records. Specific agencies, third-party insurers, and situations often require particular information, such as HIPPA. In some states and under certain federal agencies, a rule of thumb is to maintain records for 7 years following termination. For an excellent compendium of forms and guidelines, *The Clinician's Toolbox* (Zuckerman & Kolmes, 2017) is highly useful. As with informed consent forms, many clinicians are quite careless in maintaining records. Legal and ethical monitors often follow the maxim "If it isn't written, it didn't happen."
- **Failure to consult on complex issues.** Always maintain peer and expert resources to consult with on complex issues and keep a record of the results.
- **Lack of training and experience to deal with complex dynamics.** As described, this work is too complex and fraught with minefields to attempt without proper training and experience.
- **Engaging in inappropriate dual relationships.** This includes treating one partner while engaging in conjoint therapy with the couple (Gabriel, 2005).

SUMMARY

Ethics in couple therapy are more complex than in individual counseling and therapy. In addition to all of the individual ethical mandates, couple therapy requires some additional considerations. Therapists are advised to use checklists and decision-making frameworks such as those in this chapter as guides to practice and to review them regularly. We also recommend professional consultation whenever questions arise. However, a basic foundation in self-awareness, work-life balance, networking, essential competence, and a strong sense of professional boundaries are the essence of ethical practice. Rather than being "rule governed," an attitude of being "self-directed" in an informed manner will allow us to maintain our own integrity and serve the best interests of clients throughout a satisfying professional career.

3

Intimacy, Love, and Commitment

"Let there be spaces in your togetherness, and let the winds of the heavens dance between you."

Kahlil Gibran, *The Prophet*

"Love is a many-splendored thing."

Sonnet 73 (Shakespeare) and 1955 film

Love, sex, intimacy, commitment, attachment, connection, living together, partners, paramours, affection, roommates, monogamy, polyamory, adultery, polygamy, etc.

What do these words evoke in you? What do you believe characterizes a close relationship? Emotional attachment, contiguity, sex, intellectual resonance, social compatibility, time together, shared values, similar backgrounds? All of these, or just one? We don't pretend to know; many will say that it's in the eyes and hearts of the beholders—how we define our relationship is all that matters. There is little solid evidence to take a firm stance on what elements a close relationship should include, but there are certainly societal structures, cultural values, and personal and moral standards that may determine whether a relationship is close. Some would say, "I can't define it, but I know one when I see one." In order to avoid such ambiguity, we will attempt to provide some evidence and guidance for understanding intimacy, sex, love, and stability in close relationships. This is a major component of the work of couple therapists: aiding couples struggling with these key issues.

With all of the vagueness inherent in such an exploration of what really determines a close relationship, consider your own definition of love in the following synopsis of a definition in Sheldon Hamick's wonderful lyrics of Tevye and Golde in the musical *Fiddler on the Roof:*

In the story, Golde and Tevya have been in an arranged marriage for 25 years. As their oldest daughter is breaking centuries-old traditions by finding a loving marriage for herself, Tevya begins to ponder if he and Golde are in love. When he asks her if she loves him, she replies that they have fought, starved, and shared a bed for 25 years. With her answer, he surmises "Then you love me." She replies, "I suppose I do," and he responds, "And I suppose I love you too." Finally, the two of them conclude in harmony that it doesn't change anything but it's comforting to realize.

Is this what you would consider true love? It is certainly stable. Their relationship has established them in their community and provided a home, children, and security, but is there intimacy, sex, and romance? If you interviewed Tevye and Golde, would they say they care about these matters? And if they said yes, do you think they repress their desires or harbor resentments over their absence? This situation is similar to many you will find in treating couples. Clinical exploration about the level of intimacy in a relationship can uncover reasons for alienation and hostility, diminish persistent negative interactions and arguments over trivia, and enable couples to acknowledge their feelings and move toward greater connection with their partner.

As always, we cannot ignore how a therapist's personal views enter into the type of intimacy couples engage in (or not). Do we hold to the notion of the Drifters classic song that you can do what you will during the evening, as long as you "save the last dance for me" (Pomas & Shulman, 1960)? Do we believe with Jankowiak, (2008), "I have her/his heart, swinging is just sex?" or do we have a more integrated view of sex, love, and intimacy? Do you believe the Beatles' notion that "all you need is love" or does one's view of intimacy reflect a stronger all-or-none value system?

Definitions: Intimacy and Commitment

Throughout this text, we will be referring to committed intimate partner relationships involving sharing of affection and common responsibilities. The word *intimate* will be used in the sense of an emotional and physical closeness in a relationship that is primary for each partner and more frequent and intense than others. The intimacy may or may not be overtly sexual but involves emotional and perhaps intellectual attachment and physical touch in some manner that is reinforced by chemical and neurological effects that induce pleasure, comfort, and a sense of belonging. Each of these aspects exists along a continuum and can be freely defined by each couple, regardless of culture and ethnicity, sexual orientation, or gender identification. The nature of the bond is socially constructed (Beall & Sternberg, 1995) and unique in relation to other relationships each partner has.

The intimacy and commitment that are defined by each partner is significant in assessing and treating couples, while the impact of these concepts is often unclear to partners in a relationship. For example, the word *intimacy* is often considered a euphemism for sex, and disordered couples frequently report an absence or lack of satisfaction with intercourse, and ask, "What's normal?" We can't answer this question because each couple needs to determine what works for them. When we explore the range of intimacy—from warm touch, to kissing, to sexual contact—we often find that these are missing as well. If partners are not extremely alienated from each other, we can strengthen their connection by using approximations at the lower end of the intimacy spectrum (e.g., frequent hugs). Some people need to rediscover an awareness of pleasure in their bodies, and for this we recommend a guide such as *Our Bodies, Ourselves* (Norsigian, 2011). Referral to a credentialed sex therapist may be helpful for some couples, although we generally find that couples have little trouble reinitiating sex when their resentment and hostility are reduced and they become open to intimacy.

Intimacy and Couple Therapy

For the philosopher and Jewish mystical theologian, Martin Buber (1937/1970), the most essential form of life (and spirituality) was the I-thou encounter. Protestant theologian Paul Tillich (1952) focused on the phenomenon when he asserted that fully becoming a person may only occur in encounters with another person. Rogers (1951) frequently set the center of personal growth on relationship: between partners and between therapist and clients.

For Frankl (1959), love was described as the highest aspirational goal for human beings. He describes how his personal love for his wife and fellow human beings helped him survive the horrible suffering and personal losses in the Nazi death camps.

For all these authors, love (I-thou) was viewed as essential to living fully and the path to salvation or being versus non-being. It is the direct antidote to feelings of meaninglessness. This aspiration can be prominent in all forms of counseling and psychotherapy, particularly as both goal and method in couple therapy. Love and intimacy between equal primary partners are considered the most salient for relationship in life (Shapiro, 2016).

This makes intimacy a prime factor in working with couples. Crowe and Ridley (1990) specifically explored four aspects of intimacy in couple therapy: (a) sexual intimacy, (b) emotional intimacy, (c) physical and nonverbal intimacy, and (d) operational (daily life) closeness.

Crowe (1997) noted that many of the typical relationship difficulties commonly occur in any of these arenas of intimacy, ultimately involving underlying fears of suffocation and abandonment, and more conscious, daily life power conflicts, general bickering, and disagreements about sexuality.

Intimacy-based problems may be seen as foundational in triangulated (Bowen, 1974) situations such as affairs, extended family commitments, and parenting. Crowe (1997) also indicates that these intimacy-based conflicts may also underlie other more significant individual pathology such as in clinical levels of depression, anxiety, and unrelenting jealousy.

Attachment and Intimacy

The *attachment* history and style of each partner is fundamental in the type and level of intimacy each partner is capable of and desires; those who have faulty attachment in childhood may have lifelong struggles connecting to others emotionally and physically. From a systems viewpoint, this can be addressed conjointly with the couple, but a partner may need individual therapy to address this obstacle fully. Attachment repair may also be essential for those who have been abused emotionally, sexually, or physically, and for those with physical limitations. While we do not advocate a full analytic approach to repairing faulty attachment, an effective means of exploring this issue is through the lens of emotion-focused therapy (EFT) (Johnson, 2019).

Intimacy as a Necessary Aspect of Commitment

The authors take the position that however defined by the couple, some level of intimacy is essential for couples; resentment accumulates when it is completely absent. If we find that the relationship is devoid of intimacy and commitment is questionable, we may pose paradoxically the option of living together as roommates in order to elicit their motivation to repair the relationship or discuss whether separation is a better option for them. They are often astonished by this suggestion, and only those who decide to remain together for financial reasons or until the children are grown have decided on a solely roommate arrangement. Such an arrangement can become an uneasy truce, but one that breaks repetitive conflictual patterns and provides some relief from conflict.

CASE BOX 3.2

Living as Roommates?

When they began therapy, Mona and Robby, married for 5 years and exclusive for 8 years, reported that they had been "living as roommates for most of the 8 years [they] have been together." Mona described herself as a person with a very low libido and no interest in having children. Robbie reported that he'd like to be more sexual, but his requests had "mostly fallen on deaf ears." He claimed that their companionship and faith-based work together was what mattered most and that "Mona usually agreed about three to four times a year." Both of them reported that although it was troubling that they had such little interest by comparison to others, it was not a deal breaker. One of their therapeutic goals was to be more comfortable physically. This interaction occurred in the fifth session:

> M: I think sometimes he doesn't hug me or kiss me, because then he'll want sex and I'll say no.

> R: No. I don't hug you because you tense up and I just think that you find me unattractive.

(Continued)

M: You now that's not true. It's just that when you hug me, your hands roam and …

This interaction progressed for about 10 minutes when the therapist interrupted.

T: Let's try an experiment for the next 2 weeks. You probably won't be giving up a sexual time during that period, so let's make a pact that Mona will approach Robby once a week and hug him. Robby will hug her back in the same way she hugs him. Second, Robby will take the lead twice and Mona will hug him back. Here's the important agreement. This will be done while you are both clothed and agree that it will not go any further than the hugs.

The therapist asked them to not have sex, something they were likely to avoid during the time period. Second, he asked for an agreement that would reduce the potential threat of physical touching going further. Although they agreed, they found ways to avoid the homework during the ensuing week. This was discussed and the therapist instructed them to double up so that they could complete the exercise in the second week.

When they returned, they embarrassingly told the therapist that Robby had touched Mona's breast during one hug and then "pulled his hand away like he was touching a hot stove!"

Mona placed his hand back on her breast and told him that was okay. Two sessions later, they confessed that they had violated the agreement and had atypically satisfying intercourse later that night.

Short-Term Intimacy and Long-Term Intimacy

Although intimacy for any couple is best understood by their subjective experiences and definitions, one assessment that couple counselors and therapists are wise to make is the extent that the commitment involves *short-term* or *long-term* intimacy. The definition of short-term intimacy is that the couple "will stay together as long as on the whole there are more pluses than minuses and neither breaks a basic trust (as in betrayal)." By contrast, long-term intimacy is defined by the statement, "Whatever comes up we will deal with together."

Therapists cannot make assumptions about these basic definitions. The long-term commitment is, of course, more stable and more likely to be able to withstand the increased anxiety that therapy (like the potential for any change) may engender.

Commitment means that time and energy are consistently devoted to maintaining and increasing the connection and developing the relationship, and to upholding whatever agreements partners have with each other. Commitment also involves sharing tasks that are necessary to maintain the bond, which may include household, social, financial, child care, and other responsibilities. Commitment does not necessarily mean "until death do us part," but rather an openness to strengthening the positive aspects of the relationship and working to resolve conflicts as long as the relationship remains functional. Those who engage in polyamory or polyandry may have other partners, but the total emotional and physical attachment and commitment may be the same (to the group) as with the primary partner.[1] Similarly, those in monogamous relationships may have close emotional ties to others of either gender, but the primary attachment and commitment remains with the partner.

Consider the nature of commitment in the following situation.

Decision Box 3.1. Is This a Solid Commitment?: Keesha and Kevin, a 30-year-old couple, decide they have a solid relationship and move in together after 2 years together. They buy furniture, decorate, visit each other's parents, adopt a pet, and save together to buy a house. After a year of settling into a comfortable life together, Kevin becomes uncomfortable with Keesha's going on frequent business trips with male colleagues and having lunch on her day off with Elvin, a male colleague, with whom she has become friends. Keesha maintains contact with Elvin on a level similar to her contact and tone as with her women friends. Kevin does not travel for business and does not have close women friends, and although he does not suspect Keesha is having an affair, he tells her that he feels her relationship with Elvin is inappropriate and asks her to stop. Keesha feels her autonomy is being infringed upon and Kevin insists that this is a "deal breaker" for him if she continues her friendship with Elvin. What is your view of Keesha and Kevin's level of commitment after the relationship has been solid for 3 years and no breach of trust has occurred?

Keesha and Kevin appear committed from their 3 years together, but now Kevin feels that Keesha's views and behavior are unacceptable in their relationship. If there were an affair or abuse, it would be easy to view Kevin's stance on Keesha's intolerable behavior as weighty, but she believes as an individual she has a right engage in a valued friendship with a man.

Decision Box 3.2. What Is Your Position? Decision Point: In your formulation of this issue, would you work toward having Keesha accept Kevin's ultimatum or uphold Keesha's desire to maintain her autonomy?

Kevin and Keesha's disagreement developed because of a discrepancy in what each expected and what was occurring. Those expectations are often long standing, culturally influenced, and based in some core values. One of the determinants of such strong beliefs and feelings are the myths with which each partner grew up.

Some Myths of Intimacy

Because intimacy stands out as a particularly important part of relationships, within each culture there is considerable folklore and myths about the nature of appropriate intimacy for a couple. It is essential that we view these myths as values and beliefs that guide significant portions of couple behavior. Thus, we explore here the idea that they

---

1   It is important to note that those in polyamorous "group marriages" may define the primary relationship as having three or more members, who are committed equally and exclusively to the marital group.

should not be viewed through the common American lens of myths as falsehoods, but rather in the form of the Ancient Greek myths (guidelines for living).

Myths have two essential components: (a) a well-formed belief and (b) emotion. That combination makes them particularly resistant to being altered. Thus, the job of the couple therapist is to use these myths to diagnose and assist the couple from within their system. It is not to debunk a myth.

A brief selection of popular Western myths was presented by Diamond and Shapiro (1983) and these are briefly summarized here.

Myths Regarding the Nature of Intimacy

There are many beliefs, emotions and concerns that impact the manner of relationships. Understanding those unique influences and personal expectations can make therapy particularly effective. A number of these common myths are described here. It is not an exhaustive list. Each couple and each individual may be motivated by internalized values contained in these myths.

Myth #1: The Sexual Myth

Many consider intimacy and sexuality to be one and the same. This myth explores those relational aspects in which close physical connection defines intimacy. Many clients will hem and haw around the question early in therapy. "We are having some problems in ah, er, uh, intimacy relations." Examples of a general belief in this myth are almost ubiquitous in our culture, from advertising any nature of products with sexuality, to popular books that claim that better sex means a better relationship (and of course the book describes how we can enhance our sexuality), and the rapidly growing use of chemical and surgical means to aid sexual performance and satisfaction.

Myth #2: The Absence of Strife Myth

Partially influenced by the "got married and lived happily ever after" storybook and Hollywood endings, there can be an expectation among many partners that after marriage, strife will be absent. As one client noted, "When she called me a SOB, I thought the marriage was over!" An important diagnostic value of uncovering this particular myth is to help couples anticipate some strife in any partnership, find methods to recognize those situations, and identify ways of recovering. This myth may be held by either partner or both. Couple therapists need to help them realize that even in a bed of roses, there are inevitable thorns.

Myth #3: The Enchanting Fairytale Myth ("Love Conquers All")

A myth closely related to happily ever after is the notion that if I love someone enough and if they love me truly, all things shall be vouchsafed. Love is the answer, the magic potion, and the desired beginning of a relationship. In this formulation, the love between Tevye and Golda is but one form. The hot passion and shared delusion demonstrated by George and Martha in Albee's (2001) play, *Who's Afraid of Virginia Woolf*, is another example, albeit substantially darker.

One interesting offshoot of the enchanting fairy tale is the recent sense that a partner should get and give unconditional positive regard. That is something possible and derived from an idealistic therapist–client or parent–child relationship, but problematic as an expectation in a relationship of equals.

Myths Regarding Finding and Beginning Intimacy

Two of the most important and difficult tasks in modern life involves finding a compatible partner and beginning a relationship. Because the process is in some ways so mysterious, there are endless beliefs about the proper ways to pursue the goals and about the definition of a good relationship.

Myth #4: The Soul Mate Myth

Among many couples is a deeply held belief that there is one and only person for each of us. Once we find that person we can never let him or her go without tragic lifelong loneliness. There is a deep belief in a "Mr. or Ms. Right." We expect the fictional Prince Charming to ride in on his white horse and take us away from whatever drudgery we experience. It is interesting in how cross-cultural this belief in star-crossed lovers seems to be, from Shakespeare's *Romeo and Juliet*, "Running Bear and Little White Dove" (Richardson, 1959), the Bing Crosby and Ingrid Bergman film *The Bells of St. Mary's* (Nichols, 1945), and the story told in *Tiger Balm Gardens* in Hong Kong. Each depict the tragic consequences of such love being blocked by death, religious commitment, or distance. To the extent that each partner views the other through this lens, the more vulnerable she or he may feel. For a therapist, understanding that this is believed to be the only chance for true intimacy and love informs the sensitivity in which the couple may be successfully addressed.

Myth #5: All the Eggs in One Basket Myth

Another variant of the one and only is the sense that we get one and only one true intimate partner in life. Once that partner is gone by death or desertion, there is no other recourse. This may be particularly strong in some traditional cultures. Indeed, it is not unusual for a widow to eschew further relationships after a long-term marriage ends, even if she outlives her late husband for 40 years.

An Example of How Therapists May Use Instead of Try to Debunk Myths

Victor and Bette were newlyweds in their 60s. They met 4 years ago in a grief support group after their partners of many years passed away. After 2 years of dating, they married. In the first session, she complained that she could not "live up to the memory of Sally, Victor's first wife." For his part, Victor complained that lovemaking was "just not the same." He in particular, deeply ascribed to the "soul mate myth."

Instead of trying to talk them out of this belief of one and only one true love, the therapist explored with them, their survivors' guilt, the realities of being newlyweds some 40 years after they were courting their former partners, the meaning of being in this new relationship, and what they could do to make it work.

T: Bette, what if you cannot ever live up to the memory of Sally?

B: I don't know. Maybe I am not good enough for Victor!

V: That's not true. I just need to let go of Sally more to be with you.

T: And if you don't let her memory go?

V: I just want Bette to know that I love her too, but I don't want to lose my memories and we had three kids and now a grandson.

T: Tell Bette more about how you want to have both the memory and history and your new love for her.

B: If you told me how much you love me and desire me …

T: What would that take?

V: Don't try to take Sal's memory away. Just be with me as Bette.

B: When we are in bed, can you focus all your attention on me and have the split love at other times?

Myth #6: The All-or-None Myth (You've Either Got It or You Don't)

There is in Western culture a popular myth that there are "haves" and "have nots" when it comes to intimacy and love. Certain segments of the population are afforded a "right" to almost unlimited intimacy. This was underscored in 2016 when then-presidential candidate Donald Trump was heard on a recording (the famous Access Hollywood video) affirming that as a celebrity, he had the right to walk up to, kiss, and grab women as he desired. Although his depiction may seem outlandish, it did reflect a sense that fame, certain body types, and financial success privileged certain folks to have more rights to intimacy that they desired.

Beyond that image is a deep-rooted phenomenon we call the "reproductive bias." This belief is that the only people who have rights to intimacy are those who could produce a socially acceptable pregnancy. In part, the furor some feel about hetero-non-normative relationships is rooted in this myth. The clinically relevant part of this myth is when people remove themselves from relationships because of it and suffer from it. Groups that this impacts include the young and old, people with disabilities, minorities, people with lower socioeconomic strata of society, and those attracted to others of the same sex.

Myth #7: The Beauty Myth

Similar to the reproductive bias is the myth that beauty (culturally defined) begets intimacy. In the Dolly Parton (1974) country classic song "Jolene," a woman is pleading with a potential rival to not take her man. Her argument is that Jolene can have any man she desires with her "flaming locks of auburn hair" and other physical attributes.

We are bombarded constantly about beauty and desirability. A quick look at women's magazines such as *Cosmopolitan* indicates that before the articles of improving one's love life begin, there are manifold pages advertising products that presumably make women appear more attractive. Virtually no part of a woman's body eludes the need for some product to "improve" her chances of pleasing a potential mate. It is interesting that a men's magazine like *Playboy* focuses on gear and possessions for seduction. In our culture, it seems that a woman's appeal is about changes to physical self and enhanced beauty and men's is about his possessions or financial wherewithal.

It is clear that this myth will inevitably promote lower self-esteem and that therapy may have to be focused around being attractive enough.

Myths About Responsibility, Freedom, and Security

What is the nature of relationships? Are they exercises in wins, losses, and endless compromises? Do relationships represent a zero-sum game in which there is a winner and a loser? Does an intimate relationship thrive with teamwork? What deeper psychological needs emerge when committing to another person? Several concerns are evident in myths about the ever-present balance of security and freedom.

Myth #8: The Myth of Engulfment

Snide comments regarding loss of freedom ("whipped," "ball and chain," "I'm with stupid," "A prisoner of love," "under control," "suffocated") all describe a general sense that once one commits to an intimate relationship, there is an increase of security so powerful that it eliminates a sense of independence and freedom. The dark side of the goal of catching a mate will be a loss of self, restriction of freedom, and potential emotional suffocation.

Myth #9: The Myth of Abandonment

A corollary to the myth of engulfment is the opposite myth that intimacy and/or marriage will cure feelings of isolation, meaningless, and loneliness: "If only I could get a person to love me, I would be safe from abandonment and rejection." One version of this is the oft-stated belief by couples that they "complete" each other, suggesting a sense that they are incomplete persons without a partner. A downside risk here is that fear of abandonment may lead to avoidance of commitment. As Joey, a client in a men's group opined, "I am not scared of committing; I am scared of committing and being dumped."

The Intimate Paradox

True intimacy is both desirable and scary. Joey's anxiety is only one aspect of intimacy that may seem paradoxical. Intimacy requires both closeness and distance, connection and separateness. The French have a poignant term for this when they describe sexual connection (orgasm) as *la petite mort* (the little death). It involves a significantly deep connecting between two individuals that they temporarily become as one, followed by the needs to separate and reestablish personal boundaries.

If we were to describe this graphically, it might look similar to the figure that follows.

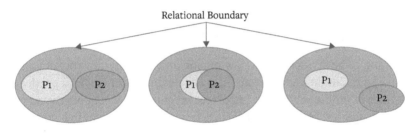

FIGURE 3.1 **Variety of intimate contact**

Intimacy is depicted here as the hard relationship boundary that must not be crossed. However, within such boundaries there are times of intense connection (middle), moderate connection (left), and distant connection (right).

Myth #10: Responsibility as Burden Myth

This belief involves a sense of obligation that comes with intimacy. Probably tracing from childhood experiences of demanding chores, many individuals see connection with another as an open path for demands: "If I love you, I have to do whatever you want, with or without being asked, or else there will be 'hell to pay.'"

Myths Regarding Differences in Intimacy

Is there a belief that the more similarities a couple shares the stronger the relationship or do opposites attract and add vitality to a relationship? Myths abound regarding how much difference or similarity is beneficial.

Myth #11: Myth of Sameness

This "birds of a feather flock together" notion involves a sense of the importance of similarity. The closer we become, the better our world. In fact, this feeling of identity is an important stage in relationship development (see stages of symbiosis and honeymoon in the next chapter). Many computer-assisted mate selection and early dates are predicated on this notion. This myth works toward being connected at the hip and against identifying disagreements or differences in a relationship.

The flip side of this myth—that opposites attract and that "absence makes the heart grow fonder"—is also held generally in the culture. In this myth, we are attracted to things that are unusual in our lives, the exotic, the novel. The basic notion here is that we do not experience the familiar with as much romantic excitement as the different. It is interesting that this myth also reflects an important (wow) stage in a normal relationship.

Maintenance and Development of Intimacy

It is one thing to be attracted to a new person and to form a relationship, but what does it take to maintain and grow an intimate relationship? Do both parties have to grow together in similar ways? How important is equity and what does that entail? How important is longevity? Many deeply held beliefs may govern the way individuals evaluate their relationships.

Myth #12: Myth of Parallel Development

A more modern myth is that members of a couple will grow in tandem. Each will grow in similar ways and mostly together. This myth may promote certain forms of togetherness. At the same time, it restricts individuation and personal separate growth. It is increasingly becoming a widely held belief as sex roles become less oriented to division of labor and more to equality.

That equality in which fairness is central may also fall into this myth. At its core, this myth—when held by couples—promotes valuing each person and each relational task. However, when taken to extreme, this myth can lead to some interesting relational problems.

Equality and Parity

Tomio and Yoko were assiduous in doing everything in equal measure. When they came into therapy, they described a pattern based on this myth of equality. Tomio was a terrific chef and he loved to cook, but he was a very poor kitchen cleaner. Yoko was very good at cleaning but described herself as a "terrible cook." Because of their shared myth of equality, they each cooked three evenings a week and each cleaned three different evenings.

They confessed that this made for an uncomfortably messy kitchen half the time and poor meals half the time. The therapy consultation involved them redefining what equality meant. Each was most pleased with a division of labor.

Myth #13: Every Problem Has a Solution

Also known as the great American myth, this involves a deep conviction that every discomfort or problem in life can be fixed by finding the right solution. If we can only find the right tool, school, religion, drug, credential, or therapist, our problems will dissolve. Of course, the upside of this myth is that couples can engage in creativity and problem solving that can be quite helpful. However, problems may ensue when nothing works and the problem persists. They can become disheartened and feel like failures.

Myth #14: Myth of Endurance (More Is Better)

Th is myth is sense that the more we go through together, the stronger our bond. It also honors a longer relationship more than a shorter one. It is commonplace at wedding receptions to identify (and invite to the dance floor) couples who have been married the longest.

A Final Reminder About Myths

These myths have great potential for a therapist to discern basic values held by partners in a couple. Although some beliefs—especially those that clash—may become problematic, awareness of one's myths is far more valuable in promoting effective therapy than is an exploration about the dangers of such myths. Such awareness can be used to promote shifts in thoughts, feelings, and behaviors in couples, often within their core belief systems. They also point us to how a particular couple finds and maintains intimacy.

Cultural Determinants of Love, Intimacy, and Sex

It is not our intent in this chapter to survey the anthropological factors involved in pair bonding throughout the world. For two excellent resources on this topic, please see

Jankowiak (2008) and Beall and Sternberg (1995). Let's examine here some issues that vary widely across cultures and play a part in our personal views and how we assess and prioritize clients' relationships:

- Attraction—Is "Love at first sight" a solid basis for developing a relationship? Is it essential for a "spark" to be present or to be "moonstruck" (which translates into Italian as "lunatic")?
- Personality types—Are similarities or opposites more enduring traits in partners?
- Love—Is it important to feel love emotionally and viscerally, express verbally, or demonstrate behaviorally?
- Commitment—Does commitment require a lifetime together, and does a breach of trust and separation indicate lack of commitment?

Attraction in Western societies, and increasingly throughout the world, is based largely on appearance (Hatfield & Sprecher, 1985). Physical beauty is a natural aspect that attracts attention, interest, and often passion. It is, however, culturally defined, and some physical characteristics may be attractive to partners in Bali but not in Beirut, Barcelona, or Boston. Globalization through print, visual, and virtual media has homogenized and idealized beauty, and dating apps and websites have reinforced appearance as an essential element of attraction.

Without an initial attraction, is it possible to develop enduring intimacy with those whom we started out with as friends? Those whose lives are based on agricultural production, such as in central Africa, view attraction and love as being integrated into their connection to the seasons and the ability to feed their tribes (though we will likely find some using *Tinder* today).

Upon inquiring "What attracted you to your partner?" many will say, "We found we had so much in common," and indeed, initial familiarity with similar values, people, places, and experiences can initiate lasting friendships and romance. But the experience of most couples is that extreme commonality (enmeshment) becomes boring, and those whose only friends are their common ones, who do the same things for recreation, who like the same movies, books, travel, and so on, and can finish each other's sentences, have little curiosity about their partner and argue frequently over trivial and large differences. The opposite pattern (complementary) applies to those who have interests and activities apart from each other and who enjoy common ones and take pleasure in hearing their partner's separate experiences (Werner, Green, Greenberg, Browne, & McKenna, 2001). As in most interpersonal dynamics, neither extreme is viable in all situations, and our perspective follows the general guideline, "Similarities attract and differences keep it interesting."

We may ask, "Is this couple in love? Does it really matter?" Love may follow the Tevye and Golde model, or the more expressive model such as saying "I love you" every day and with frequent endearing acts, including hearts and flowers. One client in a lesbian relationship stated, "I feel she cares about me because she remembers to change the oil in my car." It is difficult to describe patterns of expression throughout cultures in light of socioeconomic, geographic, developmental, ethnic, racial, and immigration factors, and globalization. One aphorism is that Asian or Scandinavian couples are not verbally romantic, but many of the aforementioned factors can disprove that stereotype. Indonesian couples, for instance, place great value on particular types of verbalized expression of love while other cultures do not use the word "love" to denote lasting relationships. Of course, all cultures place value on behavioral demonstrations of attachment, whether it is by providing resources, sharing common tasks, or merely spending time together.

Commitment can be characterized by remaining together for a lifetime regardless of the normal peaks, valleys, and serious breaches of trust (long-term), or by the example of Kevin and Keesha, who may be on the brink of separating after 3 happy years, saying, "I'm with you until our values drift apart." Kevin and Keesha may view their relationship as committed (short-term) but not permanent due to emerging value differences, but the couple who remained together for 50 years despite irreconcilable differences may hardly see themselves as committed. Conversely, if Keesha were having an affair with Elvin, would that indicate a lack of commitment? Perhaps not, but Kevin would need to be able to view the affair as an event that did not shatter Keesha's commitment to him. We do know that in some countries (notably the Middle East), a woman who looks at a man, let alone has a sexual liaison, is seen as breaking the marital bond and is subject to excommunication or death.

Intimacy Throughout the Life Span

Returning to our earlier definition of intimacy—which involves emotional and perhaps intellectual attachment and physical touch in some manner and is reinforced by chemical and neurological effects that induce pleasure, comfort, and a sense of belonging—we realize that as with all human processes, changes occur over time. As explored in detail in the next chapter, the "moonstruck" (wow) attraction and physical rush that strikes when partners first meet may occur during their teens or in their 80s, but inevitably waxes and wanes as normal transitions occur, physical changes take place, and normal interactions ensue. Intellectual vitality may be constant while physical passion wanes, or social interactions and everyday tasks may be smooth and satisfying at the same time as emotional attachment declines. These are the peaks and valleys that all relationships experience; the essential features in maintaining commitment and a feeling of being in love are

1. understanding that change is a common trajectory and
2. continuing activities on a daily basis to remain connected in a respectful manner that demonstrates that one's partner *is* his or her primary relationship, above all others. Maintaining a healthy sense of separateness (as Gibran says) provides equanimity when struggles emerge.

Life Cycle Issues Affecting Intimacy

Normal couple processes that challenge intimacy at various stages of life may occur at any stage of life. Extraordinary circumstances and losses, such as injuries, immigration, unemployment, trauma, chronic poverty and illness, and racial, ethnic, and other forms of discrimination, can be traumatic and enduring, diminishing an individual's ability to connect with a partner in a satisfying, intimate way. Normal transitions include the following:

- Distance relationships and career pressures in early adulthood
- The transition to family
- Child care, travel, career, and extended family responsibilities—the "sandwich" generation
- Financial pressures, health issues, and the search for meaning in later life

For example, in midlife, work and career factors may necessitate frequent travel for one partner, less time to share household or child care responsibilities, and less couple time. It's easy to become distanced from each other during these times. Clinicians are challenged to help couples understand normal developmental processes and at the same time to show empathy and guide couples to use coping and problem-solving skills. Consider the issues facing the following couple and how you would assess their presenting issues and develop a treatment plan.

To what extent do you view this couple's struggles as part of a normal family developmental cycle and how much do you see it as dysfunctional? Would your treatment plan involve one or more of the following?

- Short-term problem-solving therapy
- Long-term in-depth treatment
- A brief consultation to assist them in recognizing and increasing their connection
- A couple's workshop
- Reading on the "sandwich" generation
- Extended family therapy to increase family cohesion

Whether you think one or more of these or other approaches might be best, a perspective based on the life cycle of this couple is a vital part of the help you provide them. They may not be dysfunctional, but their cultural expectations, responsibilities, foundations of their relationship, and their desire and quality of intimacy at mid-life are often different from when they first met and from where they will be as empty nesters, assuming they are able to maintain their marriage.

Consider the following couple from a developmental perspective in terms of their intimacy.

CASE BOX 3.6

Fan-Chi and Lyssa

Fan-Chi and Lyssa are a couple in their late 70s who have been together 45 years and married for 5, since same sex marriage became legal in their state. They are members of the "free love" generation, had many partners, and considered themselves polyamorous for the first few years they were together. They have maintained a solid foundation and an active sexual relationship through their 60s.

Now they are loving, emotional, intellectual, and fun social partners in retirement and even though Fan-Chi feels she does not need sexual contact, she is resentful because Lyssa no longer expresses her affection through hugs, kisses, or cuddling.

How do you see their lack of physical intimacy in view of their life stage, and what approach would you take in treating them?

- Understand the situation as normal and assist Fan-Chi in understanding and accepting Lyssa's actions and look at other indications of commitment and affection
- View Lyssa's lack of physical affection as a rejection of Fan-Chi or perhaps an indication of depression
- See that each person is not taking responsibility for meeting her own needs and explore individually with each partner what her desires and needs are at this time and how they can be met

If this couple were in their early 20s and in the early phases of their relationship, we might not view their lack of physical affection as normal. We would then work to help them restore passion or refer them to a sex therapist. On the other hand, if we view relational dysfunction as "if one partner is dissatisfied, the relationship is unsatisfactory," a suitable agreement on expressing intimacy might be the goal in light of their current life stage as a couple.

The Essence of Stable Relationships

At this point we have described intimacy and commitment and some of the key cultural, demographic, relational, and developmental factors that determine what is satisfying for each couple in terms that can be used in couple therapy.

Yet, it is precarious to state definitively and succinctly what is essential in creating and sustaining stability, a quality that requires intimacy and is akin to commitment. The term *stability* will be used in this section to denote the skills and processes that create functionality and reduce conflict—or in systems terms, *negentropy*, a lack of predictability and disorder over time. In other words, if love, intimacy, and commitment are present, hostility, contempt, meltdowns, violence, and separation do not need to take place. Arguments will (and should) happen, but "fair fighting" that embodies respect, self-appraisal, and control can prevent escalation (Bach & Wyden, 1970; Lloyd, 1987). Partners who have a solid foundation do not see every dispute as a competition or a zero-sum game in that only one point of view or preference can prevail, nor will they always question different views as relationship-level incompatibility. Even some breaches of trust, such as breaking the hard, outer relational boundary, may not be experienced as lack of commitment and threaten separation.

Initial Assessment of Stability

Although there are many models from sociology, family studies, research, and theoretical orientations with elaborate constructs, we begin with approaches that are the simplest and most consistent in assessment, treatment planning, and intervention.

Although we approach couples from different perspectives, we are pluralistic and integrative in our approach. Our initial assessment may involve both the "first wave" (Jacobson & Margolin, 1979) and the "second wave" of behavior therapy (Jacobson, Christensen, Prince, Cordova, & Eldridge, 2000), including acceptance and commitment strategies. In addition, we include methods of cognitive reconstruction (Baucom et al., 1990), the importance of emotional expressiveness in couple therapy (e.g., Greenberg & Goldman, 2018; Johnson, 2019), and of meaning making in therapy (Shapiro, 2016). There is more clinical than experimental outcome literature supporting this integration (Halford, 2003).

Hayes, Strosahl, and Wilson (2009) begin with the foundation of a couple's *commitment*. Are they having a fling or a trial relationship, or are they questioning their connection with every argument? Basically, are partners open to strengthening the positive aspects of their relationship and working to resolve conflicts as long as the relationship remains functional?

Acceptance of one's partner can be difficult to develop but relates to one simple thing: Can I accept my partner's *basic* traits and behaviors without trying to change him or her? This does not mean we need to accept "deal breakers" or the fundamental issues that are incompatible with our own values or behaviors, which can include severe substance abuse, interpersonal violence, repeated breaches of trust, and other issues that need to be examined as "red flags."

EXERCISE BOX 3.1: WHAT ARE YOUR "RED FLAGS?"

Are there certain traits that are the *sine qua non* for you in a relationship? Are there certain traits that you would personally try to change in your partner (usually an exercise in futility)?

We commonly ask this question in our graduate classes in couple therapy. Here are some of their answers:

Addictions (including smoking)

Regular use of pornography

Other relationships (particularly secret ones)

Hygiene

Religious differences

Dishonesty

Serious crippling debt

Cultural differences

Problematic intrusive in-laws

Serious mental illness

Physical infirmities

We always inquire about such issues in premarital work. For some individuals (often in the helping professions), there is a tendency to take a partner on as a project to save or reform him or her or because of personal low self-esteem ("I will only be able to attract someone who needs help," or "If I save someone, he or she will love me").

As couple therapists, we need to help clients remain assertive, state their preferences, and fairly share chores, daily needs around the home, and connections with in-laws. Acceptance requires prioritizing differences and "choosing our battles" so that minor annoyances do not elicit incessant arguments. Acceptance covers many flaws and prevents nagging, resentment, and hostility.

If we are able to accurately assess a couple's levels of acceptance and commitment early in the process of therapy, we can also determine which interactions to focus on and the tools needed to either develop or strengthen skills. For behavioral couple therapists like Jacobson and Margolin (1979), these include *communication, problem solving*, and *behavior exchange*. Our purpose here is not to provide a primer on behavioral couple therapy, but to elucidate some foundational constructs and processes that are essential to maintaining intimacy, love, and commitment in a stable relationship.

Communication is the ability to express thoughts and emotions and to negotiate practical matters that are essential to functioning. Dysfunctional couples will often state that they rarely talk about anything beyond what to have for dinner or when to pick up the kids, and even when they do, a true speaker-listener transaction with clarity does not occur. Discussions between highly dysfunctional clinical couples often reveal wildly disparate descriptions of the same event, with each partner competing to insist his or her version is correct. Therapists begin to scratch their heads at this and wonder if both were at the same event.

Rather than trying to sort out the details, it becomes necessary at this point to step back and ask, "What is going on between you that your stories are so far apart?" The tried-and-true method of "I messages" (Gordon, 1970) is another useful vehicle for getting communication back on track, so long as partners have a true interest in understanding and listening to each other. A comprehensive view of communication work in couple therapy is found in Chapter 7.

For partners who have difficulty solving basic or complex issues, a valuable method is the *problem-solving* method, beginning with clear communication, openness to each other's preferences, and brainstorming potential solutions. Our approach is an amalgam of diverse approaches that draws from an extensive and diverse body of clinical and research evidence.

BOX 3.4: THE AUTHORS AGREE ON OUTCOME, DISAGREE ON APPROACH

Patterson begins with a deductive approach, closely following more behavioral and cognitive models. This approach begins with a model for problem solving and develops methods of addressing the concerns from within that model.

Shapiro's (existential) approach is more inductive, beginning with the client's frames of reference and moving to an overall theory. The clients' subjective experiences are considered more primary and the problem solving is more an act of creation than deduction.

In problem solving, each partner is asked to do the following:

- State his or her basic goal on the matter
- Express whatever fantasy or realistic approach might be taken
- Describe in detail what steps have already been taken and how he or she succeeded or failed
- Listen without comment to his or her partner's goals and solutions
- Take time to prioritize his or her preferred, realistic solutions
- Present to his or her partner

- Evaluate each solution together without criticism

One process, *motivational interviewing* (Miller & Rollnick, 2013), offers a client-focused basis for helping partners discover their true desires that lead to solutions. It draws heavily on Rogers's (1986) *person-centered therapy* in that the process begins with the client's self-defined objectives and carefully tracks solutions from a problem-solving perspective that are most feasible for the client to employ.

Behavior exchange, or equity, is a critical dimension of stable relationships and is often referred to as the *quid pro quo*, or "this for that" (Lederer & Jackson, 1968). No matter how much passion, love, generosity, and commitment exists in a relationship, partners expect that over time each will receive from each other responses that are commensurate with what they give to their partner. This balance changes over the life cycle and relies in part on the complementary nature of the relationship. One person may be happy handling finances, child care, and social planning, while the other is content to have a busy career and earn most of the income. Emotional nurturing and anticipating needs can be exchanged for doing yard work, if that arrangement is a satisfactory *quid pro quo* for a particular couple. It can also be that a partner provides financial support and does all of the housework while a partner completes a graduate degree, but that arrangement needs to become more equitable after graduation. It's never 50/50 in a given moment, but an imbalance can be accommodated with commitment over time, and each partner's *perception*—more than the actual act or item that is exchanged—is what matters.

Structures That Enable Stability

As mentioned earlier, two fundamental structural arrangements that couples tend to follow factor strongly in creating stability: *complementarity* and *symmetry* (Rovers et al., 2011; Werner et al., 2001). Complementarity is a relationship in which differences between partners are attractive to each other and improve the relationship. Complementarity is enhanced by the Bowenian concept of *differentiation* (Jankowski & Hooper, 2012). Symmetry denotes a form of relating in which couples conform to each other's behaviors, values, and personalities in aspects, and similar characteristics and behaviors are more prominent than differences. Bowen's (1966) original formulation was that partners tend to bond at similar levels of psychological and emotional differentiation, although this notion is challenged by our clinical experience, in which partners frequently display considerably different levels of differentiation. Undifferentiated individuals typically have difficulty with boundaries ("He's always so needy and intrusive!"), and those who are extremely differentiated (possibly with poor attachment histories) may have trouble with intimacy ("She's commitment phobic!" or "He needs so much alone time!"). Both symmetry and complementarity are best viewed on a continuum, with neither extreme being functional for most couples. Consider the following couple.

Eloy and Ben

Eloy and Ben are a late 30s couple who have been together 10 years, and although they have not taken advantage of legal gay marriage in their state, they consider themselves highly committed and have adopted twin 4-year-old girls. Ben is a musician and Eloy is a nonprofit executive, and, upon meeting, their different careers, personalities (outgoing/ reclusive), family backgrounds (oldest of six/only child), and personal styles (fashionable/ stodgy) were interesting to each other.

After a while Ben became somewhat critical of Eloy's reclusive style and stodgy dress, and Eloy began to emulate Ben by dressing stylishly and speaking up more at parties. They eventually began to bicker more, not over their initial differences, but in a competitive fashion due to each not measuring up to their perceived standards or due to the discrepancy between their internalized fantasy of the partner and the person in reality.

In this situation, we can see how opposites attracted and there appeared to be a high degree of complementarity, but they eventually tried to become more symmetrical and enmeshed; in their words, they were "too much in each other's faces" and were constantly annoyed with each other. Neither extreme complementarity nor symmetry worked well for them. The very factors that attracted them to one another were redefined in each person's mind. Thus, "safe, solid, predictable, and conservative" can be later seen as "boring." Similarly, "adventurous" can be redefined as "unpredictable, inconsiderate, and out of control."

The antidote: a return to more complementarity to help them rediscover their individual identities and restore their appreciation of each other's differences and how each contributes to the relational team. Paradoxically, when partners become too much like each other, the intrigue is lost and boredom and bickering ensue.

Recent Trends in Pair Bonding

As it is obvious through popular media and observing friends, relatives, acquaintances, and others, the structures and processes that couples initiate and sustain are far different today than in the mid-20th century (Julian, 2018; Pinsof, 2002; Smock, 2004).

Since the sexual revolution in the 1960s and 1970s, experimentation with alternative relational structures, and the increase in divorce rates—following the legalization of no-fault divorce in Canada in 1968 and the United States (California) in 1969—there has been an increasing liberalization in the acceptability and popularity of serial monogamy, serial exclusivity, and unmarried cohabitation, often considered a "trial marriage" to see how partners might be compatible in sharing daily routines and space. Today, more adults are cohabiting or single than are married. This may have an unpredictable effect on the nature of commitment and couple therapy in the 21st century.

Although quietly at first, gay and lesbian couples formed committed relationships and then married, and transgender, queer, and gender-fluid individuals increasingly formed bonds involving new structures and processes that were self-defined. In other cases, they emulated more traditional patterns of their parents from earlier decades.

Many asked, "Why can't we love whoever we want?" echoing the reality that despite new forms and patterns, couples today basically engage in the same routines, seek the same stability, and struggle with defining their own patterns of love, intimacy, commitment, and sex as other couples throughout the world.

Examples of Committed Relationships on the Brink

While evidence from the professional literature (Roberts & Prager, 2004; Rovers et al., 2011) and our own clinical and personal experience point strongly to elements that are vital to a functional, committed, enduring relationship, too many variables exist to discern a single pattern that works for all couples. In this final section, we will pose some brief vignettes and ask that you review them with some simple questions:

- Can you identify the level and type of intimacy in this couple?
- Are they in love?
- Are they committed to each other?
- Will they endure?

CASE BOX 3.8

Sanjay and Uma

Sanjay and Uma are second-generation Indian-Americans (South Asian) who have met through friends and are conflicted because their parents want to arrange a traditional Indian marriage for them. They have secretly lived together for 4 years far from their parents, who remain in India. They are mostly complementary in their styles and enjoy good friends and activities together.

After 2 years Uma becomes increasingly distressed over being estranged from her parents and feels generally irritated. She withholds sex from Sanjay and argues over minor details of their lives together. Sanjay understands her feelings and in the same time frame has become closer to his parents and visits them frequently.

CASE BOX 3.9

Eliza and Walter

Eliza and Walter have been married for 50 years and by all measures had a successful marriage, including grandchildren, shared activities, and a warm, intimate connection. Walter remains strongly interested in maintaining an active sex life while Eliza's sexual interest has waned since menopause. He has an affair with a neighbor and Eliza senses a diminished connection between them.

Tamar and Todd

Tamar has recently undergone surgery to conform to her female identity and Todd, her partner of 20 years, has patiently and lovingly supported her in every way. They find after a year or so that sexual contact is uncomfortable physically and emotionally. They have always had an active sex life and now wonder if their interest in each other will endure.

These three vignettes exemplify common situations the authors have gleaned from treating couples. Each couple considers themselves to be committed and they all are faced with choices that could potentially either end their relationship or open opportunities to work through an impasse, and in the process, make their relationships stronger. Presumably they are in love and have a form of intimacy that will allow them to survive their crises, but is that love and intimacy sufficient to help them weather the storms they face?

As a therapist, you will bring your own views of these dilemmas to the situation and attempt to remain neutral. Of course, you will strive to help them decide if they have the resources individually and conjointly to make the effort to stay together.

Other factors such as culture, finances, morality and religion, health, family loyalty, and each person's sexual interest will also have a significant impact. As we assess their ability and motivation, the emerging question involves how much effort we will urge them to make to work things out. Should they reach an unspecified point where they are unable or unwilling to remain together, we will be able to assist them in making plans to separate. Because both paths respect their autonomy, they are worth pursuing therapeutically.

SUMMARY

At this point, we hope that readers have developed a viewpoint on the question "Does love conquer all?" The ambiguity of love has considered the aspects of intimacy, sex, romance, and other factors. Although we believe love is a necessary component of a committed relationship, it is not sufficient. Such aspects as clear communication, the ability to effectively solve problems, sharing of responsibilities, agreement on core values, and a sense of enjoyment and friendship also contribute to a lasting relationship. But when love and intimacy fade or are disrupted by time, breaches of trust, or other life circumstances, the absence of intimacy can be pervasive and erode the partners' ability to maintain clear communication, or even to engage with each other in a civil manner as they would a friend. When we hear that emotional abuse is occurring through name-calling and use of four-letter words, we ask "Would you treat a friend that way?" On the other hand, we have seen that even in some highly conflictual couples, intimacy may endure through emotional sharing and frequent sexual congress, even as other aspects of the relationship deteriorate. We strongly recommend that the presence or absence of intimacy and its quality and depth be viewed as a critical factor and a focal point to indicate the likelihood of successful couple therapy. Long-term intimacy and commitment—to work together as a team to deal with whatever vagaries life throws at a couple—is an impressively positive sign for relational endurance and growth.

How Relationships Form and Dissolve

I am 34 years old and the longest relationship I had was my high school girlfriend. I wonder whether I even know what a real relationship entails. I do go out frequently, but after a few dates, the whole thing seems to fizzle into "the friend zone;" for me, as well as the women. I am not alone. My family history is rife with divorces, alcoholism and even some violence. I never knew my father, who left before I was born. It's hard to imagine counseling some couple that have been together for years and having trouble. I keep thinking maybe I should stick with individual therapy, at least until I get into a real relationship myself.

A description from a supervisee who asked for consultation, five years after licensure

4

Normal Relationship Development and Dissolution

When David and Sarah were approaching their 30th wedding anniversary, they were dealing with financial issues, an impending "empty nest" as the last of their three children was about to leave home, a longstanding disagreement about the role of her mother in their relationship, and a lot of squabbling. Their stated goal for couple therapy was to make it better, "the way it was, before." Despite considerable mutually experienced stress and unhappiness, there was no talk about ending the relationship when they came in for marital counseling.

For both of them, their desires harkened back to former times, when the relationship was more fulfilling. Their story is not unusual. As people grow in their lives and as the world around them changes, they go through transitions as they are confronted with the need for adaptations. Basically, if they continue to do what they did before, despite a change in circumstances, the consequences will change as well. No relationship is static over time, nor linear in progression. Instead, relationships shift and follow cycles in a variety of family forms (e.g., McGoldrick & Carter, 2003; Walsh, 1982). Piaget (1967), writing about cognitive development, referred to continual adjustments involving assimilation and accommodation. As new information enters a relational system, it is taken in. When the material is of value to the preexisting system, accommodations are made in the system to utilize the new data.

Thus, when events such as a move, having a child, a new job or job loss, issues with families of origin, or a host of others occur in a relationship, the relationship must adapt to incorporate the new situation. As it adapts, the relationship is destabilized temporarily or altered permanently. This sequence is inevitable in any longer-term relationship. Things change and the couple adapts to acclimate to the new data.

These transitional changes and adaptations are often the precipitating events that bring clients to counseling or psychotherapy. The assimilation of the changed situation may be stressful. The accommodation is often even more potent for therapeutic assessment and intervention. Transitions in long-term relationships are seldom smooth. They involve stress, disruption of homeostasis, and facing change-related anxiety. Often the short-term solution reduces anxiety but is problematic in the longer term.

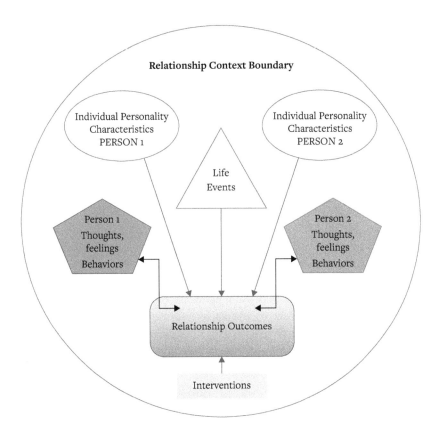

FIGURE 4.1 Multiple influences

External events frequently require adaptation and adjustment, but there are also aspects of relational development that are internal and natural phases of a growing relationship. The generic model presented here demonstrates a normative sequence in relationship development cycles.

We find the cyclical model most heuristic in developing hypotheses and in approaching couples in distress. Other authors prefer more static, single-progression models. In her model of relationship trajectory, Campbell (1980) posits five progressive stages on the path toward satisfying intimacy: romance, power struggles, stability, commitment, and co-creation. Most other authors in this area have also provided models with three to eight stages. A quick Google search found over 30 of these. Almost all were similar to, or predicated on, Campbell's approach (e.g., Diamond, 2016). The professional literature exploring scholarly research on these stages is surprisingly mostly silent (see Reese-Weber, 2015 and Rollie & Duck, 2006 for rare examples of natural stage relationship development). Richardson (2008) uses the term *seasons* to describe fellowshipping, dating, courting, engagement, and marriage (as a final stage).[1]

Halford (2002), focuses on both context and relational variables that impinge upon couples in both expected and unpredictable ways. We depict these forces in Figure 4.1.

---

1   The notion of marriage as a final stage fits with many of the myths about relationships, often following the fairy-tale ending, "They got married and lived happily ever after."

- Relationship Cycles

In Western cultures, in which arranged marriages are not the norm, so-called "love or romantic relationships" follow a fairly predictable pattern. These are important because the stage of relationship development will have a significant impact on both assessment and treatment. The time in each stage can be variable, but the sequence is quite stable.

Stage 1: Wow!

Sometimes couples actually do experience that "some enchanted evening" and meet that "stranger across a crowded room" (Rogers & Hammerstein, 1949). We meet someone and she or he appears special, unique, and a person we would want to meet again. As Eugenio described it, "Rosalie and I met at a company picnic, and we just talked for like five hours. We were the last to leave the park and I called her on my way home to continue talking." There is a spark and an openness to connect with this individual. What allows for that instant attraction has been the province of novelists, poets, and songwriters since time immemorial, but it is also the arena for therapists to understand that kind of "chemistry."

Of course, when we first meet a new person who strikes our fancy, we characteristically know very little about him or her. We may respond initially to his or her physical appearance. We may relate to something they say or the way they say it. More likely, regardless of these factors, we see something of ourselves or our expectations and fantasies in the other person. We project onto them characteristics that are desirable. By contrast, the opposite may occur, and based on such limited data, we are repelled rather than drawn to the person.

When the attraction is mutual (and in fact, finding oneself desirable in the eyes of another may be a significant component in attraction to another), the projections are enhanced (Diamond & Shapiro, 1983; Grant-Jacobs, 2016; Hatfield & Rapson, 1993; Hatfield & Walster, 1978). Fisher and her colleagues have demonstrated in a series of studies that brain activity during initial love feelings are similar to intoxication and suspension of judgment (Fisher, 2004; Fisher, Aron, & Brown, 2006; Fisher, Xu, Aron, & Brown, 2016).

Each individual sees the other as unique, different from anyone else, and clearly quite special. Describing meeting his wife of almost 30 years, David said, "I met her at a political rally. We ended up on the same bus. I remember her wearing Birkenstock sandals, a

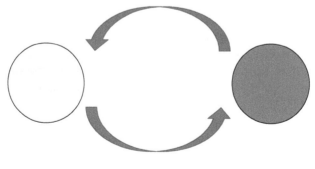

FIGURE 4.2 **The WOW stage**

peasant blouse, long hair down to her waist, and the greatest smile I had ever seen. She was the perfect woman in my eyes."

His wife Sarah, describing their meeting, said, "He was just too cute for words. He needed a haircut, a beard grooming and somehow, he was just perfect. We were from different worlds and maybe that also was really attractive."

Neither David nor Sarah had met previously. They knew practically nothing about one another, except a shared political perspective. What is important was that each saw in the other a way to relate their own selves. They projected some very positive unconscious dreams, beliefs, and feelings onto the other. One way to keep this stage in mind is to turn the word "wow" upside down. It then reads "MOM!"

Stage 2: Symbiosis

If Stage 1 goes well, the couple is drawn together as if by a powerful invisible emotional magnet. Couples during this stage usually focus on how it seems that they share almost every value, experience, and desire. They cling to one another both physically and emotionally. When apart, they talk or text constantly and always look forward to their next time together. The relationship is often very physical and each thinks of the other as a "perfect lover." As Sarah described, "Dave took his time and didn't rush things, but even when we first were sexual, it was like he was a master pianist who knew all the right notes in me. His touch was just perfect."

FIGURE 4.3 Symbiosis

They both reported that they couldn't take their arms away from each other.

Early in their relationship, they worked for the same company. Sarah described an incident about 6 months after they met. "I was at work and had to go to the city for an off site. Dave was coming up later, so I got a ride from our good friend, Michelle. About 45 minutes along the drive, Michelle asked me if I was okay because I had got very quiet and introspective. Without thinking, I told her that this was the longest Dave and I had been apart since we moved in together the second week after we met. She just laughed and asked if I was going to make it until the afternoon."

Looking back on that, noticing that she was aware of less than an hours' separation was something she thought humorous now, she added painfully, "Sometimes now, 45 minutes together is all we can take, before we need to get apart."

The major indication of symbiosis is that the couple focuses on the similarities and does not experience any significant differences. They also create a type of affective fortress against the outside world. They live in a personal bubble, as if attached by epoxy and experience things as a unit.

One example was reported by a young woman who said that on her first date, with a man she just met the week before, without a word they both walked down to the middle of the first row in a movie theater. In her delighted words she exclaimed, "I never thought anyone would do that with me!"

Along with the sense of intoxication that can accompany the symbiotic phase, a state of blurred boundaries or enmeshment (Minuchin, 1974) can also lead to a diminishment of one's identity and boredom or annoyance when one's partner does not act similarly. Enmeshed couples who develop difficulties often fail to realize that their intimate conflicts are based on being *too* close. True, lasting intimacy (detailed in Chapter 3) requires a combination of separateness and connection within a larger holding unit.

Stage 3: Honeymoon

The honeymoon stage is one in which there is a little greater sense of self and differences are more apparent. However, this is still a time of very high attachment. Differences that

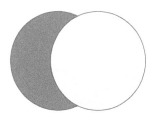

FIGURE 4.4 **Honeymoon**

are evident are seen as perfect (although, as we will see in the next two stages, their appeal may diminish quickly).

David recollected that he noticed that Sarah was "so spontaneous" during this stage. He knew that he was more cautious and conservative. He saw her spontaneity as something that made him feel freer and more able to be experimental in his own life. For her part, Sarah loved the security that came with David's more cautious approach to life. She liked the way he cleaned up the kitchen before they went to bed and "put everything back where it belonged." She also liked that he always seemed to save enough money each month to pay off his credit card and other bills and that "he still had enough for [them] to go out and have fun!" She thought it was "cute" that he carefully rolled up the toothpaste tube from the bottom. She laughingly described her own use of the toothpaste tube as "grabbing it from the middle. [Her] toothpaste always looked like it had been mauled by a herd of wild animals."

Stage 4: You're Not the Person With Whom I Fell in Love

In stage 4, a new sense of reality begins to set in. This is when both parties start to think, "You are not the person with whom I fell in love!" Each sees the other as changing. Of

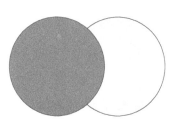

FIGURE 4.5 **YNTPWWIFIL**

course, his or her partner is indeed not the person with whom each fell in love. Remember, the initial attraction was in large part projection. Each fell in love with an image he or she created more than the actual person. While emotional attraction and desire for a love relationship may have influenced perception during the early months of a relationship, during stage 4 the other person is being viewed more objectively for whom he or she is with less projection. As one client said about his partner, "You lose all those unrealistic images when you share a bathroom with someone."

For Dave and Sarah, perceptions altered as their relationship progressed. Although there was no change in her behavior, he began to experience her spontaneity as "irresponsibility." He saw her spending and credit card debt beyond her means as a very serious sign of problems. For Sarah, his organization and orderliness seemed to be confining, controlling, and compulsive.

They argued about the no longer "cute" toothpaste tube use. They both reported that the other expected too much and wasn't "sensitive to [the other's] needs."

Another couple who met while training for a triathlon also ran into a rough patch during this stage: "He comes in the house, drops his sweaty clothes on the bathroom floor, and takes his shower. I have to pick up those soaking clothes and put them in the wash." During an earlier stage, she had marveled at his lack of concern for laundry when he needed a shower and his willingness to clean up sometime after he was dressed in non-athletic clothes. She also revealed a competitive aspect when she opined, "I'd have more time to train if I didn't spend my day picking up after him."

Ken and Mary developed another conflict over an issue that touched on values. Ken reported that they were fighting about having a TV in the bedroom. Early on they would record programs and watch together in bed, each one choosing something that the partner might appreciate. In stage 4, they became less happy about the choices the partner made. He told the therapist that he had questions about having a TV in the bedroom at all. "We should be making love, not watching reruns," he said. Mary retorted, "We only watch TV when you are too tired for anything else! Besides it helps me relax to just chill after a long day."

Stage 5: Power Struggle, Communication Breaks, Maintenance

In this stage, the areas of connection and contact are shared by the areas of conflict. There is an attempt by each person to change the partner back from who she or he is to the earlier held fantasy image. In that way the power struggle is more about process than about specific content. It is less about the facts being argued and more about getting the partner to conform closer to the projected image of who she or he is. When couples are in therapy during this stage, one major issue is the argument regarding multiple subjective realities and

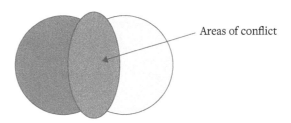

FIGURE 4.6 Power struggle, communication breaks, maintenance

whose is to be followed. Often the therapist is asked to judge the merits of their diverse. Essentially, their sense of "weness" is severely diminished.

When confronted by divergent accounts of the same event, a therapist can become perplexed. Bret complained that they had not had sex for over a month, when Eva retorted, "How about last Saturday?" As their argument ensued, Bret asked, "Who were you with?" and they burst out laughing. Without such a realization of the absurdity of such an argument, the debate could go on indefinitely. For the therapist attempting to bridge the gap, detective work to find objective truth is far less important than noting the differences in perception at the cognitive and affective levels that result in such discord over factual matters and to observe the function of the argument. At the same time, it is important to attend to the differing subjective realities to better understand each partner's needs and perceptions and to understand the consequences of these different viewpoints.

There is a marvelous split-screen scene in the classic film *Annie Hall* in which each of the partners is describing his or her sex life to the respective therapists. She is reporting that they have sex "all the time" (three times a week), and he is reporting that they "never have sex" (only three times a week). We often joke at this point and say "Be sure to keep a careful log of your activities before you come in next week!" What will become important for couple therapy is a combination of the different valuations on an agreed-on event, the function of the disagreement (distance and boundary setting), and the power struggle to have the partner experience the event similarly.

Because each person is focused on changing the partner instead of her or his image there are often breaks in communication. What each says is not what the partner hears. David recalled one of these periods in their long marriage, where he says, "She only heard what she wanted to hear. It was not what I was saying. One year she asked if we could switch up our holiday visits, because her family would be away at the time when we normally would get together. I said that I'd check with my mom, but thought it'd probably be fine. She just went off on me that I was so inflexible and couldn't ever change plans. She didn't hear me say that I'd try and it'd probably work out—by the way, it did."

Sarah quickly jumped in to argue, "He forgets that he took a long time to think it over before he said anything and left me hanging. It was like he was trying to find an excuse to say no and I thought it was just a simple change. It should have been a no-brainer." He argued back and although the issue had long been settled, they were able to experience the original feelings as if the problem was current. When resentment lingers over trivial events, the therapist must confront it and question how functional it is and the relational value of holding on to it over time.

As one client opined, "There are two four-word sentences that strike fear into my heart. One is 'IRS audit'; the other is my wife saying, 'We need to talk.' In both cases I know I will be losing something important. The only question is whether it's a critical part."

The characteristic conversation in the power struggle involves each one perceiving the other as changed. The power struggle is at its core a process struggle, with each partner trying to change the partner back to prior times in the relationship. More likely it is to get the partner to conform closer to the fantasy, projected relationship.

Working Through the Power Struggle (Recycling)

The power struggle/maintenance period is often characterized by these kinds of breaks in communication and feelings of hurt by both parties. If they can clean up the conversation and listen openly to what the partner is actually saying or doing, there is an opportunity to get clear on the partner's wishes and respond effectively. Couples who do this actually recycle back through some of the earlier stages, each time with a deeper connection than in the prior sequence. Most successful couples go through these cycles many times in the course of a relationship. David and Sarah talked about five or six such past power struggles and believed another one was on the horizon. They came in to couple therapy because they were trying to head it off before it got problematic. As they both agreed, "Honeymoon is better than fighting."

As we detail in Chapters 6 and 7, a useful technique during communication exercises is to help each partner "listen to both the words and the music" (i.e., both the literal words and the feeling tone and intent behind them). Jared and Karen related a heated argument in which Karen asked Jared to "stir the noodles." Jared did so and walked away, while Karen fumed that he did not stay until the noodles were cooked and served, which she had expected, but not explicitly requested. In replaying the interaction, Karen interjected that she is usually overwhelmed with multiple tasks at dinnertime and really wants Jared to do his part but is reluctant to ask him due to her resentment that she always has to ask him to do each task until it's done. Upon hearing that, Jared understood Karen's frustration for the first time and agreed to be a full partner at dinnertime. He did, however, request in turn a list of all expected wishes.

When clients come in to therapy with a power struggle, characteristic of this stage, and they want to improve their relationship, the therapist's job is usually focused on communication, problem solving, helping them openly discuss and manage their expectations, some skill learning, and attunement with each of their needs. Most of the time this is necessary, sufficient, and relatively short term (2–3 months of weekly sessions). It is also a good opportunity for both members of a couple to experience personal growth.

When It Doesn't Recycle

The other option when the power struggle persists is for the couple to experience a larger gap between their desires and the reality of the relationship and the specter of a split. The following generic arc of a "chronological divorce sequence" (Shapiro, 1984) explores a trajectory from a committed relationship to dissolution or divorce. The progression involves several escalations. Two actual cases are featured as examples: Sarah and David, whose marriage survived and grew from this process, and Scott and Lisa, who ultimately divorced.

THERAPY BOX 4.1: THE DISCREPANCY BETWEEN WHAT IS EXPECTED AND WHAT ACTUALLY OCCURS

Several times in relationships, when expectations go unmet, the reaction is much stronger than if the same reality occurs without any anticipated behavior on the part of a partner. When one partner envisages that his or her partner will live up to a projected image, there will be greater disappointment than if his or her behavior is simply seen as normal but different.

Very often, disappointment is the crucial element in relational unhappiness. If Mona anticipates a special evening with Al, she builds her hopes, she dreams about it, she makes internal plans for her reaction, she unconsciously is very ready to be shown some special treatment. It is much worse for her if it doesn't come through as expected than if it wasn't anticipated at all. It thus becomes somewhat important to separate out internally generated projections about a partner and the partner him- or herself.

This is often an important component in discord and conflict, common in stages 4 and 5 in the relationship development sequence. Shapiro (2013) has described this in detail with regard to Valentine's Day expectations.

One of the most common experiences couples have is when one partner is expecting a romantic encounter and the other is unaware or uninterested. Such a miscommunication can lead to considerable and inadvertent hurt.

The Multiple Stages of Dissolution and Divorce[2] in Relationships

Just as the development of a relationship may be viewed through a developmental lens, so also may dissolution and breakup be seen as an evolving process. Here we explore a generic model of relational disbanding. Each stage is best approached with a relevant therapeutic approach. The later in the process intervention occurs, the more problematic, complex and difficult it tends to be, especially if the couple desires to stay together.

Escalation 1: Acknowledgment of Developing Issue

Just about adjacent to stage 4 in the relationship cycle is a break in the "happily ever after" dream. In escalation 1, unconscious projections begin to fade with time, being replaced by the partner's actual, as opposed to desired, behavior. One member of the couple makes verbal notice that there is greater than desired distance in the relationship. This can be a result of a lessened connection than was experienced previously; real-life stressors such as work, family or school pressure; a natural reduction of dependency, and so on. Normally, as the distancing continues, one partner will acknowledge the distancing or other discontent verbally, requesting the partner's assistance in "fixing the problem."

For example, if at this stage Sara said to David, "I'm missing how we were before. I know that we've both been busy, but I think it's a problem, could we talk about it?" and had David responded, "You know, I'm glad you mentioned it. I've been feeling like you are too far away these days," the couple is en route to cycling back to the honeymoon stage or similar. They will work on the problem together and the solutions they create will be enhanced by the very fact that they are approaching it as a team and developing greater intimacy.

However, if we are exploring the development of greater distance and ultimately a dissolution of their relationship, his response might be very different. Let's explore this with Scott and Lisa. Suppose Lisa said the same thing about the distance:

1. He may interpret it as blame and deny that he has any role in it. "It's not my fault. In fact, you are the one that's been distant. I am the same I've always been."
2. He may turn it back on her and indicate that she is being inaccurate, "It's your imagination. Everything is fine. You know how you tend to get overemotional about things sometimes." He might also raise the stakes by saying, "It's your problem. You need to handle your needs," or "Are you getting your period?"
3. He may feel guilt and temporarily acquiesce, "You are right. I really messed up. I will do better."
4. He may believe that she is too needy and grumble internally that he rarely has any time to himself.
5. Lisa may choose a time to tell him that is such that he doesn't ever hear her (physically or emotionally). For example, she said that she had confronted him as he walked in the door and the dog was jumping on him. In short, she unconsciously minimized the chance that he'd pay attention. Perhaps she said it when they were in bed when he was half asleep. One client reported that she told him while he was

---

2   The term "divorce" is used here because marital dissolution is often the most difficult for couples. However, much of the process pertains to any long-term relationship dissolution.

engaged in an online video game and his attention was far more focused on that and his co-players than on what she was saying. When this emerged later during therapy, his partner said, "I think my feelings should be more important than some unknown 14-year-old in India in a stupid game."

Therapy at Escalation 1 Is Rare

Few couples consider the problem serious enough to seek outside help. When it is instituted, most of the time the therapy consists of helping the members of the couple learn active listening skills and increase their ability for negotiation and compromise. It is likely short term and quite successful unless there are other more significant issues beneath the surface of the presenting problem (Ables & Brandsma, 1991; Mashkin, 1983; Weingarten, 1990). Successful short-term treatment primarily involves each member clarifying his or her needs for closeness and agreeing to adapt as needed.

Escalation 2: Finding Support Elsewhere

Regardless of how Scott and Lisa managed to avoid closing the growing gap between them, the continuing distance and discord will likely manifest with a more intense attempt to correct the problem. In this case, Lisa found herself self-soothing by developing outside relationships with male friends in her world. Although there was not any physical sexual contact with her new friends, there was mutual complaining about unhappiness with a spouse and a developing emotional intimacy.

These intimate conversations with another person who is at least semi-available (he may also be in a monogamous relationship) may provide Lisa with an emotional connection and a sense that she is capable of more closeness with another man. This solution may take some of the edge off the problem with Scott but is adding a complicating component into their relationship.

Couple Therapy at Escalation 2 Is Also Not Very Common

However, Lisa sought out individual therapy to deal with her personal discomfort with her marriage and guilt about her feelings for her coworker. An individual therapist may strongly recommend couple work for Lisa and Scott, help Lisa explore her mixed feelings, or even view the potential of a new relationship as a reason to either confront Scott more poignantly or to consider opting out of the marriage altogether.

Some therapists may recommend that Lisa bring Scott into her therapy session and do conjoint therapy. Depending on the therapist, the couple's needs, and the situation, this may be effective. The downside risk is that Scott is entering a situation in which there is already an alliance between his wife and the therapist and he will likely feel somewhat vulnerable and threatened. This may be exacerbated by her other growing relationship with her friend. From our contextual viewpoint, where the relationship is the primary issue an individual presents in therapy, couple therapy is often more productive. While it may be accomplished by the individual therapist if alliances are carefully considered, a referral to an independent couple therapist may also be a better option. It may also be useful to bring the partner into the individual therapy a session or two as a "collateral contact".

When Sarah and David faced escalation 2, he found himself reconnecting on the Internet with an "ex" in an e-mail relationship. In response, he sought out a therapist he had seen previously. The therapist recommended a session with Sarah with a colleague. When they began to talk with this counselor, they worked on their communication and desire to make the relationship better. They both described how they "had" to find outside relationships to meet their needs for close communication. As they worked this through, they were reconnecting with each other and were able to cycle back to a more intimate form of their relationship, albeit with more sense of the real partner rather than the imagined one. It is useful to request permission for the individual therapist to consult with the couple therapist and collaborate in order to be on the same page with treatment.

Escalation 3: Report on Outside Relationship

The third escalation is often the first one that is truly heard, because it carries an implied threat. When Lisa said to Scott, "You know when I talk with Julio at work, he gets it. He really understands me," it was the first time that Scott thought there was a serious problem in their relationship. He had a characteristically strong emotional reaction to Lisa's relationship with Julio.

Many partners express anger, sadness, fear, or jealousy at this point. That outpouring of emotion, even though it is negative, is often received as a positive sign by the partner. For Lisa, the fact that Scott was so upset and was sharing it with her was far more gratifying than her unhappiness at the negative aspect of the expressed emotions. She responded with her own heightened emotions.

With the increased emotional intensity, it is not unusual for both partners to redefine their commitment to each other at this time. When this occurs, they may emerge from this "divorce sequence" and cycle back into an earlier stage of the relationship process, perhaps the honeymoon stage, and re-experience increased reconnection. Frequently, the couple's sexual activity increases as if to prove that they are the primary couple and that the "Julio's" of her world are not relevant. However, this increased focus on the relationship occurs with an implied threat and an implication that if Scott does not pay more attention to her, Lisa has already begun to develop an "out."

Grand Gesture

One of the ways a couple during escalation 3 tries to slow or fix the distancing is to indicate the depth of their relationship is to make a grand gesture. It is a time when unmarried couples may choose to "make it legal" or decide to cohabitate. Similarly, already married couples may take on a major new commitment such as getting a pet, buying a home, or having a child. While they were in this stage, Lisa and Scott took on two such commitments.

They got a dog and they purchased a condo in the building in which they previously were renting. This can be a normal and useful transition as long as it is done thoughtfully rather than routinely.

Therapy at Escalation 3

This is a high priority time for couple therapy, yet it is infrequently instituted. When couples do come in for couples work at this time, it tends to be relatively short term

(2–3 months), communication based, and skill oriented; involves fairly direct problem solving; and underscores and reassesses relational myths. It is also usually effective.

Unfortunately, most couples eschew therapy at this point because things seem much better, they are more passionate with each other, and they coalesce around the grand gesture. In the words of one client, "Who needs counseling to bring us down when everything is going so well?" He did not focus on the demand created by the potential other relationship, or on the implied threat.

Two groups of couples are more likely to seek therapy at this stage: professionals in mental health and related fields and those in which at least one had been through a prior divorce.

Escalation 4: A Rationale to Be Apart

The development of a concept of being apart is another major escalation. Sarah and David never got to this stage, but Lisa and Scott did. He recalled that she said, almost in passing one day, "You know, no one person could ever meet all of my needs." On another occasion, she opined "Marriage may well be an outdated institution. With the increased longevity expected in this century, marriage is no longer a 25-year commitment. It's more like fifty. It's hard to imagine that anyone could be happy together for 50 years or more."

Lisa said this after a night out with her female friends. To discuss the nature of modern marriage philosophically with a group of friends may be interesting, enjoyable, and a reason for thinking more deeply. Apparently, the four women present were all discussing how the essence of commitment had changed. They quoted cultural anthropologist Margaret Mead, who famously said, "I've been married three times—and each time I married the right person." Mead promoted the notion that all people should have three marriages, the first for love, the second for parenting, and the third for companionship (Howard, 1984).

When she was discussing this with her friends over dinner, it was an intellectual exercise.

However, discussing the same content with Scott is very different. In that context, it is not a philosophical discussion. It relates directly to their relationship and infers a divorce may be appealing.

At this point, the relationship is under threat both emotionally and cognitively. One interesting systemic phenomenon that often occurs during this escalation is the appearance of an identified patient (IP). As a way to maintain the homeostasis in a relationship, one of the partners may develop special needs for caring, such as an illness, injury, loss of a job, and so on. The thoughts of splitting are set aside to deal with the crisis and partners work together to surmount the difficulty. Sometimes this may become chronic.

For couples with children, the emergent IP is often a child. When Alysha and Dan were at this point, their daughter Grace, who always was a stellar student, suddenly began to have troubles at school with both her grades and her behavior. Their daughter's distress brought the couple together as parents to deal with their child's needs, and thoughts of being apart were temporarily put on hold.

Of course, that is the problem with an IP-based fusion. Unless there is also an opportunity to work on the difficulties that led to the distancing, it is likely to reemerge as soon as the dilemma has passed. Alysha and Dan were fortunate. Their daughter was referred to a counselor at the school who asked to see the entire family for a few sessions. Once her assessment was complete, she recommended couple therapy for Alysha and Dan and did some weekly play therapy sessions with Grace. The work in couple therapy got at the root of the ongoing relational issue, and as the parents seemed to relate better with one another, Grace's school problems were alleviated.

When Lisa began talking "theoretically" about a divorce, Scott developed headaches and a spike in blood pressure, followed by a painful rash on his back that was resistant to antibiotics. Lisa cared for him in part by applying a special cream to the rash site four times a day.

Therapy during escalation 4 is potentially a last chance for short-term, communication-oriented therapy; it is also a time to explore their desire for greater intimacy and the possibility of increasing their connection with each other. Once escalation 5 occurs, couple therapy typically involves structural shifts and is commonly longer term.

Effective therapy at this point usually involves a clear assessment of the therapeutic goal: to be together and make it better or find a way to split as amicably as possible. Doherty and Harris (2017) refers to this as assessing whether it is a hard (i.e., abuse, affair, addiction) or soft problem ("We're growing apart"; "I don't know what to do to be happy"; etc.). That assessment often plays a significant role not only in direction, but in the couple's commitment to the work. Any work to help the identified patient must be addressed as well as the longer-standing issues of the nature of the relationship itself. Often each member of the couple desires a somewhat different goal. For Lisa, one of the goals was greater emotional intensity, whereas Scott was more oriented toward "peaceful living together."

Once the goals are negotiated and communication has been improved, problem solving may begin. During this period, there are often relevant homework assignments for the couple. Therapists often take a more active role in working with the couple, using techniques such as role playing, translator, and traffic cop, described in detail in Chapter 7.

For example, if a symbiotic or enmeshed relationship has been identified during assessment, some psychoeducation may be beneficial. Discussing the fact that one person is incapable of fulfilling each person's needs for a lifetime may lead to a fruitful conversation on whether outside male and female friendships and time away from each other is agreeable and to what extent it is comfortable for each partner.

It is important to reiterate that this is the last time that short-term therapy to help the couple stay together and improve their relationship is likely. The next step in the progression involves structural changes in the relationship. In the next escalation, a third party is added to the relationship.

Escalation 5: A Break in the Relationship Primacy

This is often referred to as the time of an extramarital affair. This is characteristically the most difficult and most common incorporation of an alternative primary relationship and will be highlighted here. However, it is essential to note that "an affair" may not involve mucous membrane contact. It may not be physically sexual. The essential component is that something besides the partner becomes more compelling and significantly draws attention away from the relationship.

Besides the physical assignation, some other "affairs" may be with an addiction, friends, families of origin, children, work, hobbies, social media and computer games, and so on. These may all bring a major barrier into the relationship, but characteristically the sexual affair is the most problematic because it typically involves breaking a specific vow, betrayal, secrecy, dishonesty, loss of trust, and a comparison person.

Like physical violence or having a child, affairs permanently alter a committed relationship. It has been compared to trying to uncrack an egg or attempting to get toothpaste back into a tube. Because of the multiple implications of an affair, the relationship has to find new ground if it is to proceed. Not all marriages survive an affair, but many do and actually change in ways that make them more durable in the future, but it is no easy process.

An affair occurs when one person is involved with an outside person despite an expectation or agreement (i.e., marriage vows) of monogamy. This does not specifically apply to so-called "open marriages" or polyamory, which have their own form of criteria for betrayal.

These alternative forms of relationship were described in Chapter 3 and therapeutic considerations are explored in Chapter 5. When seeing clients in these latter types of relationships, it is important for the therapist to avoid being judgmental, but also not to blithely accept them. It is best to explore their motivation and the effects on their primary relationship.

Affairs are interesting in a number of ways. For one thing, they are often with a person who is unattainable or inappropriate for a long-term relationship. Thus, an affair is characteristically less about finding a new partner than about an ultimatum to the partner. This is important for therapists to understand as she or he focuses back on the impact on the relationship, not the affair per se.

Consequence/Unconscious Motivation of an Affair

It is therapeutically useful for the practitioner to view the affair in light of the primary relationship. By considering the affair as a communication between the primary partners, therapists can generate a number of potential workable hypotheses. In short, from a therapeutic perspective, it is almost as if one partner is saying, "I told you something was wrong. You didn't listen. I went to others to feel better and I told you that 'Julio' was better at listening to me. You didn't listen. I discussed the idea of how marriage may not be reasonable in today's world. You didn't listen. So now I am essentially applying an emotional 2x4 to your head to get your attention. I am having sex with someone else. Can you hear me now?" While sex is the most focused upon issue in an affair, partners often stray out of a need for connection and appreciation of their uniqueness as much as the desire for more exciting sex.

Definition of an Affair

What actually constitutes betrayal and an affair? It would seem relatively easy to identify an affair, but it can get very complicated. Is flirting an affair? Is pornography? What about prostitution or a massage parlor with a "happy ending?" Does a relationship or friendship with someone who the partner doesn't know about qualify? What about an online relationship with no physical contact? Does it have to be physical? Does an emotional affair count? Or is it considered a worse violation and more damaging? What constitutes an affair in an open relationship? From the authors' point of view, a current affair is similar to other critical matters that violate explicit and/or implicit agreements partners have with each other. Unquestionably, an affair that occurs during couple therapy at least distracts the offending person and usually results in diminished attention and affection to his or her partner. Because the secrets, guilt, and lies to cover up the outside relationship interfere with effective therapy, it needs to terminate or become known to the other partner.

Among non-sexual lines, can workaholism and unavailability be considered an affair? Does training for a marathon that involves considerable daily time consumption—which in effect puts something else in the primary position instead of a partner—count?

Affairs can come in many ways. Is a one-night drunken dalliance many years in the past as problematic as an ongoing long-term relationship? Is the other party known to the spouse?

It is important to note that an affair that remains a secret may be different than a discovered affair. Marital therapy can be extremely problematic when one partner has a secret other to whom he or she can retreat when the marital relationship becomes difficult. Secrets that do not come to light are almost impossible to address and work through.

The known affair is different. Discovery creates a crisis in the primary relationship and must be addressed. These affairs become known in a variety of ways: confession, clues left in obvious places, detective work by partners, or third-party revelations.

Many who have affairs are emotionally tortured by guilt or need the partner to know as a way of getting their attention to work on the relationship. It may be a verbal confession, or it may be indirect. Lisa sat down with "a-need-to-talk" conversation and told Scott about her sexual relationship with Julio. By contrast, Ken discovered that his partner of many years was involved elsewhere by a number of clues she left around their home (a new soap scent that they didn't use; a small gift that she claimed she bought herself; hours away during the day and evening while presumably with clients or her girlfriends; and the final clue, her birth control diaphragm being "accidentally" left in the glove compartment of a car they both used). She admitted the affair only after many hours of angry confrontations.

Some partners sense that something has changed, and although the clues may be subtle, they embark on a discovery of confirmation. When Elly came in for couple therapy, she told her husband and the therapist simultaneously that she had "proof" of his affair with a coworker. She had gone into his e-mail account and his phone logs and discovered multiple calls, texts, and messages that left little doubt. Such an invasion of privacy creates problems in itself, even though the offended partner may justify it as necessary; the person having the affair may feel and act like an adolescent with an intrusive parent. This can create resentment, often driving further distance between them.

Finally, some partners find out because a mutual acquaintance saw or heard something.

Alison's sister told her that she saw Alison's partner at dinner with another woman and asked her sister if she knew who that woman was. He had told Alison that he was at a business dinner with his male boss.

Affair Uncovered

Once the affair is known, there is likely to be a strong emotional reaction, although it may be delayed somewhat. Several couples reported that the partner seemed to take it in stride and requested details. At some point during the telling the emotion rises to significant proportions. It is useful to note that some couple counselors recommend or insist that such detailed conversations take place only during sessions, to be able to support both and contain any potential violent blow ups.

Although the emotional reactions may be intense (some have led to homicide or suicide), the outpouring of feelings usually involves hurt, anger, and fear, along with secondary reactions such as withdrawal, jealousy, surprise, or relief.

Mary said, "I'm actually somewhat relieved. I knew what I was feeling, but he kept denying it. I was starting to think I was going crazy."

- Although the betrayed partner usually suffers significant emotional pain, the unfaithful partner often does also, when infidelity is revealed or discovered.
- One of the most difficult aspects of couple therapy is confronting the "unfaithful" partner and strongly encouraging him or her to take responsibility for his or her behavior, while also helping both partners to accept some responsibility for what went amiss between them.
- Whitaker (1989) often said, "[I]ndividuals do not have an affair. Couples have affairs" (Neill and Kniskern; p. 164).

One primary indication that the affair may be more about the primary relationship than about a new one is when the affair is with someone who is very unlike the partner and who is frequently unavailable or inappropriate for a long-term relationship. Julio, with whom Lisa had the affair, was himself married with three young children. He came from a very different culture with quite different values. He was 25 years' Lisa's senior, underemployed, and unable to support either his family or Lisa.

The guilt build-up, desire to hurt the spouse, or to get his or her attention leads to an uncovering of the affair. Once the affair is uncovered, the intense emotional reactions may be followed by a period of attempts to punish the offending partner. Behavioral manifestations might include threats to harm the partner, self, or lover; destruction of property; revenge affairs; or similar actions designed in part to rebalance the power relationship. If the couple is in therapy during this period, ethical considerations must be carefully observed.

In response, the adulterous spouse often makes an attempt at penance, typically involving a symbolic gesture (i.e., doing something that the spouse has always wanted, such as taking a trip, shopping for a special item, or starting therapy), which under other circumstances might have strengthened the relationship. It is important for the partner who has the affair not to lose their autonomy as a form of repentance; for example to have the wronged spouse check all their texts, emails, or phone calls, and to account for their activities each moment of the day. This type of overcompensation can backfire and create resentment and further damage to the relationship. Sometimes, couples seriously compound their problems by doing something excessive or maladaptive, such as increasing their financial debt or having a child "to fix the relationship." Whatever the attempt, however, it is characteristically rejected as insufficient, particularly if the outside involvement continues or increases. This renewed extra-relationship involvement may be with the same person, or it may be with new affairs, hobbies, work, or the children. Whatever the form of avoidance, the consequence is increased distance.

Despite common perceptions, it should be noted here that although having an affair definitely hurts one's partner, some individuals may be spurred to engage with another due to lack of impulse control, hypersexuality, or a basic personality structure that does not maintain appropriate boundaries. This is a sensitive situation to address because while it can be inferred that real intimacy may never have developed in the primary relationship, it may be more of a deficiency in an individual more than a critical relational dysfunction. We could say that such an individual should not commit to a monogamous relationship, or at least not until such issues are resolved.

The wronged spouse will likely seek support against the partner from friends, clergy, family, therapists, or others. The initial focus often has a tone of "look what this ogre has done to me."

Couple Therapy at Escalation 5

This is a common time for couples to seek therapy, but getting both parties involved and committed is very difficult. Oftentimes, one person is pressured into the therapy and resistance is often quite high.

There are no easy solutions to this level of relational dysfunction, and therapy that is begun will most likely be long term and have reconstructive goals. Because trust must be rebuilt, effective change will necessitate creation of an appropriate therapeutic environment and relationships with the therapist.

Therapy When the Affair Is Still Active

Although the bases for counseling and therapy can be initiated—including help with getting over the grief, anger, feelings of betrayal, and loss of trust—no effective couple therapy can fully commence until the affair has ended! Effective therapy always creates some disruption of safety patterns and homeostatic shifts and anxiety in the clients. If one of the partners can go outside the relationship for easy soothing when things get difficult in the couple relationship, he or she can avoid dealing with the more difficult relational issues with the partner.

If the affair is with a bottle, such as an addiction, couple therapy is best begun after the person has been sober for some time or at least until rehabilitation issues have ceased to erupt in the relationship. Many therapists use a 6- or 12-month guideline. In the interim, counseling may occur, but attempts to rectify the relational problems can only commence once there is no chance to escape to the addictive substance. Studies on couple therapy during active addiction seem to show a positive effect on addiction mitigation, but little to no effect on relational satisfaction (e.g., Winters, Fals-Stewart, O'Farrell, Birchler, & Kelley, 2002). Some addiction-oriented therapists (e.g., Brown & Lewis, 1999; Navarra, 2018) do report work with couples in various stages of recovery. Their results also indicate that couple work is primarily effective on the addiction side, rather than on the relationship. The majority of couple therapists begin couple therapy only when the addiction is well into recovery.

Prognosis After an Affair

There is no quick recovery from a betrayal. There is a lengthy process of mourning the imagined relationship, healing, and rebuilding, always with the knowledge of the infidelity that occurred. Time, patience, and significant honest communication are necessary if the relationship is to continue favorably. However, it is clear from both research evidence and clinical observation that the majority of committed couples do stay together after such a rupture of trust. For both couples and their therapists there is no "one-size-fits-all" answer. However, with professional relationship counseling, there are some basic steps involved in healing and rebuilding the relationship:

1. Clear honest communication is essential. Both partners need to listen to each other. Each needs to accept what the partner is saying empathically and with an attempt at understanding. This doesn't require acceptance or agreement, but listening openly is essential. Because learning to listen to hurtful material can be so stressful, it is rarely a short process. It is rare for couples to be able to engage this way without a third party to "hold their feet to the fire," preferably a highly trained professional counselor or therapist.

2. Highly emotional outpourings are to be expected. It is imperative that the therapist both allows for and contains both verbal and nonverbal expressions of hurt, anger, sadness, loss, shame, and potentially some admissions of relief. Ideally, the intensity of expressed affect can be heard and understood.

3. The real key is for the offending partner to be entirely open to the other partner's questions as a path to reestablishing trust. A caution: The questioning partner must be carefully restrained from obsessive curiosity about minute details. It can be a delicate balance between discovering particularly hurtful details and letting imagination be far worse than actual events.

4. The therapist and the couple need to consider openly whether the chasm created by discovery of an affair is a reason to leave the relationship or if it can weather the storm. One or both partners may feel conflicted or ambivalent. If they try to stay together to rebuild a viable relationship going forward, couple therapy or effective intervention by an experienced third party requires a commitment by each to the process of therapy and to their partner.

Escalation 6: Separation

If the affair does not result in the couple redoubling their efforts to do what it takes to stay together and get past the betrayal and its aftermath, one member of the couple moves out. Although the emotional pain is characteristically high for both partners, there is also often a sense of relief.

Scott and Lisa were unable to navigate the hurt of her affair, and after a brief attempt at couple counseling, during which she was unwilling to give up her lover, she asked Scott to move out "while [they] figure[d] it out." He found a small apartment nearby and left.[3]

During a subsequent individual therapy session, Lisa reported, "At first it was a great relief to be apart, but soon after, I got really depressed, fearful, and lonely (I did see Julio a few times to help me through a bad night). I texted Scott almost every day and asked how he was doing, but it upset me that he seemed to be handling the whole thing better than me. He reported that his biggest problem is slow Internet access in his new place."

---

3 Regardless of which partner had the affair, in heterosexual couples it is most often the man who moves out.

Lisa's experience was not unusual. Frequently the person who is left in the couple's home has a harder adjustment. Although the partners who have left are missing their normal routine, access to various appliances, and other personal property and accoutrements of a relationship and comfortable life, they do not have the constant reminders of the relationship in every corner of their living space. They may experience a new freedom in a new environment that will be hard to lose.

In response to the separation distress, many of the partners who were the offenders in escalation 5 make promises that cannot be kept. "I'll do anything if you'd just be willing to try again." These "promises" often open the door to potential reconciliation. Often the couple will get together and begin talking. However, without an unbiased third party available, the conversation frequently hits emotional triggers and reverts to former patterns and "the fight."[4] Characteristically, the talking goes well for a while, but as each becomes more vulnerable and open, they become more threatened as well. When the fear arises, despite each partners' best intentions, it is common to respond defensively and with blaming. This is how the discussion turns into old patterns with renewed anger, disappointment, and distancing. Thus, attempts at reconciliation paradoxically end up having the opposite (distancing) effect.

It is not unusual for couples who are separating and even divorcing to reconnect temporarily in bed. They may have sexual intercourse during this period, often described as an expression of hope to be back together and to alleviate a loneliness that they feel when separated. Most often, both parties will describe this love making as tender, caring, and hurtful in the current context. Scott described these nights together with Lisa as "bittersweet; familiar and comforting and at the same time unfulfilling."

Therapy at Escalation 6: The Four Questions

As one might guess, escalation 6 is when the couple has agreed that separation, whether temporary or permanent, is the best course of action. Couple work at this stage usually begins with discussing four key matters and getting agreements before the physical separation takes place. Couples who do not make agreements about these matters are open to far greater hurt, usually quite quickly.

Therapists are advised to introduce these topics and to be fairly insistent that the separating couple address them:

1. Children and child care arrangements
2. Finances and spending
3. Agreements about their relationship and meetings
4. Other relationships

What is very interesting is that although these are very obvious, many separating couples have not fully considered all of them. Scott and Lisa did not have children, but they were surprised by each other's initial answers to these questions. Lisa said that she assumed that finances would remain the same, with Scott paying a larger share of the expenses to keep her in their former joint residence. He was assuming that he would pay for his place and she would pay for hers, and if that meant that she had to move to a smaller

---

4   "The fight" is described in depth in the therapy section on enactment.

place "that was only fair." Lisa also expected that they could get together frequently and talk and maybe continue to be sexual. Scott believed that, although they may connect at times, the distance would increase and the gap between meetings would stretch out. Finally, when Scott said that he expected to begin dating, Lisa was shocked. Although she was the one who had an affair and was still in contact with Julio, she didn't anticipate the implications of Scott doing likewise.

It often takes a few sessions to get these ironed out. The couple often engages in a lot of avoidance, requiring a considerable determination for the therapist to keep them on point.

Second, the therapist needs to address the major issue of what occurs in therapy:

1. Do they treat the separation as temporary and keep meeting as a couple trying to work through the difficulties?
2. Do they treat the separation as a step toward divorce and continue to meet to make the process as painless as possible?
3. Does one or both want to continue in individual therapy?
4. Do they stop meeting as a couple altogether?
5. What referrals should be made for individual therapy?

At times these discussions can become contentious, with one partner attempting to blackmail the other. For example, Lisa could have told Scott, "If you are going to date other women, then let's file for divorce now!" The therapist has a sensitive job to negotiate without bias. He or she must try to prevent one partner from holding a hammer over the other's head while exploring the reasons for such a demand, perhaps interjecting some psychoeducation about optional arrangements during the separation.

The nature of continuing therapy is quite different based on the answers to these questions.

Escalation 7: Support for the Split

Both parties characteristically seek out support during a separation, and many friends and family members will support a continuing splitting of the relationship. The advice to break apart often comes from a desire to help a loved one who is in pain. Of course, some friends may support the attempts to get back together.

Scott's best friend was particularly supportive, declaring, "You know you can count on me whatever happens. I've known you both for a long time and I like you both, but you and Lisa have had a lot of basic differences since the beginning and maybe being apart will be best for you both." He invited Scott to dinner with him and his wife and was generally available to go on long walks while Scott talked.

Lisa's friends, who were also at the late night gathering just prior to escalation 4 (the rationale to be apart), were also supportive of their friend, but less so of her trying to stay in the relationship. As Katie, who had known Lisa the longest, opined, "You know, Scott was never that exciting for you. You met him after the tumultuous relationship with Barry and he was a welcome relief, but you have said on many occasions that he prefers to stay home and read, play computer games, or watch TV rather than to go out. Maybe this break is really you getting back to who you really are."

The Surprise Defections

In general, both partners find supportive friends to help them make the break. However, there is one almost ubiquitous exception. Almost every couple who goes through a divorce has friends, often a couple, who "disappears" from their life. The couple in question is almost always a surprise. They are often long-time friends who would be expected to be supportive. Instead, they are nowhere to be found.

For Scott and Lisa, the couple who became unavailable had been close friends from college who lived within walking distance. They were in each other's wedding parties. As Lisa reported, "It's amazing that Jenna just disappeared off the face of the earth. She and Jorge were almost like brother and sister to us. At first I thought they took Scott's side because I was the one who had the affair, but when I asked Scott how Jorge was, he just said that he hadn't heard from either of them in months."

The reasons for this disappearance may relate more to the other couple than to the separating one in therapy. Often, they distance themselves because of a fear of contagion when their relationship feels a little rocky also. The threat of a close friend couple breaking up may just be too fearful. Another reason for losing friends at this time is that they were mostly friends of the couple, rather than one individual. This point provides a prime opportunity for the therapist to discuss the need for friends in a relationship as "yours, mine, and ours." Without maintaining individual friendships, couples can become overly enmeshed and uninteresting to each other and fall into dull routines. Having individual friends can also be seen as an insurance policy; there's always an opportunity for activities with friends, with or without their partner.

Divorce Attorneys

A second form of support for the split is the introduction of a professional to make the split permanent. When attorneys are brought in, their work is often directly conflictual with couple counseling. When attorneys do their job well, they help their client get out of the relationship as whole as possible. When both sides have a litigious legal counsel, the financial and emotional pain can be increased dramatically.

Litigation in family law can be used to get a best deal for a client and to hurt the opposing side. The greater the latter motivation, the greater the cost for a divorce and the longer the anger lasts. There is no shortage of high net-worth individuals whose highly public divorces have gone into the millions of dollars in legal fees. In one local case, legal fees had reached the $2 million mark, prior to discussion of custody or property settlement. More famously, the divorce of Frank and Jamie McCourt involving ownership of the Los Angeles Dodgers sported legal fees of "upwards of 20 million dollars" (Grigoriadis, 2011). When that level of litigation is part of a dissolution, chances of reconciliation are almost nil.

The emergence of family law mediation has somewhat altered the landscape. Rather than litigiousness, mediation tries to find middle ground where each partner is harmed as little as possible in a settlement. Family law mediators often are skilled in some counseling techniques and will work in greater coordination with couple therapists. However, their overall goals may be inimical to each other.

During the separation and divorce process, even at this late date in the trajectory toward the permanent split, couples may still get together socially and sexually. If there are children involved, they have to work out the best possible parenting arrangements. Mediators and judges are prone to placing the children's needs first as well. Couples who work out the parenting arrangements amicably tend to have better longer-term relationships and minimize the impact on the children. Although, based on her 25-year longitudinal study, Wallerstein (2000) indicates that the long-term impact of divorce on children is often substantive. It is usually sobering for the therapist to discuss not only the benefits of avoiding litigation and agreeing on custody and property settlement at this time, but also to emphasize that they will be co-parents forever for their children and potentially their grandchildren; long-term grudges, bickering, and divisiveness can be detrimental for the whole family.

Therapy During Escalation 7

During the time of separation, divorce, and general movement away from the relationship, couple-oriented therapy often ceases. Working with individuals going through this stage of dissolution involves identity issues. Often, divorcing people respond as Alison did, when she repeatedly asked, "Who am I alone? I went from my father's house to the college dorms to sharing an apartment for a short time then to our apartment together. Now it's 25 years later and I don't think I ever even thought about who Alison is. I am still Mrs. W."

The individually oriented therapy during this period involves both pragmatic concerns about places to live, finances, and being alone. Moving from a division of labor lifestyle to having to develop all the skills of living on one's own can be daunting. As Alison remarked, "When Chris moved out, I didn't even know how to work the complicated TV and music system he set up." For his part, cooking, laundry, and getting up to speed with the needs of a college sophomore daughter were all new. While none of these skills in and of themselves are insurmountable, the sudden need to handle many new things is challenging. Alison related, "I let him come over to do his laundry (with instructions) if he simplified the TV, so I could watch a show when I wanted. I am getting the hang of it and even saved a show on the DVR by myself!" Even though trends in recent decades have shown that more men in heterosexual relationships share household and family tasks, they are often dependent on women to be the household manager and may initially appear lost when faced with ordinary chores (Krantzler, 1974, 2014). By contrast, in such instances newly divorced or separated partners may often feel liberated, discover themselves in new ways, and break out socially as never before.

The themes that develop in longer-term therapy include foci on grief and mourning; individual development; intrapsychic work, particularly with fears of replication of the same relationship with a new person; family-of-origin issues; worries about additional failures; and mortality. Therapy may well last for over a year and must be considered a lengthy process.

Although the particular divorce date may occur at any time during this period, even months or years afterward, the event itself can be jarring. For example, despite the fact that he was in a new and better relationship and was finding a new much more gratifying career, Scott reported, "When Lisa came over with the final paper (divorce decree), I was shaken." He added later, "Lisa and I spent the whole afternoon together, talking and crying."

Therapists can anticipate some regression, longing, or second thoughts around the date of legal dissolution. Thus, support, empathy, and sometimes gentle reminders about the reasons for the divorce are helpful.

Escalation 8: A New Start

There aren't any myths or customs in our culture for the recently divorced. Often, there is a period of mourning, followed by an attempt to carve out a new individual life. Almost every divorced person vows "not to make the mistake again," but unconscious repetition compulsion or a pull toward the presumed security of the status quo may lead individuals into just such arrangements. Often after reflection, an individual may strike out on a new life path.

Homemakers may enter the business world or go back to school, and businessmen and women may opt out of the corporate world and adopt a new lifestyle.

Scott, who had been moderately successful as a project manager at a high-tech firm, decided to take classes in a masters-level counseling psychology program. After a few terms, he took a leave of absence from his job to go to school full time. A few years later, he completely switched career fields. Lisa, who had previously relied on Scott for her stable life, began training as a tax specialist during the April filing period and then went on to work at a CPA firm.

The bigger shift for Scott was that he began to connect with friends and associates in a much more open and authentic manner, greatly encouraged by ongoing individual therapy.

Learning About Oneself in Relationships

The essential task at this stage is to discover more about self and relationships. There are three common ways to do this:

- Withdrawal and introspection
- Multiple relationships
- Involvement in the "greatest relationship in world history" (with a classic flaw)

Approximately a third of the population favors each of the methods. Sometimes people may cycle through more than one. The essential component is that the form of learning chosen be ego-syntonic. For example, people who are more introverted are far more likely to learn through introspection.

Withdrawal and Introspection

This method allows individuals to focus inwardly and to learn about who they are in relationships by first learning about themselves. These people often experiment with spiritual programs, retreats, classes, and recreate their home life. They seldom date or look outward for insights.

Multiple Relationships

This method allows individuals to learn about themselves and social relationships through several different types of relationships. Characteristically more extraverted, they find solace, comfort, and learning in interaction. Frequently, there is considerable sexual contact and experimentation. Deeper emotional involvement is less likely than discovering parts of the self in different relationships. As Carol described, "I think I am doing *Sex in the City.* I am intellectually stimulated by Fred, I like the political work that Sid is doing, Tony is not much intellectually, but has a great body and is an exceptional lover, and Mark is someone I can talk to about anything."

There is characteristically less deep emotional involvement, and one-night stands (hooking-up) are common. When deeper involvements are attained, they are mitigated by not being the only relationship. For example, Carol admitted that she felt a little guilty about being sexual with all of them, "but not guilty enough to stop."

"Greatest Relationship in World History, except ..."

Some individuals throw themselves into a relationship that is the "soulmate" dream, *with a significant flaw.* The flaw is built in because this is not the time to get into a more permanent relationship and it guarantees that the relationship is time limited or has an upward limit. As Lee described, "Carmen would be the perfect mate for me if it weren't for (the flaw)." For Lee, Carmen's "flaw" was that she was married and had three young children. Beth, an athlete who swam distances and ran marathons, developed this intense love relationship with a man who was paraplegic. Some common flaws include wrong age, sex, religion, interests, socioeconomic status, lifestyle, incarceration, or marital status. For Cecily, the flaw in her relationship was that her lover was undocumented, having overstayed his student visa, and had little chance of getting a green card because of trouble with the law.

The flaw is essential. It protects the divorcing person by enabling him or her to be totally in love without having to face a long-term commitment. The relationship is an affirmation that the divorcing person is truly a good person, a good lover, and not a failure.

One form of this is reflexively going back to one's former spouse, an old flame, or connecting with a high school or college classmate they always wanted to date.

Robby had an affair with his now-remarried ex-wife and sought out women he hadn't seen in decades, including his high school sweetheart 35 years ago.

Basically, regardless of approach, this period is the time to learn on relational training wheels. During this time, many will develop their "top ten" list of attributes and activities they prefer in a new partner. This can become an elusive quest, and a therapist may be helpful to explore with the person what emotions and needs are essential versus desirable and to prioritize basic needs over superficial ones. It is also helpful to discuss "red flags" they may see in a potential partner as well as "deal breakers" (i.e., what could be a sign of a basic incompatibility and what issues—such as children, moving, pets, unhealthy lifestyle, etc.—they absolutely would not tolerate).

Therapy During Escalation 8

This is a time for individual therapy. Different clients are seeking different forms of therapy. Some are looking for support and skill training. This group is focused on the need for skills to develop new relationships. Their dating skills are both unpracticed and outdated (existing essentially at the level when they met their now former relationship). This is less of an issue for those coming out of short relationships than for those who have been out of the dating market for a decade or longer.

Most clients seeking therapy at this stage are focused on better understanding themselves and ways to avoid making a similar mistake in the future. If the method is ego-syntonic, therapy involves support and exploring a different form of single life. Issues such as loneliness and attempted adaptations to alleviate that discomfort are common. Sometimes, fairly unhealthy ways to deal with a sense of loss, failure, and even fears of mortality are avoided by use of drugs, alcohol, frenzied activity, and other psychologically induced symptoms.

Carol, the person with multiple relationships, said, "I think I almost had a panic attack when I found myself with no activities, no men, no plans one weekend." When her therapist asked her to say more about those feelings, Carol responded, "Well it was a long weekend," laughed, and then became very solemn and inquired, "Will I ever be okay alone, when my life is not filled up with activity?" This began some important work regarding her family of origin, relational history, and fear of introspection.

Often, individuals faced by emotional pain will respond with avoidance or, by contrast, immersion. One form of adaptation that may involve both is to either remarry, or if it is prior to legal divorce, to "give it another try." Although definitive statistics are unclear, there seems to be a surprising number of couples who actually divorce and remarry.

Of course, a person can also symbolically remarry by quickly finding another partner who seems on the surface to be different but allows for a repetition of the pattern that existed in the earlier relationship. This often follows a common naïve belief, expressed well by Jonas. He concluded, "The only reason my marriage failed was I simply chose the wrong person. I was so attracted to her physically, I just lost sight of anything else."

Jonas's ex-wife was physically a tall, slender, very attractive woman, but she was also selfish and expected others to provide more care for her than she was willing to offer in return. After a few years of "feeling like her servant," Jonas opted out of their marriage. Jonas, however, had little time to explore his own real needs when he met a new partner. She was unlike his ex-wife in age, race, height, and physical appearance. However, because she came to the relationship very insecure, she also "turned out to be" very demanding and needy and Jonas was back in the same marriage, albeit with a new partner.

Lisa, who had an affair during her marriage to Scott, had what seemed to be an opposite experience. When she was with Scott, he was the stable one in the relationship. She could be more spontaneous, knowing that he would provide security. Prior to being with Scott, she was in a relationship with Barry, who she described as "irresponsible and often engaging in some shady business." Sometime during the latter stages of the relationship with Scott, she began to find him "overly cautious, boring, and tuned out to her needs."

Once she began dating, she was careful to look for men who would not be so cautious and boring. She actually met Sam through a location-based dating app that allowed her to swipe right if she liked the looks of a man who was in her physical vicinity. Sam swiped right also, and they hit it off well. She reported that it was the first time she had "hooked-up with someone that way" and that she "didn't even know who he was or anything about him." Nonetheless their relationship developed, and Sam was soon living in her apartment. She described Sam as 180 degrees different than Scott. He was "between jobs" and had lost his license because of DUIs and a failure to appear in court. He also apparently had left college with only a few units to complete and had begun several jobs in the past few years only to quit fairly precipitously.

For the therapy with Lisa, the most significant part of this relationship was not about his irresponsibility, but about how she managed to get into the same relationship she had with Scott. She just switched roles. She became the security and Sam was the freedom side of the equation. Helping a client to understand that she had replicated the *relationship* and that her model for relating was split between freedom seeking and security might be less effective than encouraging her to face a different form of relationship: one that was more equal, far more anxiety provoking and intimate, something she had avoided most of her adult life.

For both Jonas and Lisa, therapy involved facing the internal, unconscious pressures that contributed to the failed marriages. Special attention was paid to relational myths, fears of intimacy, and small experiments with doing something different and facing the fears of the unknown. In a sense, when a marriage dissolves, individuals get the opportunity to redo some of their relational errors in adolescence, albeit in their adult bodies.

Escalation 9: Becoming Truly Single

At least in North America, people who divorce are very likely to remarry. Statistics vary, but most indications are that remarriage (or an alternative long-term monogamy) occurs for 80% or more of divorcees. This has famously been described as the "triumph of hope over experience" by Samuel Johnson (Boswell, 1791/1986). Most individuals today find greater fulfilment in relationship than in a more solitary single life. With the cultural shifts toward greater acceptance of same-sex marriage, the number of euphemistic same-sex "confirmed bachelors," "bachelorettes," and "spinsters" has decreased. Research strongly indicates that men are more likely to remarry quite quickly, often within a year (Shapiro, 1993). This quick turnaround usually does not allow time for introspection and opportunities to explore both oneself and aspects of relationships that may be essential for future relational success.

If we consider the sequence people go through, it is single, married, divorced, single. It is an interesting question to reflect on how and when one goes from a divorced status to a single status. Ava, who was married for over a decade before a divorce, was one of many who reported, "It's funny. I realized that I was single when I unconsciously check the "S box" on a government form instead of the "D box.""

Therapy During Escalation 9

This trajectory from relationship beginnings and cycles through dissolution is a potentially useful way to get a handle on the progression and the stages in which clients may be. By knowing the stage of development and dissolution, more targeted therapeutic approaches are likely, with both greater empathy for clients and sufficient support for them to make attempts at change in their behavior, emotions, and ways of thinking about where they are in a potentially lengthy process.

As is discussed throughout this text, knowledge of the clients' developmental relationship capacity allows for far more targeted and effective interventions. Doing a careful assessment and asking directly which path they believe they are on as a couple throughout various points in therapy can minimize frustration and unfocused discussion. A couple who comes to therapy with one or both partners seeking a way out of the relationship needs guidance to assert their desires and resources to achieve their goal. A couple who needs to improve an otherwise good relationship has different needs from one whose relationship is nearly broken and requires mending and new tools to overcome resentment and recreate intimacy. Knowing, for example, that a couple is deciding whether to remain together requires far different approaches to therapy than for couples who have already made a decision and want help in affecting the outcome. David and Sarah needed help in bringing them back together. Scott and Lisa ultimately needed help in getting apart and beginning anew. Best therapy requires meeting the clients' needs.

SUMMARY

Intimate relationships often begin with a "spark," an electricity, and a "knowing" that this person seems to be "that special one." This initial phase is bound to change, and every relationship, whether short term or long term, experiences waxing and waning over time. Some are blissfully harmonious over a lifetime. Some become excessively problematic and end in dissolution. The majority experience major challenges both from within and without. Although there is no standard trajectory through the early, middle, and later stages of a relationship, there are natural developmental relational stages. Five progressive interlinked stages are delineated in this chapter.

There are also stages in the challenges faced by couples in the termination of relationships. A generic pattern of nine escalations in relational dissolution is presented along with specific interventions appropriate for each stage.

Therapists are advised to take a developmental perspective on all relationships. Whether a couple presents with a 6-month or a 60-year relationship, the stage of development of the relationship and any escalations toward break-up provide a foundation to examine the partners' individual and mutual expectations, desires, histories, and potential.

We begin with clients' stated desires to improve their relationship or to separate as amicably as possible. Normally, therapists work with a couple to improve their communication and dynamics to allow them to cycle back to better times in the relationship, or conversely to confront structural gaps that make separation more likely.

When separation and/or divorce appear inevitable, therapists support inescapable feelings of sadness and relief at the same time as they as they intervene to diminish progressive escalations. These interventions play a major role in assisting the couple to grasp the severity of their interpersonal dissonance and to navigate through the divorce process with a minimum of destructive litigation, revenge, and resentment. Finally, careful attention is given to the positive and negative aspects that led to the formation of the relationship and subsequent separation and/or divorce. Therapy that continues throughout the separation and divorce phases and thereafter allows for recognition of each partner's role in the dynamics of the relationship and enhances the potential for healing.

5

Couple Relational Transitions

Growth is painful. Change is painful.

But, nothing is as painful as staying stuck where you do not belong.

—N. R. Narayana Murthy

Transitions

When do couples find their way to the counselor's or therapist's office? They only infrequently come in to work on their relationships while the status quo and predictability is holding well. More often, couples enter therapy when their routines are no longer providing the usual balance of security and freedom. In short, therapists frequently meet clients when either internal or external circumstances force changes in that balance.

Each escalation described in the chronological divorce sequence represents an example of such a break. In each, at least one partner requests a change and a commensurate shift in the relational status quo. When the escalation becomes significant, a new homeostasis is required to keep the relationship alive and moving in a positive direction. This requires a transition from one process state to another.

Transitions come in two basic forms: normal progressions in life cycles and sudden unexpected incursions. They both represent times in a couple's life when their adaptations are no longer working as well or the emotional cost of keeping the status quo becomes exorbitant.

Normal Life Cycle Shifts for Couples

From the first glimpse to the last day a couple is together, numerous predictable and unforeseen events occur in the lives of couples, some welcome, others devastating (Carter & McGoldrick, 1988; McGoldrick, Preto, & Carter, 2015). Whether the commitment is "till death do us part" or "let's see how it goes," there is no certainty that things will remain the same. At a basic level, is such stability possible or desirable? Partners bring their individual experiences, emotions, and psychological dispositions to each phase of their lives together, and functional couples draw on their coping skills to adapt to predictable phases such as pair bonding and commitment, marriage, children, empty nest, and decline. When difficult or tragic circumstances arise, functional couples draw on their foundations and skills and employ outside resources to cope effectively.

Those who lack basic histories and successes in communication, problem solving, and commitments to equity and intimacy, or who are volatile and constantly conflictual, have difficulty with both predictable and unforeseen phases and experience crises or *entropy*, in systems terms. In more normal, non-pathological couples, those who persist in holding onto earlier patterns and structures when they are no longer relevant[1] can experience stagnation and conflict as well.

Socioeconomic Factors

In addition to individual characteristics that may impede adjustment, economic, social, cultural, disability, and other systemic factors often affect a couple's ability to manage transitions successfully. For example, poverty, discrimination, and immigration status pose barriers for couples in matters such as housing, time spent together, and basic nutrition and often result in separation and cycles of generational disruption.

The difficulties encountered by middle- and lower-middle-class couples just to stay afloat financially and socially have been noted prominently in the literature and the media. At the opposite end of the spectrum, the recent opportunities that have emerged for instant wealth for some dual-career couples and those in the financial and tech industries often require long days, constant travel, frequent moves, and "outsourcing" of parental responsibilities, ranging from IVF to surrogates to full-time child care for dual earners (O'Neil, Fishman, & Kinsella-Shaw, 1987).

Necessary Readjustments

Many stresses are common at all socioeconomic levels. It is normal for sexual attraction, frequency of contact, and overall intimacy to wax and wane throughout the life cycle of couples, particularly during major life shifts such as schooling, marriage, pregnancy, and post-partum and shifts demanded by needs of in-laws. Such issues have implications for the level of relationship satisfaction and the potential for alienation, resentment, infidelity, and persistent conflict. One of the therapeutic imperatives is to understand common patterns, normalize them, and actively help couples make sex and intimacy enough of a priority to keep the relationship vital and not let it fall by the wayside (MacNeil & Byers, 2009; Tucker & Aron, 1993).

In the area of equity or sharing of responsibilities, research on lesbian couples reflects a tendency toward equal sharing, perhaps due to similar gender traits and less adherence to traditional gender roles (Patterson, Sutfin, & Fulcher, 2004). By contrast, Slater and

---

1   As one client indicated, "Once we had our baby the old 'DINK' (dual income no kids) pattern was well past its 'use-by' date."

Mencher (1991) argued that "[l]esbian family life is completely empty of images of normal progression" (p. 373). Although this comment is dated, and potentially prejudicial and more contemporary developments may provide a more nuanced general pattern of managing transitions, it also suggests that traditional American heterosexual role patterns have ceased somewhat to be the norm for many diverse couples and may have to be negotiated without customary precedents.

Predictable Changes in Relationship Trajectory

Although it is clear that life cycle transitions vary along multiple dimensions, common ones do exist that require collaboration and can engender both great excitement and anxiety. Some are briefly described, here.

Beginning

Questions during the early phase of a relationship may include "We've just met—will we see each other again? Are we compatible? Interesting to each other? Are there deal breakers? How often should we see each other—on dates, or your place or mine? What is the nature of our first trip together? When to have sex? Are we exclusive? When to meet the parents?"

> Steven and Ben have both recently affirmed their gay identities and are excited to have met each other on a dating website. Because of their relative inexperience with dating, they are uncertain how to proceed: who should take the initiative, how often to text or call, what the next venue should be, and so on. Steven has dated women before and always felt that having sex early in the relationship allows him to know better whether to proceed with the relationship. Ben mentioned that he comes from a strong religious background and that sex should be reserved for a fully committed relationship.

These are standard uncertainties for many couples who just meet, with the fine details different for each. Typically, this couple will not come for therapy at first, but individual clients may raise these questions. Rather than weighing in on the relationship itself without the partner, the therapeutic focus is primarily on the intentions and values of the individual.

- Is this a good time for them to have a committed relationship in terms of work, finances, travel, and other goals?
- Are there deal breakers (such as sex before marriage)?
- Are they on the rebound from another recent relationship and would benefit from the experience of being single a bit longer?
- How do they perceive their values being in synch?
- Can they initiate a conversation about these important issues?

When they do present in therapy together, these questions and their answers may be quite significant for each. Many couple therapists recommend an individual session for each to ask these and similar questions to help them decide how to proceed.

Considerations in Moving Toward a Committed Relationship

Once a relationship forms and seems to be working out, a question often arises about moving in together: Will the new habitat be one of their places or a new jointly chosen place? Decisions arise about merging possessions, sharing expenses, and sharing responsibilities and friends. What agreements will be made about continuing to go out with single friends (male and female)? Will larger commitments be made such as getting a dog or cat or buying a house? What to do if one is offered a new job out of state?

> Amar and Natalia have been dating for 8 months, met each other's families, and seem to have similar values, interests, and enough different activities to maintain vitality in the relationship. Although Amar's family likes Natalia, they are disappointed that they were not able to plan a traditional arranged marriage for him. Natalia works for a multinational tech company in which it is common to move out of state or to another country in order to move up the career ladder. Amar's family lives nearby and he is determined to continue working for a local nonprofit agency. The obvious question with which they are struggling is where should they go next in their relationship?

Due to the high-pressured jobs and spiraling economy in today's world, these questions loom larger for those interested in deepening their relationship than they may have a generation ago. Although at first glance they may seem insurmountable, our experience is that in most cases they can be worked out.

Rather than work on logistics and speculate about unknown scenarios in therapy, our focus is on the present dynamic between the couple: *How committed (determined) are they to continue their relationship? Is each willing to negotiate and compromise individual needs and goals for common ones as they arise? Is either partner certain of a "deal breaker"—a situation that they absolutely would not accept?* If there are clear, hard answers to these questions, partners may decide that their individual situations make it too difficult to stay together. In other cases, assisting them to decide to wait and see how their relationship deepens as they move ahead may be welcomed.

If they decide to move in together, it is useful to explore their prior experiences living with roommates or former lovers; their needs for cleanliness, tidiness, and time alone; and their ideas of sharing finances, household chores, and other common tasks. During this "nesting period," there is a tendency to spend most or all of their time together to the exclusion of friends and family. While this may strengthen their bond, it often causes a rift with others and a sense of loss of familiar persons and activities. Thus, working out time with extended family and deciding whether and how often to go out separately can be important to discuss, especially if a friend group is mostly single and may include an ex-lover.

Other issues can become significant, such as whether to get a pet and the motivations for such a commitment, whether to do the chores or hire someone, how to align different schedules, and so on. Discussions in therapy may help them focus on their commitment and ability to prioritize issues. Negotiation and compromise with a third party keeps the discussion from getting into the "deep weeds." The therapist's role here is to normalize the predictable issues and to "listen to the music more than the words" by focusing on the dynamics (process) and trusting that open exploration will allow them to get past minor issues.

Questions Regarding Deepening the Commitment

After some time together, most couples will decide at some point to make a formal or informal commitment to each other. The most common traditional method is to become married.[2] Questions that arise include the following:

- Is it time to get married or consider other more permanent forms of commitment? Wedding planning may be somewhat treacherous as financing and multiple friends' and parents' needs and wishes are considered.
- Is a religious ceremony important or will a city hall or elopement be a choice? Will children follow and when?
- Is a family affordable now or later?
- What to do with pressures from parents?
- How will professions/jobs be managed?
- Who should take time off when children are born, or will there be child care from nannies, grandparents?
- What to do about infertility or unexpected pregnancy?

Bruce and Heather are both 35 and have gone through the initial dating phase, moving in together, and discussing priorities and compromises, and they have lived together for 18 months. They grew up in middle class, Midwest families and want a traditional wedding with their own personal touches. Heather's parents have agreed to pay for most of the wedding and have begun making most of the decisions, to the dismay of Bruce's parents. They've considered eloping but have decided to use some of the relationship dynamics skills and priorities they've learned together.

After reaching a compromise, they have a beautiful wedding and are almost immediately asked about having children. They have agreed they would like three but want to wait until they've experienced time as a married couple and want to save to buy a home. Some of their friends have urged them to consider IVF and surrogacy—as they have done—due to their ages, but Heather is very healthy and wants to conceive and bear her baby. Heather earns almost twice Bruce's salary, and they've agreed that after Heather and Bruce both take parental leave, Bruce will be the stay-at-home parent for another 6 months. His parents believe that this should be the woman's job and Heather's parents have offered to care for their baby while both return to work.

When they arrive at therapy due to ongoing pressures from friends and family, it appears that they are highly functional and are encouraged by the therapist's acknowledgment of their togetherness and conviction about their values and priorities. They wonder about how they may proceed with their plans and diffuse the pressure they feel from close

---

2 Obviously this sequence may be different for those in arranged marriages or in cultures that restrict severely premarital contact between single individuals.

friends and family without offending anyone. Because we see this as a transitional point for them to strengthen their couple relationship, we help them focus on consolidating their unity as a couple, developing clarity on their own beliefs and preferences, and helping them stand firm as a team in the face of potential rejection and criticism from important friends and family. For example, the therapist may remind them of their success at prioritizing and compromising with their families of origin and encourage them to use these same skills in moving ahead as a couple. As part of this individuation from their families of origin and friends' opinions, we explore how other challenges—such as parenting, allocating time for family and friends, and decisions to use outside childcare versus grandparents—can be addressed in similar fashion.

From Couple to Family

One major predictable challenge that couples face is the transition to parenthood (Cowan & Cowan, 2012; Holmes, Sasaki, & Hazen, 2013), which requires shifting focus from the dyad to a triad and beyond, with all the attendant responsibilities that ensue for decades. Couples often anguish over decisions of whether, when, and how to have children, and those who decide to remain childless may encounter extreme pressure from their extended families or retroactive feelings of lost opportunity.

Many couples have the choice taken from them by an unplanned pregnancy. They are simply thrust into the role of expectant parents.[3] Other times, particularly in second marriages, children are already present.

> Eli and Briana are in their early 30s, have known each other for 5 years, and moved in together 18 months ago. They are secure financially, get along well, and have a good foundation for their relationship. Six months ago they had their first child, who was born healthy, and have both sets of parents available to help them. Nonetheless, they have struggled to find time together, sex has been challenging after childbirth, and Eli feels that he is in second place to the new baby. Briana's parents have weighed in and advised Briana on caring for the baby in ways that bother Eli, and he feels criticized by them when he occasionally goes out with his old friends.

We begin therapy by inquiring about their prior expectations for having their first child. Neither had anticipated some of the challenges they are experiencing and are concerned about feeling distanced from each other. As we normalize this transition, they smile and seem reassured. They realize that a new level of individuation as a couple is needed in order to establish their ground and to resist their parents from being over-involved. They welcome recommendations for reading about infant care and for a new parents workshop at a local community college. They volunteer that they can arrange for a sitter on the weekends so they can have a date night together. As a fundamentally sound couple, brief consultation is typically sufficient for them to negotiate this normal transition together.

---

3 Sometimes the unexpected pregnancy is a serious problem for a couple and alternatives such as adoption or abortion are considered. Considerable therapy around such a decision is recommended.

Questions Around the Middle Stage of Family Transition

Some time after a family is formed or a long-term pattern emerges, additional shifts in the relationship become necessary. Often these are times of multiple, potentially conflicting demands:

- How does a couple balance developing careers or job loss with children's schedules and needs, personal interests, and couple time?
- Are there needs to save for escalating costs for private schools or higher education?
- How does a couple adjust to a world and friendships that revolve around children's needs, particularly unanticipated ones?
- What needs are there in saving for retirement?
- What relevant issues emerge regarding health issues and caring for aging parents?

Couples With School-Age Children

Families with school-age children will often find themselves shifting from shared experiences with older acquaintances and friends to spending far more time with the parents of their children's friends. The only thing they may have in common is a child's soccer team or fellow band members. It is a period when personal development often takes a back seat to children's activities.

> Noel and Callie have two children, Debby, a 16-year-old daughter, and Matt, an 11-year-old son. They will often reflect that everything they do is "for the children." Callie has been her son's "classroom mom," spent extra time tutoring her daughter during a rough patch in middle school, and is planning to visit colleges with her this summer. Noel spends all weekend taking their son to soccer tournaments and coaching his Little League baseball team. He describes leaving work at 3:00 p.m. to attend one of the kids' soccer games and then after dinner going back to the office or working at home until near bedtime.
>
> They spend weekends and vacation times on family outings and "worrying about when Debby will return home after an outing with friends," one of whom is her "boyfriend." The enduring issue that they are facing is not only finding time with their own friends, but, more importantly, alone time together.

Frequently, questions arise around the needs of family and contrasting couple needs:

- How much time should we spend on careers and how much on parenting and family?
- Do we put money away for retirement or for college?
- How do we keep our relationship as a couple alive, aside from family time?
- How can we keep alive relationships with friends and peers with whom we share something besides children's activities?

Questions for Couples at Midlife With Grown Children

Maurice and Adriana are in their 50s and have typical "sandwich generation" challenges. Both sets of parents live in another state and are retired with major health issues and limited income. Maurice has been laid off from his managerial job for 6 months due to downsizing, and Adriana is providing adequate income from her job but is also traveling most of the time. Their children are in their late 20s and one is doing well while the other is at odds professionally and in her relationship. Maurice is trying to adapt to being at home while searching for a job, frustrated by multiple rejections or no responses at all, and feeling diminished because he has to rely on Adrianna's income. They both feel they should help their struggling daughter and the son who is doing well feels pressure to help them both. At the same time Maurice and Adriana are trying to get their parents the medical assistance they need and discuss assisted living with her parents.

In therapy, Maurice and Adriana expressed concerns that their financial pressures and the issues with their parents and children are causing them to bicker constantly and to feel distant from each other. It also resulted in some depressive symptoms for Maurice. Stress reactions, relationship difficulties, and depression following loss of employment and income for extended periods of time, particularly for men, has been noted frequently (Howe, Levy, & Caplan, 2004; Mattinson, 1988)

As they explored their unique struggles, emotions, resources, and constraints, their therapist was able to normalize their experiences as a generational issue, made more complicated in the current economy. This allowed them to avoid blaming one another and explore their strengths and problem-solving resources as a couple. In this case, they could understand better the incompatibility between their desire to help out as family and the conflict between helping others and prioritizing their own health, finances, and stability as a couple. At one point, he reminded them of the speech on airlines and worked with them on "putting on their own oxygen masks prior to helping others." They also considered together other less-tapped community resources such as consultants, support groups for aging parents, and job seeking at middle age.

In sessions, one primary focus was exploration of options to better manage ongoing stress, household responsibilities, and Adrianna's travel schedule. All of these interventions were relevant to their cultural expectations about fulfilling family needs.

Boomerang Children: A Modern Phenomenon

Once the children are grown and left to lead their own independent lives, most couples will have some time to be on their own again, after many years as parents. Often, that trajectory can be interrupted.

Presumably, after midlife there will be time to be alone again as a couple, to have fewer day-to-day family responsibilities. Many couples look forward to some deferred relationship maintenance: relating again as a couple without the mediation of parenting, a refocus on recapturing dreams or doing things long desired, planning for retirement (including a savings push now that school and tuition costs are relatively done), and so on.

A surprising number of economic and familial events may force a postponement or make the anticipated empty nest less likely. One of the most common involves the return home of now-adult children (another is the need to care for aging parents). As marriage and childbearing is postponed by the children's generation, there is now often a gap in time between beginning adult life and becoming self-sufficient (Casares & White, 2018).

There may be cultural expectations that unmarried children (especially women) return to their family home. Another powerful force for millennials that may make post-college independence unlikely is the discrepancy between salaries for starting jobs, college debt, and housing costs.

> Doc and Eve have one daughter. At 24, Amber had always done what was expected. She got into a good college, graduated in the top third of her class, and landed a job at a company at which she had interned during the summers. Soon after graduation, she moved in with roommates to share costs and begun a serious relationship with a man she met through mutual friends. Her salary at her job allowed her to pay her share of rent and her regular living expenses, living essentially as she did in college. It did not cover her repayment of some college debt and her parents were still subsidizing some expenses, such as her cell phone bill on their "family plan."

> When two of her roommates moved out, she could not afford the additional rent and moved back in with her parents. It allowed her to reduce expenses, pay down her loans, and save for future rent. The couple now had a third adult child in the home and while Amber was a "good roommate," her living with them as an adult created some tensions. Although she was contributing to the household, she was also regressing to a more dependent relationship with Doc and Eve. They also had to deal with family "rules" about her relationship in the home.

Amber is not alone (Furstenberg, 2010; Parker, 2012). According to the U.S. Census Bureau (Vespa, 2017), between a quarter and a third of young adults are living with their parents—a dramatic increase in a single generation. Most "boomerang kids" like Amber return to the home because of necessity, not for an easier life. They are quite likely to feel guilty unless they find ways of contributing something to compensate their parents. There is something of a conundrum between an expectation that the parents will take care of them as if they were still adolescents and the need to act as independent adults. As Shapiro (2012) wrote, "Your twenty- and thirty-something children may be welcome in your home, and in many cultures are obligated to stay until they begin their own families, but a free ride is ill advised" (p. 128).

When they discussed this in therapy, Eve, a self-described "helicopter mom," kept stressing how much they loved Amber, how she was being responsible in her work, and how easy she was to live with. By contrast, Doc indicated that he felt obligated to help out Amber, but it was interfering with plans of "a second honeymoon" and more alone time with Eve. He said the financial burden added to their retirement concerns and that they were arguing about postponing a long-planned cruise to celebrate their own independence. As Ward & Spitze, (2007), indicate, these differences and related conflicts are not unusual.

Questions Around Later Life Transitions

As couples age, there are increasing shifts and often a new focus on mortality as they adjust to health changes, losses, and retirement. Often, both couple and individual sessions center around finding meaning, maintaining social and family relationships, and managing family strife and distance. There are also inevitable losses of family, friends, colleagues, and personal capabilities that shake personal foundations.

> Spencer, 70, retired for 5 years after working as a bank manager for 40 years and his wife of 38 years, Bessie (70), is a retired teacher. Spencer has heart problems and is on medication and Bessie recently had a hip replacement. Their children live across the country, and while they have many friends and are active church members, they struggle to find ways to use their time productively. Spencer, in particular, is attempting to find new purpose in his life since his identity was embodied in his career. They also have concerns about providing equitably for their three children in their will and agreeing on arrangements for their burial. Bessie has consulted their pastor who referred them for couple therapy.

Similar to mid-life couples, the existential struggle to find meaning in later life becomes prominent and intensified with aging and impending mortality. The couple therapist begins by exploring their perspectives on vitality and decline during the aging process, especially in regard to their religious beliefs. A consultation (with signed releases) with their pastor who knows them well may provide useful context. An assessment of their physical and mental health and their resources will help provide a direction for them to gain hope and activate social contacts and activities in order to restore a new sense of vitality in their lives.[4] One exercise that may provide useful discussions is to ask them about their personal and couple "bucket lists."

Their concerns about being fair to their children in their will and settling their burial agreements also warrant attention and will provide relief for them as they address these issues openly and effectively in therapy. This does not require the therapist to be knowledgeable about the details of these matters, but rather to support and affirm clients' individual preferences and to elicit the couple's communication and problem-solving skills to accomplish their objectives. Some explanation, guidance, and perhaps handouts and referrals may facilitate this process.

Adjusting to Long Separations

Separations between partners have occurred from time immemorial, arising from the need for hunters and gatherers to travel to distant locations in order to provide safety and sustenance for their loved ones. The pattern today is not too different from earlier times, although the context may be different.

Migrant farm workers travel seasonally to garner resources; immigrants journey to a foreign land as a result of extreme weather, famine, or persecution, often with the chief wage earner leaving first; employees of multinational corporations are often required to work for long periods in foreign countries. Perhaps no group continues to experience more separations from loved ones than the military.

---

4 Working with this couple may provide a particular challenge for a young, beginning therapist. The couple may rightfully question the ability of someone who has not experienced their longevity and difficulties of aging. They may also be skeptical of a therapist who does not integrate their religious views into treatment, making an appropriate referral a major consideration.

Navy submariners deploy for 6-month periods; Army, Navy, Marines, Coast Guard, National Guard, and Air Force personnel have been assigned in recent decades to war zones for up to 2 years with multiple repeat deployments. What is the effect on intimate relationships when mandatory, undesired separations such as these occur?

Without making a blanket statement about these couples, therapists must consider multiple factors:

- What foundation did the couple have prior to deployment?
- Did they solidify their commitment through engagement, living together or marriage or was it open ended?
- What was the experience of each partner during separation? Was there illness, trauma, isolation, or opportunities for growth and adventure?
- Was the couple able to stay in touch frequently during separation?
- Did either partner have another romantic or sexual relationship during separation?

Calvin and Alysha dated for 1.5 years and married just prior to her deployment during the Iraq war. She signed up for the National Guard during college 10 years prior, wanting to serve her country and take advantage of GI benefits, never anticipating a long deployment to a war zone. They decided to get married in order to have the chance to be together when the opportunity came, but Alysha's 6 months in an unknown location did not permit that. Upon her return, she was shaken by her experiences, and Calvin had adjusted to being on his own. After 1 year, they had begun adjusting to married life when Alysha was deployed to Afghanistan for a full year. Her military specialty did not allow for her to return home during this time, and Calvin was only able to visit her in Germany for 3 days at a time.

At the end of the year, Alysha was experiencing severe PTSD and Calvin had developed a flirtatious romantic relationship with a colleague. Both were preoccupied and distant from each other and had experienced so little time together as a married couple that they decided on a trial separation.

The extreme circumstances and dangers presented by military life pose challenges not usually experienced by other couples who endure long separations, but the disruptions and the separate, often disparate experiences are similar to what other couples with long-distance relationships go through. These couples often yearn for the routines that others experience, and the challenges they face are much harder to overcome, but many endure.

A prolonged and highly significant form of frequent lengthy absences and breaks in relationships can be found in Navy families, particularly those of submariners. It is not unusual for a deployment on a submarine to last 3 to 6 months on a rotating basis. Families are run by a single parent for as much as half a year. Similarly, deployments in any service (including National Guard) in war zones may be extended. This can involve adjustment to being an only parent in the home and considerable anxiety about more permanent losses in warfare. Although military families can be mutually supportive, adjustments to loss of a partner and difficult adjustments when they return can cause particular tensions.

Jan called requesting couple therapy about a week before her Ensign husband Ed returned from duty on a nuclear-powered submarine with the U.S. Navy. They had followed fairly traditional roles with Ed as the wage earner and Jan as the homemaker. Parenting was primarily Jan's role, though Ed was the strict disciplinarian when he was home. He had been gone for close to 6 months. She had seen him only for a long weekend in Yokohama during that time. During his absence she had been in charge of the household, which included herself, three young children, and her mother. She organized the family and had finally got things going the way she preferred. With Ed's return, he would struggle to find his place in the reorganized household and would want to reassert his own preferences as "head of the household."

Decision Box 5.1: As a couple therapist, what issues do you think may be a primary focus?

1. Helping them reconnect intimately after such a long absence and limited electronic communication for 6 months
2. Helping Jan keep her control and organization anticipating another deployment 6 months from now
3. Helping them both deal with the shift from little to no contact to almost 24-7 contact while he is in port and having extensive off time in the home
4. Helping Ed reintegrate with his family after a lengthy period in which a new parental hierarchy had been established with Jan's mother
5. Redirecting Jan's attention from control and her outside friendships to an intense period of marital connection
6. Helping them deal with personal changes they both have made since last being together

---

Another common situation in military and occasionally corporate relationships is the "plum" assignment opportunity that occurs shortly before retirement. The partner who has been willing to move multiple times now feels settled and reluctant to accede to what had normally been expected. They may willingly agree to a temporary separation, but new challenges arise when they reunite.

Ben is a career Army non-commissioned officer with the rank of master sergeant. He and his wife Ida have lived in 11 places around the world during their 32-year marriage, and Ben has been asked to accept a choice assignment at a foreign embassy for 1 year in a country that is inhospitable to military families and where dependents are "non-command supported"; families have to live on the local economy, not the base.

After much discussion, they acknowledge that they have weathered numerous prior separations, and Ben decides to accept the assignment. With their children grown, Ida, who is recently retired, develops new interests and friendships and is enjoying life on her own. When Ben returns, he looks to resume the same routines and patterns in their marriage as before, but Ida desires to retain much of her newly discovered independence.

What should the therapist look for when Ben and Ida bring their dilemma to him or her? As with Calvin and Alysha, many of the same questions are prevalent, but greater potential for growth exists due to this couple's long history. They want to remain together, and separation would shake their world and that of their extended family and friends. The most pertinent questions involve whether lingering unresolved conflict or resentment persist, what Ida desires more as an individual, and whether Ben is open to personal change and how he adapts to Ida's new sense of self.

Addressing Transitions

Everyone who has dated and considered whether to deepen a relationship will recognize some of these core issues (Miller, Yorgason, Sandberg, & White, 2003). It therefore isn't a matter of whether challenges will come, but whether there is a foundation, resources, and a process to meet them. Individuals cannot know at the outset whether a relationship will endure, so it is necessary to approach meeting a potential partner with eyes wide open, a sense of humor, healthy curiosity, and antennae attuned to potential "deal breakers" that will sooner or later derail collaboration and negotiation as predictable and unexpected events occur throughout the life cycle.

It is not uncommon for well-intentioned, functional partners' individual interests to grow in different directions with a reduction in the joy and intimacy they once had, even in relationships that have endured gracefully and without intense conflict over a period of time (Acevedo & Aron, 2009).

Transitions shake up the system and require acknowledgment and accommodation. Usually it is one partner who leads the shift, based on personal dissatisfaction, growth, or a new phase of personal differentiation. Once one partner begins to make and insist on changes in a long-standing status quo, there is likely to be conflict. Often, that conflict looks like one person pushing toward new freedom and the other holding tight to the status quo.

Just as with high-conflict couples (Fruzzetti, 2006) and those who lacked a solid foundation from the start, they face the dilemma of whether to attempt to accommodate each other's differences and pursue greater vitality, to live with ongoing discord, or to separate. As therapists we may also need to accept that high-conflict, severely dysfunctional couples sometimes choose to stay together for financial, parenting, or dependency reasons.

Despite therapists' best efforts to help a couple enhance their functioning, it may be an easier decision for those who have been highly conflictual to separate than those who have undergone many life-cycle phases together peacefully and grown apart. In any case, careful discernment and professional consultation may be helpful in discovering the best resolution. Couples during difficult transitions present challenges for therapists to remain impartial regarding the ultimate outcome and *facilitators* rather than deciders.

Stages of Therapy for Normal Transitions

When couples come in for therapy in anticipation or in the midst of a normal transitional period, several steps are recommended:

1. Encourage the expression of emotions, especially those created by the tension between maintaining the status quo and facing anxieties about the unknown. Often one of the partners may feel pushed to make a premature shift in the relationship.

For example, during the retirement/older age transitions, there may be a tension between downsizing and moving to a retirement community or closer to children and grandchildren and maintaining the home, keeping lots of possessions, and so on. In therapy, it is important for the couple to communicate more clearly at an effective level. Thus the one pushing for change may be looking to simplify life and feel freer of demands of the old household, while the other sees letting go of material goods, such as books, music collections, old clothes, and "projects" as a way of losing their history or, more frightening, losing their future.

2. Normalize the transition. Helping couples understand that what they are struggling with is a common struggle, such as finding couple time while being parents of young children. When couples recognize the inevitability of change, they are likely more prone to address it as a team instead of as opponents with different visions.

3. Help the couple find and build a new homeostasis.

4. Work through any remaining lingering doubts and anxieties. This includes a plan to anticipate future anxiety about the unknown and backsliding into old patterns that have by now become anachronistic.

5. We have found that it is useful to schedule follow-up consultations 3 to 6 months and a year after termination of therapy. That date on the schedule is often referred to by former clients as a "safety net." It is important to note that although they may cherish the offer, many couples cancel such appointments, especially if relational matters have settled and they are doing well.

Sudden Unexpected Transitions

The relational disruptions described so far are normal changes that most couples go through in the course of a long-term relationship. They all involve evolution in the homeostatic balance of a relationship. In some ways, they tend to be fairly predictable, shared by others in similar circumstances, and although they involve a need for change, they are primarily at a sub-crisis level. In these transitions, the status quo grows increasingly unsatisfactory and adjustments to a new homeostasis must be made. Although any major changes in lifestyle—such as the transition to family from couple—are stressful and challenging, they usually do not threaten the existence of the relationship itself. Couples need to negotiate these changes; make the necessary compromises; and reset expectations, behaviors, and workloads both within and outside of family life.

There are other transitions that are brought about by crises, unexpected and unanticipated changes that may come about quite suddenly. These cannot be considered evolutionary as much as traumas that shake the core of the relationship itself. Although there are many possible crises, we recommend a standard clinical approach that involves crisis management, emotional expression, stabilization, rethinking commitment, decision making, working through, and finding a new homeostasis. We will explore a few of these in depth as examples of methods, and although the content may differ, the process for treating crisis-oriented dilemmas is somewhat similar.

These crisis-oriented transitions require structural shifts in the relationship and are often quite long term. Often, when couples are facing such issues, their needs are urgent and therapy must have a quick and emotionally intense beginning. For example, a couple that is enmeshed and has been extremely close, doing nearly everything together, including finishing each other's sentences, may need a "dose of asymmetry" in which they focus on their individual desires and activities in order to restore vitality and reduce conflict over trivial issues.

Infidelity

Prior to passage of no-fault divorce laws in Canada (1968), California (1970), and shortly thereafter in the rest of the United States, divorces primarily required a court finding of fault of one of the marital partners. The faults that allowed for divorces were serious offenses such as convictions of a felony, cruelty, abandonment, and *infidelity*.

The disruption of a relationship because of adultery has been well recorded in the arts and literature for centuries. In addition to two injunctions in the Ten Commandments regarding sexual activity outside of marriage and coveting a neighbor's wife, there are several references in the Bible to both infidelity and the presence of concubines.

In modern-day Western cultures, infidelity remains a common reason for the dissolution of relationships. It is one of the most difficult issues to overcome because of a sense of deep betrayal, rejection, and violation of a specific spoken or "understood" vow of faithfulness in a monogamous relationship.[5] When couples present with a discovery of a recent or ongoing affair by at least one of the partners, therapy requires some special considerations.

Regardless of the therapist's personal views, the most salient factor in assessing infidelity of any sort is each partner's perception of the event and the healing of the relationship insofar as possible. Nonetheless, couple therapists must be prepared to have a clear position of their role in dealing with affairs. One of the most challenging circumstances is when one partner, surreptitiously or otherwise, discloses an affair that is unknown to the other. This happens frequently with one author (Patterson) who routinely conducts individual interviews as part of assessment in couple therapy, or occasionally through a phone call or text or when one partner is late or in the restroom. Basically, in considering the right of an individual to confidentiality, couple therapists need to keep in mind that the *couple* is the client, and to act in their joint interest. In this regard, complex clinical, ethical, and legal issues come into play. Some issues for therapists to consider are the following:

- Is there a clear explanation of confidentiality regarding secrets that are disclosed individually in the informed consent for couples?
- What is the understanding between partners regarding intimate involvement with others?
- Is the affair in the past, one time, or ongoing?
- Does the therapist comingle or maintain separate records for individual interviews?
- What is the effect on the partner who keeps the secret?

---

5   Sexual contact in so-called "open marriages," or polyamory, may be somewhat exempt from the trauma; however, even in these there are lines that once crossed are considered infidelity.

- Particularly if ongoing, does the involvement compromise the integrity of the couple's therapy?
- What will be the reaction of the unknowing partner if it is discovered that the therapist kept the secret?
- What will be the response of the offending partner if the therapist discloses it without permission?

What Constitutes Infidelity?

Glass (2002) defined infidelity as "a secret sexual, romantic, or emotional involvement that violates the commitment to an exclusive relationship" (p. 489). We expand that definition somewhat to include those contacts that do not necessarily involve mucous membrane contact or even physical proximity, such as is experienced in cyber infidelity (via various forms of social media) or non-physical emotional affairs. Indeed, for therapeutic purposes, we include as affairs for treatment not only sexual, romantic relationships with a person outside the monogamous dyad. The treatment may be quite similar for anything or anyone who replaces the partner as primary. Included in this expanded definition are addictions (electronic as well as substances), relatives, vocations, and avocations.

Frequency and Discovery of Affairs.

Mark, Janssen, and Milhausen (2011) report that approximately 23% of men and 19% of women have reportedly participated in sex outside their primary couple relationships. According to Allen and Atkins (2012), even in the modern era of no-fault divorce, infidelity remains one of the most frequently cited reasons for divorce. For this reason, it is not uncommon for a couple to enter marriage counseling or therapy because of the effects of a discovered or revealed affair. However, as Gordon, Khaddouma, Baucom, and Snyder (2015) indicate, a sexual affair does not necessarily spell the end of a primary relationship.

It is important to note that affairs may come in many different varieties and treatment considerations may vary considerably. Those infidelities that do come to light may be revealed in many different ways. The person who has had the affair may confess because of guilt, a desire to hurt the spouse, or an attempt to do something to improve a problematic relationship. Affairs may also be discovered by a partner checking up on suspicious behavior. One couple came into therapy to deal with an affair when he found her diaphragm (birth control barrier) in the glove compartment of their car. Another affair was discovered when a partner observed some disquieting behavior between his spouse and another person at a social event. Still others have found incriminating text or voice mail messages, have overheard a conversation, or have been informed by a third party.

Once an affair is out in the open, therapy is often instituted. Affairs that never come to light in the relationship or in therapy, or those that are passively sanctioned, are beyond the purview of this text and unlikely to be the reason for people entering therapy.

Types of Affairs Described in Therapy

One-Night Stand(s)

These involve a single encounter with a third party, often while on a solo out-of-town trip. During the first year of a now 35-year marriage, Malcolm reported that he had a sexual interaction with a woman he met at a conference. Arjun, who was in an arranged marriage, described a one-night sexual congress with a woman whom he met while on an overseas assignment, several years prior to coming into therapy with his wife. These were both single events, confessed to several years after they occurred. Janet had a more enduring policy. When she and her husband of many years were in the same locale, she was "fully monogamous and a faithful wife and mother." However, as he discovered later, when she was traveling on business, she considered herself "single."

A modern form of these one-night affairs may occur when partners use social media to seek out "hook-ups" with partners with whom no enduring relationship is desired or possible. As Erik described it, "I used to go to massage parlors for 'happy endings.' Then I discovered this app where if someone was close, we could agree to hook-up—no questions asked."

Extended Long-Term Affair That Is Over

Another form that affairs may take is of a repeated pattern. Despite being married almost 10 years ago, Cal maintained an ongoing sexual relationship with a woman he dated when he was single. He repeatedly lied to his wife telling her that the other woman was "just a friend" and that he had to work late some evenings. He quit only when she threatened divorce. However, by the time they entered therapy, the lies and secrets had severely damaged any trust between them.

Extended Long-Term Affair That Is Ongoing

Chan was in a same-sex relationship with Danny for almost 20 years. During that time he had an ongoing sexual relationship with another man for almost a decade. He was unwilling to relinquish it, even after Danny discovered it and they came into couple therapy.

Semi-Agreed-To Affairs (Break)

Sometimes, extra-relational affairs may occur when a couple is separated, without a clear understanding of unspoken agreements. When Marcus and Lurline decided to take a break in their long-term relationship, he was not aware that for her this involved dating and even the potential for sexual relations with others. When they came into therapy, he reported feeling betrayed and tricked, whereas she reported that they were not together and she was free to experiment. Often when a couple decides to take a trial separation, they fail to negotiate specific behavioral terms. This can lead to one or both feeling cheated.

Cyber Infidelity

There is some question about what constitutes an affair in modern society, particularly when the unfaithful partner never meets the "other person" physically. Subotnik (2007), using Cooper's (1998) earlier formulation, describes the "triple A" engine of Internet infidelity: accessibility, affordability, and anonymity to indicate the ease with which extramarital connections may be made online.

Such unions may well be experienced as an affair to a partner. Marlene reported that her husband's online activities with someone he met online constituted an emotional affair. Although he did not consider himself to be bisexual, and he was flirting with another man he never intended to meet in person, she experienced that relationship as a threat and a betrayal. Marlene was much more concerned with the emotional connection the two men had online than the lack of a physical meeting. She also felt that his attraction to the other person was a direct reflection on her.

Several authors have demonstrated that there is a gender difference in such reactions. According to Buss (2018), Brase, Adair, and Monk (2014), and Formica (2009), men seem to report greater distress when there is physical sexual contact; women more through emotional relations. Feelings of betrayal also seem to follow along these gender lines (Donovan & Emmers-Sommer, 2012). Thus men, stereotypically, are usually more threatened by physical sexual contact and women by emotional connections.

Serial Assignations (e.g., Tinder, Grindr, Bumble, and Similar Social Media)

One form of modern-day "bar-hopping" involves brief sexual encounters that are aided by proximity and mobile apps. As Tammy described it, when she was out at a mall, "I would just check around to see who was available. If I liked his looks, I'd just swipe right and began a chat and meeting." She added, "I don't think it's cheating on Tom, because I never get involved with these guys."

Tess reported, "I have been married four times and there has never been a time when I was sexual with only one guy since I was 14." She actively sought out sexual partners on her mobile phone and frequently had a "zipless" (Jong, 1975) sexual encounter; "I just take a long lunch break," she confessed.

Affairs That Do Not Involve a Sexual Component

Some affairs do not involve direct sexual contact. They involve placing work, hobbies, children, parents, computers, or addictions in primary place and their partners somewhat secondary. Certainly, alcohol or other substance abuse can take precedence over a relationship with a partner. Many a marriage has foundered on the shoals of addictive needs superseding emotional intimacy.

Similarly, intense and relatively exclusive relationships with a child or family member may get in between the relationship of a primary couple. Even after 10 years with Keoki, Kelli was still more connected and more intimate with her twin sister. When he requested that she spend more time with him, he reported feeling excluded and used terms like "secrets about our marriage" being shared between the two sisters. In addition, although it is normal for intense bonding between parents and infants, some people do not let go of that intimacy and build a boundary around themselves and a child to the exclusion of the spouse. This kind of triangulation can be experienced as something akin to an extra-marital relationship.

Vocations and avocations may also serve as a wedge between partners. Priya described herself as "a golf widow," indicating that her husband of many years placed golf far ahead of their relationship. In their relationship, her husband Amit also worked very long hours and frequently was unavailable on weekends to be with her and the children.

CASE BOX 5.1

I Don't Want Him, But I Don't Want Anyone Else to Have Him Either

Is this a betrayal?

After 10 years of marriage with diminishing sexual connections, Marianne determined unilaterally that she was through with sex forever. She did not consult Ted. She simply cut off any future sexual connection and requested that he sleep in the guest bedroom. After 2 years, Ted met Sal, a married woman, online and began to engage in cybersex messages. Sometime after, while on a business trip, he and Sal met in person and they spent a weekend together. Neither has any interest in anything beyond a sexual relationship, which continued in a "same time next year" fashion for almost a decade. Marie was infuriated that Ted had strayed, even though she wanted nothing to do with him physically.

Decision Box 5.2:

1. Is Ted's behavior a betrayal?
2. Does one person have the right to permanently end part of the relationship unilaterally?
3. Would it be different if Ted told Marianne what he intended prior to engaging in his relationship with Sal?
4. Would you recommend negotiation in this case?
5. Would you recommend separation in this case?
6. Where do you side with one or the other personally?

Whatever the situation or our personal views may be, the tension that occurs with couples is most often due to the secrecy when an outside relationship occurs. As in the previous example, even if Marianne rejects sex, she may nonetheless feel betrayed if she does not have a clear agreement with Ted that he is free to be involved with others or that he will tell her when it occurs.

An extramarital affair usually creates a major disruption in a relationship. It is a common reason for couples seeking treatment. Couple therapy for such intrusive boundary violations is usually structural in nature in that it goes far beyond communication issues. Therapy may also involve atypical interactions for any theoretical perspective. For example, although both CBT and existential approaches to couple therapy characteristically focus primarily on the present and future, treatment following an affair often involves some considerable family-of-origin and other historical foci.

Assessment

Discovery of an extramarital affair is usually quite disruptive in a relationship. When couples come in for therapy, they are often in crisis. High levels of emotional pain and expressed negative feelings are common (Morrissette, 2012; Witte & Mulla, 2012).

Early assessment requires some evaluation of both parties' emotional stability and of any dangers to individuals. For example, it is wise to do an assessment for potential domestic violence or suicidality. Snyder and Doss (2005) recommend a safety plan be established if there is any indication that one or both partners may become physically aggressive. Holtzworth-Munroe, Marshall, Meehan, and Rehman (2003) and others strongly recommend against couple conjoint work until any such threat is minimized or eliminated.

This assessment of danger must continue for some time, because as Ehrensaft and Vivian (1996) and Shapiro (1984) indicate, it may be dormant until the therapy begins pressing into specific matters, particularly regarding new revelations about explicit sexual activities that were included in the extradyadic relationship.

Additional ethical considerations about safety involve assessment of and recommendation for any possible sexually transmitted diseases. Couple therapists may recommend or even insist that both parties are tested early in treatment. The results of the testing may magnify the hurt and pain but may be a physically essential step. Sarah discovered that her partner's assignation with another woman had left her with chlamydia. Untreated, that could have led to infertility.

It is also important for therapists to evaluate each partner's ego strength and emotional capacity for the difficult emotional work that may be required as part of treatment. The clients' relative capacities for subsequent approaches to counseling are important early consideration. For example, some couples are fully capable of connecting family-of-origin, early attachment, and other relational issues to an understanding of how the grounds for an affair may have evolved. Other couples may be able only to deal with psychoeducation and very pragmatic, instructional interventions.

Finally, it is important to get an early assessment of the couple's treatment goals. First of all, the desires of each partner regarding continuation of the primary relationship must be assessed. Do both members of the couple want to stay together? Do they want to confront this betrayal to see what can be salvaged? Do they want to work through the multiple issues in infidelity to establish their relationship on new grounds? Treatment for couples who are unwilling to go through the arduous process may involve short-term consultation focused on how to split up as amicably as possible. By contrast, for couples who want to retain the relationship, therapy may involve an agreement to work through the difficult emotional and cognitive issues in longer-term work. Although normal couple therapy may last for 2 to 3 months, dealing with infidelity (or other structural breaks) commonly lasts a year or longer. It is important for couples to know up front what the likely therapy will entail.

Common factors of assessment include several aspects of the context in which the affair occurred. We find it useful to know, for example, the following:

1. The length and strength of their current relationship (including whether they are legally married)
2. Prior relationships and how they ended, particularly if infidelity was a cause of dissolution
3. Whether the couple has children, particularly in the home, and the impact of the extramarital relationship on them currently and in the future
4. Financial considerations, together and apart
5. Any history of affairs in the relationship, in their generation in the family, and in their parents' generation
6. Whether both partners have had extra-dyadic relationships, even if only one is suffering because of the partner's affair(s)
7. The implicit or explicit understanding partners have had about intimate involvement of any type with others

Treatment Goals and Process

Couple therapy with infidelity often requires a number of stages. According to Spring and Spring (1996), there are three stages of healing: (1) normalizing feelings, (2) decision to recommit or quit, (3) rebuilding the relationship. We believe that there are potentially more stages to treating infidelity. The process necessary to recover from an affair or similar structural insult to a relationship includes crisis management, emotional expression, stabilization, rethinking and revising commitment, decision making, forgiveness, working through, and finding a new homeostasis.

Treatment: Emotional Outpouring/Catharsis

Feelings of betrayal are unlikely to easily pass or be forgotten. Most individuals who feel cheated in a primary relationship have a number of strong negative emotions about the infidelity. These typically include hurt, sadness, anger, and fear. The first steps of therapy involve expression of these raw emotions. Such emotional outpouring may last many months. Often, it may seem like a grief reaction where at least one person is mourning the loss of the imagined relationship and their psychological security. Until the emotions are expressed and there is some sense that both the therapist and the offending partner have heard the level of hurt involved, it is unlikely that significant movement will occur. It is important to note that this process is often not a linear experience. High levels of affect and upset may reemerge at any time.

It is preferable to have the relatively full expression of the hurt, angry, and sad feelings to emerge and be discussed in joint meetings. As Butler, Seedall, and Harper (2008) note, "We doubt the prospects for complete couple healing where only the unfaithful partner is able to assess, examine, and attend to all the percussions and repercussions of infidelity in the couple relationship" (p. 271). However, it is our experience that in some more severe cases where the sense of betrayal is compounded by history or trauma, some preparatory individual sessions may be advisable. It is vital for the therapist to carefully monitor the offended partner's reaction to details of the affair and to question whether the disclosures should continue due to their traumatic impact.

During sessions in which intense emotional interactions are being expressed, vulnerability for both partners may also be high. The development and maintenance of a strong therapeutic alliance with both partners is essential. This is also a period of secondary assessment. Once the details and emotions are out in the open, low levels of trust, poor emotion regulation, fear of intimacy, and psychopathology must be evaluated (Gordon, Baucom, & Snyder, 2004).

Treatment: Stabilization

After the emotional expressivity has modulated somewhat, the therapist must help the couple re-evaluate their goals for treatment and for the relationship per se. The period of stabilization often involves a decision process, a rethinking of commitment, and a motivation to move forward despite continuing emotional hurt. This is the beginning of rebuilding trust, an essential component of reconciliation (Rider, 2011). Plans may begin for behavioral manifestations of trustworthiness and trusting. The stabilization period may be considered one in which a trend develops from making unreasonable demands to more reasonable ones. While these negotiations are being considered, the therapist must help the couple find the most viable decisions.

During stabilization, it makes some sense to introduce some understanding of the precursors and causes that led to the affair. This is the period in which some historical insight may be most useful. Snyder and Mitchell (2008) indicate that an improved understanding of both one's own and one's partner's developmental history, and the manner that these experiences have influenced both current and past relationships, may provide some understanding of how infidelity has occurred. Any understanding of how the betraying partner could make the decision to engage in an extradyadic affair may be helpful in later forgiveness and rebuilding.

It is also useful to devise some safety-oriented behavioral measures to help rebuild trust, such as more transparency, access to personal phone and e-mail with passwords, frequent check-ins, and so on. After Cindy's affair with a coworker, Phil negotiated for access to her personal e-mail, texts, and phone records. He also extracted an agreement that they would talk more frequently during the day and indicate what was going on. Finally, he asked her to limit any contact with her coworker to business: no lunches or drinks together, no coffee breaks except in larger groups, and avoidance of projects that included just the two of them. Although this may seem somewhat cumbersome, it was what Phil needed to begin trusting her. As trust begins to rebuild, it is necessary for the therapist to guide them back to normalcy where such restrictions are no longer needed.

Treatment: Rebuilding

Often, it is essential for a couple experiencing the aftermath of an extra-dyadic relationship and feelings of betrayal to rethink and revise their commitment. Based on such decisions, plans for future interactions with each other and with other people may be made. Any rebuilding now must include knowledge of the infidelity and clear plans to address the security issues.

In sessions, the consequences and meaning of the affair are explored and initial plans for informed decisions about the nature of the ongoing relationship are tested out. To do this successfully, it is essential that the affair has ended and no contact between the offender and outside person is ongoing. In situations like that of Cindy and Phil, where the third party is a coworker, specific plans may be made about the kinds and limits of ongoing contact. Some couples may find it best for the offending partner to get a transfer to another department at work.

One powerful component of rebuilding is forgiveness. It is important to state that forgiving does not mean forgetting. An occurrence of infidelity is a permanent part of the ongoing understanding of the relationship. However, forgiving the affair allows a couple to move on. Gordon, Baucom, and Snyder (2004) employ a forgiveness model to treat affairs that includes three common components:

1. Gaining a more balanced view of the offender and the event
2. Decreasing negative affect toward the offender, potentially increasing compassion
3. Relinquishing the right to punish the offender further or to demand restitution (see also Morrissette, 2012)

Treatment: Working Through

In addition to reconciling the loss of trust, secrecy, sense of betrayal, and vulnerability of each person, there are some additional psychological factors that may be relevant to understand. Later in treatment, a more in-depth understanding of the consequences of the affair may be useful. Among the factors to be explored are the effects the affair has had on the primary relationship. What did the affair allow the primary couple to address? What did it allow them to avoid? How has it damaged the relationship and what are the enduring implications?

In addition, an exploration of the meaning of the infidelity to each partner may be relevant. Furthermore, an understanding of how the affair may have been a solution to another problem may be examined. Finally, the manner in which an affair seemed a viable solution to a primary couple's intimacy issues can be addressed.

Treatment: Finding a New Homeostasis

The final stage of treatment involves developing a new homeostasis in the primary relationship. If confronting the affair does not permanently damage or end a relationship, how may the scars from the process allow for a new status quo? What new insights about self and spouse does each partner take with him or her? Do each emerge with a new sense of empathy and compassion? A more realistic sense of the partner? A heightened warning alarm that things may be going less well than hoped?

The therapist role in this rebuilding process may be the skeptic, the one who brings up these important questions. She or he may have to suggest that the new plan needs much more sophistication. She or he may help the couple develop a much better "DEW" (data early warning) line. She or he can then help them consolidate what they have learned about one another during the process; reassess their relationship, both in terms of desires and in terms of reality; and help them make decisions about how they want to proceed with this new knowledge and experience.

Finally, we believe therapists have to help couples set more effective boundaries, pay more attention to self-care and emotional regulation, deal with inevitable flashbacks and regressions in the process, and anticipate future feelings of insecurity and anxiety. It is essential to predict the potential partial backsliding and provide methods to share them and address the issues. This may well include some scheduled follow-up sessions.

Sudden Unexpected Losses

By adding a third party to a relationship, affairs may be a fairly obvious break in the structure of a primary bond, but it is clearly not the only unanticipated intrusive demand for a relationship transition. Any unexpected loss can throw a couple system off its balance. Almost any sudden trauma can do so. We will briefly describe a few examples.

Treatment follows a similar process (albeit very different content) as the therapy described for affairs:

- Emotional outpouring
- Stabilization
- Rebuilding
- Working through and finding a new homeostasis based on the new reality

Major losses of life, limb, dreams, finances, or property may be causes of considerable relational disruption. After any major disruption[6] or significant loss, a couple must reassess their new and current relationship.

Property Losses

Dean and Tisha lived in North California for many years. Soon after launching their youngest child to college and beginning to discover what an empty nest might bring them, their home and all possessions were destroyed in one of the wildfires that ravaged the area in 2017 and 2018. Although they got out without physical harm, they were now living in a trailer with their three pets. Their work had been tied to their home location and they were struggling to keep enough finances going to keep two children in college and to take care of their basic needs. Although they had insurance coverage, the settlements were slow to come and their losses were only minimally reimbursed, for which they felt retraumatized.

After seeing an emergency therapist, provided by a service agency, for six free sessions, they were referred to a couple therapist who was willing to see them pro bono. The therapy

---

6 Although it cannot be considered a major loss or trauma, many couple therapists can point to examples of a kitchen remodel or building a new home as precursors of divorce.

notes after the initial session described Dean as depressed and Tisha as very anxious. They also both spoke of the loss of their history along with their possessions.

Having established a good therapeutic alliance, treatment consisted of several months of a combination of emotional outpourings and practical solutions to everyday problems that involved housing, food, and work. Once their living situation was improved and initial trauma explored, they began to resolve into acceptance of a new reality. Because they had a long-term successful marriage, they were partially able to support each other during a slow rebuilding process. One issue that remained difficult was Tisha blaming Dean for the lack of more complete insurance and his reticence to find new work in the town in which they were now living. This issue was explored with the therapist at length and her childhood history of emotional abandonment was a key factor in both their understanding.

The therapy went along fairly well for almost 9 months, when they decided to rebuild their home on their old lot in the destroyed neighborhood. That return to their devastated community re-traumatized both of them. They also had to work through the conflictual experiences of their son and daughter both taking leaves of absence from college to help with the rebuilding. Although it helped considerably at a physical level, Dean in particular felt a lot of guilt about needing help from his children.

Their experience mirrors that of survivors of Hurricane Katrina (Osofsky & Osofsky, 2013) and similar disasters.

The Biggest Loss

The most devastating loss for a couple reportedly involves the death or severe disabling of a child since most people hold the expectation that their children will outlive them. The discrepancy between that belief and (particularly sudden) loss of a child typically brings extraordinary shock, trauma, and disorientation, especially when couples have been primarily focused on their children, possibly even to the detriment of their relationship (Dyregrov & Dyregrov, 2017; Price & Jones, 2015; Ungureanu, 2017).

> Otis and Deanna got that dreaded knock on the door from a member of the Armed Forces with information that their son had been killed in action. That information is one that is dreaded by almost all parents. For Otis, it was "worse than the kiss of death. [He] worried the whole time he was overseas and now the worst has come to pass."
>
> When they first came in, just 3 weeks after burying their son, Otis was inconsolable. By contrast, Deanna spoke lovingly of her minister who encouraged her to look at the time she had her son rather than the time when he was gone. She was fully experiencing that during our first meeting. She described how her son was in heaven and she looked forward to joining him when her time came.

Both their reactions were signs of dealing with grief, but the fact that they had such different reactions had distanced the two of them. Instead of being able to offer each other support, they felt more isolated and alone in dealing with the loss. In the early sessions he shed tears, weeping almost constantly, while she tried to tell him that it was "God's way." His anger and hurt at that pushed them further apart. It was 3 months into the therapy when she began to cry about the loss. The therapist was able to help Otis find empathy and to express it by holding Deanna. That was the first moment of stabilization and the earliest signs of rebuilding. Later, they had a return trauma when information reached them that their son was killed not in combat but because of errors committed by other U.S. forces.

That by itself was traumatizing, but it was compounded when Deanna insisted on going to formal hearings about the incident with a few other parents. Otis refused to go, saying only that nothing would bring his son back and it was too painful to hear details. This pattern reflects that each partner must experience grief and renewal in their own way, while neither interfering with nor rejecting the partner during healing.

It was a full year in therapy before they began to bring their healing into rebuilding their personal relationship. This couple also had to address their daughter's reaction to the death of her brother. She was very angry at her mother for apparently not understanding how awful she and her father felt.

After approximately 19 months in therapy, Otis and Deanna were able to find ways to work together again as a team and to reform their relationship along new lines as the parents of only one surviving child. Their daughter and her husband subsequently provided some particular relief by becoming pregnant and promising to name the grandchild after her slain brother.

As for affairs or losses caused by natural disasters, this loss responded best to a similar process (extensive emotional expression, stabilization, rebuilding, working through, and finding a new homeostasis based on the new reality). The unique component of this loss was the opposite ways that the two individuals mourned (see, for example, Hooghe, Neimeyer, & Rober, 2011). The therapist had to provide emotional sustenance for both during sessions in which they could not offer each other support. It is fairly common that grieving is very individual both in terms of manner expressed and timing. Part of the therapeutic task is to help normalize that for a couple and to find ways for them to be supportive rather than judgmental, despite their different experiences. In dealing with a severely ill child, coping has been shown to be significantly enhanced by empathic communication and understanding of a partner's emotional reactions (Koivula, Kokki, Korhonen, Laitila, & Honkalampi, 2019).

It is important to note that while Otis and Deanna lost a 22-year-old son, the loss of any child, even one in utero through miscarriage, can be devastating for parents because there is the loss of the actual child as well as the loss of the dream for that child. Denial and repression often occur after miscarriages, and therapists need to sensitively address the grief and deep loss that occurs with the loss of an unborn child.

Other Significant Losses

Deaths and disabilities of other family members or close friends may be less devastating but may also have a significant impact on a relationship. Losses of parents, for example, can bring up a sense of insecurity or anxiety about one's own mortality. Three years after the death of her father, Toni had intermittent periods of sadness, depression, and withdrawal from her husband of many years. Although the relationship with her parents was complicated, she "always felt like they would be there for [her]. Nobody else offer[ed] the same kind of security." Later she said to her husband, "You have always been a good husband and supporter of our family, but you are 12 years older than me and what will I do when you leave me too?"

His reassurances that he had no intention of dying anytime soon didn't provide any comfort, and he expressed frustration at her withdrawing from him emotionally and sexually during these "down times." In this case, the couple therapist recommended a grief group for Toni, prior to beginning couple therapy some months later.

Among more devastating losses, violent accidents or murder often have a major impact on surviving couples. Charlie's boss was shot at work by his former lover. Although he didn't see the actual shooting, Charlie was among a group of coworkers who discovered the body. He responded initially with little affect and assurances that they would keep the business running without their former boss. Ilsa, his long-time partner, kept trying to get him to "open up to his feelings of sadness and grief," finally making an appointment for both of them as a couple to "work on communication."

It was some time before his fear, horror, and sadness emerged in a discussion regarding his increasing lack of interest in joint activities.

Similar losses such as developmental disabilities or medical crises such as a cancer diagnosis and treatment can have a wide impact on a relationship and require a similar therapeutic process.

> Geraldine and Petra married when same-sex marriage became legal 4 years earlier, and Petra was recently diagnosed with breast cancer. They both agreed for her to have aggressive treatment and were optimistic that they could continue their active lives together. Petra found the treatments to be quite debilitating and had to reduce her work schedule. In subsequent examinations, it was not clear that the cancer was in remission. As her income decreased, Geraldine found herself struggling to keep up with their household expenses and managing their responsibilities and activities. Petra felt diminished as a partner even though Geraldine was quite willing to step up and do whatever was needed.

It became apparent in the first session that this couple was in shock over the diagnosis and the new reality they were facing. In their usual pragmatic, "can-do" fashion, they expected that they could manage day-to-day affairs and keep up with their lives as usual. Acknowledging their shock and trauma allowed them to pause and adjust emotionally to an uncertain future, and Petra found herself more willing to accept Geraldine's generous support. The therapist found it necessary to delve into an existential mind-set herself and to not solely focus on the pragmatics of their daily routines. With consultation she also resisted the urge to bolster the couple's optimism when evidence to support it was not forthcoming.

Financial Setbacks

> Shortly after they retired, Gene and Faith suffered identity theft. It was not their fault, but they were victims of a breach of security at a major national company. Before they could get new bank accounts and passwords, their savings were drained. Their direct deposit Social Security checks on which they relied for ongoing living expenses had also been redirected to the thieves. Although their bank accounts were insured by FDIC, the reestablishing of their identities and the compensation from insurance were painfully slow and the costs to get it going were tough for retirees on a fixed income.

They had to face both the loss of their assets for some time, a loss of their faith in their safety as retirees, and tremendous vulnerability. Unfortunately for them, they both responded initially by blaming each other for not fixing the vulnerability earlier. Both of them opined, he or she "always wants to fix the barn door after the horse is gone!"

After the emotional expression of fear, anger, and hurt, they found themselves dealing with vulnerability by accusing the partner. Therapy aimed toward minimizing the blame and helping them support one another was quite lengthy.

The effects lasted for some time even after they had reestablished identities and reclaimed almost all of the lost funds. They were far more anxious and felt tremendously more vulnerable than before. Gene and Faith were fortunate in two ways: They could resolve the issues in under 2 years, and their therapist was able to be particularly empathic and encouraging, having been personally victimized by identity theft herself a few years prior.

Identity theft is a silent and behind-the-scenes crime (Golladay & Holtfreter, 2017). Other crimes such as robbery, burglary, or extortion also represent financial losses, but add the dimension of physical safety. Couples who have been victimized in an armed robbery may have long-lasting adjustment disorders (Beaton, Cook, Kavanagh, & Herrington, 2000) or PTSD (Boudreaux et al., 1998). They may find that they feel unsafe and anxious in situations in which they formerly had no problems. Similarly, burglary, such as in-home break-ins, can leave couples feeling violated and feeling insecure each time they leave and worried when they return.

Connie and Martine came home after a vacation to find that their apartment had been broken into, ransacked, and many personal belongings had been stolen. Six months later, they described in their first therapy session an ongoing fear that the thieves would return and also a prevailing sense of being personally violated. The initial therapeutic conflict involved Martine's wish to move out of their place and start anew somewhere else and Connie's defiant attitude that she would overcome the lingering feelings.

Their differences in how to deal with such a crisis was not unusual: fight or flight. After encouraging the initial expressions of anger and fear, the therapist began to help them normalize both reactions and find ways to support one another. The rebuilding of their relationship required an understanding that despite their different reactions, no rejection of the other person or relational threat was evident.

Ann was making a deposit when there was an armed bank robbery. In addition to emptying the cash drawers, they grabbed all the customers' wallets, watches, cell phones, and handbags at gunpoint. The thieves were caught within 10 minutes of exiting the bank and all the money was recovered.

However, that only partially alleviated Ann's distress. When she got home, she immediately called her partner (Trey). By the time he arrived home, she was shaking uncontrollably. Later he took her to the ER, where they admitted her and gave her a sedative. The next week in therapy, Ann mostly expressed anger and irritation at Trey as if he were the perpetrator. Although he tried to be understanding, he became very angry that he was being accused.

During the next several weeks in therapy, the therapist had to process her feelings of a "near-death" experience, her wish to be protected, and her anxiety being expressed as anger. It was some time before the therapist could help Trey support her, find ways to express empathy for her ordeal, and get back to their normal relationship.

Stages of Therapy for Unexpected Transitions

When couples come in for therapy after a trauma or unanticipated external crisis, treatment stages diverge somewhat from those of normal transitions:

1. Carefully assess ego strength and current resources within each person and within the relationship pair, especially when trauma is involved.
2. Encourage the expression of emotions, especially those sympathetic nervous system reactions (fight/flight) to the incursive events, whether a sense of betrayal or one of fear for one's safety and security. Help couples stay with the effective outpouring instead of making premature behavioral changes, unless necessary for safety. For example, if there is need for safety, food, or shelter, these must precede other considerations.
3. Normalize the reaction to the trauma. Helping couples understand that what they are struggling with is fairly characteristic for anyone who has survived a robbery, dislocation, or affair. When couples recognize that they are not alone, they may be more prone to operate as a team.
4. Help the couple acknowledge their new reality and build a new homeostasis.
5. Work through any remaining lingering doubts and anxieties. This includes a plan to anticipate future anxiety about their loss and backsliding into previously successful but now ineffective methods of dealing with couple issues. One example of this is for the offended partner in infidelity having a revenge affair.
6. Schedule follow-up consultations 3 to 6 months and a year after termination of therapy. That date on the schedule is often referred to by former clients as a "safety net." It is important to note that although they may cherish the offer, many couples cancel such appointments, especially if relational matters have settled and they are doing well.

SUMMARY

Like all systems, couples seek the security and predictability of a balance or homeostasis. At such times, comfort may lie in the processes that they can count on. Relationships tend to be consistent during such periods. However, at times, internal or external pressures may disrupt the homeostasis and create an increased tension between the apparent safety of the status quo and the anxiety of change and the unknown. These are transition times in the life of a couple. Successful movement through transitions often involves confrontation with a new reality and a need to make often difficult adjustments.

It is during such transitions that couples most often seek therapy. In this chapter, we explore a variety of transitions, both natural and predictable and those that are quite unexpected. Almost all of them represent a significant loss of stability, particularly in the process of the couple relationship. A number of specific forms of transitions are described. Therapeutic interventions for such loss and the restabilization of the relationship are provided for both types of transitions. Throughout all types of transitions, it is important for the therapist to not get lost in the details of the event, but to remain focused on the interactional dynamics of their relationship and to help them to maintain their togetherness as a couple.

Process of Couple Treatment

My first couple is coming in at 4:00 p.m. on Thursday. I've been worrying since the phone call a week ago and am sweating and panicking now.

All I know about them is that they have a Hispanic last name: a culture I know little about.

Journal note from an MFT student in her first practicum

6

The Initial Contact: The Pre-Treatment Phase

How Does a Couple Get to You as the Counselor or Therapist?

Depending on the professional work environment, clients may come to see therapists in a variety of ways. Each situation and each new couple require individual consideration. In addition, there are common factors in how we begin with new couple clients.

Next please! If you are working in an agency, a walk-in clinic, or a large practice, you may have what Whitaker (Whitaker & Bumberry, 1988) called a "blind date" with your couple clients, because your name matched with their request on some roster or schedule. Carla said,

> I heard the supervisor ask the receptionist, "Who is free at 4:00 p.m. on Thursday this week?" I heard her say, "Carla or Tom." To my horror, I heard my supervisor say, "Assign this new couple to Carla." When I went out to greet them at the appointed time, I met a couple in their 40s. They were sitting on the same couch, but about as far apart as was possible by the dimensions of the cushions. They were both on their phones, not talking to each other. The first thought I had was they are much older than I. Would they even want to see me?

Although Carla's anxiety was elevated in this situation, it may not have been much less had she met her clients in a more typical manner.

Couple therapy, at least the first several times, can be daunting, even for well-trained practitioners. It can seem so much more chaotic than individual therapy, requires unique skills, demands different approaches, and adds complexity to what has already been described as "the impossible profession" (Shapiro, Peltz & Bernadett-Shapiro, 2019), a term originally coined to describe psychiatry and psychoanalysis by Freud (1937) and expanded by Malcolm (1981).

Before the Initial Face-to-Face Meeting

Carla saw a couple on their therapeutic "blind date" (Whitaker & Bumberry, 1988, p 53).

There was no introduction, no real preparation period. The clients came to a clinic and were assigned to her, based primarily on compatible schedules. This is a less-than-ideal way to begin. More commonly there is a preliminary process during which some attempts are made to establish rapport, educate clients on what is expected, and make a connection possible.

Referral and Appointment Making

Referrals come in a variety of ways. Some come to an agency. Others come from a third-party payer such as an insurance company panel list. They may come from an Internet listing, an Internet search, the therapist's website, or from what is essentially a blind "yellow pages" listing. Often the referral will be a personal recommendation from another professional (physician, individual psychotherapist, attorney, clergy, etc.) or from a former satisfied client. The referral source can influence significantly how clients approach the initial phone call. If they are calling from a list, they will likely be therapist shopping, calling several therapists, hoping to get a return call from anyone. This is far from personal. In the authors' experience, fewer than half of clients who use this method ever call back.

By contrast, if the referral is from a trusted source, it is likely to be more directed toward the specific therapist and the motivation to make an appointment is commonly heightened. For example, during the initial phone call, the following interaction occurs:

Clients: "We were referred by our [minister, doctor, individual therapist] to see you personally. She said she would call in advance to talk with you. Can you see us?

Therapist: "Yes, I did hear from her and was looking forward to your call."

Most clients who use this method follow through at the end of the call with an appointment. That is more likely to be successful than

Clients: "We found your name online and your office is close by so we wanted to check you out," or "You were on a list from our insurance company, but it didn't say if you did marriage counseling."

The Appointment-Making Process

Most often, the process begins with a call to a private practice or agency by one of the partners in a couple. They may have asked for a particular therapist specifically, been referred directly to a therapist, or just wanted to be seen as soon as possible. Sometimes, the therapist will be on a panel of providers for the clients' insurance.

It is important to note that the vast majority of counselors and therapists do not answer such calls unless they have a phone hour or are at their desk with unscheduled time.

Characteristically, however, we get the call from voice mail, an answering device, an answering service, or a confidential e-mail to our website.

PRACTICE BOX 6.1: AN EXAMPLE OF A VOICE MAIL OUTGOING MESSAGE

Hello, you have reached the telephone answering machine of Mary Jones (PhD, LMFT LCSW, LPC, etc.). If this is an emergency, please hang up and call 911 or the local crisis hotline. If it is not an emergency, please leave your name, telephone number, and a brief description of the reason for your call. Please say your name and number slowly and repeat if possible. I will return your call within 24 hours. You may want to add times when I can reach you. I look forward to talking with you.

It is customary to return the call within 24 hours, preferably sooner, but only when the counselor has time and a quiet place and is ready to talk with the couple for the first time. Aside from the good business and professionalism of prompt returns, it also signals to clients that the therapist takes their concerns seriously (Patterson, Williams, Edwards, Chamow & Grauf-Grounds, 2018).

Therapists differ greatly on the desired length of that initial phone call, the material discussed, whether they talk to one or both members of a couple, and how they structure the initial interview. It is generally sufficient to discuss the situation with one partner, and most keep it long enough to determine if there is a potential fit, but short enough to avoid making the call into a first therapy session. For Patterson, 20 minutes seems optimal for such calls. Shapiro and Patterson prefer 10–20 minutes. One of our colleagues will stay on the phone longer and another will insist that she speak to both parties in the couple in that initial phone contact.

The initial call is important. It sets a tone for interactions, gives clients a sense of the therapist's style and manner of working, and hopefully alleviates some anxiety that is present in almost all initial calls for couple work. The phone contact is very important for beginning a connection with the clients. The impressions from the phone call create the manner in which the couple's expectations are set for the face-to-face meetings. Nichols (1988) opines, "Strong impressions often are formed during the telephone contact. It is not unusual for callers to decide that they wish to see someone else as a result of a 'turn-off'" (p. 99).

T: Hello. My name is Kim Green. I'm returning a call from Lois Wilson.

L: She's not here right now. I'm her husband. May I help you?

T: Well, please ask her to call me back when she is available. I should be available for the next few hours.

L: Oh wait, Green? Are you the marriage counselor? My name is Lew. She told me you might call. We want to make an appointment as soon as we can.

T: Okay. Please tell me why you called and what you are looking for.

L: We have hit a snag in our communication. We have been mishearing each other and we could use some new skills and help getting back on track.

T: Tell me, did anything precipitate the desire at this time?

L: Yeah. We were talking about a parenting decision and were really on different sides of the street on it. We were not even listening to each other.

T: You have children now?

L: We have a 4-year-old daughter. The question is about having another.

T: Have you ever been in marriage counseling before?

L: Yeah. When we lived in Chicago, we saw a counselor for a few months, and she was very helpful. We actually got your name from her.

T: Can you tell me her name?

L: Dr. Blue.

T: Will insurance be an issue?

L: We have Blue Cross, but if we need to, we can pay out of pocket. May I ask about your fee?

T: My standard fee for a 90-minute session is $200.00 If your insurance lists me as a provider, your co-pay will be $35.00 per session.

L: That's fine. I'll check, but we want to meet either way.

T: Okay, I can see you as soon as Monday at 4:00 p.m. or Tuesday at noon. How will those times work?

L: I have my wife's schedule here. Monday at 4:00 is better.

T: Please come 15 minutes early to complete the paperwork [alternative: May I send you the paperwork to complete via e-mail? What is a good e-mail address?] My office is located at the corner of 2nd and State on the third floor. Let me give you directions. Do you have any questions of me?

Some therapists just rely on GPS maps. It still seems to work best to offer and go over directions, particularly if the office location or parking is not obvious. It may be useful to send an e-mail reminder 24 hours before the appointment.

PRACTICE BOX 6.2: SESSION FORMATS AND INITIAL INSTRUCTIONS

Therapists have different time frames for client sessions.

They range generally from 45 minutes to 2 hours.

Patterson usually meets with couples for 90 minutes.

Shapiro usually meets for 50 minutes

Instructions Depending on the office:

T: When you come in,

A. please just have a seat in the waiting room.
B. check in with the receptionist.
C. there will be a clipboard on the top shelf of the bookshelves. Please take it and complete the paperwork.
D. I'll come out to meet you at 4:00 p.m.

Ms. Green established several matters during this short phone call.

1. Both partners were motivated to be in therapy.
2. They had a positive experience previously and a referral from the successful therapist.
3. They defined the issue as communication problems regarding parenting (of course, that could be the entire problem, or the poor communication could mask other issues).
4. Scheduling was not a problem and an initial appointment was made.
5. She provided details of her desired procedures, fees, and waiting room protocol.

It is important to note that one of the ways she took charge was to tell the clients when she had time for an appointment, rather than ask when they could come in. Setting those boundaries will obviate clients requesting a Saturday evening, other inconvenient or impossible appointment times, and/or lengthy negotiations.

Therapists differ on whether to discuss fees over the phone unless the clients ask. It is our opinion that clarity about fees, scheduling, basic issues, and general approach are important informed consent matters to discuss prior to the beginning of the first face-to-face meeting in order to avoid misunderstandings that can derail therapy if discovered later. In this case, the husband already commented on his willingness to pay out of pocket.

SIDE BOX 6.3: POLICIES REGARDING FEE DISCUSSIONS

We have different policies regarding when to discuss fees. We both will respond directly to clients' questions during the initial phone call.

However, if clients do not ask, **Patterson** will initiate the conversation.

If not asked on the phone, **Shapiro** doesn't discuss fees until clients appear for the initial session

---

The Initial Meeting

When the couple arrives, most therapists briefly make note of their behavior in the waiting room. Did they arrive together? Are they on time? Do they sit together? Do they talk? Do they complete the intake forms separately or together or does one do all the work?

For example, one couple entered the waiting room together. She picked up the clipboard with the requisite forms and silently handed it to him. He took out his pen and began filling out the forms in exceptionally neat lettering, occasionally asking her for input on what he was printing. The manner in which they chose to complete the intake forms may reveal something about how they operate as a couple and about the power dynamics in the relationship, in addition to what answers they actually write.

The information on the intake form provides the therapist with a brief map of the terrain as the three of them embark on the journey. Characteristically, the forms are less comprehensive than those in a physician's office and are broken up into contact information, business information, living situation, symptoms, and habits that may enhance or interfere with therapeutic progress. In addition, therapists all have a copy of the ubiquitous HIPAA form to sign, releases of information forms if necessary, and contractual agreements regarding the particular practice. Copies of sample agreements can be found in Figures 6.1–6.8.

On one occasion, after viewing the forms and signing them, one member of a two-attorney couple asked in a very challenging manner, "Can I have a copy of these forms that we are filling out? I want to check them over to be sure we are protected." Understanding that this was the first chance to intervene in the couple system and also to take charge of the session, their therapist responded, "Of course, I'll make you a copy right now. Listen, if you do find anything improper here, please let me know. I would really appreciate the input." Because his query wasn't about the forms per se, but about control of the (slightly threatening) situation, the client who asked never mentioned the forms again throughout the 3-month therapy.

The initial face-to-face session is a classic first impression situation. Factors such as the ambiance of the office, available parking, and location convenience may have an effect on any subsequent therapy. More often, the therapist's appearance and demeanor

Family Therapy Institute
Therapist Name and Degree Licensed Psychologist, PSY xxxx

THIS IS A SAMPLE FORM FOR STUDENT USE ONLY. NO GUARANTEES OF LEGALITY.

TO ALL CLIENTS OF

Jerrold Lee Shapiro, Ph.D.
Terence Patterson, Ed.D.

Please read carefully and complete the enclosed forms, unless you already completed and sent them online

COMPLETE BOTH PAGES OF THE
Registration Information Form

1) READ AND SIGN:

a) THE FTI POLICIES STATEMENT
b) STATEMENT OF PATIENT'S RIGHTS
c) HIPAA Form
d) RELEASE OF INFORMATION (If appropriate)
e) Limits of confidentiality form

Family Therapy Institute 400 Second St., Suite 333 Anytown, CA, 94222
Tel. (650) 555-5555   Fax (650) 555-5556

REGISTRATION INFORMATION
[Couples/Families]
_____

Phones: H _____ W_____ C _____

Phones: H _____ W_____ C _____

E-Mail _____ E-Mail _____

Date of Birth _____ Marital Status _____ Date of Birth _____
Marital Status _____ Education: Highest Degrees _____ Degrees _____
Majors _____

Education: Highest

Majors _____
Currently a student [yes] [no] School _____ Currently a student [yes] [no] School

Employment/position _____ Employment/position _____

CHILDREN: Names/Ages _____ / _____ / _____

_____ / _____ / _____

Dr. Jerrold Shapiro is not a member of any insurance panels, HMOs or PPOs, nor does he bill any insurance companies (third party payers) directly. Monthly, he will provide an "insurance-ready" form, for you to submit to your Medical Insurance carrier. If you have any questions about this, have special needs, or confidentiality please ask your therapist. [*Therapists who are on insurance panels would simply list them here*].

FIGURE 6.1 **Sample face sheet and anamnestic information**

NAME _____ *DATE*
        Please describe the situation that brought you to FTI at this time

Please describe any previous treatment for the current or related concerns. Include the names and phone numbers (if available) of prior therapists.

Are you currently under any medical treatment or medication? Please describe.

What in your family history might be relevant for the current problem?

What is your current daily consumption of
        Alcohol _____ *Tobacco* _____ *Caffeine Recreational Drugs* _____
        Non-prescription medication _____

Please comment on any problems in the areas of
        Work
        Finances
        Relationship/Family/Living Situation Legal

FIGURE 6.2 **Basic diagnostic information**

APPOINTMENTS: *We reserve your scheduled appointment time exclusively for you. As a result, we require a 48 hour notice if you must cancel. Cancellations which are not made 48 hours prior to the scheduled appointment will be charged at the regular fee. It is possible that your insurance will not reimburse you for missed sessions.*

BILLING: *Payment (or co-pay) is due at each visit. Late payments are subject to a late payment charge of 1.5% per month until the balance is paid. Special arrangements must be made specifically with your therapist.*

TELEPHONE CALLS: *We try to return all calls within 24 hours. Charges may be imposed on lengthy calls that involve consultation or therapy. There is no charge for calls that are essentially for scheduling or referral.*

INSURANCE: *We will provide you with a monthly statement that is "Medical Insurance ready." It is your responsibility to file the forms with your insurance company. We will cooperate by providing appropriate information to your insurance carrier.*

Insurance Releases: *In order for Family Therapy Institute to provide information to your insurance carrier, you need to sign a specific release.*

CONFIDENTIALITY: *All information disclosed in your therapy sessions is normally considered to be confidential. Such information belongs to you and will be released only with your expressed written specific consent.* **It is essential that you understand that in certain circumstances, confidentiality is limited by state law.** *We are required by law to report all situations of physical or sexual child abuse, intent to harm oneself, intent to harm others, abuse of elders or dependent adults. If you are covered by insurance, your insurer may require substantial levels of disclosure to authorize payment. In addition, if you are involved in a legal action, our records can be subpoenaed by a court for certain purposes determined by the court.*

    I understand the conditions described above and agree to them. I have also been given a Statement of Patient Rights, Family Therapy Institute fee schedule and a Release of Information form.

Signature _____ Signature _____

Date _____ Date _____

FIGURE 6.3 **Family therapy institute policies**

At all times we consider our patients' rights and needs as a foremost concern. As a patient/client at FTI you have certain rights. Please read this document carefully. If you have any questions, your therapist will attempt to answer them and explain our procedures.

*Psychotherapy involves a special relationship between people. In this relationship, your therapist receives monetary remuneration in return for a close interpersonal relationship in which your personal needs are paramount. It is expected that this relationship will be honest, trustworthy and dedicated to helping you develop greater understanding and skills to more successfully live your life in a gratifying and healthy manner. Our primary interventions at **FTI** involve understanding, helping you gain insight, making suggestions and following up on your progress.*

There are two major functions of psychotherapy: crisis work and growth work.

Crisis Work: *Often, people enter couple therapy in the hope of better coping with life transitions and crises. This work tends to be relatively short term (less than a year in duration). It may involve weekly or more or less frequent sessions, depending on the nature and severity of the problem. On rare occasions, these problems can be severe enough to warrant medication or hospitalization. At **FTI** we have excellent working relationships with professionals and agencies in the area that will provide these services.*

Growth Work: *Not everyone enters couple therapy at a time of crisis. Frequently, people wish to work on long standing patterns that have puzzled or bothered them in their lives. This work involves in-depth probing, often with a focus on personal historical events, facing fears, etc.*

Because this work entails long established patterns and unconscious motivation, it usually has a longer treatment duration (a year or longer). This work normally requires weekly or more frequent sessions.

In either kind of psychotherapy or counseling, the best results will be possible only if you, as a client, work hard with us and honestly give us complete information.

It is important that you understand that the process of couple therapy may bring up unpleasant memories, and can arouse intense emotions such as fear and anger.

Intense feelings of loneliness, depression, anxiety, frustration, helplessness etc. may be aroused. In short, you may feel worse before you feel better.

Benefits from therapy can include better social and family relationships, increased satisfaction from social relationships, work and creative endeavors, greater maturity, appropriate goal setting and personal growth.

It is important that you recognize that you have the right to refuse treatment at any time. You can do this without any moral, legal or financial obligation (as of the date you inform us that you wish to leave our care). You are, of course, liable for any outstanding debts. If you wish to seek treatment elsewhere, we will provide you with a list of qualified therapists.

You have the right to ask any questions about the methods used by your therapist. If you wish, your therapist will explain her/his usual procedures to you. You have the right to refuse any extraordinary therapeutic techniques. We shall inform you of, and explain the intention to use, any unusual procedures.

>   *You have the right to a written summary of your **confidential** records and files.*

Within certain required legal limits, all of the contents of your therapy sessions will be treated with strict confidentiality, and will not be released without your written permission. At your written request, any part of your records or files will be released to another qualified health care provider or organization. If making these records public can be foreseeably dangerous or harmful to you, your therapist will inform you prior to sending said records.

LIMITS TO CONFIDENTIALITY: *Under the following situations, your therapist is required by law to reveal certain information to other persons or agencies without your permission. We are **not** required to inform you of these actions. These situations are*

>   *If you make a serious threat of physical injury to another person, your therapist is required by law to inform the intended victim and appropriate law enforcement agencies;*

>   *In cases of child or elder abuse or neglect, your therapist must report it to appropriate agencies.*

FIGURE 6.4 **Statement of patients' rights** (*continued*)

FIGURE 6.4 **Statement of patients' rights**

January 1, 2019

Normal charges for [Therapist], Ph.D.

SERVICE	TIME	CHARGES
Initial extensive consultation(office)	50–75 minutes	$xxx-xxx Couple/individual therapy (office) 50 minutes $xxx
Other fees as relevant may be listed here		

FIGURE 6.5 **FTI fee schedules**

---

can have a very powerful impact. When clients' expectations are not met, it can have a deleterious effect. Zunin and Zunin (1972) underscore the salience of even the first few minutes of a meeting. In conveying an appropriate professional image, a therapist should carefully pay attention to a practice structure and style that is ethical and highly professional and that fits one's own sense of self. This is not to say the therapist should be overly formal or self-conscious, just consistent with who he or she is and the clients who are being seen. Sincerity and congruence are far more important than a line of designer clothing. Regardless, it is essential to note that not all therapists are a good match for every client and vice-versa.

Some factors are beyond the control of the therapist. Perhaps the couple expected someone older. Perhaps they expected a different kind of office setting. Perhaps they expected a more or less formally dressed therapist. Perhaps they expected that a male therapist named Sydney, Dana, or Leslie would be female. In general, though, a warm, accepting, professional ambiance is most likely to generate more therapeutic cooperation.

The first meeting of a couple with a therapist must serve several purposes:

1. Building rapport: Approach the couple with a warm, engaging, positive attitude; acknowledge ambivalence about coming in for therapy, especially the parts of them that do not want to be there.

Licensed Clinical Psychologist, Lic. Xxxx

NOTICE OF PRIVACY PRACTICES (HIPAA)
IT IS MY STANDARD PRACTICE TO KEEP CONFIDENTIAL ALL RECORDS PERTAINING TO YOUR THERAPY/
TREATMENT WITH ME, EXCEPT
WHERE I AM REQUIRED BY LAW OR PROFESSIONAL ETHICS TO DISCLOSE SUCH INFORMATION.

I. **This notice describes how medical information about you may be used and disclosed and how you can get access to this information. Please review it carefully.**

II. **I HAVE A LEGAL DUTY TO SAFEGUARD YOUR PROTECTED HEALTH INFORMATION (PHI)**
I am legally required to protect the privacy of your PHI, which includes information that I've created or received about your past, present, or future health or condition, the provision of health care to you, or the payment for this health care that can be used to identify you. I must provide you with this Notice about my privacy practices, and such Notice must explain how, when, and why I will "use" and "disclose" your PHI. A "use" of PHI occurs when I share, examine, utilize, apply, or analyze such information within my practice; PHI is "disclosed" when it is released, transferred, has been given to, or is otherwise divulged to a third party outside of my practice. With some exceptions, I may not use or disclose any more of your PHI than is necessary to accomplish the purpose for which the use or disclosure is made. I am legally required to follow the privacy practices described in this Notice.

However, I reserve the right to change the terms of this Notice and my privacy policies at any time. Any changes will apply to PHI on file with me already. Before I make any important changes to my policies, I will promptly change this Notice and post a new copy of it in my office.

III. **HOW I MAY USE AND DISCLOSE YOUR PHI.**
I will use and disclose your PHI for certain specific reasons. For some of these uses or disclosures, I will need your prior authorization; for others, however, I do not. Listed below are the different categories of my uses and disclosures along with some examples of each category.

A. **Uses and Disclosures Relating to Treatment, Payment, or Health Care Operations Do Not Require Your Prior Written Consent.** I can use and disclose your PHI without your consent for the following reasons:
1. **For treatment.** I may disclose your PHI to physicians, psychiatrists, psychologists, and other licensed health care providers who provide you with health care services or are involved in your care. For example, if you're being treated by a psychiatrist, I can disclose your PHI to your psychiatrist in order to coordinate your care.

2. **To obtain payment for treatment.** I can use and disclose your PHI to bill and collect payment for the treatment and services provided by me to you. For example, if you request that I send your PHI to your insurance company or health plan for reimbursement for the health care services that I have provided to you. I may also provide your PHI to any business associates, such as billing companies, claims processing companies, and others that process my health care claims.

3. **For health care operations.** I may disclose your PHI to operate my practice. For example, I might use your PHI to evaluate the quality of health care services that you received or to evaluate the performance of the health care professionals who provided such services to you. I may also provide your PHI to our accountants, attorneys, consultants, and others to assure that I'm complying with applicable laws.

4. **Other disclosures.** I may also disclose your PHI to others without your consent in certain situations. For example, your consent isn't required if you need *emergency* treatment, as long as I try to get your consent after treatment is rendered, or if I try to get your consent but you are unable to communicate with me (for example, if you are unconscious or in severe pain) and I think that you would consent to such treatment if you were able to do so.

B. **Certain Uses and Disclosures Do Not Require Your Consent.** I can use and disclose your PHI without your consent or authorization for the following reasons:
1. When disclosure is required by federal, state or local law; judicial or administrative proceedings;

FIGURE 6.6 **HIPAA** (*continued*)

or, law enforcement. For example, I may make a disclosure to applicable officials when a law requires me to report information to government agencies and law enforcement personnel about victims of abuse or neglect; or when ordered in a judicial or administrative proceeding.

2. For public health activities. For example, I may have to report information about you to the county coroner.

3. For health oversight activities. For example, I may have to provide information to assist the government when it conducts an investigation or inspection of a health care provider or organization.

4. To avoid harm. In order to avoid a serious threat to the health or safety of a person or the public, I may provide PHI to law enforcement personnel or persons able to prevent or lessen such harm.

5. For specific government functions. I may disclose PHI of military personnel and veterans in certain situations. I may disclose PHI for national security purposes.

6. For workers' compensation purposes. I may provide PHI in order to comply with workers' compensation laws.

7. Appointment reminders and health related benefits or services. I may use PHI to provide appointment reminders or give you information about treatment alternatives, or other health care services or benefits I offer.

C. Certain Uses and Disclosures Require You to Have the Opportunity to Object.

Disclosures to family, friends, or others. I may provide your PHI to a family member, friend, or other person that you indicate is involved in your care or the payment for your health care, unless you object in whole or in part. The opportunity to consent may be obtained retroactively in emergency situations.

D. Other Uses and Disclosures Require Your Prior Written Authorization. In any other situation not described in sections III A, B, and C above, I will ask for your written authorization before using or disclosing any of your PHI. If you choose to sign an authorization to disclose your PHI, you can later revoke such authorization in writing to stop any future uses and disclosures (to the extent that I haven't taken any action in reliance on such authorization) of your PHI by me.

IV. **WHAT RIGHTS YOU HAVE REGARDING YOUR PHI** You have the following rights with respect to Your PHI:

a. **The Right to Request Limits on Uses and Disclosures of Your PHI.** You have the right to request that I limit how I use and disclose your PHI. If I accept your request, I Will put any limits in writing and abide by them except in emergency situations. You may not limit the uses and disclosures that I am legally required or allowed to make.

b. **The Right to Choose How I Send PHI to You.** You have the right to ask that I send information to you at any address you specify and by a means you prefer (for example, e-mail instead of regular mail) I will comply with your request so long as I can easily provide the PHI to you in the format you requested.

c. **The Right to See and Get Copies of Your PHI.** In most cases, you have the right to look at or get copies of your PHI that I have, but you must make the request in writing. If I don't have your PHI but I know who does, I will tell you how to get it. I will respond to you within 30 days of receiving your written request. In certain situations, I may deny your request. If I do, I will tell you, in writing, my reasons for the denial and explain your right to have my denial reviewed.

If you request copies of your PHI, I will charge you not more than $.25 for each page. Instead of providing the PHI you requested, I may provide you with a summary or explanation of the PHI as long as you agree to that and to the cost in advance.

FIGURE 6.6 **HIPAA** (*continued*)

A. **The Right to Get a List of the Disclosures I Have Made.** You have the right to get a list of instances in which I have disclosed your PHI. The list will not include uses or disclosures that you have already consented to, such as those made for treatment, payment, or health care operations, directly to you, or to your family. The list also won't include uses and disclosures made for national security purposes, to corrections or law enforcement personnel, or disclosures made before April 15, 2003.

I will respond to your request for an accounting of disclosures within 60 days of receiving your request. The list I will give you will include disclosures made in the last six years unless you request a shorter time. The list will include the date of the disclosure, to whom PHI was disclosed (including their address, if known), a description of the information disclosed, and the reason for the disclosure. I will provide the list to you at no charge, but if you make more than one request in the same year, I will charge you a reasonable cost based fee for each additional request.

B. **The Right to Correct or Update Your PHI.** If you believe that there is a mistake in your PHI or that a piece of important information is missing, you have the right to request that I correct the existing information or add the missing information. You must provide the request and your reason for the request in writing. I will respond within 60 days of receiving your request to correct or update your PHI. I may deny your request in writing if the PHI is (i) correct and complete, (ii) not created by me, (iii) not allowed to be disclosed, or iv) not part of my records. My written denial will state the reasons for the denial and explain your right to file a written statement of disagreement with the denial. If you don't file one, you have the right to request that your request and my denial be attached to all future disclosures of your PHI. If I approve your request, I will make the change to your PHI, tell you that I have done it, and tell others that need to know about the change to your PHI.

C. **The Right to Get This Notice by E-Mail.** You have the right to get a copy of this notice by e-mail and to request a paper copy of it.

V. **HOW TO COMPLAIN ABOUT MY PRIVACY PRACTICES**

If you think that I may have violated your privacy rights, or you disagree with a decision I made about access to your PHI, you may file a complaint with the person listed in Section VI below. You also may send a written complaint to the Secretary of the Department of Health and Human Services at 200 Independence Avenue S.W, Washington, D.C. 20201. 1 will take no retaliatory action against you if you file a complaint about my privacy practices.

VI. **PERSON TO CONTACT FOR INFORMATION ABOUT THIS NOTICE OR TO COMPLAIN ABOUT MY PRIVACY PRACTICES**

If you have any questions about this notice or any complaints about my privacy practices, or would like to know how to file a complaint with the Secretary of the Department of Health and Human Services, please contact me at Jerrold Lee Shapiro, Ph.D., 4546 el Camino Real, Suite 242, Los Altos, Ca 94022.

VII. **EFFECTIVE DATE OF THIS NOTICE** This notice went into effect on April 14, 2003.

I have read and understand the notice of privacy and procedures.

_____

Signature

_____

Signature of parent or guardian if applicable

FIGURE 6.6 **HIPAA**

By signing this document, I, (name of patient) _____ (hereinafter "Patient") hereby authorize [Therapist Name]. (hereinafter "Provider") to disclose mental health treatment information and records obtained in the course of Provider's treatment of Patient, including, but not limited to, Provider's diagnosis of Patient, to (name and functions of the person or entity to whom disclosure is made)

_____

_____

_____

I understand that I have a right to receive a copy of this authorization. I understand that any cancellation or modification of this authorization must be in writing. I understand that I have the right to revoke this authorization at any time unless Provider has taken action in reliance upon it. And, I also understand that such revocation must be in writing and received by Provider at *4546 Second St Suite 333, Anytown, Ca. 94222* to be effective.

This disclosure of information and records authorized by Patient is required for the following purpose:

_____

_____

_____

The specific uses and limitations on the types of medical information to be discussed are as follows:

_____

_____

_____

Such disclosure shall be limited to the following specific types of information:

_____

_____

_____

Provider shall not condition treatment upon Patient signing this authorization. Patient has the right to refuse to sign this form.

Patient understands that information used or disclosed pursuant to this authorization may be subject to re-disclosure by the recipient and may no longer be protected by the Federal Privacy Rule, although such information may be protected by applicable California law.

This authorization shall remain valid until: _____

Patient _____ Date _____

FIGURE 6.7 **Sample release of information form authorization for release of information**

2. Clarifying goals: Determine their individual and mutual goals for therapy.
3. Assessment: Ascertain the strengths of each member and the relationship and any individual pathology
4. Why now?: Find out the reasons for seeking therapy now and the history of the problem/
5. Relevant problem history: Learn what they have done to alleviate the problem.

Terence Patterson, EdD, ABPP Licensed Psychologist #PSYxxxx 1721 Second Street #2
Anytown, CA 99999
pattersont@usfca.edu
phone (415) 555-5555

Consent Regarding Limits of Confidentiality

(Note: In all instances, this form conforms to the statutes in the state of California and the Ethics Code of the American Psychological Association).

Confidentiality generally means that anything that occurs in psychotherapy is not divulged by the therapist. Generally, this is true, although there are some common-sense and some not-so- common-sense situations which are exceptions to this rule. I have read the *Information* brochure, and understand the reasons for these exceptions for these. I also understand that **privilege** means the client's ability to protect information in a legal proceeding. With this background, I consent to the following:

Exceptions to confidentiality and/or privilege

Mandated reporting

- If I am a danger to myself physically or incompetent mentally, as determined by the therapist's evaluation.

- If I intend to bring physical harm to others.

- If I have physically, sexually, or (severely) emotionally harmed or neglected a minor or a dependent adult.

- If I have downloaded, streamed, or accessed child pornography through electronic or digital media

Examples of situations in which privilege does not apply

o   If I bring a lawsuit against this therapist.

o   If another person is in the room

o   If a *court* requires the therapist to testify

o   If I am being evaluated for a third party.

The first three items above are extreme situations which are exceptions to confidentiality and in which the therapist MUST file a report with the appropriate agency. All factors surrounding the situation are considered and your cooperation is encouraged.

Disclosure of information

In a common-sense fashion, any time you give permission to provide information to another party, there is limited confidentiality. In these cases and in most situations listed above, the therapist can only reveal information to someone who has a *need to know*. Whenever information will be shared with other persons, their names or positions will be listed on form I.4., and every effort will be made to ensure that the receiving person also maintains confidentiality. The major situations in which the therapist may disclose such information with permission are:

- If I am being evaluated or treated for a third party (disability, custody, etc.)

- If I request or give permission for information to be obtained from or provided to a third party (therapist, physician, teacher, employer, etc.)

- If my therapist is unavailable and temporary coverage is required (emergencies, vacations, etc.)

- If my therapist is being supervised, the supervisor may know the details of the case, but is also bound by confidentiality.

- If I am using third-party coverage (insurance) to pay for therapy.

FIGURE 6.8 **Limits of confidentiality (*continued*)**

Please also note that I use the internet only for scheduling or changing appointments, and never for confidential exchanges of issues that may arise in therapy. Also, should we unexpectedly encounter each other outside of therapy, we may or may not exchange a greeting, depending on your wishes, but it is inappropriate to discuss any therapeutic issues.

In addition to the above, I understand that special circumstances apply to group, couple, parent–child, and family therapy, and any time I may involve another person in treatment. Basically, other individuals in the room are not bound by privilege and may possibly not hold all information confidential; the therapist is not responsible for disclosure by these individuals. In situations where I am in therapy with another person (e.g., a spouse, sibling, or child) and secret information is revealed by one person to the therapist, it is understood that the therapist will not reveal the information but may determine that it is not workable to continue treatment unless the person holding the secret chooses to disclose it. Should this situation arise, the therapist will discuss it with you thoroughly.

Client ____ date ____________

Client ____ date ____________

FIGURE 6.8 Limits of confidentiality

6. Relationship history: Ask about the start of their relationship.
7. Commitment: Listen carefully to both and especially try to understand and recognize the lesser-committed member of the couple. Because most texts report that the male member of a heterosexual couple is likely to be "dragged in by the wife," it is sometimes essential to "hook the male" into couple work.
8. Fit: Determine if they are the kind of clients best served by this therapist.
9. The structure of the therapy: Provide clients with some structure for how the therapy will proceed.

It is important to note that the initial session may take one to four meetings. The number is often dependent on the nature and complexity of the problem, the theoretical orientation of the therapist, any comorbid individual pathology, cultural factors, finances, and so on.

Building Rapport

As for all forms of effective therapy, the development of a healing alliance that increases client motivation, instills hope, and builds a base of trust is essential in couple work.

Many couples enter counseling with substantial anxiety. In addition to the kinds of fears that accompany starting individual therapy and the daunting concern about having to change, there are anxieties unique to couple work. A partner may fear being blamed for the couple problems. She or he may worry that the therapist and the partner will gang up on him or her.

Couple therapists need to help defuse these anxieties and encourage the couple to face their fears of vulnerability and change from a more realistic perspective. An effective couple therapist will help the clients form a team with each other and with the therapist to help alleviate their current and ongoing disquiet. Particularly at the beginning of therapy or of a session, friendly affable questions such as "How was it finding my office?" "Was the traffic bad?" and "How's your day going?" convey a sense of normalcy and welcome that allow reluctant clients to relax and begin to trust the therapist.

This should be natural, and whatever the therapist's style, it is important not to immediately delve into a series of questions or pursue legalistic information. Regardless of the therapist's theoretical orientation, and unlike some forms of individual psychotherapy, the couple therapist is not a "blank slate" for the clients to project traits, nor is anonymity desirable. The couple therapist is viewed as a person in his or her own right and related to that way, even though projection will likely be present.

When the therapist acknowledges any ambivalence, friendliness (not friendship) and warmth, he or she centers the situation by offering understanding and support. In the course of a first session, it is important to have each person describe the concern and desired goals from both perspectives. The therapist should encourage communication from each client and not allow one to dominate the discussion and the definition of the problem. Empathy for each person's position creates a sense within the couple that they can be heard and that their partners are also making sense and are understandable to others. That has a normalizing effect.

Thus, it is essential that the therapist hears from both clients during the initial session (Snyder, 2005; Wile, 1992). By listening reflectively—by repeating what was heard when each client spoke—the therapist at least gives the impression that he or she is open to and trying to understand and respect each person in the room. Successful therapists are able to identify what is working for the couple and focus on improving these strategies. This is in contrast to a therapist who acts as a detective looking for the "reason," "blame," or "culprit" responsible for the turmoil.

Some very contentious couples will sigh, roll their eyes, or smirk when their partner describes their feelings and observations. This can derail understanding and empathy. It is important for the therapist to comment on such nonverbal behavior and ask clients to put words to their nonverbal behaviors and feelings. Teaching members of a couple to understand, but not necessarily accept, each other's perceptions is critical to progress.

This can be quite difficult when there is infidelity or other betrayals or transgressions by one of the partners. If the therapist can maintain a neutral supportive stance and model empathy in the room, there is greater capacity for later change. Any expressions of non-neutrality will likely exacerbate cultural differences and lead to premature termination. For example, in couples who come from a collective (versus individualistic) culture, blame can quickly lead to shame and a full shutdown experience.

Reframing the problem areas and normalizing behaviors places a positive spin and outlook on the situation, rather than one of continuing or escalating conflict. Often therapists will respond to reports of anger, frustration, or nagging by putting it into a workable frame:

> You are saying that Rosa frequently gets angry when you don't do things her way. What is striking to me is that when she expresses concern for you, it comes across as critical, rather than caring. I wonder if you could tell her what way she could express concern, caring, and even frustration in a way that is easier for you to take in.

In this way, Rosa's expressions of irritation are reframed (translated) in a positive light of caring. From that perspective, change is far more likely. Not only does Manny see it in a new light, but Rosa, who is listening, begins to understand that she can change something and perhaps get a better response from Manny.

THERAPY BOX 6.1: A CRITICAL TASK FOR COUPLE COUNSELORS AND THERAPISTS

It is essential that the therapist acknowledge positive intentionality in most interactions, even though the partner sees them as negative or destructive to the relationship. This cannot be a false construction; the therapist must truly discern the positive intention and frame it simply so it might be accepted by the partner.

THERAPY BOX 6.2: A QUESTION OF CONTEMPORARY NOTE TAKING IN SESSIONS

Therapists differ on whether to take notes during a session. Whitaker (1988) reported that he always had a clipboard and took notes during a first session as a way to indicate symbolically to clients that the therapeutic relationship was temporary and functional, not permanent.

Some therapists prefer to avoid notes for the very reason that it seems to come between the therapist and clients and creates a decreased sense of intimate connection. Instead, they use the time immediately after sessions to retroactively take notes.

The therapist's ability to recall details may determine whether she or he takes notes. **Shapiro** takes notes only during the initial session until he gets to know the couple. **Patterson** always takes notes on a formatted case record during sessions, allowing for detailed recall after the session in order to complete the case record; clients rarely inquire nor objected to this procedure.

Clarifying Goals

Without fully knowing the couple's outcome goals for therapy, the procedures will be unfocused. There are four sets of goals that should be addressed: (a) the goals of partner 1, (b) the goals of partner 2, (c) the therapist's[1] goals, and (d) mutual goals.

---

1   It may seem odd to include the therapist's goals here. This is not to say that they supersede the couple's goals, but following the assessment the therapist may well identify issues that are more fundamental to their personal relationship than what clients present. For example, it is common for couples to say, "We have communication problems." Indeed, their communication may be problematic, but it is often due to lingering resentment over real or imagined past transgressions.

There is one crucial question that must be asked in the first session regarding desired outcomes. Is the goal of therapy to repair a problem? Is it to find a way back to earlier forms of the relationship? Is it to part as amicably as possible? Each requires a different approach to treatment.

If the couple is on the same page, this may be simpler, but if they have different expectations and desires, the approach can be problematic. When Deshaun and Gloria responded to this question, they both replied that they wanted to have the loving relationship back to where it was before the trouble started. He also added, "I'd like to have some tools to avoid future meltdowns."

THERAPY BOX 6.3: COMPREHENDING PERSONAL BELIEFS: A CRITICAL TASK FOR THE THERAPIST

Lilli is the "leaver" and Walt the "leavee". The leavee may have known that his partner wants out but is prepared to fight it and may whine and beg or become depressed and feel lost and isolated. Walt may require extra attention and perhaps a separate session or a referral to an individual therapist to help him through this transition. It is also critical for the therapist to examine his or her personal values around separation and divorce as it is easy to steer the couple in the therapist's preferred direction.

By contrast, Lilli and Walt had very different answers. She said she didn't know "if [she] want[ed] to continue the relationship at all. Maybe the best thing would be to end it now and to leave while [they] can." He replied, "I love Lilli and I just want it to be better. I know we can work it out."

For Deshaun and Gloria, the couple therapy began quickly. For Lilli and Walt, several sessions had to be spent determining the best course of action. They ended up agreeing to split as amicably as possible. That therapy was clearly quite different in approach, scope, and outcome.

Diagnostic Information: Pathology and Strengths

Individual pathology is a salient component of couple problems. Therapists doing the initial assessment must always be aware of ICD/DSM-level criteria. If it is determined that one or both members of the couple are dealing with issues that might derail any couple therapy, referral to individual or group work either concurrent with or prior to future couple work is advised. Many therapists from humanistic or CBT perspectives avoid considerations of formal diagnostic criteria, but ethical, clinical, and legal mandates indicate that mental health professionals have the responsibility to treat or refer clients with psychopathology, so it is wise to bear the formal criteria in mind during the assessment phase and to act accordingly.

This is especially true with individuals with psychotic ideation, mood disorders, debilitating neuroses, addictions, and personality disorders (formerly known as Axis II disorders). Any of these will inhibit success in the couple realm.

More important is some form of assessment that encompasses each couple's needs to be understood from the perspective of their individual and joint strengths as well as their weaknesses. The most effective therapy always involves attention to traits and behaviors that hinder progress as well as activation of the strengths. Typically, an effective couple therapist tries to enter the couple system through things they do well.

Carlson (2007) described and demonstrated his approach to couple counseling by beginning with a focus of strengths in the relationship. He began a session with, "We know about the problem that brought you in, but what has been going well in the relationship?" In so doing he was able to allow a couple to view the problematic aspects of the relationship in a broader, much more positive perspective.

Assessment Tools

Some, especially more experienced, clinicians rely primarily on the initial interview and clinical judgment for assessment. However, many prefer to use standardized or proprietary assessment instruments to assess for both psychopathology and strengths. One of the advantages of such inventories is the ability to track progress with follow-up administrations (Bagarozzi & Sperry, 2012; Lambert, 2010; Wood & Crawford, 2012).

The most commonly used form of assessment is the genogram (McGoldrick, Gerson, & Shellenberger, 1999). Some other more common instruments used are the "Areas of Change" questionnaire (Fals-Stewart, Schafer & Birchler, 1993), the Dyadic Adjustment scale (Busby, Crane, Larson & Christensen, 1995; Spanier, 1976), the Family Adaptability and Cohesion Evaluation scale IV (FACES) (Olson, 2011), and the Locke-Wallace Marital Adjustment test (Locke & Wallace, 1959). An extremely comprehensive tool is the Couples' Precounseling Inventory (Stuart, 1987) which assesses 13 aspects of couple functioning from each partner's perspective and also compares each partner's projected response to each item.

Structured interviews, clinical observation, and history obtained from clients about previous treatment and from collateral (referral) sources are also important methods of gathering data for assessment and treatment planning.

Why Now?

One of the most important questions in establishing the couple limits and needs is an understanding of what prompted them to make the appointment when they did.

Jose and Bernard appeared for their first appointment with a goal of deciding whether to get married, soon after the law permitting gay marriages was passed in California. Initially, they claimed their questioning was less about personal commitment to each other and more about their cultural and political environments. Jose (30) is a third-generation Mexican-American. He is one of six children from a large extended family. At the time of the appointment he had come out to his siblings but not their parents. Bernard (34) is the sole child of Chinese parents. He came to the United States for school several years earlier and became a citizen a year prior to the appointment. His parents do not know of his sexual orientation. Jose and Bernard have been together as a couple for 4 years.

J: We want to make a formal commitment, but there are problems to go public.

T: To get married would be in essence outing yourselves to both sets of parents.

J: Yeah. That would not be pretty.

T: How so? What would the expected reaction be on both sides?

They smiled, almost a grimace at one another, and Bernard explained:

B: My parents don't even have a way to think about my being with a man. When we went there on a trip, Jose was "my friend," "my roommate," and we slept apart. They would be both astonished and ashamed.

J: I think mine would also be unsettled to some extent, but less of a reaction than Bernard's parents.

T: What do you anticipate?

J: Well, first of all, they may have an inkling or at least a sense that I will not be marrying a woman anytime soon, and then my cousin is in a lesbian relationship. Although they make comments, they don't really seem that upset about the relationship. With my folks, anyone who is single sleeps separately in their house.

T: So, it seems like a discomfort, but for Bernard, it seems more problematic, even if they are in China. Might they go so far as to disown you?

B: (With moistened eyes) Sounds like you know them. Yes, they probably would, and I might never see them again. My family is very traditional. We are Catholic and when my uncle (mother's brother) married a woman who is Confucian, they did not go to the wedding and have only recently begun to talk with him again, after 9 years.

T: Those are some daunting problems. What else is playing into the decision?

J: Well, this may sound stupid, but if we married now, some may think of us as opportunists. You know, like we are joining some bandwagon of gay marriages. We went to the mass ceremonies at City Hall a few weeks back and it was a little too popular for me, for us.

After confirming with Bernard that he felt similarly, the therapist continued:

T: You've been basically in hiding and under the radar for a long time and now to suddenly be in the sunlight ... ?

J: Yeah, that's part of it. For sure.

T: What else?

J: We would be the first of our immediate circle to do it if we went now.

T: And?

J: We might stand out from our friends.

T: Do you have concerns about rejection from them as well as from family, albeit for different reasons? It is still rejection and more isolation.

J: (Exhaling). Yeah. It's just so new and we don't know what might happen.

T: To clarify, do you want to make a formal commitment *and* go public? Or is it possible to do so without coming out to everyone?

B: We could do that, but we don't want to hide who we are forever.

T: Is it important for each of you to let everyone know now or would it be okay for you to do it gradually?

Bernard and Jose do face daunting external challenges before they can even begin to look at issues between them in the relationship. In one way, the legal status change allows them more freedom, but it also comes with serious pressure. Their therapist at the time was able to help them put an immediate decision about whether to get married *now* on the shelf until he was able to work with them on their cultural and cross-cultural issues as well as the interpersonal issues that plague many couples.

They came in to make a decision about whether to get married. Their goal was to get clarity about that decision. Their therapist worked with them on reaching clarity, primarily helping them agree that they did not have to rush the decision.

Often, couples appear for therapy with goals that are prompted by external factors. Lee and Lisa, who had experienced interpersonal turbulence for several years, reportedly came in for clarification about whether to stay together or to separate. The reason for their facing the decision at this time was a pregnancy scare.

Others are prompted by a third party, a referral from a professional, pressures from families of origin, or financial issues. Often, a friend, family member, clergy, or physician expresses enough concern that a referral is made. At times, a single event or argument goes off the rails and is so out of proportion that the couple (or their immediate community) recognizes the need for third-party help.

Some couples prefer preventative measures. When Len and Liz made their first appointment, they reported that they had been bickering lately, mostly about a disagreement about with which relatives they would spend holidays. As Len described on the initial phone call, "We know we can work this out, but we want some help and some skills to head off similar disagreements in the future."

Couples who are doing well may also request a "checkup," like getting a diagnostic for the car before going on a long trip. They may have been prompted by a class on family life, a religious organization, or a friend who has experienced "pre-marital" or "pre-commitment" counseling. In any case, it is often a rewarding, preventive experience for both clients and therapist.

The answer to the question "Why now?" will often be a starting point in developing a therapeutic alliance and contract with the clients. It also provides a context from which therapy can proceed.

Exploring Relevant History

Two aspects of history are important to address early in therapy: How have they already tried to fix the problem and what aspects of their pasts might be having an influence. The latter is more relevant in some theoretical approaches than others. It is particularly important if the clients believe the impact of their histories is playing out in this one.

Hal and Connie were a couple in their late 40s when they came in for therapy. This was the third marriage for both, and they had been together for 5 years at the time. At the beginning of the first meeting, the following was disclosed:

> C: We had an affair when we were both married to other people, and now I worry that Hal is out with other women when he is not home. I have been a real bitch to him when he comes in 10 minutes late, and I know my jealousy is the reason why my other marriages ended.

> H: She is very jealous and the only time I ever cheated was with her. I just don't know what to do. I tell her where I'll be every day and she checks up on me, but I am not doing anything but work. I married both of my ex-wives because I was lonely and hoped that marriage would fill in that hole. Last week, I near panicked because I got caught in traffic and I knew I'd be 30 minutes late.

> C: (Laughing) He called and we talked the whole way. That's when I knew I was being outrageous.

Hall and Connie present an example of what Robert Weiss (1980) refers to as *negative sentiment override*, a type of attribution in which "negative behaviors of the partner are pervasively attributed to negative personality traits or are perceived to be done voluntarily, intentionally, or with negative intent" (Snyder, Heyman & Haynes, 2009, p. 465). This is a toxic pattern in which the object of the attribution feels he or she can never do anything right in his or her partner's eyes. Patterson's (CBT-oriented) approach to this involves dealing with it directly, through challenging and cognitive reconstruction. Shapiro's (existential-oriented) approach involves exploring the consequences of the fight (most often, distancing from intimate contact) and exploring with the couple the dangers of not having such distance, the risks of greater intimacy.

Another couple who both had suffered from STDs earlier in their lives came in in the throes of infertility. Their personal guilt was causing the problem to decrease closeness and teamwork that could have made working on the very real problem less problematic.

The other aspect of history, a couple's tried but failed attempts at alleviation, are also important. It provides the therapist with a sense of how their system works, shows ground that has already been covered that might not be fruitful, and provides clues to what might be an alternative approach. It also gives the therapist a sense of their respective strengths and their resilience. It's therefore important for the therapist to inquire about what attempts have been made to address the couple's issues, through therapy or other means.

One couple reported that they tried to tough it out for some time without success. Jen and Joe were particularly interesting. They said they tried some self-help books and a workshop for couple communication and then reported almost proudly, "We have seen some other marriage counselors, but they were not helpful."

Their therapist thought, "So one thing you do well together is defeat therapists." She did not say it aloud. Instead, she asked who the therapists were. Their answers indicated that they went to some of the better-known and respected couple therapists in the area. So she asked, "What did they all do that was ineffective?" Jen blushed and replied, "Well, you know what therapists are like!"

T: Tell me specifically how they were alike.

J: Well all they are interested in is S-E-X!

T: Thank you for sharing that. So, if I want you to leave therapy here, all I have to do is bring up that subject.

Both of them nodded and laughed.

T: So, as you see it, what's the core of the issue that doesn't have to do with sex?

Discussing what failed in the past allowed the clients to build a collaborative alliance with their therapist and also provided some initial direction. Even if it shows only roadblocks, it allows for the therapist and clients to get to know each other and begin working with some chance of early successes.

With Jen and Joe, it was likely that there was some fairly important sexual issue for them to discuss openly in therapy, but they were clearly unready to do so. Indeed, about seven sessions into the therapy, they volunteered that their relationship had become essentially non-sexual. It is important to note that only when the therapist was willing to leave things unspoken for some time the couple was able to risk disclosing the issue.

Carl Whitaker would often say that therapists are defeated from the start, in that couples and families have their routines worked out and can do their dance, and it's tough for the therapist to step in. While this may be overstated, it highlights the difficulty of entering into an entrenched system without finding a key to allow a couple to be comfortable talking about their most intimate issues (Whitaker & Bumberry, 1981); timing can be everything!

Sometimes, that "dance" may seem a little like a runaway freight train. Therapists who want to join and change the pattern are well advised to avoid standing on the train tracks with outstretched arms. Instead, it is best to slowly get up to speed, jump on board when the train hits a long slow grade and while on board shunting the train onto a more productive track from the inside.

An Emotional Assessment

There is a personal assessment that is more subtle. What is it like for the therapist to be in the presence of this couple? Is it comfortable? Is it anxiety provoking? Does the therapist feel lost? Is he or she angry at one or both? Does he or she feel intimidated? To which one is she or he most drawn and by who is she or he repelled? This last issue is often under-reported. It is very important.

In each couple, the therapist is likely to prefer, like, or respond more favorably to one of the members. That person may play the same relational role as the therapist in his or her personal relationships. It is essential to connect with *the partner who is initially less appealing*. If the therapist fails to do so, he or she will not get another chance. The clients will not return unless both feel accepted.

At Jill and Bobby's first appointment, they seemed physically unmatched. At five-foot three inches and probably 110 pounds, Jill was far smaller than her partner who seemed to be at least five-foot eleven inches and close to 270 pounds. She was dressed very elegantly with professional-style makeup and carefully coiffed hair. By contrast, Bobby was wearing jeans and a band t-shirt. He had an unruly beard and his hair was uncombed. Unlike his wife, he slouched down in his chair. He also arrived a few minutes late for the appointment, while Jill and the therapist were waiting or more reticent.

Decision Point: Should the therapist begin talking with Jill or wait for Bobby? A pure systems-oriented therapist would surely say to wait so as not to appear to show favoritism or unbalance the system.

As soon as the session began, Jill remarked that Bobby was "unreliable and left messes all around the house for [her] to pick up, just like his mother always did." Bobby just laughed and retorted, "You don't have to wash the dinner dishes before we have dessert. If I leave my clothes on the floor after I come home from work for a few minutes, I'll pick 'em up later."

For the therapist, who was "the messy one" in his own relationship, Bobby was far easier to relate with than the "china doll" image presented by Jill. He reflected that his own partner was always after him to clean up after himself and was prone to what he considered to be "more than a little OCD." His struggle was to find a way in that first session to empathize with Bobby, but also to relate to Jill and her frustration. Speaking with his supervisor later, he disclosed, "I wish Jill had a blemish somewhere to be able to relate to her more easily. That kind of perfection always hits me in a funny place."

It is easy to see how any therapist could have felt a closer initial connection or disconnection to either of them. Much of that initial internal reaction is more about the therapist than the clients. Personal awareness of the potential for such reactions is essential. A clinical hypothesis might lead the therapist to inquire whether the couple was mismatched from the beginning, whether the apparent differences reflected the presenting problem in bold relief, or if this was a superficial difference that a more fundamental connection between them could resolve.

Relationship History

Couple histories can be obtained in advance through forms or taken in person during the first session. In sessions, one of the questions we like is to inquire about the couple's meeting courtship and progression to a relationship. Although this seems less focused on the reasons to come into therapy or the immediate problems, it is very valuable information. For most couples, the story is a positive memory that has been told many times in the course of their relationship. They characteristically tell it together in a well-choreographed manner. Each partner has specific lines. Among the advantages of such a story is that they work together as a team. They recall some positive strengths in their relationship and the therapist gets to experience a little more of the full picture of their relationship. Stories we have heard began the following ways:

- We first met in elementary school. Then we were friends in high school, and when we went to the same college we connected.
- We met actually during freshman week at university.
- We met through an online dating site for people of like interests.
- We worked together in the same department for a long time and then one night it just happened.
- I was laid up in the hospital with a broken leg (skiing) and she was my very attentive nurse.
- We practically had an arranged marriage. Our grandmothers fixed us up.
- We met on a (location-based) dating website. We actually hooked up before we had a relationship.
- We were both in the choir in the same church group.

Unless the story indicates major problems, it is primarily a way for a couple to connect with the therapist and each other. These beginnings may present a challenge for the therapist to examine his or her own biases about whether there was any substance to their initial connection. It should be stated that all of these ways of getting together have the potential to work out, but for some, a solid foundation may never have developed. An example of a far less pleasant beginning was the following, during which the husband did all the talking.

> We were both at this bar and getting pretty wasted. We ended up closing the place and neither of us could drive, so the bartender pointed us to this motel across the road. Well, she got pregnant so we got married down at the City Hall.

Because neither of these people made an active decision to be together, their commitment was a lot less stable. By the time they were referred, they had three children, several menial jobs, a mountain of debt, some domestic violence, and what could best be described as a "that's just the way life is" attitude. Their therapist spent several sessions just to get them to commit to change and to work together at anything. During the sessions, their children were in the waiting room, noisily leaving it in disarray.

Is There a Match?

Not all clients and therapists are right for each other. When clients don't think the therapist is right for them, they cancel or don't come back for future sessions. It is important that therapists also make a determination whether she or he is right for these clients.

Sometimes the match is just not there. Sometimes the couple would benefit from a specialist. Sometimes, the therapist is just not experienced enough or ready to work with certain kinds of problems. Sometimes, individual therapy or addiction treatment for either or both partners is warranted before couple therapy ensues. There are a host of reasons to refer, and a therapist needs to be careful to avoid taking on clients as a way to learn on the job. It can be trying on the ego (and a potential limit on financial success) to admit to being out of our depth with a particular couple.

In such cases, it is ethically and professionally responsible to make a good referral, rather than just drop out or to proceed uncomfortably. If one's ego is not engaged, making such referrals is relatively easy.

> From what you have told me and the problems you are facing, I want you to see a specialist who has particular expertise. I have her card here and I will be glad to call ahead to make sure she knows I am referring you to her.

Clients rarely have any problem with such a referral and are likely to follow up. We recommend a follow-up call to the referred therapist and/or to the couple.

Russ and Jonna were such a couple. They were deeply in debt, had some significant legal problems, and were dealing with a custody battle with her ex-husband. The therapist to whom they were assigned at the clinic was untrained in debt management or custody. The likelihood of a court appearance was also beyond his realm of expertise. Because he did not know a local resource, he told the couple, "You are dealing with tremendous stress and pressures. I want to get you to the very best person for help. I am going to do some research and will call you later this week with a name."

> Cleo and Katie seemed increasingly uncomfortable with the therapist during intake.

When she asked them about it, they replied, "We were hoping for a therapist who could understand what it's like to be a lesbian couple. You seem straight."

> T: I am straight. Does it seem that I am missing something or were you looking for a lesbian therapist?

> C: Yeah. Someone in a lesbian relationship.

> T: I'd be happy to refer you to someone who fits your expectations if you'd like.

One couple came in with the following dilemma:

We have a long-distance relationship and both travel for work. We need a therapist who does the work through telecommunications. The most we expect to be in the Bay Area together in the next 2 months is today and one weekend. We also prefer to have Sunday meetings, because we are usually free then.

The therapist they saw was neither comfortable nor qualified with the arrangements for telecommunication couple work, nor Sundays. He politely declined and referred. To the best of his knowledge, the couple never followed up with the referral list.

If Referrals Are Hard to Find

We both work in the San Francisco Bay Area and, like most large cosmopolitan areas, are blessed with a whole host of competent specialists from whom to choose. If therapists are working in rural communities or are restricted to a certain list of providers by their insurance company, there may not be many choices. This is something that has to be discussed with the clients and a solution found, given the circumstances. The APA (2017) code was revised to accommodate the contingencies around rural communities, and although treating a couple with whom you may have another connection or aren't entirely qualified to treat isn't inherently unethical, the bywords are to "proceed with caution!"

Related to this rural issue is the likelihood of running into members of client couples in other situations. One of our colleagues will not accept couples who go to the same church as she does. Another works a few towns away from home to minimize such interactions. However, as it is for all clients and therapists, it is possible to run into them in supermarkets, schools, business meetings, and so on. If that occurs or is likely to occur, the nature of any interactions needs to be spelled out. This is especially problematic if only one of the partners has incidental contact.

I recognize you as a parent at my daughter's school. We are likely to run into each other several times during the school year. Do you think that will be in any way problematic?

Who's in Charge: The Battle for Structure

One issue that often arises in the initial session is an initial skirmish in what Whitaker and Keith (1981) called "a battle for structure." The structure in question involves a multitude of factors including the way the couple functions and their relationship with each other and with the therapist.

Often, this is expressed early when each person presents a litany of complaints about his or her partner as the wrongful part of the couple. Once they are both done, they turn to the couple therapist as judge and ask, "Okay, who's right and who's wrong?" This question reflects a number of levels of interaction, most importantly it keeps alive the process status quo of blaming the other and avoiding facing the fears of the implications of individual personal responsibility. Should a therapist fall into the trap of accepting this judicial role, thereby letting the couple define the therapeutic relationship, the clients' extant system can determine the way the therapy will proceed.

Should the therapist take on the role of judge it will likely have the impact of helping the couple avoid intimacy, maintain their interpersonal distance, and keep alive their characteristic ways of doing things: the ways that have created the problem. It will also allow the couple to dismiss the therapist as "not understanding" at least one perspective.

Instead, the therapist must take control of the process, refocus it by being empathic with both opposing positions, reframe the problem as something that occurs out of the confluence of opposing views, and redirect them to a team approach to problem solving. In short, couple therapy may begin by sensitively and carefully unbalancing the current couple homeostatic balance and building with them a new, more effective and collaborative approach to responding to difficulties. Deflecting the couple from being "right" and winning the debate can be done by asking each partner to listen sensitively (but not necessarily agree) to the other partner's perspective and acknowledging the emotions and intent behind his or her statements. Often, reframes of blame and criticism are helpful; for example, switching from "You're always nagging our children" to "I really care about how the children respond to you" can elicit empathy and a more positive response.

Consider the following example. Soon after this heterosexual couple comes in, she bursts into tears as she describes how nobody in her life, especially her husband, listens to her.

He: I do listen. I just don't agree.

She: You see, he doesn't ever listen. He just gets angry at me because I am hurt by his inattention.

He: (angrily) I don't get angry. You just won't take no for an answer.

She: (crying) Well, you never say yes.

He: What about last week when you demanded that we clean out the garage for the entire weekend?

She: It needed to be cleaned out. There is no room for the cars.

He: (very irritated) Hey. It's my car that's out on the street. Yours gets into the garage. And besides, I did spend the weekend cleaning. Which, I might add, you criticized.

She: Well you never finish anything right (bursting into tears).

If the therapist gets caught up in the emotionality and pain she is exhibiting, he or she may inadvertently or subtly take the wife's side by asking the husband, "What about her suggestion about the garage makes you angry? She seems really hurt right now." In such a case, the couple may not return. What that therapist did was allow the couple to define the nature of the interaction. Further, by joining in on one side, the therapist proliferated the problematic cycle.

A more successful approach might involve the therapist responding to the wife, "You like things done a certain way and it really hurts when you feel like your husband doesn't care the way you do. And you (addressing the husband) feel pushed around by her emotional certainty and see her requests as demands, which irritate you. It seems like you are locked into a pattern in which you both get hurt. I wonder if we could explore some alternative ways to look at this and other concerns."

Another approach involves less immediate empathy and a little more distance. The therapist might say to the couple, "This isn't the first time you folks have had this fight. In fact, it seems very old and familiar. Tell me how it ends." Possible answers are the following:

We just agree to disagree and leave it at that.

We go to our mutual corners to calm down (and he usually sleeps on the couch).

We put it off until we can talk more calmly, but it never happens.

We just escalate to yelling, name-calling, and insults.

The therapist pursues the answer and asks, "How does that work out?" When they say that it does not work out well, he or she can suggest that the three of them may have to find a better alternative.

The Contract

The final aspect of the initial session is to inform the clients what to expect and the methods to be used. Every therapist has some ground rules, and this is especially important for couple work. Here are some common ones:

1. Format. It must be made explicit who comes to each session. Some therapists see the couple once and then each individual before reuniting the couple for sessions. Other therapists only see them together with no individual sessions. Finally, some therapists will agree to see an individual under special guidelines (e.g., no secrets) explicitly laid out for both partners.
2. An expectation that both partners will come to all couple sessions on time.
3. Clients should be informed that therapy needs some time to work and that there is likely to be some additional discomfort before it gets better.
4. Clients agree to follow up and complete any homework assignments given by the therapist (this is frequently broken by clients and the in-session discussions regarding why they did not do a particular assignment are often quite fruitful).
5. Confidentiality is stressed and explained.
6. Some therapists have guidelines for respectful interactions in sessions. This can include active listening, using "I" instead of "you" statements, and consideration that the problems are more transactional in nature (relational concerns) rather than one being universally right and the other wrong.

7. General rules. Whatever other rules the therapist has regarding cancellations, one person coming in when partner is away or ill, payment, and so on.
8. Specific rules about communication outside of sessions: If one partner contacts the therapist, he or she lets his or her partner know, and an equal amount of time is offered to both. Also, that e-mail or text only involves information regarding changing or confirming sessions, not details about the relationship.

Gino, a client who was very sensitive to the contracted rules, came in one day and sheepishly reported that his partner was ill with the flu. He added, "I didn't want to just miss the session, but I worried about the rules, so I brought a signed agreement from Sandy and brought a small cassette recorder." He asked, "Could we still meet and would it be okay to record the session for her? I actually wanted to talk about a problem I am having at work with my boss so I thought it would be okay." Some therapists, coming from a pure systems approach, would likely decline to have the session and ask that the couple reschedule when Sandy is better. Others might inquire if there is an important reason to talk with Gino alone right now and proceed to see him and arrange an individual session later with Sandy to maintain balance. An individual session with only one partner may skew the alliance with the couple as a unit and is usually inadvisable. A major session to this was described above, in which Patterson frequently schedules an individual session or two to establish rapport and to allow each partner to talk freely.

Shared Plan of Action

It is helpful for therapists and clients to agree on reasonable goals and methods for achieving them. At the end of the initial session, most therapists give clients a sense of what they are to expect from the therapist, the kind of work the couple will have to do, and a rough proposed timeline for the treatment. In providing an estimate of the number of sessions, the therapist must issue a proviso, such as, "As long as there is nothing bigger or more critical to address, you are probably looking at 10–12 weekly sessions." If there is something we haven't discussed yet that I do not know about, that estimate may change."

The therapist should also let the clients know that he or she is willing to see them (or refer) for that duration. She or he should include any known breaks in the weekly routine. For example, he or she might let them know, "I want you to know in advance that I will be gone the fifth week at a conference and so we will either shift the day/time of that week's meeting or skip the week entirely." An alternate arrangement might be to see the couple every other week to accommodate planned travel and work schedules.

During the summary, therapists are most effective when they discuss strengths and places of agreement, get the problem areas into proper perspective, focus on the couple process rather than content, and propose next steps.

Before making a commitment, every therapist should do a personal emotional inventory to assure him- or herself that there are no evident problematic triggers in this case. Perhaps the therapist is personally dealing with similar issues or prejudices or the clients remind her or him of significant people or events in her or his own life (Patterson, Shapiro, & Kelly, 2018). For example, if a couple is struggling to decide whether to stay together or divorce and the therapist is experiencing the same issue in his or her own marriage, it may be better for him or her to make a referral and certainly arrange for consultation. Similarly, if the clients are engaging in behaviors or practices that may be legal but violate the values of the therapist, he or she probably should not work with them. Triggers do not inevitably preclude making a therapeutic contract with a couple, and when questions arise it is advisable to consult with a skilled colleague or expert consultant.

After the Session

There are normal therapeutic tasks following a session with a couple: reviewing notes, looking through and analyzing any assessments, drawing up a treatment plan, proposing interventions, and so on. It is important for therapists to evaluate both cognitive and affective responses to the clients. We recommend asking oneself several questions:

- What approach to therapy best suits them?
- Where might there be blocks to change?
- What are their initial styles of responding?
- What is the potential nature of resistance to change?
- What are the implications if no change is made?
- What is it like emotionally for me to sit with them?
- How positive am I feeling about working with them?
- Are there likely to be any personal triggers that emerge?

Treatment Planning

Normally, treatment plans incorporate expressed and unexpressed areas of concern, assessment of strengths, the impact of history, and concrete goals. Each couple therapist and each theoretical position employs unique treatment plans. Basically, the treatment plan for a couple is a blueprint for future building. Naturally, the lens (theory) through which each therapist views the problems will filter and highlight data and focus the therapist's attention toward both comprehension and action. Characteristically, areas of potential concern are elaborated.[2] In couple work, we find that collaborative, team-oriented, relatively transparent treatment plans are most useful.

It is important to note that treatment plans are living, working documents. They exist to be altered as necessary. For example, when new information emerges from sessions, plans adjust to meet new needs and goals. For example, with Jen and Joe, the couple who warned the therapist that they would leave therapy if the subject of sex was initiated, the treatment plan had a note and an embargo on discussing their sexual life. Later when they disclosed that their sexual life was essentially nonexistent, the plan was altered to lift the embargo and to sensitively and gently address their concerns.

---

2 When there are third-party payers (insurance), therapists must be aware that anything in the treatment plan could violate aspects of the couple's confidentiality and have downstream implications. Some insurance companies have specific forms that must be completed by members of their provider panels. If there are issues that the couple does not want reported to a third party, these should be discussed in session. We have found that individuals in sensitive jobs in which any psychotherapy might be reason to limit their progress would rather pay out of pocket than have any detailed records sent to a third party. Among the groups with such concerns are military officers, executives in industry, and people in politics or security.

One aspect of treatment planning that sometimes gets lost is the notation and impact of early interventions. Careful analysis of the kinds of interventions that worked and those that failed are one of the more important reference points for future sessions. For example, in one case when the therapist tried to minimize emotional explosiveness in a session, the couple responded by distancing. By contrast, when the therapist joined them in higher levels of emotionality, both members of the couple actually calmed down and began to talk more openly. That note is of great value in treatment.

A useful component of treatment planning can be either regular supervision or consultation, including a peer consultation group. Many therapists make it a practice to engage with a group of colleagues on a regular basis in order to obtain feedback on cases, but also to learn about the practices of others. Ideally, peer groups should involve at least one seasoned colleague in the therapist's primary area of focus.

How Will We Know it's Working?

One of the most essential questions in goal setting is measuring success. Some theories (e.g., CBT) lend themselves to specific measuring tools. Others (e.g., existential–humanistic) use more global satisfaction measures. It is often valuable to put this question directly to the clients. Frequently clients are asked, "How will you know that we are reaching your goals?" Often their answers give us a working, if unscientific, measurement of success or stagnation.

Ed and Serena are a couple who were very skeptical about the therapy being successful, but saw it as "the last stop on a train to splitsville." They were in a racially mixed marriage and had one son and considerable in-law problems. When they were asked the question after 10 weeks of therapy, they responded in a feisty manner, "Well, do you think it's working? How are we to know?" Their therapist responded, "Well, you said that you were trying to decide if you would stay together or split and you wanted some relief from your in-laws. How is that going? Serena laughed and said, "From that perspective doc, you are a big success. We are staying together and divorcing our (intrusive) in-laws!" The therapist replied, "That sounds like your success and a solution you came up with." Ed responded, "Yeah, thanks, but you made us see how we were strong together if we just pulled in the same direction." The therapist smiled, nodded, and opined, "That seems important!"

One Proviso to Lengthy Treatment

Ostensibly, if the couple is pleased with progress and ultimate results, we can say that therapy is successful. However, we should be informed by APA code 10.10 (APA, 2010) regarding the length of continuing treatment. We are ethically obligated to terminate treatment if the client is no longer benefitting. The question becomes, "How do we know?" The answer is simple: With clear, agreed-on objectives between therapist and the couple at the outset of treatment, criteria emerge for collaboratively evaluating progress during treatment (formative evaluation) and at the end (summative evaluation). Without these, the risk of a de facto friendly relationship and dependence may occur. The larger ethical risk is that continuing treatment may be more beneficial to the therapist financially than to the client psychologically. Often it is up to the couple therapist to instigate termination with foci on transfer of training and dealing with the loss of the relationship (Shapiro et al., 2019).

SUMMARY

This is the first of four interrelated chapters that focus on the natural trajectory of couple therapy. Essentially the emphasis in this chapter is on the process from initial contact to a contract for future sessions. That contract emerges from assessment and from the desired outcome for the couple. The pre-treatment planning, core procedures, sample intake forms, and mechanisms of assessment and treatment planning are described. Best practices for initial contact are indicated and some essential differences between initial sessions for individual and couple therapy are explored. One core principle that is particularly important is the establishment of empathy for both members of the couple, despite any preexisting biases the therapist may have.

The importance of the therapist setting the structure for sessions and taking charge is different than in other forms of therapy. Even at the onset of couple therapy, it is expected that the therapist or counselor will play a more active role, albeit different theoretical orientations will have different levels of therapist directiveness.

Finally, different approaches to note taking, telephone conversations, and dealing with fees are presented.

7

The Early Phases of Couple Therapy Treatment: Procedures and Techniques After Intake

When beginning in a new field, it is normal to desire a combination of tools and techniques that make things work. All of the individual therapy skills may be needed, but when we discuss couple therapy, it is important to take a broader focus on skills, techniques, timing, and context. It also includes the ability to hold different subjective realities in mind without either having to resolve them or to determine which, if any, is more accurate. Because there are no simple, discrete set of tools or techniques that will guarantee success, becoming a couple therapist involves a fairly steep learning curve.

In considering techniques, it is important to keep in mind that techniques are *tools* rather than models or concepts. Models or theoretical schools provide a template or roadmap to follow through the deep weeds of couple interaction, provide us with a clear differentiation between wheat and chaff, and offer a path forward. Basically, tools and procedures derive from theories; they themselves are not a theory.

The techniques described here are common across most forms of couple therapy.

However, it is important to note that within some theoretical frameworks, individual preferences and theoretical and personal limitations will favor some and dismiss others (Patterson, 1997).

The techniques described in this chapter are most common in the early and middle phases of couple therapy and in short-term couple work. In Chapter 8, techniques more common in middle to later and longer-term therapy are explored.

Challenges

One initial challenge is the ability to encourage the couple to relate directly to one another in their normal fashion with the therapist (a third party) present and, conversely, to insert oneself into the middle of an ongoing twosome and create a temporary therapeutic triangle in which changes can be instituted.

A second challenge is finding the moment for intervention. As in most human endeavors, timing is essential. In early stages of couple therapy, this means waiting patiently for those optimal moments when members of a couple are receptive. A therapist may discern fairly quickly what the couple needs to do to resolve an ongoing disagreement, but she or he has to be able to set the stage and allow the couple to either come up with the solution on their own or to be ready to hear it from the therapist. One example of this is a disagreement we have heard from many couples as to the appropriate time for Christmas presents (Christmas Eve or Christmas Day). It is clear that the "problem" will be resolved with two presents, one at each time, or each person receiving a present at his or her preferred time. However, only once the therapist readies the couple by helping them communicate respect for each other's heritage will the "obvious" solution be the acceptable solution. That is because something very important and unspoken is being negotiated, while the topic of discussion is about Christmas present timing.

Becoming an Anachronism

It is important to restate a message from the first chapter. One of the great benefits of couple work is that both members are present and the therapist can work with them in real time to help them make significant changes in a very short period of time.[1] We need to remember here that the couple has worked out their dance (Kershaw, 1992) over time, and the therapist is an intruder into their system. The couple is with the therapist for 1–2 hours and then has roughly 166–167 hours together without her, until the next weekly meeting.[2] In such real-time active therapy, the essential transfer-of-training possibilities are greatly enhanced.

Of course, one of the most important aspects of this therapist role is that it must become obsolete. The therapist must extract him- or herself from the dyad as soon as possible after helping them develop some valuable new skills.

Enhanced Focus on Process

All couples develop a system, and all systems find homeostasis. The homeostatic balance typically operates to keep the relationship predictable and secure. In a sense, even the more problematic and painful issues that couples face are the result of an adjustment that

---

1   Unlike individual therapy in which the therapist has to rely on the subjective experience and report of his or her client, in couple therapy both subjective realities are present and he or she can observe the impact of one on the other.

2   Although weekly meetings are the most popular option for couple therapy, some therapists meet more or less frequently, and some do marathon (multi-hour) sessions separated by more lengthy gaps.

preserves the relationship. The presenting symptoms or difficult interactions have to be seen by the therapist as a couple's way to maintain the status quo, even if it is problematic and helps them avoid the fears of facing the unknown. Most of the time when couples come in for therapy, the normal equilibrium is disrupted by some internal or external events. These events may be unpredictable, spontaneous, and unexpected, or they may involve normal life transitions and a couple's reactions to those transitions. They always involve instability and disruption of the status quo. Couple therapists normally discern the consequences or function of the symptoms by exploring the process within the couple and between the couple and the therapist.

Regardless of the tools a therapist employs for assessment, he or she must develop an ability to focus intensely on process, on the couple interaction, and on the consequences of their combined behavior and interaction with the therapist. This skill of focused attention goes beyond clinical observation, characteristic of individual therapy. In couple work, there are far more data to consider simultaneously. Note eight vectors of interaction to attend to those depicted in Figure 7.1.

Thus, in addition to keeping our eyes on our roadmap, we are observing multiple verbal and nonverbal interactions while "listening to the entire composition, rather than just the lyrics." Of course, the actual words, or data, are nonetheless important to attend to as well.

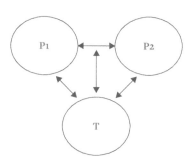

It is a challenge to tolerate higher levels of ambiguity and to detect the couple system, their unique patterns of interaction when their discussions are chaotic and pressing for a "righteous victory." An old military saying seems apropos here, "When you are up to your ass in alligators, it's hard to remember that the reason we came was to drain the damn swamp."

FIGURE 7.1 **Couple interactional matrix**

Skills and Roles

Describing group treatment, Shapiro, Peltz, and Bernadett-Shapiro (2019) describe six interacting roles that a therapist plays. These roles or skills are similar to those important in couple work. They include information disseminator/educator; catalyst; orchestrator; model; reinforcer/context adjuster; and topographical witness. Successful therapy requires a melding of these skills. It is rare when any one will work without the others. Different skills are more germane at different stages of the trajectory of therapy and, at times, two or more will be used simultaneously.

Information Disseminator/Educator

When couples come to a marriage counselor, couple therapist, or couple specialist, they expect that the provider will have some expertise that can be shared. This psychoeducational material is perceived as potentially useful in making their lives better. Sometimes, a couple with a lack of knowledge about potential or real roadblocks, misconceptions, and misunderstandings may respond well to new learning.

The information role is often quite salient early and toward the end of therapy. Basic information offered about what is to be anticipated and the procedures, expectations, nature of homework (if applicable) recommendations, and the like fit into this role, as does the planning for termination, transfer of training to home life after therapy, and any referral or follow-up instructions.

In addition, when therapists *normalize* feelings, thoughts, and behaviors for one or both partners, they are often fulfilling the psychoeducation role. In a sense, any theory-based intervention has an educative component. It is also the case that some specific information about options may be surprisingly useful, especially when a couple is in the midst of a dilemma about whether to stay together or separate.

Catalyst

In couple therapy, it is expected that the therapist will be far more active than is customary in individual work. Therapists act as a catalyst when they bring attention and sharper focus to a particular thought, feeling, behavior, or interaction. Therapists may, for example, identify and highlight nonverbal behavior in session or refocus the couple to consequences instead of trying to detect motivation. They may press the couple to interact in the here and now rather than on historical insults or gripes. They also catalyze when they "say the unsayable," encourage couple *enactment,* explore family-of-origin issues, press for insight, describe examples of arguments in detail, or keep the pressure on an interaction when the clients have an unconscious avoidance pact.

It is also important for the therapist to act as a catalyst when interventions fail to gain traction and resentments keep spilling out in both subtle and overt ways. The therapist then needs to highlight those recurring resentments and identify ways to keep them from interfering with progress.

Orchestrator

The orchestrator role primarily engages the couple in teamwork with each other and each with the therapist. Humphreys (1983) refers to this as the primary skill—establishing two-way couple communication. In a sense, it brings together conflictual aspects of the relationship and needs with resources.

Enactment—encouraging the couple to engage like they do at home—is one example of a combination of catalyzing and orchestrating. Another example can be when a therapist turns to one member of a couple who is talking to him or her and redirects that person to speak directly to the partner. Similarly, when one of the clients is in a dilemma, the therapist may ask the partner to be helpful and provide something of value. The therapist orchestrates when he or she has the couple relive examples of unsuccessful home conversations in his or her presence. Finally, the therapist's active engagement with one of the partners in a couple, offering empathy and support, can bring a corrective emotional experience and hope to both that member and the partner.

Model

Human interaction is a very complex acquired skill. It has long been known that a major component of most complex learning is imitation (Bandura & Walters, 1970). In their enhanced expert roles, counselors and therapists often serve as powerful role models. They can demonstrate more effective forms of communication in interaction with each partner and with the couple system. As they interact with the couple, they may well exhibit authentic, honest communication in the here and now. They may show the couple by example how to be flexible and open to new learning and perceptions of the partner. Counselors and therapists may also model genuine caring for others, sincerity, assertiveness, and the ability to accept and express anxiety directly. They may show an array of conflict resolution skills, such as by making "I" rather than "you" statements. Clients can learn and incorporate these skills vicariously before trying them out personally (imitating them) in interaction.

A powerful aspect of this modeling is *integrity*; just as the clients are expected to be honest in their interactions with each other and the therapist, the therapist displays integrity by means of his or her competence, presence, and honest feedback. Integrity may also be conveyed by the proper portrayal of credentials, accurate and consistent billing and scheduling, and a variety of other aspects of the frame in which treatment occurs.

This makes the model role particularly significant in couple counseling and therapy. In addition, many of *the role-playing techniques* can demonstrate modeling. For example, the *doubling or alter ego* technique—speaking out loud a client's unspoken desires or feelings—may make listening easier for a partner. By restating things in a way the other partner can understand, the therapist models more effective communication and acts as a universal interpreter.

Dispenser of Reinforcement

Because couple therapy can be an anxiety-provoking situation, a therapist is well suited to increase or decrease structure in the environment to make the engagement more effective.

When there is too much anxiety present for effective interaction, he or she may add structure. When there is too little anxiety for effective work to occur, he or she may reduce structure, perhaps by encouraging the couple to interact with one another with more ambiguity (fewer instructions).

One manner of controlling structure is through judicious selective reinforcement.

Behaviors such as head nodding, "mm-hmms," smiling, and increasing attention provides nonverbal assurance for the couple, letting them know that they are on the right track and they are making progress. Such reactions both reduce anxiety by adding structure, and it usually helps partners feel better about themselves.

In dispensing reinforcement, the therapist also acts as a model. Clients learn quickly how to please the therapist by acting in accordance with his or her apparent desires. With couples, each partner is rewarded for being open, listening carefully, reflecting back to his or her partner what was heard, sharing personal feelings instead of

judgments, and showing acceptance and willingness to be experimental. Reinforcement can be a particularly sensitive matter in couple therapy. It is essential to discern when to withhold any sign of side-taking by avoiding affirmation when a partner is attempting to prove him- or herself right and his or her partner wrong in an argument. Of course, with issues such as domestic violence, safety takes precedence over neutrality.

Snyder (2005) demonstrates this very well when he asks a husband to tell his wife directly about one of his needs. When the husband complies, Snyder comments, "Good job," before turning to the wife to ask what she heard.

Taking a Topographical Perspective

A major characteristic of all multi-person therapies (group, family, couple) is the importance of observing process from a "view from 5,000 feet." From this perspective, the emotional/psychological system between members of a couple is more evident. It is far easier to envisage consequences of actions and reactions by members of the couple from a more distant perspective. For example, a common therapist interaction may be something like, "Mari, each time you have mentioned Deshawn's mom, I noticed that he responded first by disagreeing with your perception."

The therapist who is focused on the system can begin to appreciate how the symptoms, unresolved arguments, and different viewpoints can support the status quo and security and inhibit even useful changes. It is also possible to experience more clearly any anxiety that is generated by potential shifts in the homeostatic balance. This skill requires that a therapist experience the content of the clients' verbalization within the couple context. Sprenkle, Davis, and Lebow (2009) operationalize one aspect of this skill as "conceptualizing couple difficulties in relational terms" (p. 35).

The "view from space" also allows the counselor to engage the couple at different levels of consciousness and thought processes and opens awareness of the possibility of reorganization of the relational system (Sperry, Carlson, & Peluso, 2006).

Levels of Couple Therapy

Although in reality there is more of a continuum than a discrete split in the kinds of techniques emphasized in brief and longer-term therapy, the focus in this chapter is on common techniques for the essential basic communication skills. In Chapter 8, the more complex and structural client needs are explored. We consider the goal of effective and accurate communication a *sine qua non* of couple work. This is a necessary step that may also be sufficient for successful therapy. It is also the most commonly described issue in textbooks.

For some couples, poor communication effectively obfuscates the ability to address deeper, more complex issues. In short, when Cody and Mia fully understand one another, they may have to face some far more difficult problems. Thus, it is important to facilitate clear communication while consistently probing for problem interactions, the resentments that may impede progress, and the consequences of their occurrence.

Early Skills

The most basic skills involve developing the therapeutic alliance, or *connecting* and engaging, and an initial detailed *assessment* of the presenting problem, couple strengths, the clients' process individually and together, and other potentially more problematic issues, such as individual pathology. The part of this that is new for individual therapists is the relational assessment (Sprenkle et al., 2009).

As described in Chapter 6, this is begun in the initial phase, which can be as long as three or four meetings. Effective couple therapy involves an interplay between the therapeutic relationship, the skills of the therapist, assessment of the couple needs and resources, the ego strength of the clients, coordination of interventions with client goals, and timing.

During the initial interview, therapeutic skills involve (a) taking control of the situation, (b) progressing through the intake procedures, (c) connecting personally with each member of the couple, (d) assessing for pathology and strengths, and, as in every session, (e) leaving the couple with a sense of hope that either their relationship will be improved, their stalemate will be resolved, or their joint unhappiness will be resolved through separation. Most therapists take contemporaneous notes, at least during the initial interview.

Connecting

The primary skills and techniques involve setting the stage for the therapy which is to come. At the outset, including the initial phone call, the earliest tasks involve developing an alliance with both individuals and beginning assessment of the couple needs and the capacities of the therapist. Many of the techniques used in both connecting and assessing were addressed in Chapters 4 and 6 and will only be briefly reviewed here.

Connecting requires establishing a relationship with each partner and with both of them as a couple. Most therapists do this by using open-ended questions and giving each an opportunity to respond to him or her and to each other. It has often been said that if there is no real connection in session one, there will not be a session two for a retry. If there has been an opportunity to review intake forms before the session begins, they can serve as a launching point for the interview.

One approach is to begin with specific friendly questions about the couple's problems, but also about the couple's overall life and what they do well. As described in the intake procedure, it is recommended that therapists inquire about their initial meeting and courtship. Finding couple strengths may also often involve brief forays into work, other interests, and things that go particularly well. For Cary and Tyler, there was both acknowledgment and praise for each other as parents, despite the precipitating crises with which they entered therapy: sexual dysfunction and financial disagreements and woes. Tyler praised Cary's intelligence and she lauded his ability to fix "anything." Hearing this, the therapist made a note to use these strengths later in helping them find their ways out of the current dilemmas. An opportunity arose during the fifth session: She empathized, "It must be so frustrating to be so smart and so good at fixing things to have this lingering problem." Such interventions illustrate a key *tracking* skill that builds on the clients' interests, language, competencies, and affect.

Pacing

Therapists usually try to adjust to each person's style, language, and pace. For example, among millennials, particularly women, the speed of speech is often more rapid—possibly a shorthand that reflects a modern-day "texting culture." People from some ethnicities and cultures tend to speak slower and softer while others speak with greater volume and amplitude. Some use "blue" language frequently, which may or may not be comfortable or proper for a particular therapist. Whatever the style of communication, it is useful to try to get on board as much as is feasible.

This does not involve faking a connection or identification that is not there, but rather respecting the clients sufficiently to agree to operate at least in part on their process of communication.

Supporting the Strengths

By understanding what a couple does well and uncovering the positive statements, a therapist may approach them with hope-instilling interventions that reflect competence and teamwork. "I know you came in with a very serious problem. Yet I just noticed how you two can also be helpful to one another, especially when you described how you trade off chores around the house and both enjoy long walks along the river."

Here Comes the Judge

Couples come to therapy to work out persisting problems that often involve power struggles in an attempt to avoid feelings of suffocation or abandonment. They also enter with a sense that the therapist will judge which of them is the "better" or right one in a two-person conflict. It is a zero-sum game in which there must be a winner and a loser—a very poor model for success. Therapists must therefore assiduously avoid the judicial role in favor of building teamwork and togetherness that result in win-win solutions.

One effective way to do this is to point out that while neither is perfect, they are both well intentioned, and they have worked out a "dance" together where they sometimes step on each other's feet and sometimes fall down, but it takes two to develop the pattern, for better or worse.

THERAPY BOX 7.1: OLD JOKE PURPORTEDLY FROM THE TALMUD

Two men were arguing assiduously without relief or end. They decided to go the learned Rabbi to determine who should win the argument. The Rabbi listened carefully to the first and opined, "From your perspective you are right, and it makes sense that you would care so much." Then the second one told his side of the story and the Rabbi said, "From your perspective you are right, and it makes sense that you would care so much." By then, a third person came by and said to the Rabbi, "These two men have a completely different story. They cannot both be right!" The Rabbi thoughtfully paused and said to this person, "You are right also."

This joke may provide us with the essence of the therapist stance in couple work. Each person needs to be heard, accepted, and appreciated for his perspective and, by reference, for him- or herself. Each member of a couple has to feel that the therapist understands her or him and is not criticizing what he or she perceives, what he or she believes, and the way that he or she processes information.

Note that the therapist may not agree, but respects the person's position and thinking. To be effective, the therapist must be able to make human contact with each and engender the ability to respect the position of each partner. Not all matters will be relatively equivalent. A therapist must also note when one partner is being particularly unreasonable and work to help the couple adjust to more normative interactions.

The early skills involve getting both parties to talk to the therapist and for him or her to listen to each, reflecting back what was heard (modeling good listening).

After warmly welcoming the couple and making some "social remarks," the therapist may begin addressing the couple:

T: I spoke with Ben on the phone, so I'd like to begin with you, Kris. What are your goals for this counseling?

After Kris speaks for a few minutes, the therapist must summarize then turn to Ben and ask about his goals.

T: Kris just said she wants more communication and quiet time together and more help around the house. I am interested in what your goals are.

Note that he does not allow Kris to set the agenda by asking Ben to respond to what she just said. There is plenty of time for that later. It is also important for the therapist to gently interrupt a partner who "goes off" in a seemingly endless array of complaints about their partner:

T: Kris. There is a lot here, let me interrupt for a moment and summarize what I am hearing. It seems important. It's a lot to take in and I want to be sure I get it right."

After summarizing, he or she should acknowledge that there may be more for later, then turn to the partner and ask for his or her goals, not their complaints. Some therapists like to begin by focusing more on the *here and now*, with an acknowledgment that it may not have been easy emotionally to come into the therapy.

T: I wonder what it's like for each of you to have made the effort and commitment to come in today. Where are you at this moment? I spoke with Ben on the phone, so Kris would you go first?

K: I am surprised that I am as nervous as I am. I've wanted this for a long while, but my stomach is doing flip-flops.

T: It's more anxiety provoking than you expected. Is there anything in particular or is it just the anticipatory anxiety about doing something new?

K: I am worried that I will not have the right words to describe my unhappiness.

T: And Ben, what's it like for you to be here?

B: Well … I didn't really want to come. The way I grew up was you solved your own problems and didn't go to therapy unless you were really nuts.

T: That's quite a change and a lot of courage to try something this new. So, how can I make this useful for you?

It Wasn't My Idea

There is often an initial crisis point for future therapy that must be addressed in the first session. This is when one member of the couple feels dragged in, blackmailed, or coerced by the other or is just coming to avoid an undesired break-up, incessant nagging, or worse argument. Instead of a buy-in or responsibility there, the partner feels extorted. The therapist has precious little time to convert him or her into a client and them into a therapy-ready couple. This must occur before the therapist has had a chance to discover whether the less invested member is personally ambivalent or if he or she is carrying the system-based reticence for the couple. Thus, if this member assents quickly to partaking in therapy, the homeostatic pressure may press the initially more interested partner to back away or be more reticent.

When Lee and Andi came in for a first session with a counselor at their Parish church, his reluctance was palpable. He interrogated the therapist about her credentials and whether she was independent of the church. He also wanted assurances about confidentiality vis a vis the pastor and other congregants. The therapist carefully answered all his questions and focused almost entirely on his needs for therapy with his very motivated partner.

At the end of the first meeting, Lee told the therapist that she had answered all his questions and he was prepared to go ahead and "see what counseling could do for [them]." It wasn't until they were in the car on the way home that Andi said she thought the therapist wouldn't be best for them and canceled the scheduled future sessions from the car before they arrived home. Lee was fine with her decision. Such termination after the first session can also occur when couples are merely "therapist shopping" or with those with perfectionistic or suspicious tendencies, in that they are not easily satisfied in relationships in general.

Sometimes the reticent partner may pepper the therapist with personal questions about age, marital status, children, number of couples treated, and so on. Regardless of age and experience, the therapist must maintain a professional and leadership stance in order for the session to be effective. Sometimes this involves answering such questions directly before asking the implications of the answer for the questioning client:

When a couple came in recently, the woman asked the therapist with some intensity, despite the presence of a gold band on the therapist's third finger, left hand, "Are you married?" The therapist responded, "Yes. I am. Tell me how that could be important for you."

By reinforcing the reality that coming in for therapy is not easy and by expressing understanding of some considerable reticence or ambivalence, the therapist shows that she or he understands the effort that partner is making. Selectively joining with each member, especially the more reticent in the presence of the partner, serves several goals: (a) helping everyone feel heard; (b) indicating to a partner that his or her spouse makes sense to a third party; (c) making everyone feel more welcome; and (d) showing respect. It also brings to light the suggestion that the problems they are facing are couple interaction or relational issues, not a right/wrong matter.

Doubling to Connect

Wile (1992) provides an interesting model of connecting and allying with each member and the couple, per se. Wile does this in a more dramatic way than most therapists. After carefully alerting the couple that he will be moving around a lot during the session, he gets out of his chair and kneels next to each, empathizing and reflecting what each is saying, using a technique that is often referred to as doubling or alter-ego (Wile, 2006), an adaptation from psychodrama (Hollander, 2002). Doubling is an important skill in couple work and is enhanced as the therapist gets to know the couple and their process more intimately.

For example, kneeling next to one partner and speaking for her, he might say, "Correct me if I'm wrong. What I hear you saying is (directing it now to her male partner) 'I wish you would anticipate my needs sometimes, like when I come home late from work if you could have a glass of wine or tea ready and sit with me while I debrief from my day.'"

Once she affirms that he heard her correctly, he asks the partner to respond to the message as if she had verbalized it directly.

Connecting and Assessing

As therapists join with the couple and form the requisite alliances, many further their connection by focusing on couple goals. This enhances both the therapeutic relationship and assessment. It is essential to ascertain how closely their goals match to determine the nature of treatment. It cannot be stressed too strongly that therapy cannot proceed very far if the clients' goals are not in accord. If Alan is looking to improve the relationship and Alice's goal is to split as amicably as possible, the therapist will have to spend considerable time just to get them on the same track, before he or she can counsel them.

At the same time, the therapist's comprehensive assessment is essential in providing thorough feedback to the couple on the full dimensions of their relationship. The therapist then has the task of combining each partner's objectives with the therapist systemic view, in a collaborative manner.

Typically, the therapist will work hard to get the clients to honestly explore and agree to goals. However, if either is less forthcoming or not fully aware of his or her personal desired outcome, the therapeutic work may well be compromised. The couple may also not be on the same page as the therapist in terms of their time, fees, and willingness to address their problems thoroughly.

Miracle Question

Sometimes getting to an enhanced connection and alliance as well as assessment and goal setting may be assisted by a variety of techniques that tries to reset the clients on goals and hopes rather than complaints about the partner. One method is the "miracle question," often associated primarily with solution-focused therapy (de Shazer & Berg, 1997; Hoyt, 2015).

The "miracle question" asks the client to engage in a fantasy of the problem miraculously going away during the night while she or he is asleep, and on awakening discovering that it is gone. Further questions involve what would be anticipated with the problem gone. How would the person and partner notice that it was gone and what implications were there for the relationship? Bader and Pearson (2016), using a modified method or query, "What would make you glad if everything worked out great today?"

This kind of question externalizes the problem, focuses on positive goals, looks at what might be achievable, and emphasizes hopes over the problems. The technique is designed to reduce anxiety and negativity, and it often is successful. However, it is important to note that the homeostatic glue in a relationship may be disrupted by changing something prematurely, until the expected release of complaints is entertained. It is important for any therapist to understand that the problem, like any symptom, may be both debilitating and functional. The problem in question may actually be part of maintaining the status quo. If it disappears too quickly without a supportive replacement, its loss might create far more anxiety and result in the couple bolting from therapy.

Song and Rex had a long-standing argument about the role his mother should play in raising the couple's children. When the therapist prematurely asked Song a form of the miracle question in the first meeting, she said that if his mother's intrusiveness was gone as a problem, their lives and that of their children would be just perfect. Rex responded angrily, "So I should throw my mother out in the street and then who would watch the children after school, when we are at work?" Note the potential significance of cultural factors in maintaining and potentially altering the complex relationships.

> T: Rex, you seem to be quite upset by Song's fantasy about how your dilemma might go away.

> R: She wants to get rid of my family and bring shame on me.

> T: So you are seeing a change in your mother's role as "dumping her" and creating shame.

> As he spoke, Song began to withdraw and shake perceptively. She became teary-eyed.

> T: Song, you seem to be having a strong reaction here.

> S: I don't want to cause pain to Rex or his mother. I just want to stop arguing about it.

Several sessions later, the couple began to talk about the fear and vulnerability of being alone together, something they had never experienced, except on short vacations. They reported that if they were not arguing about his mother, their children, or work, they barely knew what to say to one another. Those issues of vulnerability and intimacy became the nucleus of the later sessions of therapy. It is important to note that the proposed "solution" of eliminating something aversive actually made things worse, because the problem supported their homeostasis, as uncomfortable as it was. A potentially important question arises as to how much intimacy they desire and can tolerate.

Assessment

There is no substitute for accurate assessment of each partner and the couple relational system, but it is also important to understand that assessment is neither static nor linear. Indeed, as a couple begins to work in sessions and between sessions, their interactions may start to change. Assessment is an ongoing component of couple work, and it will shift as couples get more into their conflicts and their interactions become more intense. For couples who have been less than fully truthful with one another, either consciously or unconsciously, interactions will change as the truth emerges.

Some critical aspects of initial assessment were detailed in Chapter 6. Continuing assessment may involve here-and-now questions, history evaluation, the meaning the couple gives to the difficulties, the level of importance it holds, and the goals for therapy. Those goals may evolve as therapy proceeds.

One aspect of assessment is some determination of the couple's strengths. How have they handled disagreements or crises in the past? What overlapping and complementary skills does each partner bring to bear when things aren't going well? The questions about assets are balanced with the presenting problems and long-term liabilities.

Early questions that might be repeated in several sessions are effective for assessment and also open discussions regarding communication:

1. What's going well in the relationship (Carlson, 2007)?
2. What would be helpful to discuss today (including reactions to the last session)? What was it like at home since our last meeting?
3. What does it feel like to be here right now? What's it like to be back?
4. Who first noticed the problem and how long ago (placing the problem in a specific stage or escalation on the chronological divorce sequence in Chapter 4)?
5. What led you or your spouse to consider it a problem?
6. Who else has an opinion about the problem? (exploring some aspects of the context and of others who may be involved in promoting or containing the problem and exploring current escalations)?
7. What other possibilities have you considered regarding the nature of the problem?
8. Are there times when the problem doesn't occur, and what is different about those times (the exception question, De Jong & Berg, 2002)?
9. On a scale of 1–10, where 10 is the worst, how severe is the problem now? What is the worst it has been? What would indicate progress (scaling questions, Bertolino & O'Hanlon, 2002)?

Communication

When couples begin therapy, they often state that they need to work on "communication." In essence this means that what is intended in speech is heard inaccurately or at least, differently. For all forms of couple therapy, accurate communication is a necessary starting point. It may also be sufficient to help a couple emerge successfully from their difficulties. Most couple therapists begin a series of techniques designed to foster clear communication. Once clear communication is established, more major changes may be necessary.

Active Listening

There is a vast array of techniques involved in the communication aspect of couple therapy. One of the most basic is to assign temporary roles of speaker and listener to the members of the couple. In this way, one person speaks, preferably using "I statements" and expressing their vulnerability, and the partner listens without interrupting. Then the listener says back to the speaking partner what she or he heard.

> T: Rose, you say that Ken doesn't hear what you want to communicate. Would you be willing to tell him in here what you want him to know? As you speak from the heart, I will ask Ken to listen and reflect back to you what he is hearing. Would you be willing to do that (looking to both of them)?

> R: Okay. I want him to—

> T: Sorry to interrupt. Please speak directly to Ken and begin with what you want, rather than what you want him to do.

> R: When I get home from work after you do, I would really appreciate it if you would start on dinner. Nothing big, just chopping veggies for a salad or turning on the main meal. That would make me feel great and less pressured to come home and get the meal going immediately.

> K: You know I am exhausted when I get home and need some rest too.

> T: Ken. What did you hear Rose saying? I think you skipped a step here. Look at her and tell her what you heard.

> K: When you get home you are exhausted and would like me to start the dinner preparation ... and that somehow that would make you feel good.

> T: Rose. Is that what you were saying?

> R: Yes. I think I want us to make dinner together. It would make me feel closer to Ken (turning to Ken), closer to you.

T: Ken. Is that something you would like?

K: Yeah. I like doing things with you, but I am so tired when I get home, I feel like I need to just chill for 30 minutes.

T: Rose, what are you hearing now?

R: Well, what about my rest time? Don't I get any?

K: Respond like Ken did as a listener. What did you hear? Tell him!

R: Ken. You say you need a 30-minute break when you get home.

T: What else did you hear?

R: You like to do things with me like make dinner together.

T: Well done. Ken?

K: Yeah, that's what I said. So, how can we make this work?

This more-clear communication can lead to some active problem solving. The technique, often called *active listening*, asks the listener to concentrate, understand, recall, and respond to what is being said. Both active listening and its close correlate, *reflective listening* (Rogers, 1951) focus attention on what the speaker is actually saying, instead of waiting for one's turn to respond in kind.[3]

Focusing on listening skills and responding first to what the partner is actually saying often helps couples get out of normal interactive patterns of misunderstanding. While engaged in this manner of communication, the listener may not agree, but, before offering an alternative perspective, demonstrates that he or she is paying attention and trying to understand what his or her partner is saying. Once their communication is more certain and there are fewer misunderstandings, problem solving to resolve disagreements can follow with fewer impediments.

It is important to note that some critics of this technique, such as Gottman and Silver (1999), tend to view it as a standalone intervention instead of one method to help alter ineffective communication in a couple integrated into a larger plan. The couple may find it tedious if the technique is focused on it excessively; the therapist's tracking of the couple's reactions and modification of the approach is key to its success.

Bader and Pearson (2016) demonstrate an interesting alternative to the active listening exercise. They ask one member of the couple, "What is your partner's biggest complaint (in the relationship)?" Once clients describe the complaint, they are asked to

---

3   It's easy to go down an arduous path here by discussing various ways for making dinner together happen. For example, there could be an exploration of each having "decompression" time after work, how this would occur, and so on, and a brief foray into these issues might be useful, though not to the extent where the focus on intimacy is lost.

rate their confidence that they are accurate on a 10-point scale. This is then confirmed with the partner.

Many couples are able to accurately describe the complaint and are affirmed for that by partners and therapists. With a better sense of reassurance that they are being heard, the couple can begin to deal with other corrective communication-based techniques.

Enactment

Enactment (Minuchin & Fishman, 1981) is essentially getting the couple to engage in the therapy session the way they do at home. These "Civil War reenactments" are essential for both assessment and treatment. When the couple engages in their characteristic fashion, the therapist can assess the intensity, interactive emotional "lighter fluid" used to ignite the conflict, places where their discussions go off the rails, and their style of fighting and avoiding more intimate interactions. She or he may also determine where the strengths lie in both individuals and in the relationship.

Most of the time the therapist does not need to do much to get a couple into enactment. Usually, they will just bring in a problem from the week between sessions or the therapist can ask for a specific example of a conflict. It will typically begin with an agreed-on issue or the following:

T: Can you give me an example?

C1: I can't think of a good one.

T: Bad ones are fine. In fact, they might be better.

C2: Oh. What about last Thursday?

The only thing the therapist needs do after that is to let it occur in the session without intervening. To get a good sense of the conflictual interactions, the therapist usually has to observe this enactment a few times, before beginning to intervene.

T: I was noticing that the discussion seemed to go okay until it started to escalate. Is that your impression also? That it suddenly escalates and goes downhill fast after that? If it's okay with you, let's go back and look at where and how it went south.

It is hard for anyone, especially for new couple therapists, to allow people one is hired to help go off on a very unproductive conflictual conversation without intervening. Yet, without knowing in real time how the problems develop, evolve, and escalate, it is much harder to engage in successful interventions. As a general rule of thumb, however, it should not exceed a third time through. More than that, it may appear as if one were trying to do therapy with George and Martha of Albee's (1966) *Who's Afraid of Virginia Woolf?*

One intervention method after 5–10 minutes into a circular argument is to ask, "How is this going? Do you want to spend more time paying to do here what you do at home?" It is critical to stop arguments that escalate defensiveness, involve derogatory labels, and seem to shut down cooperation.

Traffic Cop

Somewhat embedded in enactment is the ability of therapists to find ways to interrupt an ongoing conversation and redirect it.

The most common use of the traffic cop function is to stop one partner from speaking and encourage the other to respond. For example, when Mica got on a roll providing in detail a litany of her partner's multiple deficits, the therapist interrupted her, saying, "That's a lot of important information all at once. Let's break it down and let Stefan respond to the first item and then progress from there."

Copyright © 2012 Depositphotos/ Krisdog.

Traffic cop often may be perceived as "rude" by one or both partners. Indeed, the therapist is cutting a person off, perhaps in mid-sentence. Indeed, the ability to truncate problematic conversations is a powerful and potentially uncomfortable skill that has significant value for the therapy. Many therapists actually use hand signals such as an outstretched palm toward the one he or she wants to stop and indicating with his or her fingers that the other partner may begin into that potentially dangerous verbal intersection. Partners can also be urged to use signals to indicate that they want a break or want to redirect the conversation.

When the therapist cuts off Mica and requests a response from Stefan, it might be causing some consternation for Mica. It is wise for a therapist to acknowledge that he is cutting off one of the partners.

M: (In an irritated voice) You are cutting me off!

T: I am. I am very interested in how Stefan is reacting to what you are saying.

M: I am not through.

T: Yes, and as I mentioned, if you want a useful interaction with your partner, we would best go point by point.

M: Are you saying I am talking too much?

T: I am saying that it is difficult to respond to any of your important perceptions when there are more than one to choose from. I wonder, Stefan, what it's like for you to hear Mica say you don't help enough with the household tasks.

The therapist can be fair and must be firm, here. It is no easy task to cut off a diatribe from an angry person, yet if it gets to a piling-on situation, it will only be a fight, or the partner will withdraw. By being in control of the session, the therapist can get the couple to experience an alternate way to handle difficult conversations.[4]

In this case, the couple had fallen into a pursuer (Mica)-withdrawer (Stefan) pattern and the more she talked, the more he withdrew, which in turn led to her doing more pursuing. By altering the manner of the flow of verbalization, the therapist can begin to break into problematic enactment patterns and help couples find alternative, more productive paths.

Universal Translator

It is our position that every couple is cross-cultural and bilingual in multiple ways.

Because of this, individuals hear messages differently, attribute different meanings to perceptions, and "connect the dots" in different ways than their partners. Each person has a unique manner of taking in information (representational system), processing it within his or her own cultural frame and history, and expressing that information, colored by his or her perceptions and beliefs. Partners are different in their styles, and designing a common ground (without United Nations–type headsets) requires some ability to translate one's language into the hearing capacity of the other.

For example, one partner may be more comfortable understanding and using the language of emotions, while the partner is more cognitive. One may be more visual in the way he or she perceives his or her environment, while the partner represents his or her perceptions more kinesthetically (Bandler & Grinder, 1976). Chapman (2015) has described this phenomenon as speaking different "love languages." The couple therapist is in a position to help them understand better not only what the partner is communicating, but how both are expressing themselves.

Frank is a very well-organized software engineer. He primarily processes information in a visual manner. He prides himself on being logical. Missy, a marriage and family therapist, is far more kinesthetic in how she understands her world. She is much more focused on feelings and characteristically speaks a very emotional language. They were discussing in therapy a disagreement about planning a summer vacation.

M: Ideally, I want to go back to our cabin in the woods on Moosehead Lake. It's so romantic.

F: Well, look at it this way. We have a total of 7 days. Even if we fly into Portland and it is more expensive than Boston, we are looking at a day's travel each way and a 4- or 5-hour drive. That brings us down to maybe 4 days at the Lake. Look, I have a map of Maine here on my phone. Besides, nobody has been in the cabin since last summer when Rob and Kelly went up there, so we'd spend at least 2 days getting it in shape and another getting the boat out, ready, and in the water."

---

4   Such instances illustrate the importance of the therapist being assertive and balanced. Mica is irritated and may feel that the therapist is taking Stefan's side. The therapist needs to explicitly state, "I am concerned how Stefan is reacting to your comments, and I am not taking his side; I certainly want you to be able to fully say how you feel and be sure to be heard."

M: (Dejectedly) It just seems like such a great thing to do. It'd bring back some great family memories of when I was a kid.

F: You know the cabin isn't really the one your family had. That one rotted out and was replaced with the new cabin. We all pitched in on it in 2014.

M: (Raising her voice). So what would you like for our vacation?

F: I thought we could fly into Boston and spend a week at the ocean. Maybe, Nantasket Beach.

M: (Sarcastically) Why don't we just drive to Lake Michigan and stay close to home?

F: Well, you did say you wanted to go back to New England. I am trying to figure out the logistics within the parameters you initially set.

M: You have no sense of romance or even caring about me.

F: Look, the data are as clear as the nose on your face. Just look at them and we can make the best decision.

M: Screw your data. I don't even want to be stuck in a cabin with you for a week anyhow.[5]

Although both are discussing vacation plans, they are communicating about it in such different ways, the partner is unable to decipher the code. Frank is not hearing Missy's emotional language, and she is ignoring his visual-logical stance and communication.

What the therapist can do here is to serve as a *universal translator*, taking what Missy is expressing and putting it in the language of Frank and vice versa.

He may make statements such as the following:

T: Frank, I know it doesn't look like this, but Missy is saying that she wants to recapture the romance from her past and share it with you this year on vacation. She wants to have a conversation about romance, before discussing the nuts and bolts of the vacation realities. Then, turning to Missy, asks, "Is that close?" If she assents, he then asks Frank to respond to Missy's request, even though he is not picking it up in his natural manner.

The therapist could also reflect to Missy what Frank's language is about:

F: Well, you did say you wanted to go back to New England. I am trying to figure out the logistics within the parameters you initially set.

---

5   This is clearly a point at which the discussion deteriorates and commands therapist intervention. It's important to return to the focus on romance rather than where they end up going.

T: Missy, I will be Frank for a moment. When you told me you wanted to go back to New England, "I wanted to please you and decided to come up with plans to explore how you would have the vacation you wanted. I really feel good when I can do things for you (again checking, and if Frank assents). Right now, I am feeling sad and a little irritated that when I try to do what you say you want you get upset with me. Missy, try to respond as if Frank had said those words."

If the therapist interprets incorrectly when he asks the partner and the answer is no, then the therapist can ask, "Well, what emotions/thoughts are you trying to say? What would you like your partner to hear?" When the therapist spoke to Missy, he put Frank's words into her more affective language, and when he spoke to Frank, he translated her emotion into cognitive concepts to be explored.

The universal translator role often involves both speaking and understanding both languages and also being able to role play, speaking for each client as an interpreter of his or her partner's language.

Role-Playing

Often called the "grandfather of the techniques" (Shapiro, Peltz & Bernadett-Shapiro, 2019), role-playing has several common functions in couple therapy. These include the universal translator procedure; aspects of psychodrama (Corsini, 1957; Moreno & Moreno, 2011); role-playing significant others; acting "as if"; role reversals; behavioral rehearsal; the empty chair technique (Glass, 2010; Greenberg & Goldman, 2008); the use of inanimate objects, such as hand puppets to speak "truth"; and doubling or alter ego (Shapiro et al., 2019).

Role-playing is among the most common and effective techniques. In such scenarios, the therapist asks the clients to suspend their usual reactivity and to respond by acting in a different manner. He or she may ask one of the clients to play a role. He or she may take on a role and play one of the partners (albeit in a more healthy form of interaction), or he or she may ask the clients to switch roles—to play the other just to experience what it is like to face oneself in a relationship. It is interesting to note that couples can do this remarkably well, often after a brief period of self-consciousness, and enjoy the experience of being the other member of the dyad. This is an effective method to ensure that partners have an *affective* experience, critical to behavioral change.

Many of these techniques are revisited more specifically as structural interventions in the next chapter. The doubling technique, described briefly, is described here.

Doubling as a Form of Role Play

One form of role playing is the doubling or alter-ego technique, an approach that dates back at least to Jacob Moreno and psychodrama (Moreno & Fox, 1987) and Gestalt practices (Perls, Hefferline & Goodman, 1951). In his *Collaborative Couple Therapy*, Wile (1992) both describes and demonstrates this technique in his couple therapy text and also in a video showing him working with a couple. As described, Wile's approach is quite dramatic. As the couple speaks, he kneels next to one of them and role-plays alternative ways of expressing the points that allow for greater receptivity. He will make "I statements" instead of "you statements," and he translates angry or avoidant comments into more collaborative and open communication.

For example, one partner might say, "You never lock the doors before you go to bed each night." Intervening, the therapist might translate that and, speaking more authentically, might say, "I worry for our safety and am anxious when I come home late if the doors are not locked and the alarm isn't set."

The therapist would then confirm that is in fact the message the person wants sent by asking the original speaker, "How close is that?" Then, turning to the partner who characteristically responds with, "I am tired with your constant criticism," the therapist asks him or her to respond directly to what the therapist interpreted. The greater likelihood is that the partner, hearing some vulnerability, will respond with less anger and more cooperatively, "I am sorry. I do get forgetful, especially when I am tired and fall asleep reading a story to the kids. I didn't know how anxious you got."

Doubling, like many role-playing techniques, provides excellent modeling of intimate talking and translates what the partner is saying into far more usable (honest) language. Instead of criticism, the partner hears the more vulnerable emotions expressed. The therapist also interrupts a near-automatic escalating exchange with one that offers more chances to respond congruently.

Psychoeducation

Often a couple's disagreements are related at least in part to a lack of relationship education, or a discrepancy between what is expected and what actually occurs or is realistic. In the role of information disseminator, the therapist may fill in gaps that are both educative and reassuring.

"Psychoeducation" is a term more often associated with behavioral, cognitive behavioral, and solution-focused therapeutic approaches but is an important factor across theories of couple therapy. Indeed, every insight-oriented or existential/humanistic interpretation has a significant component of information.

More directly, there are some areas of therapy in which some information is necessary to both truncate the course of therapy and to move it forward. For example, Lebow (2014) indicates the value of providing information about individual disorders, problems, skills, and family processes. In particular, people in relationships in which substance abuse, domestic violence, depression, or other disorders are present often benefit from information and recommendations about handling the individual problems. Couples often routinely ask, "Is it normal to argue/want independence/feel bored at times?" After some exploration, it can be reassuring to simply answer and provide whatever data on the topic that is available.

Arguing

One area in which psychoeducation has been reported successful is in the area of ongoing escalating arguments. Many years ago, Bach and Wyden (1970) provided a manual for fair fighting that was a popular success as a trade book as well as advice for therapists. Often, a therapist has to teach a couple how to fight in a way that does not make matters worse. It usually involves setting up rules for disagreements and communicating directly one's personal desires rather than a critique of the partner's many faults.

Similarly, therapists may educate clients on dangerous forms of verbal fighting such as Gottman and Silver's (1999) four horsemen of the apocalypse: criticism, contempt, defensiveness, and stonewalling. These are similar to warnings issued by Brown and Brown (2002) about conflictual areas in relationships. They indicate that escalation, invalidation, withdrawal, or negative interpretations make finding resolution much more problematic. When these occur, it is important to provide an intervention (even in the earliest sessions) to decrease the amount of animosity, which can prevent progress in therapy.

When clients are aware of these and want to repair their relationship, they learn to avoid them in difficult conversations.

Discrepancies Between Expectations and Actual Experience

Often in relationships, each partner has specific expectations about what forms various aspects of the union will take. These expectations may come from personal history, cultural and parental norms, prior relationships, fantasies, relational myths, or impossible-to-keep promises. These can be especially complex when they go unsaid and the partner is not aware. As one woman opined about her "oafish husband,"

Katie: He should know that I hate having anyone touch my feet and the most tender thing is to have my eyelids kissed.

T: What happens when you tell him these things?

K: I shouldn't have to tell him. That's just basic.

Another example is common around Valentine's Day, where one partner expects to be surprised with a very particular gift but feels it wouldn't mean anything if the partner was informed.

Josh expressed with considerable anger that his wife of 7 months was always interrupting the ball game without "any idea what is going on. Even when I tell her it's the fourth quarter, she acts like it's irrelevant." In his mind, interrupting a game at a crucial moment was the equivalent of talking back and arguing with a preacher during a church service; "It's like sacrilege."

Because expectations are often deeply buried in values and unconscious processes, they are often quite important, albeit unclear to the partner, who grew up with a different set of assumptions. Often it takes a long time in a relationship to learn, comprehend, and respond to those unexpressed ethics. It is useful to inquire as part of the assessment what types of expectations each partner had going into the relationship and how these have changed over time. Very often, troublesome issues are based on implicit expectations that have never been discussed, but the partner is nonetheless disgruntled that they are not being fulfilled.

In-Law, Family-of-Origin, and Extended Family Issues

Horsley (1997) uses psychoeducation and *reframing* in dealing with in-law problems. In particular, she focuses on information about and *normalizes* life cycle transitions. Horsley notes that this also serves to externalize the problems, making them more matters of course and growth than pathology. In addition, Beaton, Norris, and Pratt (2003), conducting preventative seminars about potential in-law problems, take a very similar view: getting both parties to understand that the partner's view is normal, if different. Foundational issues around relationships with in-laws are also part of Bowen's (1974/2004) concept of *differentiation of self* and are valuable in clarifying ambiguous alliances between partners and their in-laws.

Parenting

Parenting issues also seem to respond well to psychoeducation. Whether it is normalizing stages of development or particular difficulties, parents are often eager to learn about improving their skills. Morgan (2012) notes that therapists can help couples develop awareness of dynamic tensions between security and freedom needs in both children and parents. Morgan (2012) uses psychoeducation "in which it is possible to take into account another perspective alongside their own, so that an internal dialogue takes place from which new thinking can arise" (p. 82). Cudmore (2012), however, cautions that in Morgan's interventions, psychoeducation is mediated by an atmosphere that emphasizes "listening, receptivity, exploration, and the search for meaning" (p. 86). That is not always the case.

Kerig and Swanson (2010) underscore the importance of understanding the impact of marital distress and triangulation on children, which has a reciprocal effect of increasing parental stress. In situations where parents have widely different styles and one may even use harmful practices toward children, it is essential to provide parent education either directly as part of the couple therapy or to refer the couple to parenting classes, reading, and support groups. A number of empirically based online parenting programs may appeal to couples as well, such as parentingwisely.com and functionalfamilytherapy.com.

Transition to Parenthood

Going from being a couple to being a family is one of the most significant life transitions. Yet there is little formal education on the implications for a couple (Shapiro, 1993). Childbirth education classes essentially end with getting the infant home safely and some nursing instructions.

Many couples struggle with the essential combination of physical, social, and emotional strain that accompanies the birth of a family. Psychoeducation can ameliorate some of that stress. For example, Johnson (1996) writes, "As I begin to work with parenting couples, I look for small, attainable goals, giving high priority to basic health and relationship needs, such as food, sleep, and time alone together" (p. 231). She prioritizes these needs over psychological and relational distress. Often, she notes, "just reassuring a couple that their experience is predictable and that it will pass reduces the tension and allows further progress" (p. 231). A perilous aspect of this transition is when the normal intense focus on a child's needs, physical healing for the new mom, and exhaustion from interrupted sleep diminish the couple's romantic and sexual relationship and persists beyond the infant and toddler phase.

Several authors on the transition to family explain to couples the significance of switching from "hard" to "soft" emotions and understanding the differences between approaches to solvable and unsolvable problems.

Infertility

Another area of life in which there is a precious dearth of useful psychologically oriented information is for couples who are experiencing infertility (e.g., Berk & Shapiro, 1984). Couples experiencing infertility are frequently referred by physicians to therapists, and those seeing therapists often are referred to infertility specialists.

Infertility, defined usually as failure to become pregnant after a year of trying (18 months for women over 35), is related to a developmental crisis, an extensive emotional reaction, blame and shame, a concern that one's body has let her down, and life dreams having been shattered. Couples dealing with infertility and invasive infertility treatments often suffer from anxiety, depression, and relational stress.

Two common forms of psychoeducation in dealing with infertility are (a) basic normalizing information and (b) stress-reduction techniques. For example, the fact that roughly one-sixth of all couples who are trying to conceive are not fertile in the usual 12–18-month window (e.g., Blank, 1985) often provides surprising news and welcome relief. Of course, this does not change their infertile status, but it allows them to explore options and discuss emotions far more effectively as a couple. Techniques such as progressive relaxation, meditation, exercise programs, doing things as a couple, and setting aside specific times to discuss the conception problems (as opposed to always or never) can reduce stress.

There may also be some evidence that such stress reduction increases fertility, although to date, the research on that is not uniform (Galst, 2018). It is not clear whether stress causes infertility, but there is considerable evidence that infertility causes long-term marital stress (Daniluk, Leader, & Taylor, 1987; Mahlstedt, 1985). In addition, Domar, Smith, Conboy, Iannone, and Alper (2010) report that distress over infertility cause many patients to abandon fertility treatment prematurely and to avoid sex with their partners. Takefman, Brender, Boivin, and Tulandi (1990) report that psychotherapeutic interventions may attenuate psychological distress, thereby reducing treatment duration, lowering medical costs, and reducing dropouts.

Unwanted Pregnancy

Psychoeducation may also be helpful in exploring options caused by the opposite of infertility. Although the stresses here may be compounded by significant differences between members of the couple, the high degrees of emotional upset, shame, fear, loss of dreams, and the like are psychologically similar to the distress in infertility. In addition, there is often significant time pressure to arrive at possible decisions.

Bibliotherapy

One form of homework-style psychoeducation is provided by assigning or recommending relevant trade books. There are many good trade books on the market for couples who are dealing with common stresses. Some involve approaches to difficult conversations, life transitions, dealing with mental disorders, parenting, extended family, and so on. A list of some useful trade books for couples can be found in Appendix A.

Sometimes, couples will enter therapy, citing a book or an assessment tool they found on the Internet, and ask the therapist his or her thoughts:

> C1: We read the book on "love languages" and realize that we talk in different ways and don't understand each other. I am an "XYZ" and he is an "ABC." What can you do for us to help us understand each other's love language better?

> T: I assume you are talking about the Chapman (1995) book. Are you saying you want to be more aligned with each other in important conversations?

In another couple, the wife was dealing with partially regulated bipolar disorder and her husband was expressing confusion and doubts.

> Husband: Is this bipolar disease treatable? The medication seems to go in and out and I can't predict what wife I will wake up to in the morning. Is there anywhere I can go to find out something that will help me understand what she is going through and what I can do when she is either way up or way down?

> T: We will be working to identify these issues as we go on in therapy. If you want to read something from your wife's perspective, you may want to read a copy of *The Unquiet Mind* (Jamison, 1996) or *Loving Someone with Bipolar Disorder* (Fast & Preston, 2012).

When using bibliotherapy, it is essential to discuss what clients learn from the books or articles. Sometimes, trade books have fairly simple descriptions and one-size-fits-all solutions that may ill suit a particular couple. In the discussion with the couple, the therapist can suggest modifications that are germane to the couple.

Sometimes, of course, the therapist is unaware of the material about which the clients are referring. For example, one couple began therapy by referring to their enneagrams.

> C1: Look, we just want to be clear if a 5 and a 9 can be compatible. If those are incompatible, we probably should just break up now.

> C2: I don't see why we are even talking about breaking up. We get along fine. I just need more alone time than you do.

> T: Tell me what differences you see that are problematic and tell me which work out okay.

> C1: Look, if you don't understand the Enneagram styles, there is no way you can help us.

T: Well. I may not have the level of knowledge of your Enneagram styles that you do, but as long as we are here for this meeting, let's see where there are compatibilities and incompatibilities.

C1: Well what is your E-style?

T: What I am aware of at this moment is that the "personality styles" have the potential for understanding, but they may also be a source of distance. Before we get back to long-term styles, let's take a few moments to explore what is occurring in the room between the two of you and amongst the three of us.

Sometimes, despite a lack of knowledge or particular belief in something the clients have read, a focus on the here and now can be fruitful. Often when a client reads something, it is assumed that a therapist is knowledgeable about that also. Sometimes, bibliotherapy is a convenient way for clients to face the anxiety of coming to couple therapy, and the content quickly dissolves as therapy ensues. Sometimes it is valuable for clients to feel like experts on something that will impress the therapist.

In the Enneagram couple example, however, despite the therapist's best efforts, this couple canceled the next session and did not return to counseling. Both authors have experienced this dilemma, especially when partners have read an Internet column or taken a "compatibility test" that has no validity. After discussing its meaning to the couple, it may be useful to refer them to a validated instrument such as the Marital Satisfaction Inventory (Balderrama-Durbin, Snyder, & Balsis, 2015).

Normalizing

A crucial aspect of psychoeducation and joining involves *normalizing*. Often a couple will see a problem and catastrophize about it, blowing it way out of proportion. This is often related to family-of-origin issues; fears of the unknown, including those of rejection or abandonment; worries about loss of security; history of prior relationship failure; and so on.

In such situations, whenever possible, the therapist may *reframe* an issue or conflict in a more positive light, help redefine a partner's motivation, or may indicate that the conflict and stress felt is normal. For example, when the therapist informed the couple dealing with infertility that one-sixth of all couples have a similar experience, it helped diminish their stress levels. Like all techniques, normalizing must be used carefully and judiciously. Otherwise, its effects can be diluted and keep the couple from dealing with some difficult concerns. Indeed, even if stress of a certain kind is normal, it may still be a painful issue to confront, especially in situations where a loss has occurred.

Parenting

One area of life where normalizing often occurs is in parenting. One parent wants to be more lenient; the other more strict. Perhaps one wants to enrich their child's life with structured activities, classes, tutors, and so on, while the partner prefers more unstructured play time. A therapist may intervene with a comment such as, "So, you are very much wanting your child to have as rich a learning environment as possible and to keep up with other children in the neighborhood." Then turning to the partner opines, "And you are committed to free time and a chance to grow the imagination. Those both sound important." In doing so, she or he acknowledges the positive intentionality in both positions and indicates that they both have something to offer. In this way, she or he normalizes a dilemma and shifts an ongoing battle into the potential for a working alliance.

Sometimes, a partner believes that a particular behavior is somehow abnormal and needs attention. For example, "My husband roughhouses with the boys and I worry that they will become violent and aggressive." Once the therapist affirms that the roughhousing is within reasonable bounds and unlikely to cause any physical harm, she may wonder aloud about how (more generically) moms and dads treat children differently. She or he may then encourage the client to tell the husband her fears, rather than her judgments. It may also be important to let clients know that they do not have to agree on everything. However, agreement on major values or acknowledgment of differences may be important.

Children will always navigate between parents knowing that Dad's rules and Mom's rules are different. Indeed, by the time they are 2–3 years of age, children are usually quite adept at approaching the parent who is most likely to agree.

Sometimes, a parent is simply unaware of characteristic developmental stages and perceive a child's behavior and the partner's reaction as problematic. One dad came in complaining that his 2-year-old is obstinate and won't listen to instructions. He added, "My wife makes it worse because she consoles and hugs our daughter when she is being a real pill." A little helpful information on how 2-year-olds are and what they are accomplishing developmentally by being difficult may be very helpful before turning to the parents to come up with a mutually agreed-on course of action. Of course, if a particular behavior is clearly harmful to a child, the therapist's skill in framing comments and attending to the parent's reactions is critical when pointing out the effects of such actions.

Cultural Differences

Normalization is often important when there is a culture clash. For example, one couple came in with a major disagreement about church going. She came from a devout Christian family and wanted them to go every week to Sunday services. In his family of origin "[they] went to Mass once a year. Palm Sunday was [their] day. That way [they] avoided the Easter crowds." He continued, "Our family went out on trips and did fun things on the weekends." The therapist had to indicate that the problem was that the two "normal" approaches to church going were in opposition. She quickly affirmed that both patterns made sense and asked, "What do you do with other disagreements?"

Another example of this has come up more than a few times in our practices. This is when to give Christmas gifts. Hugh was locked into Christmas Eve, and Charlotte Christmas morning. Each saw the other as wrong and intractable. At one point in a session, Charlotte sputtered loudly, "How can it be Christmas Eve? What about Santa Claus?" It was clear at the outset that the obvious solution, to give presents at both times, was unacceptable, because in the words of Charlotte, "Christmas Eve is just wrong." Once the therapist could normalize both traditions, the couple found a way to explore the underlying power struggle about whose holiday traditions would be honored and what it meant to each to fail to continue their family-of-origin traditions. It took each person feeling respected to be able to share his or her respective vulnerability before moving on to a mutually acceptable solution.

Other important examples of cultural clashes are when women are expected to be subservient to men, when corporal punishment of children is common, and, in mixed cultural couples, when arranged marriages are customary for one. The therapist then treads a fine line between respecting the culture while exploring the degree of separation and acculturation of each partner and how a particular parenting practice may be detrimental to the relationship or the family.

Normalizing Requires Validation

Whenever possible, it is very helpful to *validate* each person's perspective as long as it is within reason:

> "So, I can see that your goal is more harmony in the household. I wonder what about the approach makes it difficult to achieve. It seems logical that it would work, but it does not." (Turning to spouse), "Maybe you could help out here. How could Mary achieve her goal of more harmony with a slight adjustment so it would work better for you?"

Reframing

An aspect of validation (and doubling) is *reframing*—finding the positive in an action.

Nagging, for example, can be decoded as an expression of caring. Anger may be interpreted as a demonstration of depth of caring and how much a client wants to work out a dilemma. Although reframing has been associated and proliferated in the couple and family literature by strategic-oriented therapists (e.g., Haley, 1973; Watzlawick, Weakland & Fisch, 1974; Weakland, 1990), it is easy to make reference to the positive intentionality of Rogers (1951) and other humanistic therapists since the 1950s.

It is often powerful to find positive intention in a partner's actions, and at the same time to point out that the behavior was not received positively. Basic speaker-listener exercises can provide greater understanding of this discrepancy.

Some essential qualities of reframing involve recasting a complaint as a wish or a personal fear. Another is responding to a rising tone of voice with a more neutral vocal or calmer, nonverbal expression. After a social gathering at her work, Randi came in furious with Don, her husband of 10 years. She quickly began with, "He is such a pervert. He was flirting with my boss's wife, my coworkers, even the server lady." Turning to her husband she screamed, "You humiliated me so much I didn't think I could go into work on Monday!"

Don replied weakly, "You said you wanted me to be social for a change and to get involved with people at the party. Did you forget that I spent most of the evening talking with your boss? And I wasn't flirting. I was just trying to be more social."

After relating carefully and empathizing with each person, the therapist turned to Randi:

T: For his part, Don was trying to do what he thought you had requested. Unfortunately, it seems like it didn't work out the way you wanted.

Randi (R): (Calming a little) Well, he didn't have to try to seduce every woman at the party.

T: (Reframing) Don, Randi is expressing anger that reflects a hurt and she feels threatened by your apparent attention to other women in a flirtatious manner.

D: Well okay, but her jealousy sometimes is out of control. I would never cheat on her and I wasn't even flirting. Myra, the boss's wife, was saying that her husband had a harem at work and all I said was that they couldn't hold a candle to her. I was just trying to calm down a tricky situation.

R: So, what about when she smiled at you and touched your arm?

D: Yeah. That felt weird. And you may remember, I made a quick retreat to the food table.

T: Don seems to be saying that in an attempt to defuse a situation, it somehow got worse and he made a retreat.

R: Well, what if I wasn't there? What would he have done?

T: Randi's jealousy is an indication of how much she cares about you and worries about your relationship.

D: (Noticeably calmer; sighs) I know. I also know I probably should have checked in more with you at the party.

T: Randi, would that have been helpful?

R: Really helpful. If he could just see how much I love him and how scared I am that I could lose him ...

T: Tell him that directly.

It is easy for the therapist to get "lost in the weeds" in following this exchange. The basic issues to discern here are *trust*, whether Randi basically trusts Don's commitment to her, and Randi's use of the label *pervert*, which is an extremely negative, significant escalation that offends Don. This exploration may uncover other instances and require the therapist's focus on the basic relational issues between them.

All of the roles and techniques described are common in the early phases of couple therapy. Many may also be used in the longer-term work described in the next chapter.

Summarizing the Norms Underlying the Techniques

1. Conducting an *assessment* to identify core relational structures and processes
2. Keeping a *focus on fundamental relational dynamics* rather than the *dispute du jour*

Benson, McGinn, and Christensen (2012) offer five additional core principles that transcend theoretical approaches in couple work:

3. Taking a dyadic rather than an individual perspective (exploring the *couple as a system*)
4. Finding constructive ways to deal with emotions, especially emotionally driven inciting
5. *Saying the unsayable*. Bringing public those often avoided, emotion-based private behaviors and each person's internal experiences
6. Fostering productive communication by enhancing both clear speaking and attentive listening
7. Bringing resources together with needs. Emphasizing and using the couple's strengths and positive behavior to address their needs.

8

Advanced Treatment: Techniques and Skills in Longer-Term Couple Therapy

T his chapter is focused on the third of the four phases. It is important to note that these phases of therapy are not always distinct, linear, or easily segregated. We are separating these chapters on techniques more for the purposes of elucidation than for a sense that anything in couple therapy is so clear cut. The methods described in this chapter rely on the building blocks described in Chapter 7; clear communication is both necessary and sufficient to meet some treatment goals.

In this chapter, we explore the skills and techniques that are used when more serious problems are no longer obfuscated by misunderstanding. The clients may disagree on how to approach such a problem, but they can both agree that it is real and that when one partner perceives a problem, the other person must engage.

The techniques and skills needed here may involve a number of therapeutic interventions including confrontation, problem solving, family-of-origin and cultural exploration, structural alterations, and referrals to specialists.

Longer-Term Issues

Sometimes, better communication is not easily attained or, when it is, leads to revelation of more fundamental problems. This is when longer-term therapy is needed. Some of the problems that expand the third phase of couple therapy include the following:

- Intractable (unsolvable) problems
- Unresolved resentments or "baggage"
- Chronic or acute trauma

- Financial hardships and disagreements
- Finding fault (demeaning, insulting, or negating partner)
- Seeing a relationship as a zero-sum game (with winner and loser)
- Intrusions from the larger context
- Individual pathology

Many of these issues are accompanied by, or caused by, problems in the primary relationship structure. Often, structural problems in a relationship involve a third party. This can be any person or issue that takes precedence over the two-person relationship. It may involve work, hobbies, a child or parent, addictions, or infidelity.

Structural Problems in Relationships: Triangulation

As Minuchin and Fishman (1981) describe, some problems in family therapy involve family constellations or processes that apparently solve one set of problems but may exacerbate others. One of these is what Bowen called "triangulation" (Titelman, 2012). A common form of triangulation is when a member of a couple maintains a primary emotional attachment to a family member (child, parent) of another generation as a way of getting needs for intimacy met outside of the couple relationship.

When Lorenzo and Leah came in for couple therapy, they claimed that they had grown distant through their 25-year marriage and that there was little emotional intimacy shared.

However, it was clear that his relationship with Cleo, their oldest daughter, was very emotionally intense. They shared several interests, worked together, and frequently talked long into the evening after Leah was asleep. Although Leah also had a "good" relationship with their daughter, she frequently felt like a "fifth wheel" when they talked about the business. For this family, their daughter Cleo had helped meet her dad's needs for greater connection and partnership as she was being groomed to take over the family business. That was a plus for everyone in the beginning, but as it progressed, Leah was being left out. In return, she withdrew from Lorenzo and Cleo, which accelerated and widened the marital relational gulf. It was also convenient for Cleo, whose husband of 3 years was described as "a workaholic in a startup company." Minuchin (1974) described this as a "detouring triangle" in which Leah was bypassed and Cleo became Lorenzo's primary emotional and functional partner.

For Rona and Dave, a similar multigenerational relationship occurred. Although they were married for 5 years, her primary connection was with her mother, who lived 2,000 miles away. In the first session, Dave described,

> Our life is always about her mother. All our vacations are travels back to St. Louis. She (Rona) is on the phone with her mom for hours every day and late into the evening. The only time I get to have her alone is when it is after her mom's bedtime in Central Standard Time."

When the therapist inquired, Rona went into a long rambling description of her mom's aging, failing health, and need to be close to her. She asked the therapist, "Would you please tell Dave that talking to your mom every day isn't a sin?"

For Rona, her very close, enmeshed relationship with her mother was an effective, albeit subconscious, tactic to be less intimate with Dave. However, while it provided predictability, it was pushing him away more than he would like.

For each of these couples, there needed to be a shift in the relationship structure such that the marital relationship was primary and the cross-generational boundary was strengthened. The structural shift that was desirable was to have the therapist hold the child-parent relationship securely and allow the marrieds to shift their focus onto each other. Once they tried that, the therapist's job was to support them as they faced the fear of intimacy in the primary relationship.

For Lorenzo and Leah, because their anxiety about intimacy was rising, the recommendation was made for Leah to increase her contact with both Cleo and Lorenzo. One intermediate idea that the couple tried was for Leah to take Cleo to play tennis with her on some weekend days and for Lorenzo to take Cleo's husband to a few sports events with him. This allowed for some reduction in intensity of the bonds between father and daughter. The next step was to have Lorenzo and Leah find a way to spend some more private time together. In the short term, those private couple times were somewhat threatening to Lorenzo. In response, the therapist supported him to make the shift and see the benefit in being closer to Leah while having a more even relationship with Cleo.

For Rona and Dave, the attempts to reduce the bonds between mother and daughter were more problematic. Rona's father had left the family home several years prior, presumably because he also could not break into what he referred to as "the affair" his wife was having with their daughter.

Although the therapist had explored with the couple the potential risks of increased intimacy and the value of avoidance, it may have been premature to make what seemed like a logical recommendation: that the next time they planned on traveling to St. Louis, Dave and Rona would take a day or two alone in another city like Chicago "as a second honeymoon." Although they tried it, when they were in Chicago, Rona spent both evenings after dinner talking to her mother on the phone. Dave's hopes for a "sexual honeymoon" were dashed.

It is possible that the therapist's recommendation of a second honeymoon was premature, in part because the significant issue of intimacy avoidance had been insufficiently explored, either for its meaning and value, or with successive approximations to make a change less of a giant step.

A few weeks later, Dave asked to come in alone because Rona was in St. Louis for several weeks with her mom. Their therapist was hesitant but made the appointment with an agreement that Rona would also be able to have an individual session later.

D: Rona went to St. Louis. I don't know if she will be back anytime soon.

T: Say more about what prompted this.

D: She just said her mom needed her and left the next morning. I tried to call a few times, but she only texts me back with short messages that she really needs to focus on her mom. I asked if her mom was ill, but she didn't respond.

T: Where does that leave you?

D: I think I am out. This is not a marriage and I don't want to spend weeks on end wondering what my wife is doing halfway across the country while I hold down the fort.

As the therapist discovered subsequently, their marriage did end shortly later. According to Dave, Rona stayed in St. Louis in her mother's house. At their last session, he reported that he had hired a divorce attorney.

One could argue that the intimate failure in both relationships was either a precedent or symptom of the softening cross-generational boundary. More important, however, was that whatever the reason for having a stronger bond with a child or a parent, the shift from a same-generation boundary to a triangulated one became a significant issue in blocking the essential primary relationship.

Whenever there is a weak boundary around the couple and a third party, there is need to explore the structure in which the couple is embedded and potentially to make some significant changes, once both members of the couple agree on a common goal and view of the problem. Although this occurred for Lorenzo and Leah, it did not work out with Rona and Dave.

Interventions for altering these patterns begin with labeling the triangle, its usefulness, and its deleterious effects. The therapist should explore how the triangle relationship is functional for the couple, either in terms of giving them something (e.g., a close connection) or by avoiding something (e.g., threatening levels of couple intimacy or anxiety about the unknown). Having determined its functionality, the therapist can then help the couple meet those desirable goals within a single generation, instead of across generational boundaries. The triangulation needs to be reframed as a reasonable, yet imperfect attempt to solve a real problem.

One way to address this is to point out to the couple the high emotional cost of such a partial solution.

The Therapeutic Triangle: An Exception to the General "No Triangle" Position

One method that may be very facilitative in this process is to create a therapeutic triangle. This serves as a less problematic intermediary, helping the couple experiment with alternatives in a relatively safer relationship.

To create a therapeutic triangle, the therapist inserts him- or herself in the middle of the conversation between the members of the couple, listens, translates, and expands the repertoire of possible responses. When Billie and Joan—two women who had recently married after 10 years together—were continually going back into their characteristic "big fight," the therapist asked them each to talk to her and then she translated.

B: I keep telling you that I can't deal with any "open marriage" relationships. It's selfish and just plain betrayal.

J: First of all, you are changing the rules now after your past experience and I want to be part of the decision.

T: This seems like a discussion that has gone on a lot.

B: We have never agreed on this and she is unwilling to be reasonable.

J: (Voices rising) Me? You are the unreasonable controlling bitch. Nothing is going on. You just want to lock me in the apartment with no friends.

T: What's bringing this up now?

B: Joan's ex-husband is coming for a visit and she wants him to stay in our guest room. She has a long history of hooking up with him when she sees him.

J: (loudly) That is not—

T: (Interrupting the conversation) What I am hearing, Joan, is that Billie is fearful that your history with your ex will get in the way of your relationship.

J: I haven't been with any man in over 5 years and nobody else since we were married (actually since we decided to get married).

T: Billie, because Joan has been faithful to you since you were engaged, she is hurt by the idea that you think she would have sex with her ex-husband.

B: I'm just not feeling safe leaving the two of them alone in the apartment all day while I am at work.

T: Joan, respond specifically to Billie's fear, without agreeing or disagreeing. Talk to me while Billie listens. Imagine I am Billie.

J: I know you are scared, but I feel an obligation to Carl while he is visiting.

T: The first part of that worked well. I felt reassured. Let's try it without the justification.

J: I don't want you to be fearful, jealous, or mistrusting.

T: Good. It means a lot that you are sensitive to my feelings (as Billie), and I hear that you have a dilemma regarding Carl. (Coming out of the role and talking to both clients, the therapist continues) Is it possible for the three of us to come up with a solution that respects everyone's feelings and is practical as well?

Over two sessions, they decided that Carl could stay for a weekend when Billie was present and that he would stay with other friends during the work week. They also agreed that the decision was final and the reasons not be discussed with Carl or other friends (underscoring the primacy of the couple relationship).

Affairs: Broken Structures

One of the more dramatic and difficult forms of structural breaks in a relationship is the occurrence of an affair. As was discussed in Chapter 4, extramarital affairs are particularly difficult in a relationship. Whenever another person is introduced into the emotional mix in a primary relationship, triangles occur, boundaries are broken, and basic fears of abandonment and betrayal can be activated.

Although many relationships can weather this storm with considerable therapeutic work and time, infidelity frequently results in a crisis for the relationship. It also requires a rebuilding of both trust and decisions about the form of the relationship moving forward.

Statistics on the percentage of marriages that "survive" affairs are notoriously inconsistent. In addition to the lack of replicative empirical evidence, there are also questions about cause and effect: whether the affair caused the break-up or a developing break-up led to an affair. If we are pushed to make a rough estimate of the population of couples we have seen in therapy, it seems that approximately 50–70% of relationships that are changed by an affair are not irretrievably broken.

Structurally Oriented Techniques

Techniques that address structural issues may target intrapsychic, interpersonal, or systemic aspects of clients' lives. The particular approaches employed should be dictated by theory, the nature of client needs, and pragmatics.

Relevant techniques that address structural problems include exploration of several, often interrelated factors:

- What the relationship means to each of them and the discrepancy between that perception and what an "ideal" or model relationship looks like for each
- Understanding what the positive value of the current structure (security of the status quo) does for them as a couple
- What they would have to face if changes were to occur
- What risks they are willing to attempt to make changes

Methods to address these questions may be considerably enhanced if the "problem" is presented as external to each person instead of as the property of one's individual pathology.[1] Therapists often interpret the presenting problem to the couple as a solution that has had unfortunate side effects or as something in the interface between them. Once again, the real focus needs to be on the "dance" between them, or the "us," rather than on either individual.

Leon and Marissa came to couple therapy after some long-term financial and parental hardship. They reported that they had "lost touch with each other" in the process of

---

1 When individual pathology does in fact, represent the major reason for discord, individual treatment should either replace or operate concurrently with couple work.

dealing with Leon's 11-month job loss, near bankruptcy as a result, and their daughter being expelled from high school. They said that they had worked together well to get over the crises and Leon had finally found a new position, but now they "were just not connecting" like they used to.

After working some on their connection to the therapist (an Asian American woman with African American clients), on their capacity to listen to one another, and assuring herself that their ability to discuss matters was sufficient, she asked them to detail the problems and solutions. Marissa began the fifth session:

> M: About 2 years ago, Leon's company was acquired by a bigger one and he was one of many who got laid off. At first, we didn't worry because they had outplacement help and he's been employed since he was 15, but then as the months dragged on, and with no jobs in sight, we had to dig into our savings and retirement and my job barely covers the mortgage.

> T: Leon, what position did you hold?

> L: I was a manager and had 16 direct reports in three projects.

> T: How do you see what happened?

> L: Well, the company was basically subject to a hostile takeover and after the new management came in, they replaced all us managers with their own people. They also took the company in a new direction that I thought was not a good idea. It's XYZ company. You probably read about it in the news lately.

> T: I have. Didn't their stock tank last week?

> L: Two weeks ago. That's not the end of the bad news either. This is confidential right? I still have some insider info. If I didn't, I'd short the stock even now.

> T: Yes. It is confidential and I won't personally trade any single stocks if I am working with a principal in that company. So, what happened next?

> L: Well, I got 12 weeks' pay and outplacement services, which didn't do much, and I started sending out resumes. It was very frustrating. I finally got my new job with my old boss, when she left the company and went into the new one.

> T: (Providing both assurance and psychoeducation) That's the way it is today. Resumes fall into the black hole and you never even get rejections, just nothing. At your level, you did well to get something so quickly. Most people have a 12–18-month lag.

> M: That's what he told me, but it still was scary, and I worry that it will happen again. You know my dad was an accountant for one company for 40 years.

T: That world seems far away now. You also mentioned your daughter having difficulties.

L: About 6 months into my unemployment, Mar and I were squabbling a lot and I was home with Sasha more, and she began to just get into trouble at school. Not real big stuff, but she cut some classes and got into a verbal fight with another girl, and then she and her boyfriend broke up. She wouldn't talk to me about it and Marissa was working extra hours, so she didn't have much of a chance to get into Sasha's difficulties like she usually does.

M: Well. I didn't feel bad about her breaking up with that kid. He wasn't very nice to her and was always more selfish than he should have been.

L: Once I got called into the school, we went into high gear … grounded her until she talked to us … got her into therapy. That's the therapist who said we should come to see you. We waited until I got the job because even the co-pays would have been a strain, what with Sasha seeing her lady every week.

T: Where does it stand now? And what about your son?

M: He's fine. He just puts his head down and keeps going ahead. He's motivated to do well like his dad (acknowledgment of strength to build on). And Sasha seems to have straightened out some. My mom came to stay with her while Leon began his new job and they have a nice relationship.

L: My mother-in-law is very kind and loving but won't put up with any crap. She is tough as nails when she has to be.

T: So, the ship seems to be righted now. What is happening between you? (Silence)

L: We just aren't as loving as we usually have been. We aren't doing as much together. I don't know. I love Marissa with all my heart, but sometimes she seems a million miles away.

(Marissa nods in agreement)

T: Well, let me tell you, what I am hearing is you had a real work-related financial crisis and that you pulled together to weather that very scary storm. Then when you started to get into squabbles, Sasha suddenly gave you a reason to pull together even more, including involving Marissa's mom. So basically, you have been in crisis mode for almost a year and living on adrenaline. It sounds like you did the best you could in a "war zone," but now the war seems over and you find yourself licking your wounds separately.

L: So, we're like soldiers with PTSD?

T: What did you use to do that had to be dropped while you were battling for survival?

M: We gave up movie nights and barbeques with friends and even drives out to the coast or up to Napa.

T: Some of those are potentially expensive. How well have you replenished your retirement funds and reserves?

M: We have a ways to go, but we are now banking a good part of my take-home.

T: Great. That's an excellent plan, but what are you doing together for fun?

M: Not much.

T: Okay, I'm going to ask you to have a weekly date night and choose to do something that won't cost an arm and a leg.

L: We used to go out with friends and have evening picnics down near Santa Cruz on the beach. (turning to Marissa) Would you be open to that?

When she looked skeptical, the therapist observed aloud:

T: You look skeptical.

M: Not so much that, but I thought Leon would say that he would give me one of his special massages. That's almost free.

T: (Orchestrating) Ask him!

M: Leon?

L: You don't have to ask again. That's a much better choice.

They had trouble planning for the time alone to do the massage but managed the evening before the sixth session. It was more pressured and less satisfying than either remembered. The therapist attributed it to the external stressors still playing a role and she asked them to try again. By the third time, they both reported more closeness. This was reified in the next couple session when they sat together on the same couch instead of separate chairs.

It is important to note that the massage intervention requires a lot of intimacy. The therapist would have been more cautious had the suggestion not come from Marissa.

For Leon and Marissa, the structure that had to be altered was a shift from essentially sympathetic nervous system reactivity to a more playful, relaxed (parasympathetic nervous system) ambiance.

Boundary Resetting

Often, when couples have concerns about boundaries, the therapist may make suggestions about alternatives. The boundaries may concern other people and/or the members of the couple itself.

For Andrea and Lanny, the issue began when their first child was born. Andrea believed strongly in having a family bed, in which the entire family slept together. She argued that it was good for their baby and made nursing easier. Lanny agreed reluctantly. Although it was not a concern during the first few months of the new family, increasingly he experienced the family bed as a detractor to the couple's sex life and to his getting a good night sleep before going off to a stressful job. Andrea argued that the family bed promoted bonding and attachment, made it easier for the baby to get to sleep and stay asleep longer, and facilitated nursing. Besides, she stated, "I am not ready for sex now anyway, so it doesn't make a difference." We can see here how Andrea's insistence and Larry's acquiescence sets up the potential for the difficulties they are having.

They came into therapy when their "compromise" had Lanny sleeping in the den on a pull-out sofa bed. They were both unhappy about their negotiated agreement. When they came in, Lanny was holding the baby Damon, in a sling-like baby carrier.

The therapist quickly moved to understand aloud that Andrea was responding to the needs to be a good mother and Lanny was trying to protect and provide for the whole family as a good father and husband. After assuring that each understood the positive intentions of the partner, he began to help them negotiate a different kind of compromise.

> T: Andrea, with your idea of co-sleeping with Damon, is this a temporary or permanent notion?

> A: What do you mean?

> T: I was just wondering if co-sleeping was for infants like Damon or is it a permanent new arrangement?

> A: Well. I haven't really thought of that much, but it wouldn't be when he is in school.

> T: What's your thought about that Lanny?

> L: I am glad to know that we won't have school-age children in the bed. I thought you might even want teenagers to sleep with us.

> A: No.

> T: So, the issue is that you agree that at some point, there will be a shift back to an adult bed and a separate children's bed. The solution is to determine the time frame.

> A: How do we do that? And just if Damon isn't in the bed, it doesn't mean I am ready to have another child.

T: Whatever the solution, you want a clear agreement that you will not be getting pregnant again anytime soon.

L: You should know that Damon came as a failure of birth control. Don't get me wrong. We are both very happy to have him, but he was a surprise.

T: So, if Damon is in the bed, another "pleasant surprise" will not occur.

L: Yeah.

T: (Resetting boundary) I'd like to suggest a small experiment. It has two parts. One night next week, after Damon falls asleep in your bed, put him down in a bed that is next to your bed, same room, but not *in* the marriage bed. The second part is that you agree to no sexual intercourse that night. Would you be willing to try that?

They reluctantly agreed to try it, with Andrea showing understanding by commenting:

A: Like when he takes a nap. I lie down with him, but get up after he is asleep.

T: It's only a one-night experiment. We can talk about how it works out next Tuesday.

Once the therapist had them adjust slightly the sleeping arrangements, he was able to help them find more effective verbal compromises that were protective, but with a softer boundary.

Lisette (36) and Carol (25) had a different kind of boundary concern. Lisette was a principal in a small business with her brother and sister. She had responsibilities as an owner and as the primary marketing person. Carol worked as a teacher in a local elementary school. Their boundary issue was that once they had moved in together, Carol had become increasingly insistent that Lisette have only common social contacts and that they share an e-mail address and phone passwords.

Lisette came into therapy complaining that Carol's "jealousy" and intrusiveness was driving her crazy. Carol, in turn, reported that she had to be in a faithful relationship and that Lisette had a long history of lovers before they met. She also said that Lisette was her first female lover and that it was "all new to [her]." She reported that when Lisette drank at social events, she became very flirtatious, "with other women and men, too."

They had experienced several fights about Carol checking messages on Lisette's phone and asking her pointed questions about the identity of each caller. The current crisis concerned Carol's deleting a business call from a woman Carol assumed was a potential lover. Lisette reported that it almost killed an important deal for the company.

To deal with the loss of boundary here, the therapist had to set some boundaries of her own very quickly. First, she had to evaluate whether the jealousy was pathological, whether Lisette was indeed untrustworthy, and whether Carol was in need of individual therapy. Second, she had to confirm that they wanted to stay together as a monogamous couple. A few things can be assumed in this case. First, that this type of enmeshment is not workable and that their individuality needs to be reestablished. Second, that checking e-mails and messages and intercepting phone calls places Carol in a "one-up" parental position and engenders resentment on Lisette's part. It is important for the therapist to hold these assumptions as a basis for disentangling them. In addition, basic, adult-level (rather than parental) trust needs to be rebuilt for the relationship to be successful.

She began by setting two priorities. She made a referral for Carol for individual work, and then she set a goal of finding a way to help Lisette reassure Carol about the relationship while maintaining her professional boundary.

She explored with Lisette the drinking and flirting issue. It turned out to be a relatively minor single event when Carol was present and clearly identified as her partner. She also explored with Lisette the possibility that she seemed to be withholding information as a way of encouraging jealousy.

> T: Lisette, I know that it is important that you have company secrets and have to draw a line between personal and professional aspects of your life. We need to find a way to get that clear. I am also wondering how much you mix the professional and business matters and where Carol might feel left out.

> C: The problem is that it is business and family. Her sister's husband makes it very clear that he disapproves of our lifestyle and relationship. If we ever decided to get married (looking tentatively at Lisette), he'd be that baker who refuses to make us a cake!

> L: It's true. Barry is a jerk and even after all these years, I don't know why my sister married him. He doesn't work, just lives off the family business, and is always trying to force his way into jobs in the company.

> T: So, you agree on Barry. I want to bring us back to how you could do the opposite of Barry and have a personal life and a business life that doesn't get corrupted. What have you tried to do to keep those separate (setting the need for a boundary)?

> L: I think I should have my business cell phone, like my phone at the office—away from spying eyes.

> C: Why can't I know who you talk to? Why does it have to be a secret?

> L: For the same reason I can't text you hourly when I am at work and you are home. It's too much, and it interrupts my flow at the office and then I come home with more work to do.

> T: So, you have set some limits regarding texting.

> C: Yes. But I am not happy about it. We agreed that if I text her, she'd text back unless she was in a meeting, but that she wouldn't initiate the texting.

T: I wonder if that would work with the phone and e-mail as well? I have a potentially strange idea about e-mail. Would you be open to trying something new? I warn you in advance, it would take some work.

C: What do you have in mind?

T: I'd like you to try two separate e-mail addresses: one for Lisette at the company and a second for Carol and Lisette as a unit. You'd have to have an agreement that the personal e-mail comes to the joint account.

C: How would I know that she isn't using the business address for personal contacts?

L: You have to trust me. I could show you the list of e-mail, but I don't want you getting in and deleting stuff by yourself.

C: My therapist said that if you wanted to cheat, there was no way to stop you anyhow. I am just scared to be rejected.

T: We can talk here about those anxieties and how you both generate fears between you, but we need to also find ways for you each to have separate parts of your lives.

As might be expected, as they developed better boundaries, their fears of intimacy emerged as the major relational issue in therapy. It was only once the boundary was reset that they could face those larger fears. Carol's fears of abandonment were matched by Lisette's fears of vulnerability. As long as they were fighting about the boundaries, they protected themselves from facing deeper levels of intimacy.

The Larger Context

Sometimes the couple issues are nested or embedded in much larger systems such as extended families (Horsley, 1997); poverty (Minuchin, Colapinto & Minuchin, 2007); immigration and acculturation status (Inclan, 2001); social, religious (Walsh, 2009) and community groups; cultural demands (Kelly, 2017); friendships; disconnection and isolation; and so on (Jordan, 2017). Madsen (2011), for example, advocates careful attention to the greater context ("collaborative helping") as it bears on the presenting problem.

The exploration of the larger context, within which systems hold sway, has often been referred to as the "biopsychosocial" or "ecosystemic" approach to couple therapy (Lebow & Rikart, 2008). It is also reflected more generally in developmental psychology. For example, Bronfenbrenner's (2006) bioecological model of child psychology can be a useful guideline for consideration of extra-couple influences.

Two of the major advantages of systemic approaches—which take into account the larger social environment in which a couple operates—are *circular causality* and *equifinality*. Rather than a linear cause–effect approach, these theoretical assumptions presume that a change anywhere in the system will have ripple effects throughout the entire structure.

Interventions can be broader in scope, and may be individually based, couple based, or more generally systemic. Thus, the couple's families, friends, work, community, and the social, environmental, and political context are considered in assessing their impact on interpersonal dynamics.

Techniques Used When Issues Arrive in the Larger Context

In dealing with larger cultural ecosystems, some additional techniques are more germane.

Family of Origin

To explore multigenerational transmission of patterns that lead to discord, genograms—especially those that highlight couple relationships across ancestral lines—can be particularly useful (Banmen, 2002; McGoldrick & Gerson, 2008). While focused on family-of-origin issues, the therapist may offer interpretations of the psychodynamic, developmental interactions based on each person's childhood and family history (Scharff & Scharff, 2004). Siegel (2010, 2015) underscores the importance of working with psychodynamically oriented, generationally transmitted issues such as couples' splitting and projective identifications. She also explores the most important transference-countertransference issues in couples work and methods to address them.

Whether or not a psychodynamic approach is taken, Satir (Banmen, 2002) underscored the considerable value in looking at intergenerational patterns. One member of a couple, for example, may report that there has never been a divorce in either side of his family. His partner may report just the opposite: "When I look back at my family history, there is only one couple that hasn't separated or divorced, and they are miserable together."

Those patterns create both conscious and unconscious expectations and thresholds of tolerance for what the current relationship may bring. One of them may assume that once married they will be together for life, while the partner expects that it could end at any juncture. When both partners come from a long history of disruption in relationships, they may be more prone to let a fairly small disagreement go to the relationship decision level almost instantly.

When Ellen and Ross were referred for therapy, they had been squabbling about a number of small issues. The precipitating reason for making the appointment is the fight they had over a brand of toilet paper he had picked up when he did the weekly shopping.

E: If he can't do the simplest thing like follow the list for shopping, I don't see much of a future for us.

R: Yeah. Her parents got divorced about how much fat content should be in hamburger. This is nuts.

E: It's just so disappointing. I can't trust him at all.

T: Wait. You can't trust him at all?

E: No, he's a good person and I know he'd always be faithful, but I really wanted the soft TP and he got a bargain brand.

R: I cannot be worrying about which brand of toilet paper to buy. I grabbed one off the shelf and she's making it into a federal case. If it's that important, you could just do the shopping.

E: No. You see what he's like. If he screws up, I get more work.

After several sessions, their family histories and personal dating history emerged. There were numerous divorces in her family, including parents, grandparents, brother, and sister. In addition, she had been the one to end all of her prior relationships. By contrast, Ross's parents and grandparents were together and his sister was engaged to her high school sweetheart.

The therapist was able to work with them by helping them explore the different patterns and to help them develop a scale of disagreements that were well below relationship decision levels through a process of values clarification and prioritization. What was most fascinating is that the major issue for each was trust and security. He managed it by focusing on permanence and keeping everything together, and she by being hypersensitive and wary of any "disturbance in the force"—potential ripples—for escape.

When exploring trans-generational genograms, family values, traditions, and patterns become clear. Consider a pattern in which several generations of a family endured multiple affairs, domestic violence, addictions, or significant losses. In one genogram, deaths in military action were present in each of five previous generations. What implications does that have for a couple? Often, expectations about relationships are built up over generations. Although it occurred almost 9 decades ago, the impact of the Great Depression of the 1930s can still have a powerful effect on the grandchildren and great-grandchildren today. Boszormenyi-Nagy and Stark (1973/1984) describes such patterns as the "family ledger."

Adam's immigrant grandparents went from upper-middle-class to soup kitchens and bread lines in the early 1930s, and then were devastated again by the Holocaust in which most of their relatives in Europe had been exterminated by the Nazis. He recalls vividly a very traumatized aunt who was liberated from a concentration camp and lived with his grandparents. Somehow the fear and trauma from those ancestors' experiences had been transmitted to him. He worried constantly about finances, abandonment, and being singled out and persecuted for being Jewish.

He was introduced to Shlomit by a "matchmaker yenta" at the temple during High Holidays. Shlomit, an Israeli Sabra, grew up on a Kibbutz and came from a fiercely independent family. She was in the United States working on a PhD at the university where he was an assistant professor. Their differences were very attractive, and they soon developed a relationship and moved in together. After a year, they were very much in the "You're not the person with whom I fell in love" (YNTPWWIFIL) period, described in Chapter 4, and struggling with their different expectations and backgrounds. That is when they came in for therapy.

While Adam had an already comprehensive genogram and family tree, Shlomit had no information prior to her grandparents immigrating to Israel. The conflicts could be viewed through those differences. As cautious as he was, she was care-free and experimental. Her history was marked with risk taking; his was very conservative.

The conflict that brought them to seek therapy was his marriage proposal, which she met with a suggestion that they move in and live together and see what happens next. The proposal activated her anxiety about being tied down, and her response encouraged his fears of rejection and abandonment.

Their therapist encouraged them to explore each other's genograms and to try to understand the multigenerational transmission on their values and concerns. He also underscored their shared desires to be together for the present and to live together. The question he added was when they could decide about a permanent relationship. After several months of working to bridge the cultural and developmental gaps, they were in a better position to evaluate whether mutual empathy was possible and how much they could appreciate what the other brought to the relationship. In Shlomit's words during the last session, "I know I want the grounding Adam provides, but he needs to hold me less tightly." As in the earlier case of Lisette and Carol, enmeshment in the form of clinginess, dependency, and mistrust often results in alienation and resentment.

Socioeconomic Status and Racism

Socioeconomic issues can be quite influential and serious. The degree of resources individuals and couples have readily available significantly impacts the issues that emerge in therapy. Lower socioeconomic levels and poverty are associated with more uncertain living conditions and job security, higher rates of relationship and family instability and divorce, lower education levels, a greater number of unwed single heads of households, and a greater amount of time expended trying to keep afloat (Kelly, 2017).

When the dangers of having enough food and shelter enter the picture, couple counseling may be greatly impacted, and interventions may well be more tied to the need for survival. Under conditions of poverty and privation, there are significant problems with relationship quality, stability, and coping resources (Conger, Conger, & Martin, 2010). Focusing on the higher incidence of poverty in marginalized populations in the United States, such as commonly seen in Hispanic and African American couples, Boyd-Franklin (2003) explored how stressors in the influence of racial, sociopolitical, and cultural factors negatively affected the formation and structure of relationships in these subcultures.

It is not hard to expect that the stress of eking out a marginal existence would add strain to any couple relationship. Sarmiento and Cardemil (2009) have shown that couples who experience the combination of racism and limited economic resources are often characterized by less constructive communication and relationship satisfaction and by increased likelihood of aggression in the relationship. The increased time demands required for survival also impacts parenting roles (Cowan & Cowan, 1992). Finally, living conditions for these couples include racism, poor school systems, and violent communities.

In working with couples in the lower socioeconomic strata of society, therapists must connect with the couples by demonstrating an understanding and awareness of limitations, cultural values, and environmental barriers. Sound therapeutic alliances are especially essential. One interesting component has to do with therapeutic distance during sessions. Our experience with some cultural groups, especially African-American couples in general, reveals an expectation on the clients' part of more openness by therapists. For example, they may question whether the therapist is married, has children, is gay or straight, and so on. Many therapists, trained in traditional therapeutic methods, find such questions disconcerting and intrusive. However, a willingness to be open with clients about non-sensitive characteristics may be helpful, before inquiring what the meaning is of the answers.

C: Look, are you married? Do you have kids? You look very young.

T: I do look young. I am married, coming up on 5 years. No kids yet. Tell me what's important about that for you?[2]

Most of the work with clients who are close to or below the poverty line will occur in low- or no-fee agencies. Sometimes couple therapy may also involve areas that are more often the purview of social workers, such as getting clients in touch with important available resources.

Therapists may also be asked to intervene on behalf of clients with agencies and institutions. For example, a recent intern who was seeing a Hispanic couple had to intervene on behalf of the pregnant woman for essential prenatal care that required a number of administrative hoops with no instructions in Spanish. In fact, the bilingual intern said that she spent over 6 hours just to get the care for which her client was entitled. The intern ruefully observed, "[B]efore I was in the MFT program, I worked for a medical insurer, and even I found the procedure crazy."

Kaslow (2005) and Lindblad-Goldberg, Dore, and Stern (1998) indicate that sometimes couples will need more than clinic care. When they are unable or unwilling to come to the agency, some agencies will reach out and do home-based care. Such care for difficulties in daily living is necessarily brief, problem-solving oriented, and designed to enhance the couple's resilience. Unfortunately, the inclusion of home visits that was more common in the nascent era of family therapy is currently quite rare due to scheduling difficulties, staff shortages, changes in the training of social work case workers, and various theoretical orientations.

Other accommodations may include child care, alternative means to reaching clients who may not have or share a mobile phone, transportation to sessions, and some kind of food present at the therapy location.

Socioeconomic Status and Values

Although values are always individual, there are some general differences in personal values and behaviors that correlate with levels of socioeconomic life. It is often an error to treat couples from lower (or higher) socioeconomic strata based on middle-class

---

2   For therapies and theories that require a tight therapeutic frame, such as classic psychodynamic therapies or behavior therapies, answering instead of interpreting questions may be improper.

values that are common in psychotherapy (Falconnier, 2009; Grimes & McElwain, 2008; Rojano, 2004).

One dominant misconception is the middle-class belief in the value of building toward a better future by delaying gratification. By contrast, many clients from lower strata of society may be far more focused on immediate and practical needs. This can be reflected in missed sessions, late arrivals, and fewer, highly focused sessions. A couple therapist, faced with such value incongruities, may mistakenly interpret these behaviors as a lack of motivation instead of a lack of information about what therapy has to offer and development of reasonable positive expectations. Ethnicity, race, and socioeconomic status play a strong role in the expectations clients have of therapy regarding its length (short term versus long term), level of self-disclosure, secrets, and whether it should be values driven or pragmatic.

One expectation common in couples who live a day-to-day existence is that they will be looked down upon. Therapists must work to meet all clients where they are and focus on the additional difficulties that these hardships may cause. In short, the external stressors must be taken into account as well as the couple dynamics. In such couples, for example, under- or unemployment may be a significant factor in relational stress, as are regulations of aid programs that favor single parents over intact couples. When extreme external conditions impact individual and relational functioning, it may be helpful to encourage a balance between accommodation and advocacy.

Another issue of concern is that people who live in poorer housing areas often have greater risks to their safety and that of their children. These families may not have supervised play dates for children, but they do have the same kinds of worries about their children's health and safety. In high-risk neighborhoods, even "free" visits to a local park, community center, or playground may be fraught with dangers for children. Eamon and Venkataraman (2003) describe a complex domino effect that is instigated by economic adversity, which leads to psychological stress, marital conflict, and less supportive parenting. Extended family members and others are often key supports to stressed parents (particularly single parents) and need to be considered and included in therapeutic interventions.

Garcia and McDowell (2010) describe the significance of external factors that can marginalize couples: race, gender, and social class. They describe how a deficit in social capital reciprocally limits life choices, social influence, and material resources. They argue that by analyzing class and social capital, therapists may avoid pitfalls of "rescuing" clients, supporting middle-class values, and situating problems solely within the family. Today, being an undocumented immigrant or refugee severely limits opportunities, creates chronic tension, and results in marginalization and often separation of families.

The bottom line is that in working with couples from lower socioeconomic strata, their entire ecosystem must be taken into account and middle-class values and opportunities may not be assumed. Sometimes, helping clients to find external resources—an atypical activity in couple therapy with middle- and upper-class strata of society—may benefit the process as well as serve as a precursor to the more intricate couple dynamics and system treatment (Levy & O'Hara, 2010). Therapists of all disciplines need to step up and facilitate and advocate for clients so that therapeutic interventions can be implemented.

With one couples group at a community clinic, the four couples in the group had to pay less than a dollar a session for their treatment, but they received child care at the center, bus tokens worth double their fee, and snacks were present at sessions. Because of these accommodations, attendance in this group was more typical of couples from less marginal backgrounds. The therapy work each week began with their discussing their day-to-day stressors before evolving into talk of the relational difficulties. It seemed that the contextual discussions were essential both as therapy per se and as a basis for opening more interpersonal and intrapsychic issues. What was particularly interesting is that the four couples also formed a post-therapy social support group in which they shared child care and information about job opportunities.

The Other End of the Economic Spectrum

Many therapists will work with couples who have a surfeit of social capital, wealth, and privilege. These couples often come from family wealth; have earned high incomes over years, or perhaps quickly through a startup and stock options; and have quite an advantaged life. They had access to enriched preschools, elite private educations, and contacts to enhance their careers. Yet for all their largesse, the emotional and relational problems are often quite trying.

For most couple therapists, some parameters of these clients' lives are as unknown as those at the opposite end of the spectrum. Most therapists do not come from great wealth or know the values of such lifestyles, nor of the social strata in which these folks travel. Thus, learning the socioeconomic context can be challenging. It may also have the added problem of envy, like when the clients say they will miss two sessions because they are going on a friend's private jet to some exotic resort.

Fitzgerald (1926) captured this notion in his short story "The Rich Boy": "Let me tell you about the very rich. They are different from you and me. They possess and enjoy early, and it does something to them. ... unless you were born rich, it is very difficult to understand" (p. 5). A more recent observer, football coach Barry Switzer was quoted in a widely disseminated December 14, 1986 *Chicago Tribune* article: "Some people are born on third base and go through life thinking they hit a triple" (Shatel, 1986). The 2018 film *Crazy Rich Asians*, based on Kwan's (2013) book, portrays some of the advantages that extreme wealth can bring.

Frequently in our experience, these folks will use "retail therapy," exotic gifts, or financial talk as a way to avoid their here-and-now relationship issues. Again, as is with any cultural group that is less known to the couple counselor, the context plays a huge role. If we engage with these couples, we must clearly understand their expectations and social context. In one case, the therapist was stymied in the attempt to assess a couple's equity in sharing responsibilities and discovered that nearly every aspect of their lives was "outsourced," including scheduling their couple therapy sessions.

During the fifth session of couple therapy, Justin and Momi were describing multiple problems with their two children, "unreasonable" expectations from his parents, and a significant drop in the stock market soon after the 2008 recession. Although they had suffered losses in the market, their wealth was sufficient that it would not impact their lifestyle in any material way.

M: We need to be careful about our spending now, and Justin is just convinced that he should get a timeshare in a helicopter to avoid the traffic battles when he has to go into the city. We are going to go broke, but he keeps spending.

J: We are not going broke, and in the long run the chopper is going to pay for itself in time saved, and in contacts with the other owners.

T: Momi is concerned that the spending is going to interfere with your lifestyle. What can you say to address that?

J: She is always concerned when I spend anything but doesn't even think about going off on spa and shopping weekends in Park City. (Turning to her) The last time you went, you said we should buy a condo there.

M: Well we didn't buy it, did we?

T: There are two issues here: one concerning the amount you can spend and a second about who has which rights in your relationship. Tell me quickly and roughly where you stand financially after the losses in the market.

J: We have over $25 million left.

T: And what's your current burn rate?

J: Maybe half a mil. We are fine. The losses are paper losses. We didn't panic sell, although I should have doubled up on a few holdings. As I keep saying. We don't have to change anything.

T: (Adjusting to the cultural norms expressed) Let's divide the issues into two types. Problems money can solve (we'll call those PMCSs) and problems money cannot solve. I'll let you and your financial advisors focus on the PMCS. Let's refocus here on who has which rights, what the two of you need to face as parents, and how to deal with in-laws.

It is tempting for the therapist to become frustrated in dealing with the "one-percenter issues" of such wealthy clients and easily dismiss the impact of basic relational dynamics.

Immigration and Acculturation

Other external forces affecting couple relationships involve immigrant and refugee needs, assimilation, and acculturation processes. The generation that moves to the new country must be dedicated to preserving as many of the old country and its traditions as possible. Their children, the first generation born in the new country, are the bridge (and often the language translators)—with one leg in the old traditions and one in the new. Their children (third generation) tend to be far more oriented to the new culture.

In working with immigrant families, it is essential to understand the normal demands of the cultural matrix for each of them. To use the Japanese terms, the Isei are the generation that moves, the Nisei are the first generation in the West, and Sansei are the second generation born in the new country. In a Nisei couple, the therapist must be willing to work with them within the dual demands of being bicultural (and probably bilingual).

Mitsuo is the eldest son of a second-generation Japanese-American family in Hawaii. Sachiko is the youngest of three daughters whose mother was Nisei and father Sansei. They had both been born and raised on Oahu, had graduated from the University of Hawaii, and married after a 2-year courtship. Although their families were polite with each other, there was not a lot of closeness because they came from different strata of life in Japan.

Their issues arose when Sachiko gave birth to their first child. Both mothers-in-law were eager to be part of raising her, but they arranged to do so on separate days so they would not encounter each other. They did agree that their grandson would go to a Japanese preschool and take Japanese lessons. Although neither parent wanted to do this, they also were worried about defying their mothers' wishes.

Mitsuo and Sachiko felt they were caught between two generations, families, and cultures. The baby was just about 1 when they self-referred for therapy. It was essential that the therapist join with them in the middle of the dilemma, focusing on having to disappoint either their parents or themselves. It is also important to assist them in examining whether their views of their parents' positions are absolute or whether some accommodation can be made through respectful dialogue.

T: So you want a regular local preschool and your folks want a bilingual Japanese school. That's a terrible dilemma when the Japanese sides want one thing and the American parts want the opposite.

S: Yes. It is the choice between our parents or our children.

T: I wonder if it's that clear-cut? I recognize that you left yourselves out of that mix. That even complicates it more.

M: We are trained to be obedient and honor our parents and our ancestry. But we also have to be good parents to the children.

T: You both said children. I know about your son.

S: (Laughing and blushing) Oh. No. Not yet. But the pattern we set with Toshi is one we will keep.

T: (Smiling) So, now is the time to decide to try to work things out and risk the shame. Are the two of you on the same page?

M: I am more traditional, and Sachiko is more Americanized. Also, her dad is more Hawaiian in spirit and he just wants what's best for his grandson. My parents are both very firm on this.

T: I am interested in how you both feel about this decision. No commitment, but please talk directly to one another now and I will listen (enactment).

For this couple, the immediate problems reflect other larger interacting systems. The therapist must be aware of the cultural-familial pull on the couple and of their own desires. After having learned that Japanese school was a 4-day-a-week after-school program, he wondered aloud about the importance of keeping the Japanese culture in this generation.

T: How important is it to keep the Japanese language and culture alive for you two?

S: I have a lot of respect for my cultural heritage, and we got married at the Shinto temple. I speak Japanese at home with my parents. So, I'd say it was important.

T: And for you, Mits?

M: My mother has very limited English; my dad and my uncles are mostly more mixed because of work.

T: Do you speak Japanese at home?

M: Not much. I learned it mostly to figure out what my parents were saying that they didn't want the kids to hear (laughing and pausing, looking at Sachiko). Can I tell about your sister?

She averted her eyes, looked down, and slightly nodded.

M: Her middle sister, Reiko, married outside to a local guy (non-Japanese), and her mother basically cut her out for 4 years. They even pressured Sachiko to not talk to Reiko. It's getting better now because Reiko has a child and the "Obaba" (grandmother) gene clicked in. But Sachiko doesn't want to be disowned like Reiko was.

T: Do you believe that would really happen at this point? The decision about schools has much bigger consequences in her family. How about yours?

M: My dad really likes Kimo (Reiko's husband), and he would be accepting with whatever decision we make about Toshi, although his preference is Japanese preschool, probably mostly to avoid conflict with my mom. My mom wouldn't be as rough as Sachiko's, but she is pretty strong in her beliefs.

T: So, you are caught between a rock and a hard place, and I hear it is more your mothers than the rest of the family. The more Japanese approach would be to listen to your parents; the more Hawaiian thing would be to listen to your own hearts. Are you on the same page here?

S: We are mixed up. Sometimes we both agree on one side or the other and sometimes we disagree. I usually lean to the tradition. It'd be best if Toshi was old enough to choose, but he's way too young.

T: I assume you both went to Japanese school.

S: We both hated it, but we didn't have a choice until we were teens.

T: That seems important. What would you as parents do if you could have your way with schooling your children?

Note that the interaction did not resolve the dilemma, but the couple began to explore more with each other what they felt best and to agree on a unified (team) approach to working on the very real acculturation, generational problem. Of course, this is not unique to Japanese families. We have heard the identical dilemma, rooted in assimilation, regarding Chinese school, Hebrew school, traditional East Indian weddings, arranged marriages, Catholic schools, and so on. It requires the therapist to recognize the external stressors and work with the couple with attention to such tensions on their couple relationship. The goal of these sessions will often be for the couple to not be split, but to find a way to operate as a team in facing the external pressures.

Acknowledging the external will allow the couple to feel safe enough to explore the more internal pressures that are the usual couple therapy turf.

THERAPY BOX 8.1: TWO PERSPECTIVES

Both Shapiro and Patterson would begin this process in similar ways. However, the normal turf for Shapiro would involve the meaning attributed to such choices, the tension between the security of the cultural status quo, and the fears of the unknown (independence). Patterson would focus more on cognitive distortions they may be creating and work with the couple on reality testing, given the contrasting cultural demands.

Advanced Techniques

Many of the more advanced techniques involve more active interventions for therapists. These often begin with feedback and confrontation.

Feedback

Feedback, a term used in electronics for a century, refers to situations where the output of a system is looped back to the input. A form of this is the loud screech sound when a microphone is placed too close to a speaker in a loudspeaker system. The term has been adopted and adapted by modern researchers in many fields. In psychotherapy, the term is used primarily as a form of confrontation in which the therapist comments on the client's behavior. Claiborne, Goodyear, and Horner (2001) define three components "(a) information provided to a person (b) from an external source (c) about the person's behavior or its effects" (p. 401).

In couple therapy, there are several active feedback loops: between therapist and clients, between members of a couple, and between clients and therapists. Whether the feedback is positive or negative, it is designed to influence the receiver to alter course and either do more or less of something. Therapist feedback involves objective comments and reframes based on observation, inquiry, history, and perhaps couple inventories; it shouldn't involve loud screeches!

One of the more dramatic examples of this occurred in New Britain, Connecticut, at the initial meetings of what was to become the National Training Labs in 1946. Groups of individuals focused on social justice, interracial sensitivity, and intergroup under-standing were led by experts as part of the research of social psychologist Kurt Lewin. Members of the groups that met during the day asked to be present in evening meetings of the group leaders, in which the daytime group behavior (primarily process rather than content) was discussed. This became so popular that it evolved into t-groups and later to all multi-person therapies when systems theory began to be applied to family therapy in the 1960s and beyond.

Feedback is important in any couples counseling and therapy in which there is atten-tion paid to circular versus linear causality. Rather than finding blame in one partner, the therapeutic inquiry explores any part of the relational system between individuals that is causing difficulty. Any subsequent attitudinal or behavioral change in one part of a system is shown to affect the entire system, without a need to detect a particular starting cause. In general, searching for "why" (the cause or origin of a problem) leads the couple into the weeds, reliving blame and escalating arguments.

In couple therapy, therapists have the right and the obligation to comment on behav-ioral and emotional client interactions. They observe client interactions and make remarks related to their theoretically based understanding and relevance to clients' prior behavior. Reviewing relevant studies on the use of feedback, Claiborne and col-leagues (2001) claimed that results show that feedback was positive or neutral in all studies reviewed.

Letty and Mark had been in a long-term relationship and were in therapy because of recent fights about whether to get married. After they ran through their typical argument a few times in front of the therapist, he intervened with some feedback.

> T: I was struck with something just now. Letty brought up the idea of getting married. Mark went into some detail about the potential wedding location and plans, and as he was speaking, Letty looked down and away and turned her body position away from Mark (descriptive feedback).

> L: (To T) I was listening. I just don't think he really wants to do it.

> M: (Getting irritated) I just took what you said and started to talk about the wedding you brought up.

T: (Emotional feedback) Mark, you are trying to get on board with Letty, but she doesn't seem to come with you there. What am I missing? Letty, did Mark skip a step here or was your wedding request a way to create more distance?

L: He didn't say he wants to marry me.

T: Letty is saying that when you jumped into planning, you missed her desire to hear you commit verbally.

M: What do you think planning a wedding is?

T: Let's start by telling her if you want to get married.

M: She knows I do.

T: Tell her directly and say it like you mean it, without irritation.

M: Well. It is irritating. She always brings it up and then it goes nowhere.

T: So initially, Letty turned away when you were discussing plans, and now Mark is saying he wants to wed in a non-romantic manner. I guess that is the way the two of you work together to express your ambivalence (a strong, slightly critical statement).

Once they argued with the therapist about his perceptions, they got into discussions about some financial and familial issues that were of concern, if they were to marry. Without the therapist's feedback about their behavior, they may have kept the loop alive without resolution and increased frustration.

Confrontation and Saying the Unsayable

Confrontation is considered a stronger or more direct form of feedback. Sometimes when a couple is stuck, a firmer intervention is advisable. Two methods to shake up the system involve confronting either or both clients or saying what they are avoiding.

To some extent, any interpretation, feedback, or observation of behavior during a session can qualify as confrontive. Psychotherapists are at their best when they make asocial (Beier & Young, 1984) responses to client verbalizations, or provide feedback about the actual message received, regardless of what was intended. When a therapist makes an asocial response, it interrupts the automatic, unreflective reactions and creates a situation where there is more unknown into which the client may be encouraged to experiment and explore (Shapiro, 2016).

In a simple example, when a couple reports that they had a good week and got along well, the normal social response may be, "Great, that's terrific." For a therapist, however, it is an opening less for praise but for greater understanding. Thus, he or she may respond, "That's interesting. Your interactions with one another today don't seem to reflect that. What specifically did you do differently?"

Another therapist may inquire,

T: What's it like to be telling me this?

A: Well. I guess we are kind of proud that we could get along so well.

B: Yeah. Maybe we're cured?

T: Well, it's certainly a plus to have a such a good week. Based on that, what would you like to address today (taking them out of the talking about past successes and more into current avoidance)?

THERAPY BOX 8.2: WHAT IS CONFRONTATION IN EXISTENTIAL PSYCHOTHERAPY?

Confrontation is often envisioned as an aggressive challenge, disputing the facts or conclusions that a person might draw. Many students watching an old "Gloria" video of Fritz Perls or a 1970s-style encounter group with a non-professional leader, such as the Synanon addiction approach, conclude that an "in-your-face" approach characterizes a true confrontation.

Actually, from an existential perspective, confrontation is common but far from aggressive and never a challenge of another's perspective. In this approach, a "heavy confrontation" usually involves holding up a mirror to a client and requesting assistance in understanding the discrepancy.

Sometimes the discrepancy is between two different client statements. A therapist might query, "Joe, I'm a little confused here. A few minutes ago you said that you are devoted to your children and are a 'pushover' when they want something. Then you just reported that the children, particularly your daughter, were annoying, out of control, and undisciplined and that you just need to 'escape' the house on weekends. Help me understand those apparently different experiences."

Other times it is a discrepancy between verbal and nonverbal messages. The therapist might say, "You are saying something that seems very sad and frustrating, and at the same time you are sitting back with your hands behind your head and smiling as you say that. I am confused as to how I might put those together."

Notice that in both cases the therapist offers the apparent contrasting messages back to the client and requests clarification. She or he is not saying that one of the messages is incorrect; she or he is indicating a understand the client's full experience better.

She or he may also offer her or his personal process experience: "You just told me something that seems painfully sad. And you are smiling as you say it. I wonder if I am more sad than you" (Shapiro, 2016, p. 179).

When confrontation is most successful, it involves placing incompatible actions and goals in front of the clients, rather than getting into the face of the couple and challenging them.

A form of this is the necessary confrontation when clients do not do homework they agreed on.

T: I must say I'm surprised you didn't get to fill out the forms I gave you and arrange a date night in the past 2 weeks. Perhaps you really didn't think they were a good idea?

C1: I was traveling for 10 days and we didn't have much time together.

C2: And I had an extra busy week arranging activities for the kids.

T: I feel somewhat handicapped in helping you make progress if things don't occur in between sessions. Is there a way we can modify the plan to make sure that it's done or do either of you have another idea?

It's important for the therapist not to be seen as a task master who chides children for not doing their homework, but to assert that certain tasks are essential to achieving success according to the therapist's working model.

Often confrontation may add the technique of *therapeutic amazement*.

THERAPY BOX 8.3: THERAPEUTIC AMAZEMENT

This is a collaborative strategy that brings curiosity and apparent naiveté by the therapist to encourage clients to assess more cogently or reassess the interface of their goals and behaviors. Shapiro (2106) describes the technique as "bringing the clients into the therapist's mind as he comes to awareness of a pattern without obvious sophistication." (p. 231)

Confrontation With Therapeutic Amazement

After living together for several years, Kathy and Ahmed came to therapy saying they had decided to "tie the knot and begin a family." They described being very happy about the decision and had support from both families of origin.

They came in after a celebratory romantic evening they spent away at a hotel they had visited when they first got together. After making love, they were luxuriating in a hot tub, when they got into a major fight. The argument carried through the weekend and was still creating a lot of anger and distance when they came into therapy.

The content for the disagreement was their very different approaches to the wedding. Kathy was into planning in detail. Ahmed just kept focusing on the honeymoon and marriage after the wedding, which he considered something he was doing for others, particularly parents.

K: I don't know what happened. We were in this wonderful place and feeling great and then out of nowhere he shut down.

A: You need to understand that we were in this wonderful hot tub overlooking the ocean and, if I may say so, in post-coital bliss. I had no blood in my brain and was far from thinking when Kathy started up about the color of napkins and flowers and how they couldn't clash with her dress or the bridesmaid dresses.

K: Well you could care a little about me.

A: I do care about you a lot. What I don't care about is color coordination and napkins. And besides—

K: Iinterrupting) Well, it's the biggest day of my life and I want it to be perfect.

A: I don't know who you are anymore. I have known you, lived with you, went through a cancer scare with you, supported you when you lost your job, and not just financially. We have been through some tough times together, but now you seem like a "Bridezilla."

K: You won't even stay in the room when my mom and I talk about the wedding

T: (Confirming the budding enactment) Is this how it goes at home also?

A: Well it may be a little restrained here.

T: (Therapeutic amazement, sounding slightly confused) So, let me get this straight, you are feeling really close and connected. You are sitting in a hot tub looking out at the ocean and the night sky, and somehow a sequence begins between you, and at the end, you are feeling distant. Interesting!

K: What do you mean? We just went from one pleasure (lovemaking) to another (wedding).

T: (In a halting, questioning tone of voice) It would seem like an easy transition between pleasures, but somehow the two of you went from a warm afterglow to cold, distant morning. Correct me if I get this wrong, but it looks like the intimacy was great and then you two collaborated to create more distance.

A: I was fine. I just can't handle the incessant wedding planning.

T: My sense is that both of you acted in good faith and you agree on how great the evening was earlier. There is just something curious about the timing, and you know how therapists are always looking for hidden messages. (Turning to Kathy) You want everything to be wonderful for your wedding, and Ahmed, you want everything to be great for the marriage and your life together. That all seems so positive. So, what was the possible advantage of more distance at this point instead of more vulnerability and connection? Help me understand this.

K: To be honest. I wanted to get out of the tub, go to the bathroom, and take a walk, but I didn't want to ruin his mood.

T: And?

K: Like Ahmed would think I didn't care enough or something.

T: You may want to ask him that now.

This led to a more open discussion of how they both avoided the specter of potential rejection by getting into cognitive disagreements. They actually described that after the first time they made love, they ended up in a philosophical discussion about the nature/nurture issue. Is this a persistent avoidance pattern, or does it uncover differences between them that they cannot accept? One path of exploration might be to ask Ahmed that even though he's not interested in wedding details, he can understand and accept the importance Kathy places on them. Another may be to focus on Kathy's desire to do something different and instead of negotiating her desires, initiating a conversation that would likely create a break in mood.

Confrontation as Curiosity

In general, confrontation works best with a question or expressed confusion rather than a command or statement at the conclusion of a detective hunt for the true villain. Thus, a therapist may "confront" a client with the divergent aspects of desire and actual experience. Libby and her Air Force husband of 22 years had been in couple therapy for five sessions when they began to describe their ongoing battle over house chores. They agreed on who was to do each chore but disagreed on timeliness and completeness of the job. They also disagreed on getting their teenaged daughter to do her share. In their well-practiced roles, Libby was the "unsatisfied critic" and Roland was the one who was both too easy on the daughter and when he got around to finishing a job.

L: We really got into it this weekend. We had agreed to clear out Kelly's bedroom for painting (looking sharply at Roland as if anticipating his disagreement), but Saturday passed and Sunday was almost gone. When he and Kelly came back Sunday afternoon after her soccer game, they showed no interest in doing anything but lazing around.

R: She was acting like a drill sergeant inspecting with a white glove and was all over both of us. I just told her I'd get it done, but she needed to turn up the heat and she just went off. She stormed into Kelly's room and started to tear the place apart as if the painting was in 20 minutes instead of tomorrow. Then Kelly freaked out at what her mom was doing and the two of them got into it, and when I tried to calm the situation, Libby turned on me also.

L: So, he just got in his car and went to who knows where for an hour. When the therapist looked at him as if to ask where he went, he replied,

R: I went to the Commissary and did the grocery shopping and picked up some dinner.

T: So, this is the battle you seem to have frequently, and it never seems to get resolved.

L: That's why we are here. You need to tell Roland that he is spoiling Kelly and needs to shape up.

T: I don't know how that would work. What do you think Roland? Would a command from me make a difference?

R: No. I get orders all day. I don't need them at home also. Besides, the room got painted on Monday just as planned.

L: That's what he's like at home also. (Mockingly) "It'll get done."

T: Here's my confusion, Libby. You seem to be in charge of what occurs in the home and you do your best to get everything right and get your family on board, but somehow it doesn't work out as planned. How come?

L: It's Roland. He just won't listen and now Kelly is taking after him.

T: What's it like to seem to do everything properly and have them not work out?

L: I am frustrated all the time.

T: I can believe that. Roland, can you help out here. How come when Libby does everything right, things drop through the cracks?

R: It isn't that things don't get done. It's that they don't get done to her exacting standards and on her time frame. Kelly played the entire soccer game and just needed a shower and to relax for a while. She didn't need to begin moving furniture and take everything off the walls.

T: So, you think Libby's desired jobs are right, but you disagree on the way they are done and the timing. (Turning to Libby) Would you agree with that?

L: He doesn't understand. If they did the job on Saturday when I wanted it done, then there was time for relaxing and shopping after the game. Besides, I played soccer in high school and college. At Kelly's age, you don't need a whole day of rest after a game.

T: Here's what's confusing. You seem to agree on the jobs and the large picture timing, but you get into a power struggle over how it's done. So, things do get done. Libby, I wonder if you are caught in a trap, ending up as the frustrated master sergeant. As things are, you need to get Roland to change to win, and Roland needs to do nothing to win. That seems like a guarantee of loss for you and a pyrrhic victory for Roland. And at the end of these painful confrontations, you both feel righteous hurt?

In this scenario, the therapist confronted with curiosity and also by stating what was occurring in their relationship rather than what was expected. At one point, the therapist asked Roland,

T: What would happen if you did it on her timeline?

R: Then she'd have ten more things for me to do.

T: And?

R: I'd have no more life.

T: (Turning toward Libby) Roland is saying that his whole life could be used up with demands and he'd have no say.

L: (After a pause) Well. He is right about one thing: I always see the half empty glass so I am always on top of what needs to be done. It's a long list that keeps growing. I am not happy about that, but …

T: I am wondering, and this may be something the two of you have already tried, but what could Roland teach you about prioritizing and having some more fun, despite the endless array of things that are not done?

Roland and Libby display patterns that couples engage in when they have been together for an extended period—a dysfunctional homeostasis that keeps them together but tense and resentful. Key issues to explore here are the following:

- The detouring triangle aligning Roland with Kelly, bypassing Libby (Minuchin, 1974)
- Whether either or both partner's positions are extreme (Libby's obsessiveness and Roland's laissez faire attitude) and need to be modulated
- The balance of tasks and responsibilities between them—does Libby have the major responsibility for the family and Roland is her helper (equity—see Patterson, 1995 and Parker & Wong, 2013)?
- Differences in parenting—are they playing "good cop/bad cop"?

Paradoxical Interventions

One of the common interventions described in the systems therapy literature involves paradoxical interventions. According to Hirschman and Sprenkle (1989), more than 75% of AAMFT members claimed to have used such methods. Because these methods can be counter-intuitive, dramatic, and designed for rapid change in couples, they are worth a closer look. They may well take the form of instructing the client to do the opposite of what was intended, such as keeping or exaggerating the symptoms.

Paradoxical intention was first discussed by Frankl (1959). Erickson (1965, 1980) also used them in his hypnotherapeutic work, and Whitaker (1989) demonstrated their use with couples and families. Neither Frankl nor Erickson, both exceptionally experienced and intuitive clinicians, made a particular point of focusing on client resistance and responding in a paradoxical manner. Yet observing them made it clear that they naturally understood the clients' need to hang onto the status quo and avoid fears of the unknown and subsequently joined clients in those avoidant methods.

Paradoxical interventions came to the mainstream with Haley's (1973/1993) "Uncommon Therapy," an intensive study of Erickson's work as a clinician. In this text, focusing on strategic therapy, Haley[3] outlined the technique of paradoxical intervention. Coming from a pragmatic, solution-focused background, Haley did not underscore in his book the importance of Erickson's intuitive understanding of unconscious resistance. Instead, he focused more on the behavior change that such techniques produced.

The innovations were picked up and integrated into the strategic systems approaches to family therapy by the Mental Research Institute (MRI) group in Palo Alto, California, and other strategic therapists (e.g., Watzlawick, Weakland, & Fisch, 1974; Weeks & L'Abate, 1982). By the end of the 1970s the work had spread and was being used extensively in the Milan School in Italy (Selvini Palazolli, Boscolo, Cecchin, & Prata, 1978).

Because of the "astounding and dramatic success" of paradoxical interventions, Gurman (1988, p. 129) noted the widespread use of the technique and a corresponding lack of empirical evidence. This is of course compounded by the failure of many practitioners to explore the centrality of resistance that was a core of Frankl, Erickson, and Whitaker's "intuition." In a sense, the technique provided the form but not the essence, timing, or contextual understanding necessary to be used effectively.

---

3   Jay Haley held an MA in communication. Although he did not have a degree in any of the mental health fields, he became one of the most significant figures in strategic (systems) family therapy.

THERAPY BOX 8.4: MISCONCEPTIONS ABOUT PARADOXICAL INTENTION

It is essential to acknowledge here that Frankl (1959) first introduced the construct *paradoxical intention* as a therapeutic technique. Erickson (1965) also used the concept in his ground-breaking hypnotherapy work. They used the technique so intuitively that others who later adopted the technique misunderstood the timing and scope of its use (e.g., Haley, 1963, 1976).

Shapiro (2016) carefully delineated the conditions under which paradoxical intention would be therapeutically effective. *Paradoxical intention* applied to resistance (defined here as an unconscious pull toward the status quo [security] and away from the anxiety related to change [freedom]) works consistently well when well timed. However, when applied to behavior in general, the impact is more random.

Examples of paradoxical interventions may include the use of reframing and restraining (Davidson & Horvath, 1997). In reframing, described in Chapters 6 and 7, the therapist sees the positive intentionality in a client and may point out to the couple that dropping particular behaviors (or even symptoms) may force them to encounter greater problems. This concept draws on the notion of maintaining homeostasis and the adaptive nature of dysfunctional behaviors and symptoms.

Similarly, therapists may predict and normalize relapses for clients who are undergoing rapid changes. Restraining (Weeks & L'Abate, 1982) may be described as apparently holding the clients back when they are moving hastily in the desired direction. Because the therapist is joining the resistance and pull to the status quo, the clients may be more prone to facing more bravely the fear of the unknown. It may also force a couple to join together to resist the therapist's directive to hold onto the symptom by rebelling and rejecting it; both ways of achieving the desired result.

Erickson (1986) dramatically demonstrated restraining at the initial Evolution of Psychotherapy Conference. He was challenged by a man who claimed he could not go into a hypnotic state and was reticent to even try with Erickson, "because if the greatest expert fails, that means [he] will never be able to" (Erickson, 1986). Erickson agreed that it might not be possible, especially with a large audience observing. By supporting the client's resistance instead of assuring the subject that he could do it, he actually made it more likely. As he began the demonstration in front of the large audience of mental health professionals, he cautioned the man to "be careful not to go into any sort of trance too quickly." The client fell into a deep hypnotic state in a matter of minutes, while Erickson talked on about the difficulties one might have in forcing anything to happen.

The paradoxical part of these methods is that instead of encouraging clients to stop a symptom or to overcome their fear, the intervention honors the reasons for avoiding the fear.

In a couple session, Annie and Paul had been struggling with a long-term problem with intimacy. They described a classic pursuer-distancer pattern where he relentlessly pursued her and she constantly withdrew. After several sessions in which they came closer to communicating in less threatening ways, they came up with a plan to have a week-long vacation away.

T: That's an interesting plan to get away just the two of you with no distractions.

A: Well, we think we can try it. We've been practicing a lot with open communication and we think this will be a big test to see if it works.

P: I am pleased that we will try, and I will restrain myself from pushing Annie and she will tell me if she is feeling pushed into anything she doesn't want to do.

T: You have a plan and both seem at least partially confident about it. Is there any prep you can do beforehand to be more confident?

A: Like what?

T: I was wondering what it would be like if Paul came on strong like he used to do when he wanted to be close to you.

A: You mean now (with a fearful tone)?

T: We could try it now, but I was thinking over the weekend as a test.

P: Like what? We have been doing really well. What do you have in mind?

T: Now, I have managed to bring doubts into your confidence. Maybe this won't be a good idea, but I was wondering what would happen if you both agreed to take a short turn at being the aggressive one. I have a probably crazy idea in mind. What if we set aside 1 hour on Saturday evening? You said you were going to be home and agreed that it was the experiment time. For the first half hour, perhaps Annie could really push for more connection with you in a particular way that is pleasing for her. Just see how you respond. Be as natural as possible but feel very willing to back away. Then reverse the roles. Finally, talk about what it's like to be on either end of that conversation.

In the ensuing session, they reported that they tried the homework, but never got past the first part. Paul replied,

P: I found myself backing away hard when Annie came on even moderately strong.

A: I asked him to help cook our dinner and was affectionate when we were both in the kitchen.

P: And I was really uncomfortable with that, because I didn't know where it would lead.

T: Your fantasy?

P: To the bedroom (embarrassedly).

A: I knew it wouldn't, so it was okay.

T: So, the fear had to do with physical intimacy when you weren't ready or in the mood yet?

P: I don't know, I just felt anxious.

T: Of course, it's a new experience for you, and I'm wondering if you can recognize and move past your discomfort with not knowing or planning what was coming next. Maybe that's a message to own, that you really want to end up in the bedroom with Annie? Perhaps all three of us are moving too quickly and need to bring up other issues. So, on the trip you have planned, what do you anticipate getting in the way?

The session soon turned to what they would have to face if it didn't go wrong. The therapist responded, "You know if it appears to be going well, and you feel understandably anxious, you can use a safety word to create some distance."

Note that by being the discouraging factor in the therapeutic threesome, it left the clients (a) feeling better understood, (b) having more normalized doubts, and (c) able to respond more positively by arguing with the therapist, only this time toward change instead of stasis. This is characteristic of the use of "paradoxical" intervention.

Problem Solving

Although direct assistance in solving problems is atypical in some forms of therapy, it is fairly common in couple work. Sometimes, couples just do not have sufficient knowledge or resources to solve a particularly difficult dilemma.

Problems come in two forms: those that are solvable and those that cannot be solved. The latter are issues in a couple's life that have to be endured and to which adjustment to an intractable situation is necessary. Some forms of chronic illness, disability, or loss of a loved one may all be examples of growing to accept and endure rather than to fix. They may require a focus on the development of problem-solving skills more than a particular solution.

Unsolvable (Endurance) Problems

Cedric and Winnie had been married for almost 40 years when she was hit by a rapidly moving vehicle while she was crossing the street. Her left leg was shattered, several ribs were broken, and her lungs were punctured. When they came in for treatment, she was in a wheelchair and had portable oxygen that lead to her nose. They both said that the accident had severely altered a formerly active lifestyle. Winnie had been on a bowl-ing team and a runner, had completed two half marathons in her later years, and was frustrated and irritable about her current incapacity. Cedric had essentially retired early and become her caretaker.

Because of the nature of her injuries, her doctors had informed her that she might be able to walk with a cane and might get off the oxygen in a year or two, but the need for both could be permanent.

Although they were "getting through the days while (she) recovered," neither was happy. Complicating matters was an uncommunicative insurance company regarding some of their claims. They reported that their home was depressing and outings were rare and usually only to doctors' offices. Cedric added, "It was all we could do today to get to this meeting today at 2:00 p.m., and that is all we can do all day."

One of the compounding problems was that they had withdrawn from their usual social group and had not adjusted to a much less active lifestyle with others. Their son and his wife had visited regularly, but Winnie was disinclined to play cards or board games. She would occasionally watch a DVD movie he would bring over but then complained that life was so unhappy.

Their therapist recognized immediately that there were several interwoven problems: depression, loss of a social group, no replacement social group, and dependence on one another. He had to specifically ask if Cedric had any time off from care taking, and only after some real reticence did they reveal that he was essentially on duty "24/7."

He knew that several alterations had to be made but began with supporting their status quo and what they had to adjust to before slowly helping them find some help with potential ameliorative changes. Although they may see no options for change, brainstorming about all fantastic and possible solutions can help shift them from hopelessness. These included more social contact, time off for Cedric, and greater acceptance of a changed life style.

Even more challenging was a couple who had lost a young child. Their daughter had been born with congenital heart disease and had passed away at age 9. Both parents were understandably devastated and were each grieving the loss when they came in to therapy. One of the major issues they were facing was that they were mourning in very different ways. He was crying a lot, kept focusing on missing the girl, and had become overprotective of their surviving child. By contrast, her reaction was to spend much of her time in a church group, feeling blessed for the time her child lived, and being happy that the girl was "now with God." They were both very critical of, and hurt by, the other's reaction.

Of course, therapy could do nothing to bring back their lost daughter or help them grieve uniformly. The focus on this therapy was to help them get into a group of parents who had lost a child as a way to understand that everyone grieves in their own personal way. The therapist also tried to help them support each other's form of dealing with the loss. The couple therapy was primarily palliative and allowing the "tincture of time" to help ameliorate the horrible wound.

Finally, another couple had had some financial setbacks that took them from the upper middle class to the lower middle class. Through a series of lost jobs, poor investment choices, an underwater mortgage, and a very difficult electronic theft of funds, they had lost their house, much of their retirement savings, and the college fund they had set aside for their children.

Their therapist could help them adjust to a new lifestyle and make some much more modest plans for their future, but most of their material wealth, security, and dreams of a certain future were gone. Because they were now in their late 50s, the focus of treatment was on helping them adjust cognitively and emotionally.

Similar dilemmas can arise in dealing with divorces or relationship losses. Although these are beyond the scope of couple counseling per se, sometimes we inherit a client during or after a relationship split. Some of the examples include clients who have affairs and leave a relationship, a couple where a partner "discovers that [the other is] gay and want[s] to pursue that," mental health or addiction problems that spiral to extremes, severe mood or thought disorders, or individuals whose partners "just want out."

The solvable part of these issues is helping the individual to adjust to a new life. The unsolvable part is the return of the former relationship.

Many situations with unsolvable problems are heartbreaking for therapists as well as clients. In these cases, therapy is often long term, supportive, and focused on endurance and living life within the new unexpected parameters.

Life Transitions

Some unsolvable problems come naturally in the course of aging.

Couples in longer-term relationships inevitably go through a series of transitions that will impact expectations, feelings, and the nature of a changing relationship. The transition from childless couple to family, for example, will necessitate significant changes in roles, physical energy, and likely in income. Transitions that come from being procreative to companionship can represent a loss that must be accommodated. Edie described it well, "There is no way I want any more children, but menopause still hit me hard psychologically and now we're looking at each other in a new way."

Most transitions indeed represent losses from prior ways of functioning. Physical capacities wane with age. The time it takes to accomplish various normal tasks of living tends to expand. Various forms of sexual activity can be affected. Each loss requires adjustments in couple functioning. Therapists need to acknowledge with couples that things are different and normalize those changes before helping the couple find new ways of functioning together. Some of the major life transitions are detailed in Chapter 5.

The "empty nest" is one example of a change that may require considerable relational shifts. When a couple has children, their relational roles shift to being parents as well as partners. When the children leave, the couple is forced to again become a two-person unit. After a few decades of having others in the primary relationship, some serious adjustment may be necessary. Therapists can guide such couples to ways of being together that blends their prior pre-children skills with new ones. They frequently are mourning the reality that "things will never be the same as they were."

Retirement often coincides with this period and creates different challenges for couples to find ways to spend their formerly working hours together. Retirement likely requires shifts in both individual and couple needs.

Finally, involuntary retirement or unemployment can be an unanticipated transition challenge. Unemployment may be primarily affected by macroeconomic or regional economic trends. As the economy downturns, unemployment becomes more likely. With long-term (6-month or longer) male (but not female) unemployment, the incidence of marital distress and of divorce increases dramatically (Larson, 1984).

According to Baer (2016), the best predictor of divorce in heterosexual couples is the husband's employment.[4] Unemployment impacts both the individual who lost a job and his partner in significant ways, including increased likelihood of addiction and domestic violence (Luhmann, Weiss, Hosoya, & Eid, 2014), loss of self-esteem, (Goldsmith, Veum, & Darity, 1997), life satisfaction (Lucas, Clark, Georgellis, & Diener, 2004), depression (Howe, Levy, & Kaplan, 2004), and suicidality (Fergusson, Boden, & Horwood, 2007). In addition, Beck (2016), among others, has detailed the negative impact of male unemployment on partners and families.

Therapists working with long-term unemployed or underemployed clients need to be sensitive to the fiscal, psychological, and relational aspects of unemployment. Most of the research has indicated that it is male unemployment that is characteristically most problematic. Therapeutic intervention often begins with the clients' methods to find new employment and the importance of teamwork and support from the spouse. There also needs to be some differentiation between what constitutes help and what is received as nagging and disapproving.

Solvable Problems

Fortunately, many couple problems do have viable solutions. Most of the time, with therapeutic support and encouragement, couples can courageously face and overcome obstacles. However, sometimes therapists can be active in helping them to solve their problems directly.

In describing problem solving here, our focus is less on the problem solution per se, but on the development of problem-solving skills. Christensen and colleagues (2004) and Epstein and Baucom (2002) have established a five-step process for problem solving in couple therapy:

1. problem definition
2. creating a list of possible solutions
3. examining the pluses and minuses of each
4. agreeing on a mutually acceptable solution and
5. monitoring each partner's progress

A more extensive behavioral method is provided by Cordova and Mirgain (2004).

These procedures are especially viable when there is a solution that seems obvious to the therapist but is unknown or unconsidered by clients. For example, when a couple claims to have no affordable child care to allow them to go out for a few hours, the therapist may explore what they have tried, questioning whether there were family help available, friends, local babysitters that would not be too expensive, and so on. The recommendation may be to trade child care with another couple who they know well.

> C: We have no family in the area. When they visit from out of town, they do encourage us to leave the kids with them for an evening. We have friends, but they also have kids.

---

4 There is insufficient research and data on the impact in same-sex couples to draw conclusions at this time.

T: My experience is that having four children to feed and put to bed at night isn't much more work than two.

C: That's true. Are you recommending we trade kids sometimes?

T: It's a distinct possibility. How does it sound to you?

C: You know the Clark kids are about the same age and they all get along. Maybe we could give them a night out and they could give us one.

T: Is that worth checking out with the Clarks?

C: I could do that tomorrow. We have a play date together.

The therapist then monitors if it happens and what results there are. It is of particular interest therapeutically if they find ways to avoid finding a problem solution. That may lead to far more important discussions of what they fear if they achieved the goals they said they wanted (and lost the complaint/excuse).

In this way, the problem-solving recommendation will have a therapeutic yield whether it works or doesn't, leading to a deeper discussion. In fact, the more obvious the solution, the more likely having a problem is covering something more threatening psychologically for the couple.

For Rick and Codi, both occurred. They were married for 18 months when they came in for therapy and had recently bought a condominium. They both held over six-figure income positions in high-tech Silicon Valley firms. Although they worked hard, they had most evenings and weekends free. During the third session they came in looking exhausted.

T: You both seem very tired today (wondering about depression).

R: It's been a tough week.

T: What made it more difficult than others?

C: We both had big meetings on Friday and then there was the usual weekend work. When the therapist looked quizzical, she continued,

C: You know we spend the weekend catching up, shopping, cleaning, chores, washing the cars—the usual.

R: This weekend was worse than usual. We had a lot of extra laundry and then washing the floors, dusting ... cleaning the toilets was no fun.

As this went on, the therapist wondered why they were doing all those tasks by themselves and why they had no help. He was also aware that both Rick and Codi commonly responded to direct suggestions with "yes, but" answers. In addition, he wondered whether there was an unknown financial issue, despite their combined high salaries. To offer a potential problem solution, first and foremost, he knew he had to have it be their idea. He decided to intervene by allowing them their usual reactions. In short, he found a way to go with their natural automatic resistance.

> T: I am curious. What made you decide to not have a cleaning service come in and do the floor, dusting toilets, and so on?

There could be reasons for such a decision, such as not wanting strangers in their home, feeling like they had to clean the condo before the cleaners came in, and so on, but none of those arose. Instead, they looked at each other quizzically and then Codi asked Rick naively, "Could we afford something like that?" He responded with, "I think so," and asked the therapist how much something like that would cost. They also asked the therapist if he had such a service and would he be willing to give them the name.

> T: I'd recommend that you check with your friends and see what they do.

They came in the next session and reported that they had found a person to clean the condo and when they came home on Friday, everything was even better than they had hoped. Problem solved! Right? Not so fast!
As the session evolved from self-congratulatory to drifting, the therapist intervened:

> T: What are we not talking about today?

As they looked at one another warily and finally consented nonverbally, Codi began:

> C: You know we had the weekend free and no chores, but we didn't really use it well. We went out with some friends (the ones who recommended the cleaner) but not much else.

> T: What had you hoped for that didn't occur?

> C: Well. Is this okay, Rick? Rick has not had much sexual interest for me the past few months. We even tried this weekend, but he couldn't get into it and we stopped.

The therapy then took a major turn into their sexual desire issues, which had been obfuscated by floor mopping and toilet cleaning.[5]
Finally, some clients need fairly direct problem-solving advice when they are about to engage in behavior that will serve them poorly.

---

5 At this point, assessment could be made to ascertain if referral to a specialist in sex therapy would be useful. However, with a couple like this, *anhedonia* (problems with lack of desire) is most likely the problem. The classic text on this topic is by Kaplan (1979).

Doc and Savannah were in a long-term cohabiting relationship when they came in a week and a half following a party that got out of control. At a neighbor's house the prior weekend, where there was a surfeit of alcohol and cocaine, Doc had ended up in the bedroom with the hostess. He apologized, blaming being high, but Savannah remained very upset. Apparently in the week in between, the husband of the woman with whom Doc had sex contacted Savannah and recommended that the two of them get together and get even by having sex with one another.

Doc was actually encouraging this liaison during the session, but the therapist was thinking the entire time, "That's a terrible idea." She recommended that Savannah not jump into the solution, adding that she could take the action if she wanted later. Instead, she worked with Savannah to explore what it would mean to her and to encourage her to do what felt consistent with her values rather than take Doc's recommendation of the two wrongs negating each other.

> S: I don't think I should. It seems wrong. I don't even like the guy and I have never cheated in my life.

> T: It sounds like you know that it would be a very bad idea for you. That's a good sign not to do it. Let's look for a better solution that doesn't involve violating your personal values.

Fostering Resilience

In any relationship, each partner is likely to step inadvertently on the emotional toes of the other. It may be through action toward or against the other or it may occur through perceived insensitivity and non-action. Regardless of the reasons, harboring resentment and focusing on loss may be protective against further insults in the short term, but will also create walls between individuals. Repeated insults, name-calling, and cursing the other are like little slings and arrows that open up into larger wounds during times of extreme stress.

For many couple therapists, helping clients involves developing resilience to weather the daily or even chronic stressors in a relationship. Resilience refers primarily to the extent to which an individual or a couple can bounce back psychologically from the negative impact of anything, from relational disappointments to trauma.

Resilience as a construct has been widely described as a component of positive psychology (e.g., Forbes & Fikretoglu, 2018) that has several elements, including the ability to adapt and evolve to new situations after experiencing stressors. Many other authors in positive psychology include components of these abilities, including the following:

1. Having or recreating a positive self-image
2. Using effective problem-solving skills, especially novel ones
3. Flexibility/adaptability, including a willingness to attempt alternative perspectives
4. Developing an optimistic outlook
5. Being hopeful
6. Having and developing social support

In *Supersurvivors,* Feldman and Kravetz (2015) describe three commonalties in uniquely resilient individuals:

1. A grounding in what could be changed and what could not
2. An optimistic view of the future along with a slightly inflated view of the ability to control one's own destiny
3. A solid support group

When couples are in the midst of a relational crisis, they often have a tendency to shut down and to become more conservative, holding on tightly to the status quo, even if it is painful. To enhance resilience, therapists first have to help clients find their current strengths and then, with support, try to experiment with new behaviors.

Quotes from two great baseball players of the 1940s and 1950s capture some important aspects of resilience. Pitcher Bob Feller once opined, "Every day is a new opportunity. You can build on yesterday's success or put its failures behind and start over again. That's the way life is, with a new game every day, and that's the way baseball is." (Dickson, 2011; p. 80) Ted Williams, perhaps the greatest hitter who ever lived, put misses into a positive perspective, "Baseball is the only field of endeavor where a man can succeed three times out of ten and be considered a good performer." (Palmer, Gillette & Shea, 2007; p. 265)

Forgiveness

Often the healing salve for both crises and chronic disagreements is an increasing awareness of ways to enhance forgiveness and reduce distance. It is important to note that the clients do not forget what occurred. Instead, they must let go of the emotional valence and of the desire for revenge or permanent blame and distance.

Russell, Baker, McNulty, and Overall (2018) note the inevitability of hurt in close relationships, whether by commission or omission, and we would include failure to meet often unrevealed expectations. Living daily with continuing hurts can be burdensome at best and emotionally draining. Focusing on revenge, internal avoidance, or balancing the emotional hurt slate keeps primary attention to the past slights instead of a better present and future. By contrast, forgiveness is associated with benefits to both parties (Bono, McCullough, & Root, 2008; DeWall & Richman, 2011) and the relationship itself (Fincham & Beach, 2007).

However, forgiveness alone without confrontation can sometimes lead to continuation of the undesirable behavior (McNulty & Russell, 2016). As DeWall and Richman (2011) indicate, reciprocity is an important element in any longer-term positive impact of forgiveness. This matches folk wisdom. For example, in the traditional, ancient Hawaiian corrective ceremony *Ho'oponopono,* healing begins when both aggrieved parties offer mutual apology and forgiveness.

Actual effective forgiveness involves acknowledging and confronting the insulting behaviors or lack of responsiveness, refocusing inward on the reasons for the emotional pain, increasing differentiation (e.g., Scharff and Scharff, 2014), and reducing the impulse for revenge. This combination provides the partner with a signal that the hurt party is willing to continue the relationship with appropriate changes. Of course, forgiveness may be impossible or unlikely when the act is egregious. Among the "unforgivable" acts we have observed are cheating, violence, theft, or other betrayals, although these do not necessarily lead to a breaking of the relationship. When past grievances are repeatedly brought into an argument, one strategy is to inquire, "How much more do you need to mention this to your partner?" Pressing for a commitment may lead to reflection and a decrease in the repetitive interaction, but it can also lead to a process of resolution.

When helping generate forgiveness, therapists often move the entire process into the therapy sessions. There are several phases that a therapist may recommend:

1. Airing of the complaint and the manner of hurt
2. Confrontation
3. The other party hearing the hurt and reflecting back the reasons an action might be so painful
4. A sincere, heartfelt apology
5. Acceptance of the apology
6. Requesting additional hurts by both parties
7. Finding a method to move forward in the relationship or to end it

Rituals as Preventative and Corrective

One method of being more experimental to enhance both resilience and forgiveness is for the couple to create rituals that promote more positive interactions. The goal and method of such behaviors are to encourage couples to try new things or recapture old methods in the face of the formidable pull of the status quo for presumed safety. The kinds of rituals recommended are often only small steps away from the norm, are presented as "experiments," and create means for newer interactions and actions as a couple.

Therapeutic rituals have multiple functions:

1. Get the couple working together as a team instead of as individuals trying to protect themselves psychologically and emotionally
2. Develop greater adaptability in the face of undesirable or unexpected stressors
3. Break out of patterns that have become anachronistic; those that once were effective but have become increasingly unhelpful
4. Build on strengths, rather than weaknesses
5. Increase tolerance for minor annoyances
6. Increase the ability to assert one's preferences when needed

For example, when a couple is stuck in the day-to-day existence of making a living, caring for children, connecting with families of origin, doing what is needed in their community, and just keeping on top of the myriad chores that are necessary to keep a home afloat, they often seek help. They wonder if they have fallen out of love, report that they don't like their lives, often feel disconnected and may blame each other for various miseries, and have increasing escape fantasies.

Katie and Marco had been together for a decade. They described a "storybook romance," followed by marriage, children, a mortgage, and significant distancing. They both talked longingly about rare adult vacations of even a few days.

Recently they had been keeping score about who did more of the childcare and who was contributing more to household expenses. Their relationship was devolving into a quid pro quo ambiance. Their therapist recommended that they arrange for two meetings per week: a work meeting—to deal with the household, children issues, and job disquiet—and a date night. In the date night meeting, she recommended that the couple talk primarily about their relationship and engage in enjoyable things they do on a date.

> M: We barely have time to finish chores and fall into bed exhausted; when could we schedule two meetings a week?

> T: I don't know if you are saying you don't like the idea or if it's too hard.

> K: If I know Marco, it's both.

> T: How about you Katie? Do you like the idea?

> K: I like it, but it makes me anxious.

After exploring the anxiety with Katie, she turned to Marco and asked, "Is a date night something you would like if you had the time?" When he assented, she asked him to talk to Katie about her anxiety.

When she claimed that the biggest risk was that the dates would fail, the therapist increased the pressure slightly.

> T: It may well fail, and you could just be like always. Or, perhaps, it might have a potential for changing things without a downside risk, unless you want to keep the distance.

They agreed to try it and found that the most difficult part was to keep the "business" from seeping into and flooding the date night. They then explored how they could separate it, and Marco made the suggestion that they had to get out of town to really be on a date.

> T: So, when you get away, you can relax into a real date, and if you stay close to home, the business and home problems are hard to avoid. How far away do you have to get?

> K: We could go to Palo Alto (about 6 miles away) or the city (an hour's drive).

> T: Would that be enough, Marco?

> M: It's worth a try. The last time we just went to the restaurant we take the kids to, so mostly we talked about how much they would like to be along.

Rather than focus on their capacity to subvert the chance for a new ritual, the therapist continued to help them find a way to enhance the chances. Their tendencies to sabotage the novel and favor the predictable would be addressed once they had a few new rituals in place. However, if a couple continues to undermine the intent of a date night, the intervention may involve confronting by pointing out the consistent failure and what value failing has for them. It's important for the therapist to not accept the issue of lack of time and to assert the importance of reconnection if their relationship is to improve. At the same time, approximations to higher goals are important, such as "Your only goal on date night is to enjoy each other's company and not to have a wild romantic evening."

There are a number of reasons why it is wise to schedule the two meetings instead of just a date night. The most important is to designate a non-work time in their week. By scheduling a work meeting for those necessary conversations, it sets off more clearly the reason for a date night.

Date Nights

One form of resistance to date nights involves complaints about the cost. As Mindy replied, "We just can't afford to go out on our budget. Between babysitters, a meal, and a movie, it's over $100. We just don't have that kind of money." One plan of response we like is to set the date up to be inexpensive.

> T: You are right. That could easily be $100. What I have in mind is a lot less expensive. In fact, I'd like you to plan a date where you spend $5 or less (except for transportation). Most couples complain that it's not possible and then get into quite creative ways of having such a date. Some even comment, "It's like when we were in school and couldn't afford it."

Tillich (2016) describes a method he and his colleagues have for a month of weekly date nights. The first is to have one member of the couple plan the evening, especially the one who rarely plans events together. The second week is to have the other person do the planning. The third evening goes back to the first person with instructions to create a date night that would please his or her partner. Finally, the partner gets to create a mate-pleasing date. One interesting component of this ritual is that couples do know how to please their partners, and those who are pleasantly surprised by the pleasing date feel closer and better understood.

Preventative Guidelines and Behaviors That Can Be Encouraged

It is commonplace for therapists to recommend certain rituals for couples to help them navigate through the straits of life. There is no doubt that external pressures and distractions can have a deleterious effect on a primary relationship. As couples adjust to new realities and inevitable life transition, their status quo is disrupted and they struggle to get the relational ship back in line to avoid foundering on the rocks.

In addition to the scheduled work and play times to connect weekly, there are some other recommended actions that are designed for positive interactions:

1. Find ways to laugh together both at external issues and at personal frailties.
2. Hold the partner in high regard. This often involves being and expressing thankfulness, showing respect for a partner's opinion and manner, and generally appreciating what the partner brings to the relationship. Treat the partner as the most important person in the world, reminding him or her to treat his or her partner as respectfully as he or she does his or her close friends and family.
3. Stay curious about the partner, his or her history, opinions, and ways of adjusting to life.
4. Recognize that the relationship is a team effort that each adds to it. It is not the property of either person.
5. Do small romantic things. Try to recall and repeat some of the mating gifts and behaviors. Do things to let the partner know he or she is in your thoughts.
6. Try to keep sexual intimacy alive. Plan times to be together. Couples who wait for it to occur spontaneously often don't find the time.
7. Listen, listen, listen to what the partner is saying rather than finishing his or her sentences and thinking up a retort. This is a significant characteristic of what Doherty (2013) calls "intentional relating."
8. Talk to each other without smartphone, TV, or other electronic interruptions.
9. Therapists often prescribe certain rituals for couples to keep these guidelines in place.

Couples thrive when they repeat the kinds of things that were so appealing during courtship and the early days of a relationship. They often need structures or rituals to help them get back to those things that nurture them. The rituals that follow are just a small sample of ideas that experts have generated to help couples maintain the good times and prevent the harder times from taking a major toll on the relationship.

A Few Common Rituals

1. Schedule two separate times together to meet weekly: one for business and one for pleasure (aka date night).
2. Eat a meal together without electronic distractions. This may be possible only once a day or every other day, but eating and talking together without interruptions is valuable. A "check in" every day is essential, however brief, to see how the other is doing. Therapists often have couples put those special meals on a calendar to help keep sacred. Sometimes this recommendation is prompted when one or both members of the couple check their phones during therapy sessions.
3. Develop a ritual for leaving and greeting. It may be a kiss hello and goodbye. It may be a reminder of love. It may involve honoring unwinding time when a partner returns from work. One couple worked out a 30-minute buffer for the husband when his work was done, followed by his co-cooking the evening meal and reading to the children at bedtime.
4. Do something physical together on a regular basis. An evening walk, exercising together, family outings to a park, and so on are all functional rituals.

5. Being quiet and de-stressing together. One couple was instructed to turn off the evening news and to quietly listen to music and read for 30 minutes, something they came to regard as their "holy hour." This can also be called a daily check-in at a set time.

6. Floyd (2006) and Gottman and Gottman (2006) recommend what they call a 6-second kiss to indicate more connection than a perfunctory peck on the lips. Therapists who recommend this often predict that it will be harder than it sounds and that they may laugh the first few times.

7. Gottman and Gottman (2006) also recommend that each couple set aside six hours a week just for each other, an example of Doherty's (2013) "intentional time." This may be impossible for some, but at least a few hours per week are critical to maintaining a sense of "we-ness."

8. Schedule time for physical and/or emotional intimate connection each week.

9. Build traditions for celebrating holiday, anniversary and birthdays.

10. Practice having each person take a turn to declare what she or he wants without justification.

These couple rituals can take many forms and often should be planned and discussed with the therapist present. For example, with the declaration of desires, it is essential that the therapist interrupt discussions of justification, rationales, or comparative evaluations. The therapist is most effective when he or she directs each person to listen to the desire of the partner and take it in. This doesn't mean he or she agrees, only that he or she is listening and heard.

T: Cindy. Tell Bart what you want from him this evening.

C: Well, he gives great massages and I have been on my feet all day and really want one of his foot massages. It's only fair because I made him a special dinner and lunch this week and I also did two of his errands, besides—

T: (Cutting Cindy off mid-sentence) Cindy. I want you to say it again. This time I want you to stop after the word "massage."

C: But I think he owes.

T: (Cutting Cindy off again) Do you want a massage or not? (When Cindy nods affirmatively) Okay. Just tell him you want a massage this evening and when.

C: I really need a massage. Would you give me one?

T: I want a foot massage. Would you give me one?

B: I don't know what errands you did for me. I took in your cleaning and got Billy from T-ball to help you.

T: Bart. Please respond only to the request for a massage. When the two of you get into justifications, you get nowhere. So, Cindy has just asked you for a massage tonight. Are you open to that?

B: Yeah. I like to give her massages.

T: Tell her!

B: Cindy. What time would you like the massage? Oh. Would you like it with massage oil? I can get some on the way home.

Later, the therapist also asked Bart to tell Cindy what he wanted and gave them an assignment to set up a 10-minute "free ask, no justification" zone each day. To no surprise, the therapist had to also interrupt him and get him to ask Cindy directly. In similar fashion, the therapist must be alert to those who assertively express a desire to their partner and accompany it with a grievance from the past. The process must stop at this point and attend to when and how the past can be put aside in favor of trusting the partner to do better in the future.

SUMMARY

In Chapter 7, basic techniques of couple therapy were described. In this chapter, the more advanced, longer-term, structurally oriented techniques are detailed. As with the earlier chapter, all techniques must be culturally and personally sensitive to the clients; they must actually reinforce behaviors that are pleasing to each partner rather than be "stock" items that may work for some but not others. No technique should seem out of line with the ongoing discussions.

Instead they should seem natural extensions or small experiments that couples try together.

The chapter began with the need for structural shifts for intrusions that came from inside or outside the primary relationship. The therapeutic triangle is proposed as an example of a positive structure break to help fix structural distortions. Structural breaks, such as affairs, are briefly described, along with methods to create and repair relational boundaries. The basic structural concept is that committed couples must be first and foremost emotionally, psychologically, and physically aligned with each other, rather than with extended family, children, or outsiders in order to be functional. Techniques used when the larger context is involved are described. These techniques must take into account family of origin, multigenerational transmission of relational beliefs, cultural considerations including immigration and socialization, and socioeconomic-induced distress. The chapter concludes with a presentation of advanced techniques such as feedback, confrontation and saying the unsayable, paradoxical intentions and directives, restraining, and levels of affect and problem solving. Active problem solving is related to forgiveness and therapeutic rituals.

9

Termination

It occurred to me that I had seen live demos, videos, and

role plays in class of about 15 different couple therapy intake sessions and

several examples of techniques and theories for the middle of couple therapy.

What I have never encountered in my training was a single termination.

Talk about feeling unprepared!

(A practicum student about to see her first couple as clients)

All therapy is designed to be ultimately expendable. It should only last as long as significant progress is being made and the couple is benefitting. The final stage of couple therapy, like all counseling and therapy, is termination. During termination, two essential tasks are paramount:

1. Transfer of training: taking what was learned in therapy sessions and applying it to the couple's everyday life
2. Dealing with loss (saying goodbye)

Termination may be instituted by a predetermined and agreed-on number of sessions; mutual agreement to end between both members of the couple and the therapist, by the couple or one member of the couple alone, the therapist alone, or by illnesses; or external forces such as work demands, family members in need, or required moves out of the area. These external forces may at times arbitrarily inhibit the power and outcome of the therapy. For example, the clinic, health services organization, or the third-party payer (insurance) may set arbitrary limits on number of sessions. There may be an annual decision by third-party payers to shift the provider list or coverage, making the couple no longer eligible for reimbursement for services with their current therapist.

The Process of Termination

Termination of couple therapy is not simply an acknowledgment that the allotted number of sessions has ended. This phase of therapy is as important in promoting lasting success as is intake or the earlier phases of therapy proper, described in the previous two chapters.

Collaboration between clients and therapists on goal setting, creating the alliance, approaches to treatment, techniques and strategies employed, and assessment have all been shown to be effective steps in all psychotherapy (Berdondini, Elliott, & Shearer, 2012; Dattilio & Hanna, 2012; Park, Goode, Tompkins, & Swift, 2016; Tryon & Winograd, 2011; Wiseman, Tishby, & Barber, 2012). Bachelor, Laverdière, Gamache, and Bordeleau (2007) claim that this kind of collaboration is actually a curative factor in therapy outcome and Swift, Callahan, and Vollmer (2011) report that it also results in fewer premature terminations.

Goode, Park, Parkin, Tomkins and Swift (2017) and Lebow (2014) extend this to effective termination. In fact, Swift and Derthick (2013) and Tompkins, Swift, and Callahan (2013) conclude that failure to include clients in early discussions of termination robs them of the opportunity to participate in, and take ownership of, a treatment decision, which could lead to increased hope, motivation, and beliefs of self-efficacy.

Termination Process as Universal Across Theories

This focus on the importance of termination is quite trans-theoretical. Lebow (2014), using a systems orientation, Blum (1989) and Cachia and Scharff (2018) exploring termination from a psychoanalytic perspective, and Shapiro (2019) describing termination for an existential therapist, all highlight the salience of proper termination for couples therapy. Similarly, Brown and Brown (2002) offer an extensive method for termination of CBT-informed couple therapy, concluding, "Termination of marital therapy should occur when the couple has reached their goals and do not wish to work on any related concerns. Any discussion to terminate should be made both by the therapist and the couple, and termination should occur when there is some way of evaluating the results of therapy." (p. 203).

Describing termination in group therapy, Jacobs, Schimmel, Masson, and Harvill (2016) include reviewing and summarizing, assessing members' growth, finishing business, implementing change, providing feedback, handling goodbyes, and planning for continuing problem resolution. These requirements of termination are also well suited to couple work.

For most therapists, much of the termination work occurs collaboratively and consistently throughout the couple sessions, beginning with the initial contact. However, during a termination phase in treatment it becomes paramount to maintain gains and prevent major relapses. The termination stage of therapy is the time for the couple to most poignantly confront their feelings about specific endings and general losses and engage in extensive future planning.

Transfer of Training

Meaningful use of couple counseling or therapy outcome must be based on the couple's everyday life. Better couple functioning that occurs solely within therapy sessions is insufficient. The therapeutic triangle that assisted the couple to break old patterns and create new ones has to become internalized by the clients and carried forward, without the active presence of the therapist. The couple has to own the skills, adapt them to new situations, and function as a two-person unit within the cultural setting in which they live.[1] Among the essential tasks in effective termination are establishing the couple as the full change unit, capable of maintaining, applying, and generalizing what was learned in the therapy sessions in their everyday life. It also involves future planning.

One of the most common and gratifying reports during sessions is when couples relate a between-session experience in which they describe a beginning fight that they caught early and truncated. Naming their therapist, they often say, "We did a "Susan" this week. As soon as we caught the fight we both said what you always say, and then we laughed."

Because they begin as a unit and go home together between sessions, couples work on transfer of training throughout the therapy sessions both within and between meetings. However, there are special areas of emphasis that are essential during the final phase of therapy.

When Does Termination Begin?

Most therapists acknowledge that termination begins with the initial contact. Whitaker (1988) said that he used a clipboard and note taking as a message to the couple or family that there was a boundary between him as therapist and them as clients. It's a message that includes separation as part of the relationship, even as it is forming.

Many behavioral and cognitive-behavioral couple therapists also remind us that transfer of training begins with the earliest contact and initial contract. In part, they do this by using a host of monitored assessment tools and homework assignments that can show progress to goals from the first through the final sessions.

Although termination begins with the first contact, it becomes a primary focus of the therapy when the therapist or members of the couple identify the imminent end of the regular sessions.[2] Although there is often not an immediate response, perhaps reflecting a denial of the imminent end of the relationship, after the second or third reminder, the couple begins to focus both on transfer of training and on saying goodbye (which often elicits other relationship losses in members' lives).

It is essential to plan and prepare for termination well in advance. Most therapists structure approximately 25% of the total time in therapy around the tasks of transfer of training and saying goodbye. Some, such as Brown and Brown (2002), recommend a

---

1   The role of the extended family or nuclear family is typically culturally determined. Success for one couple may not resemble that for a couple within a different cultural context.

2   As mentioned earlier, weekly sessions are the most common format, but hardly universal. Usually, lengths of sessions and frequency are set by the client (or sometimes the therapist or agency) needs or what a third party dictates. The use of wider spreads between sessions is more often found during the termination process.

gradual withdrawal by implementing a reduction in meeting frequency to consolidate adaptation to everyday functioning. Thus, they recommend separating the last few sessions by increasing time intervals to both highlight that the couple will be able to adjust on their own and to minimize dependence on the therapist. However, the frequency of sessions is largely determined pragmatically, depending on the clients' and the therapist's availability.

Some Steps in the Transfer-of-Training Process

Particularly in short-term couple therapy, a specific termination is often known in advance (e.g., due to insurance coverage limitations, a known, imminent client move, a therapist transfer, a student or intern placement ending). Therapists may regularly remind clients of the upcoming date and focus attention on the best use of in-session time as the deadline approaches.

The steps in the termination process involve *summary review* of what has worked and not worked in session and in any homework. This review can be very helpful in identifying major themes addressed and areas of strength and growth for the couple moving forward.

The therapist and client can also jointly develop a *future plan* for the client's continued growth. This future plan is best when it offers realistic predictions of posttreatment life, including likely challenges, relapses, and reminders of resources to address likely future setbacks. A significant component of this is a review of the strengths the couple has developed and an expression of a positive expectation that they are now better equipped to deal with the problems life throws at them. This may also include personal resources in their lives, who could provide help and support.

It is often worth describing how when anxiety arises, the couple jointly does something to support the status quo, even when that homeostasis is disruptive and painful. When they can remember that the stresses are caused in some part by an intended protective adaptation, they can recognize it as a relational protection (that might be overzealous) and address it together.

Finally, any possible *future relationship* with the therapist might be included in this discussion (Greenberg, 2002). Future contacts with the therapist are far more common in couple work than in individual or group treatment. The possibility of future contact and the nature of such contact must be cautiously offered. If future contact is available and useful, the therapist might pose a hypothetical question such as, "What could occur to cause you to bring the problem back in for treatment?"

Under some circumstances, the therapist may not be available for in-person meetings. Is it then viable to meet by online, phone, or other means? Alternatively, therapists who operate from a psychodynamic perspective with a strong therapeutic frame (e.g., Langs, 1981) may be less open to post-termination contact.

When it is available, the offer of future availability must be proffered in such a way that does not either minimize the important work of termination or create additional sessions primarily for the benefit of the therapist (Shapiro, 2010).

Some Indications That It Is Time for Termination

Particularly in longer-term couple therapy where there is not a pre-set limit on number of sessions, the therapist and clients together have to determine when it is best to begin the termination process and end the regular sessions. Several criteria are useful in determining the best time to begin:

1. The goal of therapy is reached or discarded for a better solution
2. The couple is working increasingly well as a team, addressing problems that occur. They do this respectfully and listen to each other, valuing (although not necessarily agreeing with) the input from their partner
3. Defensive responses and negative views of the partner's motivations are diminished. Their traditional battles are viewed as ways to keep the status quo going, and they both strive to minimize knee-jerk reactions; consider their respective needs for security and predictability; and find alternative, less destructive or insulting means to achieve it
4. They demonstrate fondness and caring for one another, admiring what each brings to the relationship. They make the partner and relationship primary
5. They make evident their successes, taking what was learned and practiced in therapy and applying those skills to new challenges
6. They each take care of themselves psychologically, without requiring the partner to anticipate and compensate by filling in their emotional needs. Each focuses on personal vulnerabilities and potential triggers. Once aware, they share the reasons for and manner of activation with their partners
7. At the same time, they demonstrate openness to give and receive care taking from their partner
8. After arguments or difficulties, they are able to reset and try again, considering the interpersonal problems as relational rather than the partner's fault
9. They show regard and trust for partner's way of doing things
10. They share humor

When these are in place or well on the way to fruition, the need for ongoing therapy is not only unnecessary, but continuing beyond that point may potentially undermine the confidence in the progress they are making on their own.

The Final Goodbye, or *Au Revoir*?

One aspect of the transfer-of-training sequence is the procedure for the final session. If the therapy has been collaborative between the couple and the therapist, some mutual sharing of the personal impact of the therapy may be in order. The extent of such discussions is typically related to the therapist's theory and personal comfort. Existential and humanistic approaches (e.g., Mackrill, 2010; Shapiro, 2016), are more likely to indicate that this will be a significant part of the final session. When a therapist shares gratitude about what the therapy process has meant to her or him with the couple, he or she is telling the couple about his or her positive impact on relationships outside of him- or herself, even when those relationships are time limited.

Sometimes, clients will actually ask. When the Whites were in their 12th and final session, he asked their therapist, "So what was it like working with us? I suppose this is just like an old hat for you. You may not even remember us in 2 years." The therapist replied, "Actually, this has been a very meaningful time for me as well. I am very excited that things are going so much better for you both, and I think you'll have a great future. What you were dealing with when you came in was a really daunting problem ... It's also been a growth experience for me. I liked working with you and we all learned new things together. I really appreciate that you placed so much trust in my and in our work." Then chuckling, she added, "Besides, you are not all that forgettable!"

In a note the Whites sent to her 4 years later, they both commented on how much her last words meant to them. They added, "The fact that you were moved by our story made us both feel stronger and able to handle the (inevitable) crises that came up since." The note was emblematic of the value of closure and equalizing the relationship to enhance the couple's sense of self-sufficiency post therapy (Greenberg, 2002).

Can We Be Friends?

Particularly, but not solely in rural areas, therapists and ex-clients share a community and may run into one another in other aspects of their lives such as school, youth sporting events, universities, classes, gyms, weddings, and other celebrations or political activities. Sometimes, after couple therapy is done, a client may invite the therapist to an event.

Although all such contact is not necessarily unethical, it can be problematic, and it is advisable to discuss potential conflicts of interest with the clients ahead of the end of therapy. The general rule of thumb is to let the clients make the initial acknowledgment or initiate contact in a chance meeting and then be courteous and professional. Accepting invitations may be problematic.

Some examples of those kinds of meetings we or our colleagues have experienced is a chance meeting in the shower of an athletic club, having a substitute doctor (an ex-patient) do a physical examination, sitting close to someone at a ball game, coaching a child of a couple seen in therapy, social events, and having a former client in couple work take a graduate class in couple therapy.

This is similar to issues like gifts proffered at the last session. The general rules of thumb is that it is best to accept small gifts, preferably homemade (like baked goods for the office staff), or if it would be a cultural insult or microaggression to refuse. If the gift has great value or seems like a tip for services, it is best to politely refuse and explain that it's against policy.

Examples of such offers include a new smartphone or watch by a couple who worked at the company that makes them or offers of expensive athletic tickets by a member of a couple who worked in the front office of the team. Rather than accept, it is imperative to explore the meaning such a gift has and what consequences it might have for the clients.

Saying Goodbye

The second task of termination is for the therapist to let the clients emerge from the treatment in the manner in which they desired, as expressed by their evolving goals. This is not always as easy as it may seem on the surface. Unlike many professional and service-related experiences, couple therapy involves a very intimate connection. Therapists are involved in the communication between partners. They are privy to secrets and very personal sensitive information. The end of such interactions, although often desired, may elicit in clients' memories and experiences of other losses of people who have been close. As Shapiro (2016) notes, from an existential perspective, all significant personal losses may bring up fears of ultimate losses like mortality.

Most people are far more comfortable with hello's than goodbye's. Some languages and cultures have less discrete demarcations than is common in North America. For example, "kwaheri" expresses good bye and good wishes in Swahili, the Hebrew word *shalom* and the Hawaiian *aloha* convey both hello and goodbye (along with the former's "peace" and the latter's "love"). Other languages distinguish between soft and hard goodbyes. The French *au revoir* and the German *auf Wiedersehen* are examples of temporary goodbyes. Similarly, in Russian, *do skorova* means "until soon" while *do svidanya* is a more permanent goodbye. In North America, regardless of the specifics of the parting, endings can be problematic. The most difficult ending for a therapist is when clients cancel treatment and do not provide an explanation.

Because goodbyes are often difficult, many couples in therapy try to avoid it. This can be done by asking the therapist for additional couple sessions or a promise to meet again for check-ins, requesting individual sessions, divulging a previously undisclosed problem, or even an expression of a heretofore unknown crisis at the last moment.

When their marriage counselor Sarah began a session stating, "It's good to keep in mind that we have only three more scheduled appointments," the initial response from Dina and Bill was to keep going as if Sarah had not spoken. She reminded them again about half way through the session, requesting that the three of them focus on any "unfinished business," at which point the room fell silent.

S: Tell me what's happening now!

D: I know this is a professional relationship, but I am going to miss you. On our walk yesterday, we were talking about how much better we are.

B: Yeah, we wondered if we could see you maybe once every month or two just to check in.

S: We can discuss what kinds of arrangements would suit you best, but let's focus for a few minutes on what you've accomplished so far. (Smiling) I have a list here, but I wonder what's on your lists first.

After they discussed their successes, Sarah proceeded to work with them on transfer of training such as how they could maintain those gains, potential pitfalls, and signs that they may need future help. Not until the next session did she bring up the meaning of the ending with them.

S: You both had a strong reaction last week to the reminder that we had only a few sessions left. I wonder what our meetings ending brought up for you?

D: It was feeling a lot like when my favorite aunt moved away to Florida for retirement. She was the person who was always on my side.

B: It was worse for me. I was reminded of people who died and my losses of close relatives and friends.

S: So, losing our sessions brought up other losses for you both. Let's talk about those.

Much later, Sarah helped them build a bridge to each other for mutual support during times of hurt, sadness, and feelings of loss. These issues are important, and some sense of potential closure may greatly enhance the outcome of the entire therapeutic endeavor. Because it can be quite time consuming, sufficient in-session time needs to be allotted for the issues to emerge and be addressed.

This is especially so if the therapist asks a question such as, "Is there something that is important to you in your life that we have yet to address? Maybe something you've had no reason to bring up here as yet." Another form of this question may be, "What have we not discussed in therapy?" Sometimes a couple will reveal very surprising (and important) clinical issues. These may include histories of abuse, sexual "secrets," extended family concerns, or psychiatric and medical histories.

One couple revealed that they had met when he was a priest in her parish. He was a constant visitor to her home while her first husband was alive. He provided solace during her mourning his death from brain cancer at a very young age and was close with both her children. Several months later, he decided to leave the priesthood and they married. They said in therapy that they moved soon after that and never told others in their new community about his being a former priest. They also had neglected to mention it during intake, when they responded to a question about how they met. Their holding on to this "secret" had caused them to be much less social and less in touch with community support, including their church community. That became a central issue in the termination process.

Termination: Hard or Soft?

One of the factors that Sarah mentioned, that continuing sessions may be negotiated, has a number of implications: procedural, ethical, therapeutic, and financial. In individual therapy, promises of continuing sessions after the contracted limit are relatively uncommon. Although clients may come back for another round of therapy at some point, a "hard" termination is usually recommended, if for no other reasons than to enhance closure and impact of therapy, and because of the potential financial implications for both clients and therapists. In couple work, hard termination may be less common (e.g., Lebow, 2014), although for therapists who work with a tight therapeutic frame (Langs, 1981), such as many psychodynamically oriented practitioners, the termination is usually very firm, similar to that in individual therapy.

Soft Terminations in Couple Therapy

It is fairly common for couple therapy to have less concrete terminations. For one thing, couple work is characteristically short term and focused on a particular issue or problem. In addition, many couples return for follow-up, check-in, refresher or new concerns, especially if a new life transition makes their current homeostasis less effective. They frequently return to the same therapist if the prior work has been successful.

When the time between later sessions is stretched out, support may be offered for changes the couple has made. The therapist also has an opportunity to express confidence that the couple can handle new life crises with their new skills. This may lead to "softer" adieus. Some researchers, such as Jacobson and Addis (1993), have concluded that follow-up "booster" sessions may also minimize the pain of loss.

Avoidance of Termination

Because of the issues around loss, couples can be fairly creative in creating barriers to termination. There may be denial that the relationship is actually ending: "We can still call you, right?" They may respond to the perceived rejection with anger and reactive rejection of the therapist: "You are only seeing us for the money. Besides, it'll be great to have Tuesday evenings back." They may request additional time for weaning (and establishing their right to end their way): "We were discussing this and would like to see you monthly for a few months to make sure it's going well."

More problematic are clients who develop new symptoms or interpersonal crises: "You know, I should have mentioned this earlier, but because of Adele's snoring, we've been sleeping in separate rooms." Finally, some couples try to change the relationship: "Would it be possible to become friends in the future? Like could either of us invite you to a party at our home or go get a cup of coffee sometime?" "Would you be open to friending us on _____ (a social media site)?"

A frequent issue is when treatment has reached maximum benefit, as indicated in the APA Ethical Principles and Code of conduct: (a) Psychologists terminate therapy when it becomes reasonably clear that the client/patient no longer needs the service, is not likely to benefit, or is being harmed by continued service. (APA, 2017.) Clients may feel they have little to replace the convivial discussions they've had with the therapist, and therapists my be anxious about a decline in their caseload. All of these may be considered resistance to the fear of change and the unknown. The most effective approach is for therapists to be aware of these anxieties and help the couple understand and contain them by working with the clients on courage to face those fears.

Therapist Termination Losses

Couples are not alone in feeling the loss of special intimacy when a therapeutic relationship ends. Often, a couple therapist will have difficulty letting go of a successful relationship. One senior couple therapist likens it to the experience of launching a child and facing the empty (therapeutic) nest. There is a desire to keep in touch in anticipation of them doing well.

If the therapist does experience these emotions, such as a sense of loss or personal sadness, and if it is unexamined, there could be a temptation to subtly maintain contact by reengaging with additional sessions, or by accepting the "friend" request that comes over their personal social media account. Of course, this can be exacerbated by the therapist's personal social or financial needs. Any such issue that creates greater dependence on the therapist or fails to properly refocus the couple on their feelings of loss and out-of-therapy existence is best addressed with the therapist's own consultant or personal therapist. Although a therapist's open sense of loss with a terminating couple may be mentioned in session, the therapist's personal difficulties with termination and loss should not be addressed with the couple.

Needs for Reassurance

For providers of human services, self-evaluation of personal impact is potentially problematic. Long-term outcomes are rarely known at termination. Some assessment tools that measure or scale differences from intake to termination may be quite helpful. Sometimes the couple's self-reports are used, and frequently the therapist's internal yardsticks suffice. However, these measures may be subject to some doubts, concerns, and misperceptions from a therapist who wonders,

1. "Have I done enough to let them launch?"
2. "How can I be sure this couple has received the best that I have to offer?"
3. "Is my job with them really complete?"

Sometimes the therapist's needs may not be conscious. It is no surprise that an important motivator for mental health professionals are needs to give and receive nurturance. Many were drawn to the helping professions by personal experiences and needs. Anyone unaware of these personal influences may be susceptible to low self-esteem when they are unsure of our impact on others. As one therapist recently opined, "As long as I am seeing a couple and they are making (even slow) progress, I feel great. My problem occurs when a couple graduates from therapy. I no longer have the instant feedback in sessions. Every termination feels like my final oral exam." The end result of such insecurity can make termination procrastination tempting.

A Lack of Training in Termination

The quotation from a practicum student in an MFT training program heading the chapter is not a surprise. A dearth of experience in professional terminations is a serious problem in our field. Most graduate programs that have classes in couples train new couple therapists fairly well on how to do an intake, and some even get decent training in theory-driven techniques. Virtually none cover the essentials and intricacies of termination of couple therapy.

In the first place, few graduate programs and predoctoral internships in the United States provide sufficient classwork and supervised practice to meet minimal criteria (Patterson, Shapiro, & Kelly, 2018). Given the short time periods allotted to learning about couple counseling and therapy generally, professors in graduate classes barely have the time and capacity to teach opening skills. The only way to learn middle and closing skills in couple work is to follow some couples longitudinally through the entire process. As essential as this process is, it is taught and learned infrequently, except on the job in supervised training.

Complicated Terminations

As if the material presented so far isn't sufficiently complex, it applies primarily to collaborative, well-planned terminations. As Lebow (2014) points out, these well-planned couple therapy terminations are often not the norm. For example, the couple may simply stop coming in and be unavailable to process the closure. This is not the lengthy and psychologically important termination often described in the literature, and it is not uncommon in couple therapy.

Premature Terminations

Sometimes, a couple decides to leave therapy suddenly. If at all possible, it is important for them to explore with the therapist their thinking and decision making.

THERAPY BOX 9.1: "GHOSTING" TERMINATION

Voice mail time stamp 4:35 p.m., Thursday:

"Hi Dr. T.: This is Mary Jones. Sorry for the late notice. Joe and I will not be able to come in today for our 5:00 p.m. appointment. The sitter got caught in traffic and couldn't make it here when she was supposed to come. Also, Joe is traveling for work the next 2 weeks and the next week after that is our son's birthday. We will call for our next appointment. I think we have to pay for today because the notice is so late for our missed appointment. I'll put a check in the mail."

The couple, who had eight sessions previously, never contacted the therapist, nor did she send the check.

Dr. T. called after 3 weeks and left a voice mail. "Hi Joe and Mary. I have not heard from you folks about scheduling our next appointment. Please let me know your schedule and intentions. I will be able to meet at the usual time on Thursdays."

When he heard nothing for another month. He sent a bill for the missed session. There was no response.

Sometimes the termination is unrelated to the therapeutic alliance or the progress of therapy. Here is an e-mail message received by Dr. K.

THERAPY BOX 9.2: TERMINATION CAUSED BY EXTERNAL FACTORS

E-mail: October 7, 2018; 11:10 a.m.:

To: Dr, K.

From: Grace Lee

Subject: Another Insurance Change

Hello, Dr. K. This is Grace Lee (of Russell and Grace), and we have an appointment scheduled tomorrow at 5:00 p.m. I just got a letter from my insurance company saying that they have a new provider list. I checked and you are not on the list. I called my HR

(Continued)

Department and they said that if you are not on the list, we are no longer covered if we see you.

I called the new company and they said that there was a 6–12 month wait for doctors to join their panel. The provider recommended another therapist who we can see for three sessions. We have no idea who she is, but she is located a few blocks from you. Do you know her? Her name is Elena G. Her website says she does mindfulness and AEDP therapy for couples. What do you think we should do?

We would like to continue seeing you, but as you know we cannot pay out of pocket. The new co-pay is $25 per session, but only for three couple sessions.

Dr. K. called Marie immediately and asked her to come in for a consultation session for which she would charge only the co-pay the couple had been paying. She explained that three sessions with a new therapist would likely be insufficient and tried to work out a viable payment schedule on an income-related sliding scale. The Lees did not return, nor did she ever discover if they went to Ms. G.

Sometimes a couple will stop coming in temporarily or permanently after a particularly deep or painful session. Such anxiety-generated premature terminations are particularly troubling for a therapist.

Others who terminate prematurely are those who have difficulty expressing gratitude or other positive emotions. Instead of facing their fears of intimacy related to positive connection, they drop out. Conversely, couples for whom saying goodbye is particularly difficult in therapy (or in life in general) may truncate the painful process by ending it prematurely. In so doing, some couples need to find fault or express anger at something that either occurred or that they wish had happened but did not.

Exploring military couples in a VA setting, Doss and colleagues (2012) concluded that many couples left therapy prematurely. Similarly, Allgood and Crane (1991) reported that half or more of couples in a university or community clinic left prematurely. Both studies indicated that those couples who left therapy "distressed" had a greater reported deterioration over time, at least partially suggesting that these early unexpected terminations were a negative sign, especially when contrasted to the potential gains shown by distressed couples who stayed in therapy.

There are many questions about why premature terminations may be so common. In a qualitative study of premature dropouts from couple therapy, Jurek, Janusz, Chwal and de Barbaro (2014) indicated that premature termination was related to a parallel process in which the couple's presenting conflict was replicated in their relationship with the therapist. Thus, a couple for whom fighting was a form of disconnecting from intimate moments may be prone to break off therapy prematurely to avoid the goodbye process.

Gottman (1998) focuses on a reason for premature termination that involves a lack of fondness or mutual admiration. Brown and Brown (2002) also provide more clinical/psychological reasons for terminating therapy prior to goals being reached or the clients unilaterally making decisions to stop without therapist collaboration. These include when the couple experiences the therapy as "spinning the wheels" or relies solely on the "report of the week" between sessions, when they don't experience progress toward their goals. Of course, they may also bolt from treatment with a sense that change is coming too fast.

Brown and Brown (2002) also indicate that a personality conflict may exist between the therapist and one or both partners. Sometimes, for example, one or both partners are not fully committed to the relationship, such as when one has an undisclosed goal of leaving. Long-term polarized, unresolvable conflicts and a related mistrust may also lead to early termination. In all such cases, a referral to an alternative therapist and approach might be wise.

Describing termination in general, Lebow (2014) reminds us that "[c]lients are the principal decision-makers about when treatment will end in almost every couple ... therapy" (p. 165). Thus, a general sense of what is premature for the therapist may not be for the couple in therapy. Lebow states that termination may range from "[c]arefully planned to totally unplanned and from cases that are completely successful to those that are unsuccessful" (p. 169).

If a couple does terminate therapy prematurely and without sufficient warning, it is desirable, if possible, to get them back for at least one session, during which the therapist must address both the logistical and clinical issues. If leaving is primarily related to escaping from intimacy or too-rapid progress, the therapist can focus specifically on their manner of escaping from difficult emotions or interactions. He or she can encourage them to experiment in small ways by doing something that may be more anxiety provoking in the moment, but ultimately in their best interests:

> Historically, when relationships were ending, you either cut off emotionally or somehow ended up in a fight between you. I wonder what you would have to face if we accepted that this is the end of our relationship without either of those scenarios. Where would that leave you now?

Well-planned, organized, clinically careful terminations are by far the most desirable. The best terminations involve collaboration between all parties, review of the goals, assessment of levels of success in attaining them, anticipation of some failures and new crises in the future, and a lot of support for the couple's ability to handle whatever they have to together. Indeed, that is a major difference between short-term intimacy (we will stay together as long as the balance in the relationship is positive) and long-term intimacy (we will face whatever comes up together as a team).

Our answer to premature terminations correlates well with Goode and colleagues (2017) and Lebow (2014). It involves referencing goals and termination collaboratively throughout the therapy sessions and paying attention to achievements and positive changes, new skills, and regular sensitivity to the number of sessions remaining from the initial contract.

Follow-Up and Referral

Inevitably, couples' needs are not all met in the typically brief time frame in which couples tend to remain in therapy. To address this, some therapists stretch out the weeks between the last few sessions to aid the couple adjustment. Others schedule a follow-up "final" meeting several months down the road. In reality, more than half of the couples we have seen do not take advantage of that follow-up meeting. Yet, a much larger percent report that having it on the calendar is very helpful. If research is being done and follow-up outcome measures are needed, it must be built into the long-term plan. Such follow-up assessments need to be short to get much compliance.

Returning to Therapy

As has been indicated several times in this text, some couples will return to therapy on a somewhat irregular basis after a termination.

The Conditions for Returning

Because many couples wait until their difficulties are critical before initiating therapy, they may follow a similar pattern of delay prior to returning for additional sessions. This is one reason why during the termination process discussion should be held about when and under what circumstances it would be wise to return to therapy for a refresher or course correction or in case of a new difficult situation.

There is a tricky balance between encouraging the departing couple that they have the resources within themselves to resolve future dilemmas and creating a framework for return if necessary. One related concern is that a follow-up possibility may have unintended consequences. Knowing that there may be a follow-up session available, the couple may avoid addressing the difficult losses associated with effective termination at the end of the regular sessions. Instead of saying goodbye, they may simply say *au revoir*.

Follow-up meetings may also be particularly problematic if the therapist is in training and the term for remaining at a particular agency may well be up before the couple might decide to return. For this and many other externally driven reasons, every such discussion of return should also involve potential referrals:

> I would of course be open to seeing you again, but you should know that my position as an intern at the couple therapy center ends in June. I don't know if my next placement would work for you. So, in addition to checking with me, one option I want you to be aware of is my supervisor, Dr. Gray. She is on permanent staff here. She has been supervising me and is aware of your situation, so she would be a good person to contact.

Referrals for Individual or Group Treatment

During the course of couple therapy, sometimes it becomes evident that individual therapy for one or both members of the couple will be beneficial. Referrals to individual treatment for therapy for specific disorders, medication consults, assessment, and the like are often made during the termination process. Usually, it has been brought up early in the process and reopened for discussion and recommendation one or more additional times.

Some couple therapists will themselves accept the individual as a client. If they do, it should come with a warning that further couple work as a threesome might be compromised.

Despite all these considerations, the nature of couple therapy, especially brief couple work, is such that therapist availability for return is strongly recommended

Some Advantages of Termination

According to Lebow (2014) and others, termination offers opportunities to review with the clients their successes, changes, and increased abilities to handle future problems that inevitably occur. It also adds the benefit of collaborating with the couple, underscoring them as a functioning team that has insights and thereby equalizes somewhat the relationship between therapist and clients. By working on this together, there are opportunities for a couple to turn to one another for support rather than risk.

Whenever possible, especially when the number of sessions is not strictly predetermined, it is particularly valuable to provide a clear track of progress and an anticipation of future work that may need to occur. The clients' roles in the success may be strongly accentuated. To the extent that it is possible, it is particularly valuable to encourage couples to internalize the therapist or the therapist's role. It can be slightly embarrassing to hear a couple say (as they did with their therapist, Susan earlier), "You are going to love this: We did a (fill in your name) this week. We started to have our old argument and then we just knew what you'd say and we did it in the kitchen."

The best response is to inquire how it worked out and how they might use similar approaches in the future. Encouraging positive internalizations of the therapy and therapist will usually serve the couple well in alleviating difficulties and simultaneously enjoying some humor about the therapist together. This may also lead to a therapist's observation of situations when the couple interactions tend to become difficult, identification of the problematic patterns, and use of that awareness to reconnect instead of to distance. In particular, when the status quo is an argument, encouragement may be offered to try the alternative path of facing fears of more intimate contact by being more vulnerable, transparent, and open.

Finally, there is an opportunity to help the couple find means of support in their community and promote their use of those resources that support their relationship.

SUMMARY

Of the four phases of couple therapy, termination may seem a more unusual occurrence, especially if it involves ending because time is running out rather than a more natural sequence of coming to a close. The process of termination begins with the first couple session when the therapist sets parameters for the work and the couple and therapist determine collaboratively the goals and methods to be used in achieving the goals. Formal assessment may also begin the distancing process, indicating that this therapy will not be a permanent entity in a couple's life. Often the therapist needs to remind the couple of the imminent ending, initiate a review of progress, and examine closely what remains to be done.

The two significant and essential goals of this phase of therapy are (a) transfer of learning and new skills to the couple's everyday life and (b) saying goodbye. They are both very important. Success in couple therapy will always require that the couple be increasingly successful while out of therapy. That is the *sine qua non* of all effective therapeutic work. The therapist must become obsolete except as internalized by the couple. In addition, unless the couple confronts their discomfort with endings and saying goodbye, the impact of the work may be minimized.

It is important to note that many therapists will also experience an emotional loss when the couple leaves. To the extent that these feelings for both the couple and the therapist can be open, the easier and better the termination transition.

Frequently, terminations are complicated by external forces that can truncate the therapy and make a normal process of termination impossible. Therapists who operate more collaboratively and keep clients up to date may mitigate somewhat those sudden endings.

Finally, plans should be made for follow-up meetings and for referrals.

Advanced Considerations

I have recently left my husband of 19 years. We had a good life and have three children, but for some time I felt like something was missing. Now I have realized what it was and am going through the process of "coming out" as a lesbian (or maybe bisexual). I have been a marriage counselor with my church for more than a decade What I wonder is how much of this should I share with couples I see. Normally, I have kept my social life private, but my ex-husband goes to the same church and I worry that he will make my new lifestyle public. My new partner is also a member of the church and she wants me to make our relationship known.

From a private consultation with a former student and recent colleague

10

The Couple Therapist as a Person

W e have spent some time considering the difficulties of being a couple therapist and some of the qualities necessary to be effective. In this chapter, we
will explore some potential strengths and pitfalls of personal qualities of
couple counselors and therapists. In the first section, we look at the impact of personal
experiences on the therapy. In the second part, we explore the mechanisms by which
therapists know what they know.

Personal Relationship Experiences

All of us are prone to be more responsive to personal experience than more objective
data. To quote many former students, "I know what the numbers say, but remember that
fiasco in grad school?" For this reason, our personal relationship encounters can color
professional practice. It is essential for counselors and therapists to know themselves,
their sensitivities, and their triggers well and to be cautious in applying them to the way
they listen to clients.

Regardless of theoretical orientation, therapist self-awareness is always an essential
consideration. A therapist's personal thoughts, values, feelings, background, and the like
will always color both the data she or he is receiving from a couple and how she or he
understands and uses those data.

Recently, a therapist came in for consultation on a case that she thought was going
poorly. The couple she described was at odds with each other. There was a suspicion that
the husband was engaging in some "online sexual diversions," and there was a significant
power differential in the relationship related to his greater earning power.

The supervisor, recognizing that everything the therapist described was fairly common
in couple work, asked, "What about this couple is making it so difficult?" When the therapist had no clear answer, the supervisor (with permission) asked about any stresses in

her personal life. At this point, the therapist began getting teary and disclosed that her own marriage was ending.

She also indicated that as they were going through the divorce process, she had discovered some disquieting secrets about her husband, including a serious online gambling problem. These personal experiences were then connected to how she was viewing the couple and her difficulty seeing the husband's side of things. With that insight, the therapist was able to continue the couple work when she added case consultation from a supervisor in the community.

This is but one example of how personal factors can influence professional capabilities in therapy. It is not the only factor. Indeed, the therapist role probably needs the most meticulous taking of personal inventories because of the risk of contagion from subjective experiences and reactions, which may occur out of conscious awareness. Psychodynamic therapists usually interpret these unconscious determinants of therapist reactivity as countertransference. For current purposes, we are exploring the phenomena more broadly as one reason that most effective therapists are also regular therapy clients and keep consultants at the ready.

Minimal Personal Experience

Frequently, when clients have a choice of therapists, they choose someone who is older and/or more experienced than they are. For example, it may be difficult to have much faith in parenting advice offered by individuals who have never had children themselves. However, it is essential to emphasize the significance of training, professionalism, and competence regardless of the counselor's personal experience.

Of course, many clients do not have a choice, particularly in agencies or in areas where couple therapists may be scarce. It is not uncommon for graduate students and newly licensed individuals beginning in the field, especially when they are in their 20s, to have little couple experience. If they do have the requisite training, professionalism, and experience (as described in Chapter 2), some courage and ability to build rapport and guide the session expertly can save the day.

In response to the personal couple genogram mandated in her training (Chapter 6), Annie wrote, "Well to sum up my experience as a part of a couple, there isn't any! I am embarrassed to say this, but I have not been in a long-term relationship since my high school boyfriend and that hardly qualifies. My friends and I 'group dated' in college and I came here right out of undergrad. The only couple I know well are my parents who have been together for 35 years."[1]

Responding to the same assignment, DeSean wrote, "I have experience with one girl. We dated on and off for 7 years from the time I was 17 'til recently. We broke up because I discovered she was sleeping with other guys while keeping chaste with me. Sometimes I feel like I dodged a bullet when we broke up. I wonder, though, if I have had my one love and it's now gone."

---

1 It is interesting that many of our students think they know well their parents' relationships and can use that knowledge as a template with which to view other couples and their own personal relationships. In reality, most do not know the more intimate details of their parents' relationship and have considerable naivete about parental conflicts or many of the more private loving aspects.

Similarly, Brandon wrote, "We met at a church dance when I returned from my mission. I was a college sophomore. We got engaged the next year and married during senior year. We just followed the script and at 26 we have two little ones. She's the only girl I've been with. The only girl I ever kissed."

As can be expected, each of these potential couple therapists had minimal personal experience regarding what made a good relationship work and even less on the variety of relational styles. They all were responding in some ways to limited personal experience and internalized myths about what a relationship is or should be (one and only, soul mate, all the eggs in one basket, etc.).

It is no surprise that a person who has not had the experience of living together with someone over a period of time may well be naïve about the characteristic disagreements, adjustments, arguments, negotiations, and compromises that are normal in any relationship. They may not have much knowledge about yielding some personal power and desires to enhance a relational team.

All of these students were initially "thrown for a loop" when they encountered their first couples in a therapy setting. None were fully ready for the kinds of problems that the couples presented, nor the level of hurt and anger expressed. They were also unprepared for the chaotic ambiance of those early sessions.

Limits of Self-Knowledge

Brandon's background, values, and understanding of marriage caused him some consternation with his first couple therapy, who were clients in a church-related counseling center. She was a three-time divorcee, with a long history of alcohol abuse, in a new relationship with a man who refused to be monogamous, before or after marriage. For Brandon, who believed in one marriage for eternity, sobriety, and faithfulness, these folks seemed almost like aliens.

What values seep into our judgment despite our keen attention to being fair, balanced, objective, neutral, and willing to try to understand the world from a client's perspective? Whatever our personal experience may be, it is essential that we engage in ongoing methods to check our biases.

Assumed Similarity

As much as differences in cultural experience can be limiting, similarity of experience can also create serious blind spots.

For Dante, an Italian American New Yorker who grew up in Little Italy, his current clients seemed easy to understand. Luca, the husband, grew up in an all-Italian neighborhood in Hammonton, New Jersey. Francesca, his wife of 5 years, grew up in the same neighborhood as Dante, attended the same church, parochial schools, and colleges as he, and could compare notes on the relative merits of local New York pizza joints; Luca, whose family owned a pizza place, readily claimed that "Jersey" pizza was far superior.

It would seem that because of their common background, religion, and related comfort with one another, the therapeutic alliance would be easy to develop, and to some extent it did. They both seemed comfortable with Dante and appreciated his understanding of family guilt induction, particularly increasing pressures from both families of origin to begin a family.

Yet despite the obvious easy ethnic connection, the therapy in its fifth session was not moving much. One of the difficulties was that Dante and his wife had themselves moved west, in part to avoid the constant "Nonna" (grandmother) pressure. Because he was very sensitized to the guilt-inducing parental messages, he worked hard with the clients to help them create a firmer boundary with their families of origin. Although that served one part of the conflict, the couple's desire to please the parents and half of Francesca's ambivalence about having a child went less explored.

To some degree, assumed similarity is a precarious blind spot for many therapists. Because we think we know the people well if there is shared history, we also imagine that they are psychologically similar as well and intervene accordingly. In fact, Dante could understand the pull to please the nonna and the rift that can cause with the wife. While he worked well with the couple to create an appropriate boundary, he did not go further to uncover the complexity around Francesca's ambivalence. As Dante put it later, "For several weeks, I was missing that Francesca also wanted to have a child. She just didn't want to do it for others. It wasn't that I didn't ask about her and Luca's desires. I just took their initial word that the pressure was problematic. I missed her unspoken wish for Luca to want a family also." In the 12th session, with a consultant's recommendation, Dante asked the couple about how they were dealing with birth control, given the pressure. In very embarrassed tones, the couple said that they had "put it in God's hands" the past month.

Issues Too Personal or Difficult: Current Dilemmas

All therapists have areas of life that they prefer to avoid in their clients. They may be too personal, embarrassing, or unresolved. For example, consider how much more difficult it might have been for Dante if he and his wife were suffering from years of infertility. Exploring the ambivalence about trying to get pregnant may have pushed some of his personal buttons.

Nelson, whose wife had taken her own life during a bout with deep depression and early-onset Parkinson's disease, carefully avoided in his practice individuals and couples who were dealing with suicidality. He described it as "just too much for me emotionally." In fact, he was unable to work as a clinician for 2 years following her passing.

He had done some excellent work years ago with an older couple, when they called and asked for a refresher session or two to address some new dilemmas. Only after they were in his office did he realize that the woman was suffering from Alzheimer's dementia and that she and her husband had made a pact earlier in their 55-year marriage that they would opt for assisted suicide if either had begun to suffer from such illnesses. They had not yet procured the necessary drugs, nor an expert to help in the action.

His ethical and legal concerns were drowned out by his emotional reaction and reliving his own experience with his wife several years before. His solution was to get a consult and also to bring in a co-therapist to explain to the couple what was going on for him personally. Nelson was well able to provide empathy for the couple, but he needed his co-therapist to address the other considerable issues.

Not all issues relate to life and death. Relationship problems in one's own marriage can be very problematic in effectively hearing a couple's needs.

Sex

In their 2008 study of over 30,000 U.S. women, Shifren, Brigitta, Russo, Segreti, and Johannes (2008) reported that 43% of the female population reported some suffering from sexual problems. Large-scale studies of men (e.g., Laumann et al., 2005) indicated slightly lower, but significantly high rates for men as well. Yet, Miller and Byers (2008) and Reissing and Di Giulio (2010) indicate that counselors and clinical psychologists are often unlikely to address these issues.

Although licensing laws in most jurisdictions require that all therapists have a course or continuing education workshop in human sexuality, there are many who find the topic very difficult to explore in depth (Harris & Hays, 2008). There are many reasons for the reticence, including sexual embarrassment and shame (Mollon, 2005; Shadbolt, 2009), insufficient sexual education (Goldman, 2008), religiously based constrictive view of sexuality (Papaharitou et al., 2008), cultural stigma on certain sexual activities (Kwee & Hoover, 2008), fear of embarrassing clients that may result in withdrawal from therapy, and an exclusive focus in training on deviant or patholog-ical sexuality. Instead, counselors as well as clients often fall into a fairly constrictive *reproductive bias* when it comes to their viewpoint of "normal sexuality." They may hold the notion that any sex that cannot lead to a socially acceptable pregnancy may be somehow deviant or at least problematic. This bias obviously eliminates healthy sexuality within many populations, most notably LGBTQ clients, couples who engage in BDSM and kink, the unmarried young, older people, the disabled, those who engage in polyamory, or potentially people of different racial backgrounds (Noah, 2016). Many are uncomfortable or unknowledgeable about some varieties of sexual expression that do not conform to the reproductive bias or their own upbringing and personal sexual experience.

Some topics in couple sexual work may be important, but very difficult to broach. In a recent informal survey of advanced graduate students, the question was posed about how many of them would introduce the topic of masturbation with couples. Only 10% of the students would discuss male masturbation and less than half that number would be open to discussions regarding female masturbation, unless either was associated with forms of pathology such as addictive pornography. It is very difficult to normalize most aspects of sexuality if the therapist is uncomfortable with the topic.

Blanchflower and Oswald (2004), in a study on economics, underscored the salience of unresolved sexual problems on couple happiness and demonstrated a connection between sexual happiness and socioeconomic status. The main point about sexuality, as well as any other issue affecting couple dynamics, is that therapists must be open not only to discussing them, but raising any issue that is salient in the interpersonal lives of their clients.

Money

Ever a taboo subject, and one which therapists are frequently loath to introduce, are issues that involve money and finances. Most therapists are even less well trained in financial matters than in sexual ones. Indeed, the literature is very sparse, and it is a rare training program that even addresses the topic (Durband, Britt & Grable, 2010; Rappleyea, Jorgensen, Taylor, & Butler, 2014).

Many couples who declare that talk about their sexuality is off the table for the therapy eventually do bring up and discuss sexual concerns when they develop greater trust for the therapist. There may be even greater avoidance when the difficult topic is financial. Nonetheless, couple concerns, disputes, and conflicts often include problems managing money. One of the reasons for this goes beyond the couple's discomfort. Most therapists, having little or no training in dealing with money and finances in a counseling setting or of addressing their own financially related discomfort, are also very uncomfortable initiating or following up on this issue.

That reticence is unfortunate because as Amato and Rogers (1997) and Britt, Huston, and Durband (2010) indicate, financial problems both cause and exacerbate relational distress, hostility, and deep anxieties about security.

Therapists also need to be aware when clients have differing views of finances, one of which is anathema to her or his personal values. For example, Lin grew up in a home in which "money doesn't grow on trees" was a constant cliché. By contrast, her partner Kathleen's childhood values were characterized by a quite different cliché: "Eat, drink and be merry for tomorrow we may die." They had many conflicts about spending and saving. Their therapist, having grown up with the cliché "a penny saved is a penny earned" had a hard time identifying with Kathleen's position on the money disagreements.

In almost every couple, the therapist will find it easier to connect with one member more than the other. What is different here is that because money is such a taboo subject, these values are more likely to be generated by powerful, fundamental issues such as *equity* and *autonomy* in the relationship (the extent to which they share accounts, expenses, and financial decisions, and the level of independence each partner has or feels he or she has).

Beyond basic values, several other money conflicts may arise in therapy, which are readily addressed if the therapist is sufficiently comfortable discussing them. These include saving and spending plans, personal and combined money, money anxieties, debt, power, financial indulgence, and living within means. It is essential to understand that money issues almost always elicit strong emotions because of what they mean to each partner. As with other key issues, if basic foundational dynamics are functional, a problem-solving approach (Jacobson & Margolin, 1979) may be used with the couple to negotiate financial matters. However, when it pushes on matters of psychological freedom and security, the financial discomfort may represent additional, basic psychological concerns that may be more resistant to rational solutions.

Religion and Culture

As much as there are human universals across cultures, there is also cultural uniqueness. Shapiro (2016) notes, "Each client's thoughts, feelings and actions are embedded in a complex variety of contexts. Unique representations of appropriate or inappropriate behavior are always culturally-determined" (p. 242). Clients' primary language, backgrounds, neighborhoods in which they grew up, and values provide lenses through which they perceive and attribute meaning (Pedersen, Draguns, Lonner, & Trimble, 2007; Sue & Sue, 2012; Vontress & Epp, 2015).

Clients frequently have values that are discrepant from those of the therapist. These may relate to different backgrounds, belief systems, values, and ethics. It is essential that therapists work within the religious and cultural beliefs of the couple. One of the most notable cultural aspects in working with couples involves the discrepancies between individualistic (focused on individual growth, achievement, striving, and success) and collectivistic (oriented around the group, harmony, and interconnectedness) cultures. The former, often described as "guilt" cultures, mostly have origins in Northern Europe and the West. The latter ("shame" cultures) are more common in clients whose ancestors came from East and South Asia, Central and South America, and some African cultures.

Similarly, clients who hold different religious beliefs will likely respond in different ways to therapeutic interventions. Clients who self-describe as fundamentalist or orthodox will require different understanding, interventions, and approaches than those from more liberal, agnostic, or atheistic beliefs.

It has been noted that a common belief among the general public is that therapists are opposed to religious discussion and avoid the topic in therapy. In recent decades, Shostrom (1976), Worthington (1993), and others have emphasized the importance of identifying religious or spiritual values that may guide clients and form a basis for meaning in their lives. This can, of course, be through organized religion, secular humanism, or even atheism, and therapists can guide clients through a process of values clarification, discussed in Chapter 2 of this text. The importance of this aspect of human functioning is emphasized by Lazarus (2008) in *Multimodal Therapy*, which emphasizes a comprehensive approach to clients as complex biopsychosocial beings. Therapists need to become aware of and work within the cultural and religious values of the couple being seen. The good news is that therapists do not need to know the ins and outs of every cultural and religious group. When asked about their cultural or religious values, most clients will be very forthcoming.

Multicultural Complications

Earlier we recommended that couple therapists might view all relationships from a multicultural perspective to best understand clients in a comprehensive, contextual manner. Indeed, in modern Western society, there is an increasing percentage of intermarriage. According to two recent (Livingston & Brown, 2017; Murphy, 2015) Pew Research studies, Asian-White intermarriage is close to 40% among Asian women with White men, and half as high for Asian men with White women. These numbers increase with acculturation and assimilation to Western cultures. They also are higher along the Pacific Rim states and Canadian provinces. Among Hispanics, just over a quarter intermarry, with roughly equal numbers of men and women. Conversely, African American men are twice (24%) as likely as African American women (12%) to intermarry.

Interfaith marriages are also on the rise, with 47% of Jewish marriages (United Jewish Committee, 2004) reportedly to non-Jews. According to another 2015 Pew study (Wang, 2015) on interfaith marriages, 39% of Americans married someone of a different faith. These numbers become higher when religions that forbid such marriages are removed from the analysis.

Couples come from significantly different cultures with discrepant expectations and inherent conflicts. For example, one of the authors (Shapiro) has seen several couples where the man was first-generation South Asian (Indian) and the woman was from Los Angeles or New York and Jewish (both religiously and culturally).

Although they shared many values, one major conflict involved the length of time visiting in-laws would stay with them. For the Indian man, a visit from his parents had an indeterminate limit, often stretching across several months. By contrast, their partners were more accustomed to visits as famously described by Benjamin Franklin, "Guests, like fish, begin to smell after three days." Each of the women expressed love for their in-laws but felt invaded and described both a need "to get my kitchen back" and a chance to get away alone each day.

The therapist, whose personal values were much more aligned with the 72-hour position, had to work hard to recognize that both positions were appropriate within their own cultural frame, be sensitive to both perspectives and expectations, and work carefully to help the couples negotiate ways to deal with their distress. Coauthor Patterson describes work with such couples as "walking a fine line" between generational value differences and autonomy, particularly when parents want to arrange a son or daughter's marriage and the latter is in love with a partner of his or her own choosing.

Couple therapists need to be aware of each individual culture, the combined couple culture, and the inevitable conflicts that different traditions entail. This can be problematic, for example, when dealing with the role of women in a relationship, working with arranged marriages, traditional gender roles, understanding religious or cultural traditions that are discrepant from their own values, and so on.

Other Issues

In a recent informal series of interviews with MFT counseling graduate students, one of the questions asked was, "Looking ahead, what population of couples would you think you'd like to avoid?" Among the most frequent they identified were dishonest clients, felons, serial philanderers, pedophiles, those with a dying partner or child, partner batterers, and those who mistreat women. In all of these situations and with all client types, we as therapists must acknowledge our inevitable biases and moderate them so as not to impose them inadvertently or directly.

How Therapists Know What They Know: Communication, Context, and Process

Having explored briefly some of the common personal areas that impact the effectiveness of couple therapy, we now turn to a consideration of the ways couple therapists know what is happening during and between sessions.

Students watching live demonstrations or videos of couple therapy often ask, "How did you know that? What made you think of that? Was that something you heard from the clients, or theory, or what?" To be useful, answers need to have much more data than "It seemed like a good idea at the time," "It was my gut feeling," or "It comes with experience."

A therapist understands each partner in a couple and the couple system per se by incorporating communication, equality, problem solving, and contextual aspects. These are characteristically highlighted by the filter of theory, evidence-based practice, practice-based evidence, and common factors. Through careful observation, history, and verbal and nonverbal messages, meaning is assigned to what is said between the couple members as well as what is left unsaid. In combination, these elements provide a template for the therapist to understand the dynamics and manage current and future sessions.

There are many ways in which our attunement to the couple and the process provide guidelines for interventions. The most important perspective is to try to understand both content and process (content in context). The words spoken between each member of a couple and between the couple and the therapist convey only part of the total message. The way they are spoken and their impact on the receiver often contain more important data.

Theory

All communication is necessarily governed more by what is picked up and understood than by what is actually spoken. Two of the major functions of a theory of personality and behavior change are filtering and interpreting. Our theories inform us what aspect of the communication is relevant and what those relevant data mean. Thus, therapists who operate from a psychodynamic orientation will glean different data and interpret them differently than a CBT, systemic, or existential/humanistic therapist. All of these may lead to fruitful avenues to help the couple, but the paths can be considerably different.

We acknowledge the importance of clinicians having a solid grasp on a foundational theoretical orientation and also applaud the movement toward a post-theoretical era in which neither theory nor techniques are considered the critical factor in effective therapy. For many years, the term *eclectic*[2] has been widely used without specification of any particular approach and often connoted as using one's intuition or "going with a gut feeling." Goldfried and Norcross (1995) and others have defined *theoretical integration* in a more detailed fashion, and a professional organization and major annual conference has been developed on this premise. Lebow (1997, 2008, 2014), in some of the most articulate and contemporary descriptions of this concept, describes the wide array of models that have developed in couple and family therapy as a "pre-model equivalent of the post-model world of practice that has recently emerged" (Lebow, 2014, p. 12). This focus on common factors, diverse techniques, and overlapping concepts are being practiced effectively from a variety of perspectives.

Because of different theories, we actually "hear" different things from our clients and perceive them having different interactions with one another. For this reason, we need to be aware of the built-in heuristic biases inherent in any theory. We may also need to switch theoretical perspectives to match up better with client needs and ways of connecting.

---

2   The term *eclectic*, the creation of some new entity from parts of various sources, has fallen into disregard in many circles because it was considered to be more a "seat-of-the-pants approach" and less hardy than pure theoretical approaches or pluralism. When eclecticism has a well-considered integrative system of understanding couples and their contextual world, we think it is worthy of consideration.

Therapists are drawn to specific psychotherapeutic approaches in part by what seems to be effective for them personally. They are also drawn to theories that reflect their personal values—another reason to follow Socrates's dictum, "Know thyself," and what we view as the "guru model," having learned it from idiosyncratic, dynamic figures such as Satir, Minuchin, Whitaker, and others.

If a therapist has a free will philosophy, she or he will be more drawn to those theories than to more deterministic ones and will view his or her world through those value-centered lenses. It is important to note that this is not a problem unless those lenses have blind spots and are not ultimately discardable when necessary. In fact, all of the major psychotherapeutic theories seem to work well with some populations of couples.

Therapists' Processing Systems: The Use of Self

A therapist uses more than theory to understand clients. Shapiro (2016) describes the use of a number of inputs for a therapist. These include linear and nonlinear, internal and external, and multicultural sources of data and data analysis.

Content and Process: Revisited

The content of a message sent from clients to their partners or to the therapist comprises the words alone, as if they were written down on a blank sheet of paper, texted, e-mailed, and so on. To use a simple example, consider Mary saying to John, her husband of many years, "Sometimes you get me really mad!" What change in meaning occurs if he just told a joke and she was laughing in apparent appreciation? What if she said this in a very irritated or sarcastic tone of voice? What if she said it while smiling at him and gently squeezing his hand? What if she slid her seat away from him or looked hopefully at the therapist for acknowledgment? What if it is said by a person who comes from a collective culture where harmony is essential?

The content carries a fraction of the data available in tones of voice, body posture, emphases on certain syllables, and the relational context in which it occurs. The entire message, including the larger environment (e.g., it is said in the presence of the therapist) is the process of the communication. For the couple therapist, process requires taking in a multiplicity of data sources, some involving cognitive and sensory perceptions, some linear and others intuitive.

Another analogy is the written script of a play: The screenwriter and producer realize that many factors will determine how it will be delivered and received, including the personality of the actors, their mood at the moment, the setting, and the receptivity of the audience. It is similar with scripted plays in sports, and with even finer texture and nuance in therapy.

Linear Sources of Information

A well-trained therapist pays very close attention to what is readily observable in the couple's behavior. Verbal and culturally consistent, nonverbal cues are almost automatically integrated into the approach to understanding and interventions. It is also important to recognize nonverbal dismissals of content. For example, is there a lack of appropriate eye contact between partners or with the therapist? Is there an intensity indicated by sitting forward and talking in a pressured form of speech? Is the ubiquitous smartphone out and observable? Does a client read incoming text messages during sessions or is he or she fully present with his or her spouse?

Other sources of linear data include the intake information on forms, assessment, information from the referral source, assessment inventories, and prior history of therapy, particularly couple therapy. When Rory and Theresa first entered therapy, they indicated that they had seen several other couple therapists and "it just didn't work out."

The therapist asked what made it unsuccessful and Theresa answered, "They all wanted to know about the past and our prior relationships. It's just not something we are proud about and have decided to move on. What's done is done!" Rory quickly jumped in and said, "We are on the same page with that and want to move forward with problems we have now, not from NA and SA meetings."

The therapist, knowing that they would leave if he disagreed with the limitations, replied, "I am okay with that for now, if you will be responsible for bringing up anything from those times that *you* think might be getting in the way now. However, if I do think there is something in the past worth discussing, I will tell you and you will have to decide."

Nonlinear (Intuitive) Sources of Data

Couple counselors and therapists are often attuned to what Shapiro (2016) refers to as a wide bandwidth of multiple, interwoven channels. Some of these channels are subjective and intuitive, and the input from these may sometimes be inconsistent. The best couple therapists develop their capacities to accept data from a host of internal as well as external sources.

Remember Frankie and Johnny in Chapter 1 and her "overreaction," including a threat to divorce over his being late for a soccer game? A couple therapist may well ask him- or herself internally the question, "What does it take for me to get that overemotional?" Let's say that the answer involves a need for acknowledgment or the ability to trust one's partner. That hypothesis may then be tested by providing additional empathy and recognition and observing Frankie's reaction. If she responds positively, Johnny may then be encouraged to respond to her similarly.

Sources of Therapeutic Intuition

Nonlinear sources of data include the therapist's awareness and use of personal feelings as well as auditory and visual imagery. Therapists also may rely somewhat on symbols, dreams, metaphors, and stories in both diagnosing the couple and in intervening. For example, if the clients rely heavily on metaphor to express themselves, metaphoric interventions may be particularly useful. Modern psychoanalytic and object relations–oriented therapists use the term *reverie* (Quatman, 2015) or *therapist's mind* (Diamond, 2010) to describe the unconscious internal therapist processing.

Of course, such data that emerges when working with a couple must be considered hypothetical and carefully tested. Like all intrapsychic data, it must be considered as something that generates hypotheses to explore and not necessarily factual. Such non-linear attunement has the ability to enhance therapist understanding and empathy for the couple members and couple system.

Feelings (Kinesthetic Imagery)

We encourage therapists to be aware of personal emotions that arise while in the presence of a couple. It is not unusual for couple therapists to experience anger, sadness, joy, or any other emotion. Presuming that the therapist did not enter the session already experiencing particular feelings, emotions elicited in session may be useful indicators of what is happening with the couple at non-observable levels. Such feelings may then be used to reach clients at deeper levels.

> Walter: I know it's just seventh grade, but I think our daughter could be getting better grades and be less attached to her phone.

> Melissa: (To the therapist) I think he just worries too much. She is like all her friends. They are always having high drama about boys and it's just what girls her age do.

> T: Walt, Melissa seems to think it's normal, but you seem concerned.

> W: Yeah. She went from being this star in sixth grade with all kinds of plans for her future to this teen with interest only in social things and makeup and clothes. She also wants to get a tattoo and a nose ring, and I don't want Mel to support that.

> M: I don't, but given the choices, those things aren't as bad as others.

> T: When you said that I picked up a lot of sadness in the room.

> W: It's me. I was awake and crying last night thinking of her mutilating herself and feeling like not only was she out of control, but I was also.

> T: That's a helpless feeling. (As Walter's eyes moistened, the therapist turned to Melissa), What are you seeing in your husband's face now?

> M: I can see his tears and his sadness.

> T: Will you tell that to Walt directly?

> M: Walt, I am fearful also. I just remember what it was like to be 13 and how unsure I was. You know she's a good kid, and I don't think she'd actually get a nose ring or tattoo. I think she just tries to get a rise out of us.

W: I hope you are right. You usually are, but I do not want her to get any encouragement at home.

M: I don't want her to do those things either. Maybe we could both talk with her.

With this couple, the therapist's self-perceived sadness allowed her to be more present and to get the couple to talk more as a supportive team, coming closer to working together as parents. She had accurately picked up the father's sadness below his words. It is important to note that if had she been inaccurate and asked about sadness in the room, the clients may have corrected her and said, "No, I think I am more afraid." They could then have worked with the fear. Attention to the affect also kept the therapist from getting into the weeds about nose rings and tattoos and more on the essential focus of the couple being on the same page together in their concern for their daughter.

In another situation, a couple was describing a very difficult problem with some relatives who had borrowed some money and then reportedly could not pay it back, while living a much more expensive lifestyle than the couple who had loaned the money. The couple complained about it with an air of resignation, always ending with statements like, "Well, that's just Connie. She has always been irresponsible and she's done it to everyone," or "It is what it is."

Although the couple was complaining, their affect was fairly level. The therapist recognized his own anger about being deceived and asked, "I am confused here. How come I am the only person in this room Connie didn't cheat and I am the one who seems to be the angriest?" Within minutes, the couple was discussing their relative's disloyalty with far more appropriate levels of upset.

If the therapist can use her or his feelings to bring the emotion that the couple is inhibiting into the room, there is greater opportunity to work it through and to get past unspoken hurts. This requires a high degree of experience, self-awareness, and filtering so as not to blurt out a random statement that is not grounded in the process.

Davi and Sally had been in couple therapy several times over the years. The issue on which they always hit a dead end was her jealousy about his ex-wife and a former lover. Recently, they were at his college reunion and ran into both women from his past. Later in the evening, a fraternity brother accidentally called Sally by Davi's ex-wife's name.

Sally fumed over that for the next few weeks and they came in for couple work. Davi claimed that her jealousy was out of control. He excused the frat brother because he was drinking and knew the ex-wife and had been in the wedding party. Sally insisted he should have confronted the man. She also claimed that many of Davi's old friends had too many stories about wild parties and sexual adventures, including an "open marriage" with his ex.

The therapist had seen Sally's jealousy previously and thought it to be slightly greater than the situation occasioned, especially when she was experiencing a fear of abandonment. He was also aware that this time the jealousy had reached far greater proportions. Taking a moment internally, he wondered what would make his own jealousy and anxiety about rejection flare in the way that Sally's was. His conclusion was that it happened when he felt insufficient support from his partner.

Using those subjective data as a hypothesis to test out, he turned to Davi:

T: Davi, I know that you find Sally's jealousy troubling, and the reunion party seemed especially triggering for her. I wonder how you could anticipate such events and reassure her?

S: He could have been with me instead of his exes and frat bros.

T: Davi, what do you hear her asking you?

D: Look, it was a bad scene. I didn't expect to see two exes there, and because we had an open relationship, I didn't know what to do with my frat brother's relationship with my ex. I just wish Sally would know that I am not that Davi anymore and those people are not my life. She is.

T: (To Davi) How could you let her know?

D: Well, I told her basically that on the way home.

S: You didn't say you were unhappy about it.

T: So that would make a difference. Is that new information?

S: The words aren't new, but he seems more sincere now.

T: What could you both do now to make it better?

S: I can pull Davi aside and tell him what I am feeling before the "green monster" appears.

T: Davi, what if she did that?

D: Sally, if that ever happens again, just pull me aside and tell me what you want from me. If I knew at the party how bad it was for you, we could have left.

T: Sally, tell Davi what it's like to hear him say that you are his first priority.

That simple internal check-in allowed the therapist to understand better what each person needed and to de-escalate the situation. Whenever the anxiety can occur in real time in the therapy room, the couple can better respond to what the partner needs than to a rehashed report of the reunion that occurred previously. As a side issue concerning equality, the therapist should also be attuned to the fact that Davi could have anticipated Sally's sense of isolation at his reunion (as many spouses who don't know anyone might feel) and spent time introducing her and staying close to her during the party.

A therapist's emotional sensitivity is not the only variable offering inroads to better understanding the couple. Other forms of imagery may also be used to discern less obvious aspects of a couple's system and offer alternative methods for intervention.

Visual Imagery

Many individuals represent their perceptions visually. They *see* what is happening in their *mind's eye*. Therapists often employ visual imagery to understand what their clients are expressing, to theorize what it means, to discern what is important, and to suggest timing of interventions.

Often therapists describe their clients' communication in visual terms. These images may represent something the therapist pictures from his or her own life. For example, with a couple who had a constant power struggle that colored almost every interaction, the therapist had a recurring image of a famous 1913 silent film train crash. After the couple enacted their power struggle several times, the therapist shared the image with them and described the effect of a Pyrrhic victory.

> T: You know, as I hear you argue about which road to take to get to the city without any agreement or compromise, I keep getting an image of an old silent film in which two locomotives crash headlong into each other at high speed. In the end, both are destroyed.

> C: What do you mean?

> T: I wonder what the value is of winning if neither of you can walk away whole? In fact, I wonder about the value of winning even if only your partner was destroyed in the loss.

Another couple was dealing with increasingly high standards that they set on their own behavior. They encouraged each other to keep getting better to the point where they began to feel like failures regardless of their many successes. The therapist began with an acknowledgment of the value of seeking success and then shared a visual image.

> T: I can see how your mutual encouragement has led to a lot of success in life and has allowed you to move ahead professionally, but at this point, I wonder about how high the bar can go.

> C: Well, we can always be better if we just put our minds to it.

> T: I know that's what you believe, but I am also aware that you feel like failures when you are not number one in any competition.

> C: We can't be number one in everything, but it's worth trying to keep bettering our times in any race.

T: You know when you said that I am reminded of something I saw as a girl. It was a show called the *Ice Capades*, and at one point all the skaters formed a giant wheel so that the skaters near the center had short distances, but the girl at the far edge had to race to catch up. In every show, she was left behind and was seen racing five times faster than the others just to take her place on the wheel.

C: I remember that also. I saw that show in Oakland when I was really little. I remember feeling that it was unfair, and I was very relieved when she did finally catch up.

T: Maybe the standards you set for yourself are also a little unfair, and you have to be five times as good just to be equal.

In this situation, the cultural relevance of having to be superior to be equal was particularly powerful to the African American couple because that was their constant lived reality. The therapy continued with questions regarding being better in some, but not necessarily in all, life endeavors. With an issue such as this, it is important for a therapist to comment with images or perceptions, but not to impose his or her own values about achievement, particularly when it contrasts with the experience of a couple from another culture, for whom unrelenting 110% effort is their only way to succeed. Socratic questioning, motivational-based interviewing (Miller & Rollnick, 2013), or therapeutic amazement about the consequences may be useful methods to use to elicit true values and goals with clients who are out of sync with what they really want.

Those shared images, initiated from the therapists' personal memories, opened an avenue for the therapy to move to a deeper level instead of continuing on familiar dead-end patterns.

When the internal visual imagery keeps occurring during some blocked interaction, it may be an indication that it is time to intervene.

Auditory Imagery

Sometimes, it is what a therapist hears that has importance. In addition to listening to changes in tones of voice, inflections, and use of primary language idioms, some therapists understand their world better through what sounds they hear. Awareness of subtle shifts can allow a couple to reflect on the meaning of their interaction or to try novel ways of talking to one another.

As with kinesthetic or visual memory, sounds may also elicit powerful images. They may come in the form of conversations, sayings, or personal idioms. One intervention that is often useful with couples for whom English is a second language is to ask them to converse in their native tongue (assuming they have the same one). The therapist may not understand clients speaking in Spanish, French, Mandarin, Tagalog, or Russian, although sometimes the power and emotion of that conversation is conveyed. Most significantly, the clients will often experience far more emotion in their primary language. Once they are done, they can try to translate for the therapist. Regardless of the usefulness of the translation, that interaction underscores the primacy of the couple relationship.

Sometimes, therapists also hear things in a more primary argot or patois. It may be sayings they knew from childhood or languages spoken in their homes as they were growing up. It is also possible, with commonly spoken languages like Spanish, that a bilingual therapist may have some fluency and an ability to intervene in the native tongue.

Symbols

Many therapists and clients are drawn to various mythologies, art forms, or other representations that describe for them far-reaching truths or expectations. Some of these may be archetypal, religious, or reflective of powerful experiences. For one couple with problems around sexual desire, it was helpful to have them move a portrait of her parents from the wall over their bed. That picture symbolically had them being observed by her parents during times when they could be affectionate and sexual. It was without doubt a passion killer. Of course, once they removed the portrait and began more regular sexual contact, they had to confront their own fears of intimacy.

Our work with veterans suffering from PTSD has often involved changing the value of various symbols from their combat experiences. Often, holding on to the symbol kept alive the disquieting status quo while avoiding the unknown fears of shifting their relationships or just being "back in the world."

Metaphors

Most individuals have self-definitions that are supported by metaphors or personal stories. Metaphors are also useful in representing and expressing complex experiences. Understanding clients' metaphors and stories enhances empathy, attunement, joining, and intimacy. It also allows clients to discuss matters in greater depth and more safely because it is less direct.

Josh and Lindy described a consistent problem with their "almost nonexistent" sexual relationship. They had both grown up in a conservative religious community and had been virgins when they were married. Josh revealed with some embarrassment, "It took us the whole honeymoon just to figure out the mechanics of (and in a very low voice) sex and it seemed more difficult than we expected. Lindy finds it painful and I think I finish too quickly."

T: It sounds like sex was not as you expected.

L: We thought it'd all be natural and it'd be as pleasurable as we had heard from friends.

J: But not from relatives.

T: What did they say?

L: My mother and grandmother and two aunts took me aside at the wedding and told me what I was to expect on my wedding night. They basically said it was a woman's duty to keep her man and to have children. They insisted it was something to endure, rather than enjoy.

Lindy was referred to her gynecologist to check out the pain/discomfort. She was reassured that there were no structural problems and she could benefit from some extra lubrication for intercourse. In the next session, the couple was describing their pleasure in restoring and driving classic cars, when the therapist offered the metaphor.

T: Do you like standard shift vehicles?

They both stated their preference for manual transmissions and described how Lindy in particular liked the level of control offered by manual shifting.

T: (Recalling the classic poem "She Being Brand New" by e.e. Cummings (1926/1972) commented) Remember when you first tried to drive a standard shift? It was so complicated, both feet, both arms, balancing, coordinating. It seemed impossible and yet soon it was second nature and natural.

L: I remember it so well. My dad taught me on the farm with old trucks. I learned when I was about 13—on the farm that was normal. I taught Josh when we were first going out. I had a stick shift and he had never seen one. We used to call him the "gear-grinder."

They both laughed.

T: It's funny how new physical challenges often seem so complicated until your bodies take over and everything seems to work after some practice.

J: You mean like sex?

T: Well, you mastered shifting, a clutch, and coordinating your four limbs; maybe sex is a little like that, learning to let your bodies take over and not thinking about it as much.

L: Well you still have to think again when you are on one of those hills in San Francisco.

T: So maybe you have to do some talking and thinking in some situations, but my experience on the hills is that if I start worrying about the emergency brake and the clutch when I am stopped on a 45-degree angle, it's harder than if I just expect to roll back a bit and do it moderately well.

I just had a weird idea. What if you, Lindy, taught Josh about what makes your body feel good? It doesn't have to be intercourse, just what kind of touch is pleasant. If you taught him how to drive a standard shift …

Like Cumming's poem, we were talking about shifting gears in an automobile while we were also using that as a metaphor to talk about their new experiences with sexuality. It's also a more palatable way to encourage them to continue exploring their sexuality together rather than giving up, in the sense that "practice makes (nearly) perfect" (or "good enough").

Joining in on the client metaphors can be very powerful, especially if they fit into the natural ways clients think about their lives. Shapiro (2016) discusses sports metaphors and science fiction metaphors to break through impasses on the surface level. He also describes a client who was unable to decide if he wanted to propose marriage to his long-time partner until in therapy there was an extensive discussion about what new car to choose.

In Silicon Valley, there is a very dominant ambitious ambiance. Many clients describe that the way to solve problems at work and in relationships is to keep trying harder. Often it is useful to join their ambition but add a twist that will encourage more flexible thinking. When one couple described a "pedal to the metal" approach to parenting their rebellious teenage sons, the therapist wondered aloud whether gunning the engine was useful when the kids had jacked the rear wheels off the ground.

Gloria and Denny, two executives in high-tech firms, were diehard Golden State Warriors basketball fans who always tried to do everything at the best and most intense levels. When they came into therapy, they described being "burned out" and wanting more time together, adding that it was impossible. After several sessions, the therapist posed the hypothetical question, "suppose that Steph (Curry) is nursing one of his ankle injuries and you have a game coming up against Houston. What would you do to work around the injury?" Instantly, Gloria said, "I'd give the ball more to KD (Kevin Durant) and play more with the big men inside." Denny instantly agreed and said that they had to learn to play when one of the stars got injured. The therapist responded, "So who could take over for the two of you when you need a break?"

Using their fandom and knowledge allowed them to approach their own need for time out and they began to come up with some creative solutions. Another useful approach might be to have them understand that an effective coach drops the technical aspects of practice when the team is struggling and says, "Just have fun out there!"

It doesn't matter what the metaphors are or the therapist's knowledge of a particular aspect of life. Whatever the clients use can be employed. Metaphors with couples often involve hobbies such as knitting, gardening, or musical interests. The therapist does not need to be an expert to discuss how to deal with errors in any of those realms. For example, questions like "When you slip up while knitting, do you have to rip out a lot of work?" can lead to discussions about mistakes in the couple relationship. In short, by getting into a metaphorical discussion that is meaningful to the client, a number of powerful options may open up for the couple.

Stories

Closely related to metaphors are short stories that come from the therapist's life. Often, such stories generate powerful interventions. Although he worked more frequently with individuals than with couples, Erickson (Erickson & Keener, 2006) pioneered the use of story and light trances to move clients from seemingly intractable homeostatic thoughts, feelings, and behaviors onto productive channels.

The content of Erickson's stories indirectly conveyed considerable empathy, offered alternative paths, and conveyed hope for a better future. When therapists share personally relevant stories, they are able to work somewhat indirectly—thereby bypassing the couple's defenses—and at the same time convey emotional importance and meaning because of their own felt experiences. Erickson's success was in part due to his uncanny (practiced) ability to enter the client's frame of reference and use a story that resonated with them, and in part due to being able to use trial and error, switching stories based on the clients' reactions.

Couples who are parents often respond to the moral messages contained in well-known children's stories. Working in Silicon Valley, for example, Piper's (1930) story, *The Little Engine that Could* is a frequent model for particularly ambitious couples, especially those who have exceptional expectations for their children. By alternating that story with *Tootle* (Crampton & Gerely, 1945) a story of a train who literally "stopped to smell the roses," a therapist can help the couple to examine the total impact on the entire family of their ambitious goals for their children.

> T: You know, as you were describing your Herculean efforts to give your children the very best, I was thinking of a story I heard as a kid, *The Little Engine That Could*. Do you know that one?

> As both clients nodded and smiled, they acknowledged the long-term "keep trying" importance of that story on their approach to life's dilemmas. The therapist then continued,

> T: While that came to mind, I also began thinking of another train story, *Tootle*.

> C: Is that the one where the train went off the track to play?

> T: Yes. I wonder why that came up now?

> C: Probably because we don't play much anymore.

Another children's story, *The Runaway Bunny* (Brown, 1942), has been useful to indirectly assist couples to let go while experiencing an "empty nest" as their last child leaves home. Almost any fable, Greek myth, pop culture, or personal experience can help convey alternatives in a non-confrontive manner. After all, on the surface, it is just a story. Erickson would often begin a story with, "I don't know why I am thinking about this (he knew and was using therapeutic amazement), but I knew a couple from back East once. They were both lawyers ..."

The Value and Danger of Self-Data

The advantage of using both keen linear perceptiveness and enhanced attunement or intuition and personal reactions is clear. However, caution must be observed as well. Therapists may use such perceptions to generate hypotheses and create new opportunities for therapeutic interaction. They are best treated as data and, as such, need to be carefully evaluated. Therapists' internal perceptions and assumptions could correlate more to themselves than to the clients. Using self-referential items must also be evaluated in light of the phase of therapy and whether sufficient rapport has been established for the client to receive such a detour from standard, expected techniques.

Know Thyself

As Shapiro (2016) has indicated, the capacity of therapists to emulate science fiction and learn about clients through phenomena such as a Vulcan mind-meld is a fantasy. Self-awareness remains the best protection against overconfidence in using self-referential data. For example, a therapist going through a divorce may see a client couple's marriage through more negatively tinted lenses than one in a happy, solid relationship.

Similarly, couples who have divergent moral, ethical, religious, or cultural standards have to be understood from their reference points rather than the therapist's point of view. It can be a considerable challenge for a therapist to work within the client's frame of reference when it is incongruent with personal beliefs. For example, a couple who was considering an abortion may be problematic for a therapist, especially if the clients themselves were not in accord on the decision.

Similarly, recent "tribal" political positions may add to social, religious, cultural, and moral value system conflicts. Without awareness of their personal triggers and sensitivities, therapists may be inclined to disagree, rebut, or lack understanding—decidedly non-therapeutic positions. Awareness through ongoing personal therapy, consultation, and supervision of couple cases are the best antidotes to having such biases enter into the consultation room.

Recently, a couple presented with a problem that would test the therapist's ability to be neutral. After 3 years of a relationship, in which they did not cohabitate, the woman became pregnant. They decided to marry and came in when she was 4 months pregnant. The presenting problem was that it would be a mixed religious and racial marriage and that his parents were "diehard Trump Republicans and Christian fundamentalists." His family had already insisted both that she convert to their religion and his father declared that he would never accept the marriage. They knew her family well but had little to no contact with his parents, siblings, or extended family.

The therapist, who was from the same ethnic minority group as the woman, was aware of her own built-in bias and anger at the political/religious views of the man's family. She found herself at times wondering if the marriage should take place at all, internally envisaging a very difficult life ahead for her female client. Thankfully, she recognized the personal conflict as significant and sought supervision immediately. As she was able to pull back from her own concerns, she was able to hear the couple's attempts at solutions to the differences and to ways of addressing his family. It was particularly telling to discover that he had no interest in his fiancé undergoing a religious conversion and see his willingness to keep his family from their wedding.

SUMMARY

The chapter focuses on the person of the therapist. The individual's experiences and history are explored. Inherent dangers of assumed similarity and of cultural differences are examined. Some dangers to novice couple therapists include personally difficult issues including discomfort with sexuality, finances, religion, and cultural differences. The second half of the chapter explores how therapists perceive and process information about couples in therapy. Among the ways that therapists can use their internal processing to better comprehend couple systems are theory, feelings, and visual and auditory input. Interventions using metaphors and stories are considered. The chapter concludes with an evaluation of positive and negative aspects of internal processing and a call for awareness as the antidote to errors of personal bias. In essence, while the relationship with clients remains the essential ingredient in successful therapy, the self-awareness and filtering of how the therapist processes linear and nonlinear data and decides to reveal aspects of him- or herself largely determines the quality of that relationship.

11

Gender and Couple Therapy

CURRENT CONSIDERATIONS BOX 11.1: SPECIAL INTRODUCTION TO THIS CHAPTER

Controversy swirls when it comes to issues involving gender and gender identity. There is a considerable sociocultural need for acknowledgment about gender-based (power) disadvantage, especially when gender intersects with other minority cultural status or with lower socioeconomic conditions.

Many writers, researchers, and therapists stress the importance of reaching for acknowledgment of gender-based disparities and call for activism as part of treatment. Although such positions emerged from feminist therapy writing, it is more mainstream today within relational-cultural approaches.

Of course, we recognize that for our client couples, gender is far more fluid and variable within any specific sex-linked groupings. However, even though gender is fluid and non-binary, our gender socialization continues to focus on shaping individuals into the categories of male and female. In short, gender socialization characteristically may be considered binary even though gender is not.

Gender as defined in this chapter includes behavioral, cultural, and psychological traits typically associated with one sex, rather than inherent biological traits. We recommend specific therapeutic attention to gender when there is reason to explore with clients, meaningful power differentials, unnegotiated roles, and emerging gender-related issues. From this perspective, gender is as important as any ethno-cultural difference that manifests within a relationship. Throughout this book we treat gender and gender identification as important aspects of individuals and couples.

Our perspective here is that of clinicians working with couples. When gender and/or gender socialization power differentials contribute to discord in a couple relationship, we investigate and treat it. We explore sociocultural issues that are salient issues for the couple we are treating.

Beyond the Accusations of a "War on Women" and "War on Men"

That there are biological differences is not really in doubt and rarely a cause for dispute. The sociopsychological reasons and sources for dissimilarities between women and men are far more arguable. The general consensus about gender differences is that both nature and nurture are germane. When it comes to how men and women may differ in relationships, there is usually a greater emphasis on what is learned than on what may be inherent. Parker (1999) summarizes,

> That men and women exhibit differences in their approach to relationships is well established in the literature and is not new information to family therapists. Men and women exhibit differences because of their differing socialization, but even more important, differential power afforded them. That these differences create problems when men and women relate to one another is also established. What to do about those differences in practice with couples is less well known. (p. 1)

Whenever gender roles and expectations become rigid, they can be problematic. As Parker (1999) indicates, for couple therapists, when socialization and power differentials become a source of difficulty, the methods of therapeutic amelioration may be far more nuanced than identifying causes. Parker's method was in part psychoeducational and involved helping couples see the disadvantages of gender role socialization for the female member in heterosexual relationships. Her observations and methods have been echoed by many others in the field (see Hyde, 2014 for a review). The conclusions are closely matched by the need for similar interventions for men, described in the 2018 APA "Guidelines."

We believe strongly in the importance of dealing equitably with all clients in couple counseling and therapy. In line with this, it may be essential to address gender-oriented issues that underlie particular couple conflicts. However, we encourage caution in stereotypic notions about what are proper differences in how men and women approach each other in therapy; as such pigeon holing may interfere with important avenues to effective couple therapy.

We are relying as best as we can on extant scholarship and clinical realities of couple counseling and psychotherapy. To the extent that our perspective may appear to conflict with viable alternate views of male–female similarities and differences, we ask that you consider withholding judgment until you have considered our approach as a whole and as a heuristic and contextual way to approach couples where gender issues are germane.

An Approach to Gender Roles in Couple Therapy

Our basic approach is that therapy is directed toward the couple with whom we are engaging in therapy. Although we understand the crucial need for social change for inequalities based on gender (and other intersectional minority issues) in society, the focus here is less on global social change than on a couple seeking our assistance.

CURRENT CONSIDERATIONS BOX 11.2: GENDER CONTROVERSY AND THE 2018 APA GUIDELINES FOR PRACTICE WITH MEN AND BOYS

In 2018, the APA published a set of "aspirational" guidelines for treating males. It followed the guidelines for women and girls by 11 years and lesbian, gay, and bisexual clients by 6 years. Some of the guidelines speak to positive father involvement, male interpersonal relationships, a new focus on the needs of boys and men, addressing the high rates of aggression, violence, substance abuse, and suicidality; promotion of better health-related behaviors; and so on.

A few of the guidelines promote recognition that masculinities are constructed based on social, cultural, and contextual norms and the impact of power, privilege, and sexism on the development of boys and men and on their relationships.

After general dissemination of these guidelines in 2019, and a Gillette company national commercial that aired in early 2019 (which focused on sexual harassment and aggression and indicated that men need some work in being the best they can be), a critical firestorm emerged in psychological circles and in the media from right-wing sources such as Fox News (Ingraham, 2019) to mainstream media, the *New York Times* (Douthit, 2019), online professional responses such as *Quillette* (Wright, 2019), comic strips such as Scott Adams's (2019) "Dilbert," and near-vicious comments on social media and professional listservs. The primary flash points were the terms *androcentrism* and *traditional masculinity* and their identification as a major cause for gender role strain. In fact, it was translated frequently as "toxic masculinity," a far more egregious term.

These terms were seen as a political attack on tradition, conservatism, and men in general. What was impressive was that attacks came from many sides of the political spectrum. One poignant example of the scope of upset in both trade and professional circles is encapsulated by the title in the February 2019 *Monitor on Psychology*, "APA Guidelines on Boys and Men Launch Important—and Fiery—National Conversation" (American Psychological Association, 2019).

This underscores that discussions about gender, and the way men and women are relatively seen and influenced are very sensitive and lead to potentially exaggerated emotional/political positions.

Although at times we use binary categorizations of male and female, we do so to elucidate rather than to obfuscate, or be insensitive to any particular individuals. There are well-documented data that there are greater psychological differences within each gender than between them and that overall differences between genders on emotional/psychological domains are small (Chapin & Aldao, 2013; Hyde, 2005, 2014; Silverstein & Brooks, 2010; Zell, Krizen, & Teeter, 2015).

We thus promote assessing carefully any presenting issues before we explore the extent to which particular gender or gender role issues may play a part in the couple's issues. For example, a couple fighting over neatness/messiness in the relationship may not reflect any gender issues. However, if the issue goes unresolved as therapy advances, gender issues may be explored. These may include an expectation that because of gender, one partner is expected to clean up after the other.

In addition, *when therapy seems stuck* and the clients are not experiencing or showing movement in the direction they desire, a therapist may find fruitful ground in exploring gender-related differences as well as other culturally based variables. We may do this by first addressing some conventionally accepted male and female preferences. These stereotypes are used to clarify sex roles and culture. It must be kept clearly in mind that these stereotypic recognitions are not reified, but that they may generate useful hypotheses. Although in any given relationship, these gender-based observations and roles could be uniquely defined, even reversed, it is useful for therapists to be aware of the characteristic male/female differences and gender-related disputes, particularly when the therapy is not going smoothly. Awareness of such differences does not mean prejudice against either group. It just may allow therapists to take some safe hypothetical shortcuts to further connect with the couples they treat.

Gender in Couple Therapy

Gender, like all aspects of culture and diversity, can have a powerful impact on couple therapy. There are a number of gendered beliefs that may impact the process and outcome of couple work in therapy. For example, a common belief among couple therapists is that the female partner in a heterosexual relationship is usually the primary driver and instigator of therapy. She is perceived as the partner who desires the most change in her partner and the relationship. Yet it is also commonly believed (e.g., ChenFeng & Galick, 2015) that therapists may unintentionally set the burden of change on the woman. Similarly, a common perception is that women need to be the caretakers of the relationship and men need to be more autonomous (Knudson-Martin et al., 2015; Leslie & Southard, 2009). In short, women are posited to be in charge of security and men in charge of the freedom side of the relational equation.

Current trends that began during the women's movement in the 1960s and continue today recognize contrasting needs: for men to be more involved and supportive in all aspects of couple and family relationships and for women to be more autonomous. Nonetheless, traditional patterns and influences remain with many couples. In some cases, it may be necessary for the therapist to accept gender roles that are counter to the therapists's own beliefs, so long as they do are acceptable and functional for the couple.

Of course, each couple defines their own relationship, and these broadly believed generalizations are only useful guides as hypotheses when a therapist works directly with a particular couple. Indeed, in a given couple, any distribution or balance of responsibility of the security and freedom aspects of the relationship will be somewhat unique. This is often significant when exploring gender roles in a relationship and the locus of change. It is not unusual that the heavier burden for change is on the partner who is believed to be tending more to the relationship.

A Couple With Some Typical Presenting Issues: Melinda and Jaden

Melinda and Jaden are a heterosexual, White, non-Hispanic, middle-class-income couple in their mid to late 30s. They were referred to marriage counseling by Melinda's individual therapist. Melinda had been in individual therapy for several years and was being treated for mixed anxiety and depression that was exacerbated after the birth of their twin sons. She had complained that Jaden did not help around the house, nor did he seem to parent the boys in a consistent and helpful manner. In the initial phone call, she told the couple therapist that Jaden might not agree to come in, and if he did he would not talk about anything important. She also implied that he had marginally agreed to come in only once.

When they appeared for the first session, her warnings seemed somewhat justified by their nonverbal behavior in the waiting room and when they entered the consulting room. Jaden seemed particularly uncomfortable and paced in the waiting room. When they entered, he sat on the far end of the long couch, crossed his legs, and looked away from the therapist and out the window. Although he was an attorney coming from his workplace, he was dressed casually in sweatpants, a San Francisco Giants sweatshirt, and a baseball cap with the SF logo.

Noticing these nonverbal cues, the therapist, a middle-aged woman, deliberately walked over to each member of the couple, shook their hands, and rolled her seat to be equidistant between them. She also began with a short welcome and immediately addressed Jaden:

T: You look like you are ready for the game tonight. Are you going?

J: (Appearing surprised, smiled) No. I have to get back to the office and work late.

T: Are you as much a Giants fan as you seem?

J: Yeah. Do you like the Giants?

T: I do. When I was a little girl, my dad took me to Candlestick to see "the Willies" (Mays and McCovey). McCovey hit one to the moon ... Been a fan ever since.[1]

Noticing that he had turned slightly toward her, had uncrossed his arms, and was making some eye contact, she continued:

T: I spoke briefly to Melinda over the phone, so I'd like to get your take on what brings you in today.

J: Melinda is unhappy with me.

T: In general, or are there specific things?

---

1 This type of apparent social banter may seem superfluous and must be considered judiciously. It may set the tone that goes down a path irrelevant to meeting the couple's objectives in therapy. However, the therapist in this case successfully engages the reluctant partner by noting his apparent initial reluctance.

J: Basically, she is an unhappy person and then I can't do anything right.

T: What is your sense of what Jaden is saying, Melinda?

M: Call me "Mel"; everyone does. I am overwhelmed with three kids at home, particularly twin 6-year-old boys, a part-time job, and not enough help. So, am I unhappy? Yeah. My life is no bed of roses.

T: Jaden, you seem to understand that Mel is unhappy a lot of the time. Tell me how you can't do anything right.

J: Mel thinks that as soon as I walk in the door, I should be ready to be *on duty* with the kids. She thinks I should make dinner half the time and talk with her about how bad life is. No matter what I do, she doesn't think it's okay.

T: Does that mean there are two overwhelmed parents every evening?

M: Pretty much.

T: That seems like something we might address fairly quickly. Before we get to that, what have you tried to do so far that hasn't worked, or even something that did work a little?

J: (Looking questioningly at Mel): Well, on Tuesday, I was supposed to make dinner and I thought, maybe I could make it easier if I picked up pizza and a salad. I also brought Mel some flowers. It was good for a while, then when the kids were in bed, she started on me that pizza was not healthy food for the kids and that it was expensive to buy food out and also flowers were another expense.

T: Your sense was that Mel appreciated the effort and thoughtfulness initially, but later she was critical of your choices. Is that accurate (looking toward Mel)?

M: I did appreciate his thinking of us ahead, and I did like the flowers. But then I started to think that the kids should eat more healthy, and also we are not doing great financially because I am only working part time and it seemed like an added expense. I wasn't very nice about it and I apologized on Wednesday morning at breakfast.

T: On the one hand it felt good to be thought of in a more romantic way, even in the dinner chaos, and on the other, your role as a good mom and family nutritionist also clicked in.

M: Yeah. Exactly!

J: I accepted her apology, but I don't know why we have to go negative all the time first.

T: Thanks for bringing up an excellent example. One thing I heard was that in an attempt to get closer, it worked temporarily, but then distance was created. I wonder if that is a pattern we might explore.

She noticed when she added that very early interpretation about the relational pattern, neither seemed put off by it and both managed to nod their heads.

Gender Considerations in Couple Therapy With Melinda and Jaden

All of the gender differences described in this chapter are based on research and clinical practice. However, clear scholarly and clinical evidence on the interface of couple therapy and gender is still minimal. We draw from many studies on gender socialization, gender role strain (e.g., Deaux, 1984; Levant & Richmond, 2016; O'Neill, 2008), and on studies of individual therapy, as well as the research on couples. Our summary here does not represent absolutes, but rather ways of viewing a couple to enhance fair, equitable treatment.

In this initial session with Mel and Jaden, the therapist dealt with some characteristic gender-based issues in couple work by making some adjustments, focusing on equality, and addressing the issues indirectly.

First, she joined by commenting appreciatively on how Jaden was dressed.

Second, she sat equidistant from each member of the couple to head off any concern that she and Mel would be ganging up on Jaden.

Third, she was willing to talk about sports and self-disclosed something about herself to allow him to relate to her better.

Fourth, she quickly showed interest in his perception of the difficulties (even if he did not respond directly to her question).

Fifth, she was even-handed and relationally focused in how she laid a foundation for future work.

Though Jaden and Mel's conflict follows traditional gender-based patterns, we do not know at this point whether they have actually discussed these roles, they are comfortable with them, they have just fallen into them by default, or they are patterning their parents' roles. By approaching the couple—particularly Jaden—in these ways, the therapist was responding in a manner that defused Jaden's anticipated worries about the entire endeavor. It is important to note that this couple did return for future sessions and had a very successful experience, dealing specifically with their mutual fears of intimacy and developing plans for bridging their differing needs for family life. For example, one of the therapist's later suggestions involved their planning a free day for Mel, while Jaden took the three kids to a local minor league baseball game (a very low-cost activity). Because it was one endeavor that allowed each of them time away, they connected much better when they got back home. The key dynamic addressed here is *equity* (discussed in greater detail in Chapter 3), which has significant implications for how they define gender roles.

EXERCISE BOX 11.1: INTERVENTIONS AND GENDER

The therapist here is described as a middle-aged woman. Would the intervention about baseball be different if the therapist were a man?

Cultural and Socialization Issues in Couple Therapy as They Affect Women

For many years in the study of psychotherapy, certain assumptions of the relative status and role of women have prevailed. As we will discuss later in this chapter, a significant number of case studies involved male therapists and female clients. This may sound glib, but our understanding of women from a man's perspective and a lack of understanding of men (as clients) led to some conclusions that disadvantaged women within the field.[2] Even in couple therapy, both theory and practice commonly placed a burden on woman partners[3] to bear extra responsibility for what was wrong in relationships and how it could best be fixed.

Researchers and writers such as Hanisch (2006); Hare-Mustin (1978, 1983, 2017); Nutt, (2005); Philpot, Brooks, Lusterman, and Nutt (1997); Silverstein and Brooks (2010); and Unger (1979) began to chip away at what they referred to as a "patriarchal view" of therapy that mirrored society and gender role patterns. Exploring a larger cultural context and influences of gender-role socialization, they persuasively explored the importance of power as a significant and understudied variable in relationships.

Systems and Gender

In general, the emphasis on historical—particularly early family-based—notions of pathology began to shift in the 1970s following larger social movements such as the civil rights and women's liberation movements. Within the field of psychotherapy, it gave rise to an increased interest in systemic views of couple functioning. Notions such as *circular causality* in relationships and structural milieus began to emphasize the importance of relational contexts rather than individual pathology in couple work.

Systems therapy, which applied contextual analyses, cybernetics, and communication patterns, grew out of two different long-term psychological traditions. *Structural family therapy* evolved from practitioners of psychodynamic and family-of-origin approaches

---

2   Although we agree that the traditions of psychotherapy may have served to disadvantage women, we take issue with common statements such as Pappas's (2019), "For decades, psychology focused on men (particularly White men), to the exclusion of all others" (p. 34). When it comes to therapy per se, men have been largely understudied. This has led to an imbalance in understanding men as well as women.
3   The exceptions were in cases of addiction and violence.

such as Minuchin (Minuchin & Fishman, 1981), Bowen (1996, 1974/2004), Framo (1992), and Ackerman (1970).

Strategic family work evolved from notions of behaviorism and cybernetics (Bateson, 1972) and practitioners such as Haley (1963, 1976); Watzlawick, Bavelas, and Jackson (1967); and Fisch, Weakland, and Segal (1982). Both clinicians and scholars were applying communication analyses to therapeutic change interactions. The work was expanded and found fruition, even radical construction, in the Milano School in Italy in the work of Palazoli, Boscolo, Chechin, and Prata (1985).

The examination of systems and homeostasis in relationships refocused the field on communication and other contextual issues rather than on individual, developmental pathology, particularly that of women. However, as Nutt (2013) indicates, even these new approaches were based on patriarchal models that disadvantaged women. For example, the structural models fostered traditional roles and placed the husband at the head of the household. As Goodrich, Rampage, Ellman, and Halstead (1988) and Pittman (1985) argued, this reinforced devaluation of women in the family and hence as a partner. Despite the improvements in the view of gender equality in these new models, the mother was still viewed as the one responsible for family harmony and was therefore responsible for any disharmony or relational problems (Haddock & Lyness, 2002). Although progress has been made as a result of these developments and the increasing feminization of the mental health field in which women outnumber men (American Psychological Association, 2016) by more than 2-1, evidence and clear guidelines on other areas of diversity—such as gender fluidity, interracial and cross-cultural relationships—are lacking, and the dynamics involved continue to be misunderstood and viewed as outliers.

One of the dominant role recommendations within systems approaches was to increase the involvement of the disengaged father in a family. Although this goal was quite valuable in many relationships, it sometimes came with moving the mother out of a disciplinarian role, which feminist writers viewed as a reduction of her power. Far more influential was the blame for her somehow blocking the father's enhanced involvement. As Walsh and Scheinkman (1989) and Silverstein (2003) describe it, the impact, whether unintentional or not, was an overvaluing of the father as family savior and devaluing of the mother as a lesser partner as her only powerful role was diminished.

Hare-Mustin (1978) and other feminist writers further objected to what was called "therapist neutrality" because it supported extant power differentials and a status quo that was unfavorable to female partners. They also critiqued an unfortunate consequence of the strategic model: the notion of *circular causality*. Rather than look at a relationship from a linear perspective to uncover the essential cause of particular problems, system therapists argued that there is no specific cause–effect index. Instead, a change anywhere in the system will reverberate throughout the entire interactional matrix. In addition, because counselor and therapy training is so geared to more feminine manners of inter-action, there can be an inclination for female therapists to be more open to clients of their own gender and male therapists who espouse feminist principles to react too strongly against a male who is encapsulated in a traditional male role as the disciplinarian, "fixer," primary wage earner, and stoic one.

From the perspectives of equifinality and circular causality, issues between partners were seen as relational, with all parties mutually responsible. Although this notion had significant positive value in therapeutic approaches to couples, some feminist writers were quick to indicate that when power in a relationship was unequal, these concepts could blame the victim, particularly in cases of domestic violence or threats of bodily harm, based primarily of the relative size of each person. They also questioned Whitaker's (1989) heuristic notion that individuals do not have affairs; couples have affairs. The critique was that married men were more likely to have affairs,[4] and as Nutt (2013) summarizes, the victimized wife was then somehow blamed for her husband's infidelity.

The basic feminist argument is that protecting the status quo for those who are in a one-down minority position is less helpful than if one is in an equal homeostasis. From a therapeutic standpoint, Satir's (1967) work—which focuses on the expression of feelings, the here and now in the consulting room, and active therapeutic engagement—was far less loaded with inequality.

One of the most salient examples of these inequalities was an early notion within systems theory of the "schizophrenogenic mother." Schizophrenia was hypothesized to be a result of certain kinds of maternal behavior that involved double binds, unclear boundaries, and inconsistency. This conceptualization that grew out of sociocultural beliefs of the day and psychoanalytic thinking of the 1940s and 1950s held sway for many years. Perhaps the most significant aspect of the term was the blame leveling at the woman, who was simultaneously viewed as the marital partner with less power, who nonetheless had the amazing ability to "drive her children crazy." Today this concept is considered unfitting, and yet the forces that assigned women both powerlessness and tremendous negative influence remain to some extent in the early 21st century.

As Sutherland, LaMarre, Rice, Hardt, and Le Couteur (2017) indicate, modern sexism is more subtle and yet maintains a patronizing tone toward women. This more "benevolent sexism" seems positive but holds women as more fragile and less competent, needing male protection. The double bind that closes the loop in couple therapy is that women are viewed as weaker and as the partner who is often seen as the primary initiator of change. This contradiction leaves women as the protector of the relationship and the likely source of any problems, with no clear pathway for equality.

We take the position that relationship dynamics are *multi-determined*: far too complex to assign to simple cause-and-effect paradigms. For example, bringing the father into a more active role in a family may be an effective way to create greater balance and serve the best interest of the children. However, the strong role the mother plays must be acknowledged and negotiated between the parents. In regard to intimate partner violence, the abuse must be stopped, primarily through intervention with the abuser. Once it has ceased, it is relevant to examine the overall context of the relationship and the sequence of interactions between the partners that contribute to and sustain the problem from a systemic perspective. We believe such a formulation is a pragmatic approach that examines the objective reality that is occurring. Rather than interjecting a theoretical or philosophical perspective into assessing and treating difficult couple dynamics, it provides a wide-angle lens to examine presenting problems and collaborates with the couple to achieve effective solutions.

---

4   One consequence of increased freedom for women and their greater likelihood of being in the workplace is that opportunities for both partners in a couple to engage in infidelity has increased and the affair-by-gender gap has narrowed.

Gender and Power in Couple Therapy

To ignore power dynamics in a relationship is akin to disregarding any other cultural variable. Therapists need to be aware of circumstances in which role socialization is interfering with effective interactions and problem solving and to be able to name it as it arises.

This can involve intervening by directly verbalizing the power differential.

Yvette: I just need more help around the house when he comes home from work.

T: Such as?

Y: I want him to babysit the kids when I get dinner or help with dinner while I get the kids ready for bath.

T: (Naming the power differential) You just used two words that really resonated with me, "help" and "babysit." They both indicate to me that you are responsible for taking care of the home and children and that Rafi's job is to pitch in as a volunteer assistant. Is that an agreement you have discussed and agreed to?

Y: Well. I am a teacher, so I get home earlier from work than Rafi does.

T: Stay with me for a moment. Did the two of you agree on this or are you just fulfilling natural, socially acceptable roles?

R: She just takes over when she gets home and tells me what I need to do.

T: And how does that work for you?

R: Well. It doesn't, because I want to get things done at home also when I get home.

T: Such as?

R: I want to play with the kids. I see them at breakfast and then at dinner. So, I want some fun time with them.

Y: Well. That's it! I have to be the one in charge. He will just play with them and then give them their bath late and they don't get to bed by 8:00.

T: I'd just like to take a moment to think about how you got to be the boss of dinner, playtime, bedtime, bath.

Y: That's what a mom does. My mother did all that too. My dad was the fun parent and mom was the disciplinarian.

Note that the therapist here kept trying to refocus the couple on how Yvette was entrapped by filling an unnegotiated social role that may not serve her or Rafi. It just fell to her as a "mom's burden." If the therapist blithely proceeded to have Rafi "help" Yvette more from a traditional gender role perspective, there may have been temporary improvement, but Yvette would continue to feel overwhelmed, and Rafi would be resentful both over being told what to do and not having time to decompress after work. The therapist's "naïve" questioning along with his or her perseverance to explore unspoken decisions allows Yvette and Rafi to understand each other's viewpoints and collaborate to meet each other's needs.

There were several incidents in this therapy where the therapist asked questions about how they made decisions such as these and the toll it was placing on the marriage and family. At one point, he offered some homework to address it.

T: I have a very weird idea for an experiment. Would you two be willing to have Yvette as the fun parent and Rafi as the firm parent for one evening next week?

R: Does that mean that I have to do the kids and make dinner?

Y: Well that's what I always do!

T: It's interesting to see how hard this might be. You haven't tried it and are already arguing. No. I am suggesting that, on this Tuesday, for example, Rafi takes charge of the dinner and bedtime and asks Yvette for "help" if he needs it.

Y: It'll just work out the same. He will just ask me to do everything.

T: Maybe. But because he is in charge, you can say no or just play with the kids.

Y: But then they won't get to bed on time.

R: So, it'll be 8:30 instead of 8:00 one night. Let's try it.

It took them three tries to actually do it without sabotage by one or the other. Once they did, they became aware of their ability to set rules that were appropriate for the two of them rather than rely on some internalized social roles. The homework was focused on getting them to engage in different behavior before exploring their reactions instead of a more objective conceptual exploration of gender roles. It also forced them to consider the status quo and face the anxiety of altering it to create a new homeostasis.

DISCUSSION BOX 11.1: INTERVENTIONS AND GENDER

The therapist here is a man. Would the intervention about automatic gender-based and non-negotiated roles be different if the therapist were a woman? How so?

Assertiveness and Nurturance

Many feminist therapists and scholars draw a direct link to a common perception that women are to emphasize and focus on the needs of others above their own, a practice that promotes inequality (e.g., Coontz, 2005). According to these writers, the corresponding message given to men is that they are to be autonomous, powerful, strong, and aggressive (ChenFeng & Galick, 2015; Doull, Oliffe, Knight, & Shoveller, 2013; Knudson-Martin, 2013). In therapy, when one partner accepts responsibility for the relationship, she is most commonly the one who is expected to change.

In their study of 19 heterosexual couples, ChenFeng and Galick (2015) reported three dominant gender discourses:

1. "Men should be the authority"
2. "Women should be responsible for relationships"
3. "Women should protect men from shame"

They concluded that therapists inadvertently reinforce gender discrepancies by the following:

1. Overvaluing the man's perspective of difficulties
2. Failing to intervene when the male partner verbally interrupted his female partner or blamed her for their relationship troubles
3. Focusing on how the woman can change to help the man, without a corresponding request of what she may need from him
4. Being less empathic with the female perspective. For example, when men are asked a question by the therapist, their answers are too often accepted as factual. By contrast, women partners' answers to similar questions are then addressed to the male for confirmation

In line with ChenFeng and Galick's (2015) cautions, several studies seem to indicate that men more frequently talk over and interrupt female partners and that therapists interrupt women more frequently as well (Smith-Lovin & Brody, 1989; Werner-Wilson, Price, Zimmerman, & Murphy, 1997). West and Zimmerman (1983) refer to these as small insults that establish and maintain power differences in a relationship. Subjective observation tends to support the notion that conversational power is a prerogative that flows more naturally to the male partner in a heterosexual relationship.

It is important to note that few of these studies controlled for the amount of time each partner actually talked during a session (West & Zimmerman, 1983). In the Werner-Wilson and colleagues (1997) study, the researchers did account for the number of words in the video clips that were coded. They also studied both male and female couple therapists. However, these therapists were all doctoral students and thus less experienced than licensed professionals. Therapists are wise to observe and rebalance such interactions, if they see them occurring. In one example where one partner consistently interrupted the other, the therapist intervened by saying, "I'm going to interrupt you here Boris, I'd like to hear what Talia began to say."

In some relationships, especially those with a pursuer–distancer pattern of interaction, it may well be the woman who talks far more than the man and verbally dominates their interactions. The following interaction is all too common in therapy:

> Marnie: The problem is that Eric never says anything. He never expresses his feelings. He just sits there like a bump on a log, like there like nothing is going on. See, he's just silent now. I don't know what to do with him.

She spoke for about 5 minutes uninterrupted by the therapist, a young woman, or her partner, Eric. Each time either of them tried to say something, Marnie just kept going, sometimes indicating "I'm talking."

> T: What is going on for you now, Eric?

> E: (Quietly and shrugging) I'm sad.

> M: (In a louder voice) What do you have to be sad about? If you only would engage me, you wouldn't be sad and I wouldn't be beside myself.

> T: Marnie, I am going to interrupt you, here. Let's focus for a moment on Eric's statement that he is sad, without evaluating it. (Turning to Eric) Tell me about what is making you sad now.

This form of interruption had to occur several times before the couple could begin to talk to one another without the tidal wave of words and resultant "low-tide" withdrawal in response. Later they had to come to grips with the manner in which their pattern of frustrating one another was an unfortunate attempt to connect while anxious about intimate contact for both.

Implications of Gender and Power Differentials on Therapy

Gendered role socialization and inherent inequality have significant implications within therapy. Therapists need to be aware of gender differences, equally honor both perspectives, and explore with the couple any gender-based dominant culture pressures that hold one (particularly the female) partner more accountable for the relationship and more responsible for changes.

In her summary of qualitative studies of feminist therapy training, Whipple (1996) underscored a true meaning of feminism as equality and summarized that feminist-oriented couple/family therapy included, among other factors, personal awareness of therapist gender-role socialization, therapist encouragement of a nonhierarchical therapeutic relationship, introduction of gender-related topics into therapy, encouragement of egalitarian couple relationships, and affirmation of women's experiences as equal and important. She also encouraged a focus on gender stereotypes as damaging to both women and men. From her conclusions, it is important to note that both male and female therapists may be equally effective if they employed these guidelines.

Serena: I just cannot please his parents or any of my in-laws. They constantly criticize my parenting the kids, tell me that I should discipline the dog better, cook the way they do, and dress differently and he just sits there and does nothing.

T: J.R., is that your impression also?

J.R. My family is very critical of me also. Serena is just too sensitive to their shit.

S: That's because the biggest criticism of you is that you married me. Remember the wedding fiasco, when they threatened not to come and then they showed up unexpectedly and blamed me for not having a table for them?

J.R.: That's just their way. They are not easy. Look at what it was like for me growing up in that household.

T: (Addressing the gendered beliefs) What I am struck by here is that somehow Serena gets blamed by your family and is expected to somehow fix it on her own. You agree that they are problematic, but you somehow stop there.

J.R.: Well they are a royal pain. I won't let them babysit the kids because of my parents' penchant for corporal punishment and because of what they say about Serena (and me).

T: (Sticking to the gender issue) I just want to know how Serena ended up as the one who has to fix the relationship with your family. She ends up here with all the responsibility and none of the power to get a change done.

J.R.: Well. I guess I know better than to get into it with my folks. Nobody wins.

T: I don't doubt your conclusion. Ask Serena what she feels in these situations.

J.R.: What do you feel?

S: Invisible.

T: J.R., how do you understand that?

J.R.: I think what that means is that she (responding to T's request that he talk to his wife), *you* feel disrespected and like you are a small child at the whim of some powerful aggressor—scared, like I was in my childhood with them. It's like there's no way to be right.

T: Serena, how close is that?

S: That's exactly it, and if I may add, I hope for my support to come through and protect me or agree with me publicly.

T: Tell Serena how you can help her in dealing with this very difficult situation. Where can you take over the battle?

J.R.: Well. I think she (turning to Serena), you are a terrific mom and I like your cooking and the way you dress, and mostly I don't believe in the kind of discipline they do.

T: Serena, what are you hearing now?

S: That he appreciates me and what I do and who I am.

T: What else could he offer you? How might he take the lead in dealing with the situation?

S: I think this may be hard to swallow, but when they criticize me, I'd like you to tell them to stop, and if they continue, I'd like you to tell them we are leaving until they can be more appropriate to me. Like on Easter dinner, when they were dissing me about the bread pudding. I said "enough" to them and that just got them going more. I think your mother said, "Just being honest." I said that I could use less of her honesty and asked you to go. At that point I want you to stand up for me. You know, I do that with my parents, who are also no major bargain when it comes to kindness.

T: That's a strong statement. What's it like for you to say it?

S: It feels good … a little scary too.

T: J.R., what would it take for you to go along with her in such situations?

Notice here that the therapist did not hold Serena responsible, encouraged her assertiveness, and shifted the locus of change to J.R. The solution Serena requested was such that she would be more assertive and he would be more supportive. This both acknowledges the gendered-oriented socialization roles, without specifically naming it as such, and moves toward increasing role flexibility for each person. She also encouraged his empathy with what his wife was experiencing and tried to rebalance the extended family situation where Serena and J.R.'s relationship was primary. Finally, she encouraged both to ask for what they want and encouraged both to respond with expressed empathy.

DISCUSSION BOX 11.2: THE GENDER OF THE THERAPIST

The reader may be wondering how responses would differ if the therapist in this vignette were male. We have described her as female. As indicated earlier, both gay and straight individuals are gender fluid by virtue of biology, socialization, and personality in their views of the world, and their relationships to others. Thus, a male therapist may be more or less aligned with Serena, regarding role equity, than with J.R., and vice versa. Thus, counter-transference or subconscious bias may be influenced, but not entirely determined, by gender.

A therapist may be inclined from his or her own perspective to encourage Serena to speak up to her in-laws on her own, or to stress JR's responsibility to protect Serena by standing up to his parents. From a systems viewpoint and the couple's preferences, both are workable solutions and respect the autonomy of both spouses. Especially difficult for an egalitarian therapist to accept is a couple whose values and choices involve traditional gender roles. In this case, respect for client autonomy requires us to assume a neutral posture. As in all situations, it is not our job as the therapist to determine which type of gender roles fit a couple best, but to assist them from their own value base to work out the roles and patterns that alleviate their conflicts and are most functional for them overall. Thus, our role is to incisively question and review with the couple how these choices affect their presenting problems and to serve their interests in the most ethical fashion.

Process, Process, Process

The answer for most couple therapists is that by focusing on the process and on consequences, some of the gender role issues may be ameliorated. Consider the impact of process on Knute and Maureen, newlyweds who came to see the therapist after what they described as a "disastrous honeymoon." According to their description of events, "everything went wrong." Among the issues were the following:

1. Some unanticipated sexual disparities that they both attributed to lack of experience
2. Texts from her parents that she should have had him sign a prenuptial agreement, with recommendations and pressure for a postnuptial agreement with her parents' attorney
3. Their first argument that ended with them not talking to each other for several hours
4. The reservations for their honeymoon were lost or not honored and their having to find alternative housing
5. His anger at events and treatment of others with more anger than she had expected
6. Her withdrawal when he sought physical connection

M: Thank you for seeing us. I called because things just were not going as expected and we are both unhappy.

T: Knute, would you agree with that? How do you see it?

K: Yeah. Mo is right. We were planning on happily ever after and we are now looking at unhappily.

M: Well, we hope to work it out. We just didn't expect so many problems right after the wedding.

K: (Interrupting) We were barely married when everything started to crash down. Even the honeymoon was a disaster.

T: (Taking in what he said, but not accepting it as mutual truth) Mo, would you agree about the word *disaster*?

M: Yes and no. I mean it wasn't all ...

K: (Interrupting) Look, it was a disaster. Let's face it. In less than a week, we had our dream honeymoon fall apart, we had in-law problems, we may have financial problems, and we may have some incompatibilities we didn't expect.

T: I can't tell if you feel more angry, frustrated, or hurt?

M: He is frustrated, and he deserves to be.

T: (Not accepting her care taking) Knute, Mo seems to think you are feeling more frustrated. I wonder what emotion you would say.

K: I think I am more fearful that we have got off on a wrong footing and it'll be hard to fix.

T: So you are fearful, somewhat sad, and wanting to fix the relationship. Mo, is that new information for you?

M: You know, Knute, I don't blame you for the reservation mess and the fact that we are both inexperienced sexually, and I certainly don't blame you for my parents and all that prenup talk. I don't blame myself either, except we probably should have worked on this in premarital counseling. I know you didn't like the minister and his counseling.

T: Knute, is that how you see it also?

K: Yeah. He was just wanting to get us to sign up for his church and pledge a tithe. He never asked about what we might want to discuss.

T: So, here are two places where you both agree: Neither of you is to blame for the situation and that the minister wasn't right for any real exploration of issues. So, where would you like to start? What's the most pressing issue between you, now?

M: I know what he'll say. If the sex was better, everything else would work out.

T: (Again avoiding being distracted by the potential gender issues, here) Well, we can certainly address the sexual issues here, but first, I wonder how much you (Knute) think that's the major block.

K: I think it's the prenup/postnup issue. That's on my mind all the time.

T: Mo, you seem surprised by that?

M: I already told my parents to butt out and we would decide about that.

T: Knute, you look surprised by that.

K: I didn't know.

T: Okay, so let's begin by the two of you negotiating the first issue for us to address. I'll listen and, if necessary, will help, but you two decide.

What followed was a more equitable discussion, although, at several junctions, Mo seemed more interested in protecting Knute's feelings than her own, particularly about any potential shame he might have about being inexperienced sexually. With help, they were able to talk together, listen better than usual, and come to agreements regarding learning how to be better sexual partners and deal with external pressures as a team.

Although the therapist was particularly sensitive to the gendered issues, she did not highlight them, here. She simply pointed out her observations and worked with the process, trying to avoid falling into gender-role expectation traps. She demonstrated a form of therapeutic neutrality in which, without necessarily commenting on gender roles, she mitigated the normal power differentials that can occur in the context of couple work.

DISCUSSION BOX 11.3

This is a point where the therapist could obviously have noted the potential for greater gender role imbalance and asked Mo whether she wanted to continue taking care of Knute's feelings. Here, she took a neutral position and moved ahead without commenting. Which approach do you believe is more effective, and what would you base your decision on?

THERAPY BOX 11.1: TWO ALTERNATIVE APPROACHES

From a CBT perspective, it may make sense to discuss the gender-role expectations, label them in the couple's framework, and deductively work on cognitive distortions and specific methods to decrease unsuccessful behaviors and activate more functional ones. This method can lead more directly to transfer of training.

From an existential perspective, the approach demonstrated in this vignette was for the therapist to listen closely for gender role issues and to simply work with them inductively in the here and now, without necessarily making them conscious. The therapist and clients operate together on a search to discover what means the most and works the best for the couple

---

Two Key Issues to Explore With Women

The first and perhaps most obvious issue requires a sensitivity to and understanding of the effect of traditional gender-role socialization. Despite great strides toward acknowledging gender fluidity and equality in the past 50 years, patterns from previous eras endure. They can be insidious, even in younger couples today, because gender role patterns are largely transmitted across generational patterns. For example, limited gender roles and patterns promoted by grandparents raised in the 1950s influenced their children's viewpoints on gender roles, and these in turn were passed on to subsequent generations. *Wonder Woman* notwithstanding, some forms of popular media still portray women as traditional homemakers, who fulfill less powerful and capable roles than men, who continue to be viewed as the primary providers and protectors. The disadvantages of such discrimination for men are described later. School textbooks and children's fairy tales continue to depict boys and girls in stereotyped roles. When these views serve to inhibit a woman's sense of self and limit her aspirations, career choices, or desires for personal growth and independence, they may deeply impact the relational issues that couples bring to therapy. A keen awareness and sensitive exploration of the impact of a sense of powerlessness (suffocation) may be mandatory to help clients make their desired changes.

A second powerful influence to examine is the roles some women fall into with their current partner, regardless of their early socialization. This may reflect an inherent desire to please others, coercion by their partner, fear of abandonment, or an avoidance of confrontation. When such automatic roles are entrenched in a relationship from the beginning, and reinforced by the needs of children, work, and home, pressures ensue and likely impact satisfaction of both partners.

It is not for therapists to determine which levels of freedom and security are in a woman's best interests (from our personal perspectives), or to judge the kinds of equality that exist in a given relationship. Our job is to explore role patterns as they impact the couple's presenting issue and interfere with intimacy and growth. In the current economy, a majority of women are forced or choose to work full time, and yet surveys indicate that they continue to carry the major responsibility for childcare, household, and socialization for the family (Biernat & Wortman, 1991; Lachance-Grzela & Bouchard, 2010).

Section Summary: Power and Gender From a Gender-Equity Perspective

Considerable scholarship and research support a feminist/relational understanding of how gender role socialization can impact couple communication and relational roles. These power differentials may seem subtle at times and may be a primary cause of relational difficulties. It is clear from research on couple therapy that equality is an essential piece in couple interactions and in healing. Therapists who are aware of their own gender training and role expectations are far better suited to identify gender-oriented issues for couples and to help ameliorate them. It is essential to indicate that gender alone may be insufficient to understand the important values and beliefs of any particular clients. We have specifically reduced the variables under consideration here to highlight gender as a significant variable. However, it is insufficient to comprehend intersectionality. For example, identifying as a woman, a particular minority, and living at lower socioeconomic status levels require independent and interactive considerations.

Gender Similarities and Differences

Although numerous studies indicate that the psychological differences within gender are greater than differences between them (Hyde, 2018; Zell, Krizan & Teeter, 2015), it can be useful for therapists to look for indications of stereotypical behavior of men and women as a way to generate hypotheses. This is not to recommend that such observations be treated as facts, but rather as entry points into each member of the couple.

For example, early in this chapter, we described a therapist bonding with Jaden, a client whose partner indicated that he was (stereotypically) reluctant. She took only a few moments to bond with him over a baseball team, after noting his fan clothing. She even shared her own experience as a young girl going to a game with her dad. This is not the characteristic manner of starting therapy with a couple or an individual, but it is a common form of bonding with men. By doing so, she indicated that she was open to things that were important to him and that she was willing to share something of herself in that realm.

Joining with clients in their personal characteristic ways of being is essential in all therapy, but it may also be important to connect along gender lines until more personal contact can be made. It is particularly useful when one partner seems especially anxious or reluctant, relying more on the *creativity* and of course *presence* of the therapist than on any research theoretical-based protocol.

In the example with Melinda and Jaden, the therapist had a working hypothesis (from her conversation with Melinda) that he was entering therapy reluctantly, because of a number of concerns that were not shared by Melinda:

1. He may anticipate that he will be blamed as the reason for all the couple difficulties
2. He may expect that the therapist and his female partner will gang up on him
3. He may expect that his perceptions and interests will be lost in the discussion
4. He may believe that his approaches to problem solving will be dismissed out of hand
5. He may also worry that he will not have the "feelings-oriented" therapeutic jargon that his partner and the therapist speak

These concerns are not to be minimized. Many beginning therapists do approach couples in a male- and masculine-dismissing manner. Consider what would have been the outcome if the therapist in the example with Mel and Jaden responded to confirm his anticipated worries. The following is a transcription of the beginning of such a session.

T: Melinda, you called me. Please tell me more about the difficulties that we can address (not acknowledging Jaden not having prior contact).

M: (While Jaden stared out the window) My therapist said that if I were to work through the issues with our marriage, we should meet as a couple. Basically, I have been very unhappy for a long time, particularly since the boys were born 6 years ago. I feel like I have all the responsibilities and that Jaden just goes off to work and doesn't help me when he comes home.

T: What sorts of help are you looking for?

M: Well, when he gets home, he should co-parent; not just sit around and expect me to do it all.

T: Jaden, what do you think about that?

J: Basically, she is an unhappy person and then I can't do anything right.

T: What is your sense of what Melinda is feeling?

J: She has a hard job with three kids and a job and wants me to take over when I get home, but I am exhausted too. I work long, hard hours and need a buffer zone when I walk in the house. It's like she is lying in wait and just attacks as soon as she hears the car in the driveway. And it's not just her; the kids are all over me too.

T: You do hear that Melinda is overwrought and desperate for help when you return.

J: Well, that's another thing. She needs a break. I get it, but I do too. Give me a chance to get home, change my clothes (I am usually in a suit and tie), and then I can either help with dinner or the kids.

M: I have to do both. Why can't he get dinner done and give me a break with the kids? And why does he get the buffer, when I don't?

T: You see that the arrangement the two of you have is unequal and unfair to you.

M: Yeah, why does the woman have to always be the one to do everything?

T: We can explore that. You do know that it is a much larger social problem about inequality.

J: Well, even when I do what she wants, she is critical about how I do it. I knew Wednesday night was going to be rough, so I picked up some food on the way home and some flowers for Mel. So, what does she do? She tells me that it's too expensive and that pizza is bad for the kids.

The session went on like that, affirming Jaden's anticipated concerns.

The couple did not return for their scheduled second session.

Before addressing gender-related issues for men, let's explore briefly another set of stereotypical gender preferences in communication for men and women. These have powerful implications for effective communications for couples and for therapeutic approaches. Many couples report frustration with their partner's manner of talking and, more importantly, listening.

Functional and Intimate Communication

In 1991, Tannen introduced the notion that men and women may belong to dissimilar linguistic communities. Tannen argued that men and women communicate differently. Similar popular psychology notions have been promulgated by Gray (1992) and others, suggesting that men and women come from different conversational planets or speak in alternative love languages (Chapman, 2015). Although such work has been questioned by later research (Hyde, 2018), and gender-related disparities reportedly are small (e.g., Zell, Krizan & Teeter, 2015), there may be some advantages for couple therapists to consider potential different uses of language and conversation across gender lines, especially when the therapy gets bogged down (Shapiro, 2016). In short, we offer these potential differences as one way of reaching a couple.

Functional Communication

For functional matters, male and female stereotypical communication is often quite similar. For example, when May asks Joe, "Do we need milk from the store?" the answer is expected to be on target and direct to the question. Among potential responses are

"Yes, good reminder"

"Oops, I'll pick up a half-gallon on the way home. Do we need anything else while I'm there?";

"Any chance you could pick it up? I am running late"

"Do you want 1% or 2%?"

Had Joe asked the question, Mary might have responded in exactly the same way.

Similarly, if one of them asks, "Would you get the ladder? We need to change two light bulbs" expectations are that the issue of changing the light bulbs will be addressed in the response, "I'll get it right away"; "I'm busy right now. How about 30 minutes?"; "You know, I want the kids to learn how to do this. Let's wait for them to get home and I'll do it with them."

There is little room for different forms of communication or languages in functional situations. However, when a couple is "at war" with one another, any communication can lead to problems and misunderstandings. For example, a much larger issue can be ongoing if the response to either request is something like, "Why do you treat me like a servant? Why do I have to be the one to do everything?" "Do it yourself!" or the like. In such circumstances, there is something far more insidious in the relational communication where anger is the underlying topic, not milk or light bulbs.

One classic form of dysfunctional communication occurs when one partner expects a particular response and the partner is unaware because of the way she or he hears the communication. For example, the woman says, "It's cold in here" (expecting that her partner will immediately respond by retrieving a sweater or turning up the heat). However, he may hear it as her opinion and might respond by saying factually, "It's 70 degrees." In such a situation, she may stew over her partner's insensitivity or lack of caring, and he may be irritated that she expects him to be a "mind reader."

The resulting spat is common material in couple therapy sessions, often with a request that the therapist judge who is the wrong partner. This miscommunication can occur with either partner feeling let down and hurt because of unclear, unassertive communication and unmet expectations.

Intimate Communication

However, if we look at preferred modes of communication about relational matters, we can see some characteristic differences in men and women. They are represented in Figure 11.1.

Men	Women
Shoulder to Shoulder	Face-to-Face
Time limited	Time indeterminate
Bottom Line First	Story First
One Subject at a Time	Many Subjects Interwoven
Clear Expectations	Open Expectations
Primarily Informational	Primarily Relational

FIGURE 11.1 **Gender and communication**

Stereotypical Preferences for Men

Most intimate male conversation occurs *shoulder to shoulder*, when both parties are looking in the same direction at something outside themselves. Men talk most easily about personal relational matters when they are walking side-by-side, riding in a car, sitting at a ball game, or lying beside their partners. The lack of direct eye contact seems to enhance openness, rather than detract from the intimacy of the conversation. In addition, it may be related to the fact that men often respond better to metaphors in such discussions.

For men, *time-limited* conversations are preferred. They want to know up front, "Is this a 10-minute, 30-minute, or hour-long conversation? The answer will provide a framework (and security) for his interaction.

Men also prefer the *bottom line prior to the story*. They prefer to do a damage assessment and determine if some action (or solution) on their part is necessary. The longer he has to wait for the key pieces of information, the more upset he is likely to become.

Men also prefer to talk about *one subject at a time*. They characteristically do not have the bandwidth to connect several topics simultaneously (this is related both to biology and socialization). When the topic drifts or changes in his mind, he tries to get it back on course and refocus on finding solutions to the primary problem under discussion.

We have often observed that the easiest way to infuriate a man is to ask him to do something and then, when he begins, ask him to do something different or to tell him how to do it differently.

For men, there is a strong preference to know the reason for a particular conversation to have *clear expectations* of the outcome.

Finally, men prefer conversations that primarily gather or share *information*.

From a therapeutic perspective, there is nothing particularly unusual or problematic with these preferred ways of communicating. Interventions may readily be made using these preferences.

During a time when the interactions were wordy, rambling, and devoid of feeling, the therapist, looking directly into Doug's eyes, requested his emotional reaction to the matter being discussed. Doug responded with a rambling, circuitous series of questions about the usefulness of such inquiry. The therapist then went to the characteristic "male pattern."

> T: (Looking more indirectly toward Doug) Doug, I'd like to ask you to try a very short, 5-minute, thought experiment. If you could imagine it, what do you think a guy in your current situation might experience in a similar situation?

The intervention was time limited and avoided eye contact, was hypothetical, and was narrowly focused as speculation.

> D: I suppose when I think of it, anyone would be really pissed off at being in this situation.

> T: That makes sense to me. It does seem quite unfair and unpleasant. What do you suppose happens to *your* anger?

In a sense, we are being consistent with culturally relevant interventions by using the language and process of the client. This method is far more likely to be successful than pressing for something that is more alien for a client. Difficulties emerge in couple work when each partner is using language and conversation in a different manner.

Decision Box 11.1. Decision Point: At the point where Doug questioned the usefulness of describing his emotions, a therapist could have moved on and waited for a more opportune time. In this case the therapist used a method suggesting that Doug look outside of himself as the "other," and it was easier for him to comment on what others in his situation might do. Which do you prefer?

For many reasons, women usually prefer *face-to-face communication* with eye contact. They trust the interactions more when they are observing facial reactions. For many women, this may also be a safety issue.

For most women, an *indeterminate time for the conversation* is preferable. Talking is fun and bonding. Thus, the more natural the ending time, the better. She may opine when pressed, "I don't know how long it will take; let's just enjoy the experience."

Most women prefer the *story before* coming to the bottom line. The more involved the plot twists, the more people involved, the more speculation, the more detail offered, the more interesting the conversation, and the better the bottom line will be.

Women also tend to prefer *multiple topics* that impact one another simultaneously. The connections between stories are usually present, if not in a linear order. This offers richness to any interaction.

Because talking is an enjoyable experience, *open expectations* are preferred. "I don't know where this will take us; let's go for the experience."

Finally, communication is judged based on the *relationship* that exists during and afterward. Information is secondary to how everybody feels toward one another.

Again, there is nothing particularly unusual or problematic with women's stereotypic preferred ways of communicating. The goals for a conversation are reached and the focus on the relationship allows for additional input. Unfortunately, it seems like a cosmic joke when men and women (and again we are describing stereotypes) have to communicate with one another. It can also be an additional problem in therapy, because both male and female therapists are trained to be more "feminine" in the way we talk: feelings oriented, relationally sensitive, empathic, and for the most part open to whatever emerges. It is also usually positioned face-to-face.

Successful couple therapists have to be in a sense bilingual: listening and relating to the male member along masculine preferences and to the female member along feminine preferences. Because each couple may have unique manners of communication, therapists must be able to adjust to each person's style and pacing as they present themselves and to join with them in a relevant way.

Couple Communication

For both LGBTQ and heterosexual couples, successful conversations about the relationship are characterized by doing it the "male" way about 50% and the "female" way about 50%. It is rarely, if ever, that balanced in a given conversation. Sometimes the conversation follows a more male preferred pattern; other times it is more "female."[5]

How do couples determine what form a conversation takes? Most successful couples work this out naturally and primarily unconsciously. Therapists often have to help a couple identify and understand their partner's style of interaction and to help

---

5   The reader will note that this comment is stereotypical in itself, because roles can easily be reversed; whether therapist or client, a man may take a typically more feminine approach and a woman may follow a more masculine mode. Picture the potential dissonance when a therapist in a female mode treats a couple in which the man is more feminine and the woman is more stereotypically masculine—a good time to consult and check our own biases about gender role stereotypes!

them communicate more effectively. The determination of which form would be most fruitful in a given conversation is slightly counterintuitive. It is not determined by the person for whom the topic is most important, nor for the one who wants to influence the partner. *The essential determination of which type of conversation is held will depend on who needs to listen.*

If I want my male partner to hear something important, we are best suited to engage in a shoulder-to-shoulder alignment with clear time and goal boundaries. If I want my female partner to hear what I have to say, it will best be done face-to-face and unrushed. When Gwen was frustrated that Julius, her long-time partner had "ear lids" whenever she wanted to talk about their future, their counselor recommended that they go for a walk and, during the walk, set aside a 10-minute period to talk about her future aspirations. He inquired how it went the following week during the session.

G: (laughing) Well it worked, sort of! (When the counselor looked at her with a questioning look, she continued) When I told him I wanted to go back to school to finish my degree, he asked when and began to strategize about how we could afford the loss of my income for about 9 months. He also surprised me by asking how this fit into my desires to have a child.

T: So how was that for you?

G: Way better than I had hoped for.

T: So, the downside ... ?

G: After about 15 minutes, he wanted to stop talking about it.

J: She asked for 10. I gave her 15 and we came to a partial solution. After that I didn't want to hash it out again. I told her I was interested in helping her financially if she wanted to complete her BS, and also I was interested in planning a family. Story over.

T: So, by setting the time on your walk, you both got what you wanted. Julius, would you be willing to listen while I explore with Gwen, in here, more of her thinking? Was his interest in supporting you and of beginning a family new information?

You will note here that the therapist chose not to focus on what could be a gender issue when Julius used the term, "I gave her 15," indicating a potential power imbalance. It seems more important to help them learn how to get what they want in a conversation at this point.

Two Potential Dilemmas in Therapists' Communication on Gender

First, because gender socialization may be so ubiquitous and ingrained within cultural norms, it behooves all therapists to become aware of their personal gender role expectations and ways of responding to clients. Therapists who expect men to be stoic, protective, or dominant, for example, may inadvertently exacerbate gender-related conflicts in a couple. Such therapists may miss entirely the sociocultural context in which the couple functions.

It is no surprise that self-awareness is a most significant factor for all therapists, but gender and cultural context awareness is both external and internal. It requires an expanded sense of awareness of powerful cultural factors and potentially subconscious biases that can be deleterious to one or both members of a couple.

Second, training in counseling and therapy focuses on developing listening skills, expressing empathy, focusing on feelings, putting the clients' needs first, and being respectful of differences. This is stereotypically more female than male. All therapists are trained to communicate in the more feminine manner. This has implications in couple work when it is important for each party to listen. The "bilingual" therapist must be able to speak so that both men and women can best feel heard. By demonstrating and modeling listening in both ways, therapists teach clients to do so as well. This is why a therapist may talk to each member of a couple quite differently.

It is also necessary for couple therapists to be active, direct, and assertive. There are times to be reflective, listen quietly, and allow for silences. But it is also important at times to interrupt, to clearly state that certain behaviors—such as name-calling and hitting—are unacceptable, and to state when one person needs additional help, such as with severe substance abuse. This may cross gender lines and require both preventive explanations and closely tracking each partner's reactions.

Communication can also be complicated when the clients are gender nonconforming. When working with a same-sex couple, for example, a therapist may mistakenly expect that both will speak the same stereotypic gender language. Often, they do not, and their communication styles are more characteristic of heterosexual couples. Perhaps a therapist anticipates that each member will adopt a stereotypic role.

Daisy and Shawna are a lesbian couple who had been together for 4 years when they came into counseling. The presenting problem involved a new job opportunity for Shawna in a distant geographical location. When they began to discuss it, they self-described themselves, respectively, as "butch" and "femme," with Shawna appearing more masculine in her gender presentation. As both partners spoke, they did so in ways similar to stereotypic male/female roles.

Their therapist made efforts not to focus on sexual orientation as the impetus for their presenting concern and yet acknowledged and recognized that they were presenting in ways that were stereotypical of heterosexual gender roles. with familiar clashing gender-oriented styles. As the therapy bogged down, she discovered that both partners had high needs for affiliation, both preferred face-to-face interaction, and both were more interested in the other's feelings than in the particular solution to the current dilemma.

Once she was able to discern this, she avoided the "anticipated" differences and focused on the similarities in communication. She also directed the therapy to an exploration of what it would mean if they moved for the new job or stayed.

Cultural and Socialization Issues in Couple Therapy as They Affect Men

Whether it is attributed to patriarchy, toxic masculinity, misogyny, stoicism, androcentrism, "testosterone poisoning," or general masculine traits, men are currently held to blame for much of society's and relational ills within many academic and therapy-training disciplines in particular. As a field, we have accepted the notion described by Pappas (2019) that what we know has been primarily based on "his(story)," studies of males (particularly White males).

Several curious notions about gender and therapy can obfuscate the real needs of men and women. As mentioned earlier, the vast majority of the case studies in the history of the field have involved male therapists and female clients, hardly a prescription to understand men as clients. In fact, a majority of case studies of men often focus primarily on clients who have problems with addiction and/or violence. Of course, this also obviates possibilities to better understand women clients from a more feminine perspective. Thus, the bias in information disfavors women as it does men. Because our research and clinical literature does not actually focus on men, it has just defaulted to them without actually exploring and understanding their culture-specific needs, strengths, and areas of concern (Shepard & Harway, 2012).

Until the civil rights and women's movements in the 1960s and 1970s, this selection bias led to a general belief that women were more in need of therapy, had more deficits as people, were weaker (thus needing male protection and in a remarkably double-binding manner), and were also responsible for the health of the family. Since the first-wave feminist movement in society and in therapy, and several that followed, such as the recent women's marches, and the #MeToo movement, there has been a shift in the psychological world as well. Case studies still remain more oriented toward female clients, albeit with more female therapists. Sadly, the outcome of the change was to keep the process intact while altering the content. Now men were seen as the root of all social and relational problems (again with very few actual case studies of men).

In the 1990s "male bashing" became a popular tool of both pundits and many in the therapy establishment. Masculinity accrued pejorative terms like *traditional*, and even worse, *toxic*. These terms were spread widely and attempts were made to encourage men to become more feminine.

What does this mean for the treatment of men in couple therapy? How does it square with the well-reported notion that the male partner in a heterosexual relationship will be more reticent and fearful of being ganged up on in an anticipated female environment? If he is entering therapy with a number of fears, not shared by his partner, how does a therapist equalize the situation to engage the male partner? Once again, we acknowledge that we are highlighting traditional male stereotypes for the purpose of heightening therapist awareness of how gender may play out in couple dynamics. These roles may be reversed or exist on a continuum or not at all, but more often than not, partners' identification along gender roles plays a key role in their relationship.

Hooking the Male

Most texts and articles on couple therapy have a short section on how to engage the less interested member of the couple in therapy (Dienhart, 2001; Doss, Atkins, & Christensen, 2003; Englar-Carlson, & Shepard, 2005; Levant & Pollack, 1995; Mahalik, Good, & Englar-Carlson, 2003; Shepard & Harway, 2012). Traditionally, and in many cases today, the woman is more likely to initiate couple therapy and more likely to be the more involved client, although this may be changing today (Englar-Carlson, Evans, & Duffy, 2014; Englar-Carlson & Stevens, 2006)

Scher's (1990) 30-year-old statement is still held as accurate by many clinicians:

> The man who comes into the consulting room is usually there because he believes there is no alternative. Very few men come for therapy because they subscribe to its life-enhancing qualities. Even if they did, they would likely not see it as something for them anyway. Men are in therapy because something, internal or external, has driven them to it. (p. 323)

There are a number of reasons offered for this perceived gendered discrepancy. Most indicate that the more men follow traditional sex-role mores; the needs for stoicism, self-sufficiency, problem-solving in conflictual situations; and aggression or withdrawal in the face of partner criticism, the worse they are candidates for couple therapy. Levant (1995) reports that men are often afflicted with alexithymia, the inability of putting feelings into words, also a detriment to most therapy. It is our experience that in conversations about their relationships, men have difficulty active listening, without offering solutions, and "tune out" when a woman just wants to share her feelings and be understood.

A second variable is culturally approved male-bashing. It is well established that in many ways women are held in less-than-equal status. This is a serious social problem that seems to be changing very slowly. However, there is a corresponding notion that men are to blame for all of society's and relational ills. Napier (1991) described male bashing as a "cultural pastime." The basic notion that men can be seen as the primary reason for relational ills can be found in lay and professional settings.

In an unpublished study, Shapiro (2015), analyzed over 1,900 prime time television advertisements. When there was a man and a woman in the advertisement and one was made the fool, 100% of the time the male was the object of the humor. Women were presented as long-suffering accepters of male stupidity or as having to fix the results of ill-advised male actions. In none of the advertisements were the women perpetrators. North American culture is clear. It is okay to perceive men as fools and the object of humor. It is not okay to perceive women that way. This represents almost a full 180-degree reversal from the advertisements and values prevalent in the 1950s. In the mid-20th century, mothers and fathers were often held up for ridicule. Today, only mothers escape the "Blondie and Dagwood" comics ambiance that flourished in the 1930s to 1950s. These depictions have also made their way into popular culture through satire, sitcoms, and stand-up comedy, and their influence is pervasive.

These attitudes are reflected in professional circles as well. In a far-too-common couple therapy training program for therapists and counselors in San Francisco in June of 2000, the well-known presenter demonstrated his method by showing seven videotapes of live therapy with heterosexual couples. As he described how therapists could deal with the male partner in couple work, he criticized the men's inability to relate effectively, show appropriate soft emotions, or be empathic with their partners. These observations were made despite the fact that in two of the videos the men were crying. Few of the over 200 therapists in the audience seemed to recognize the incongruity. We do not present this to criticize the presenter, but to show how even in professional circles, it is acceptable today to hold the male member of a couple more responsible for problems. It is simply easier to find someone to blame than to explore the contextual realities. Thus, we recommend that therapists should look for each partner to share equally the burden of responsibility for problems, but to be aware of the general tendency to view men as the culprit. Viewing couple dynamics through a systems lens as a "dance" they both create can be a foundation for attributing responsibility for problems more equitably.

Finally, couples often divide labor according to current social mores. It may be that for many couples, one of the woman's roles in the couple system is to seek outside assistance. This may include social events, childcare and school arrangements, arranging medical appointments, and so on, and may not be something that the couple negotiated. It is always a good idea to begin therapy by asking the person who did not make the initial phone call to speak first, as a way to disrupt standard patterns of interaction in therapy.

Is It Always the Male Who Is More Reticent?

In our own practices, we each have had experiences that differ from this norm. Patterson estimates that the male partner has instigated therapy in approximately half of the couples he has seen in recent years. Shapiro (2016) has reported that the male partner in heterosexual relationships is more often the therapy-ready participant. This discrepancy may reflect our location in the San Francisco Bay area and Shapiro's writing on fatherhood and men since the 1980s, but it does suggest that under certain conditions, men are as interested in couple therapy as women.

Effective Therapy With Male Partners

It has long been our practice to begin with the client's current state of functioning rather than the aspirational one they wish to achieve. We believe that starting with the strengths in a couple (Carlson, 2007), rather than the weaknesses, allows for maximum growth. If a partner does something well, there is greater potential for change using those strengths than focusing primarily on the weaknesses. This also derives from the practice of *positive psychology* (Seligman, Steen, Park and Peterson, 2005).

Thus, if the male partner has trouble accessing and expressing his emotions but is very capable in his thoughts, we begin where he is comfortable and show respect and empathy for his process as well as the content. Demanding he express feelings as a starting point to eliciting more feelings is both fruitless and likely to elicit shame at being unable to live up to a counselor's expectations.

Englar-Carlson, Evans, and Duffey (2014) recommend that male-friendly counseling and a positive working alliance should include eliciting his first impressions, acknowledging his ambivalence about being in the session, demonstrating balance, using gender-appropriate language, being sensitive to potential feelings of shame, being attuned to cultural context and intersectionality, and guaranteeing no ganging up on him (unless he is ignoring his own well-being).

One area where this exception may be crucial is when a male partner is ignoring his health. About halfway through a session, the couple reported that they did not do their homework that week because he was in the emergency room twice. The therapist became insistent on his following up.

Cedric: It wasn't anything, The docs said "panic attacks," not heart attacks.

T: Two visits to the ER in a week is always something. What occurred?

C: Maybe you should tell him, Merily. I don't remember that much.

M: I found him on the floor at work, sweating and holding his chest. He had collapsed and was in pain. I called 911 and they took him to the ER. We were there about 5 hours before they sent us home. Then, 2 days later, he had chest pains again. I got scared and drove him to the ER. That time they kept him overnight for observation. He is right. The docs said it was a panic attack after all the tests came back.

C: I just haven't been sleeping and have been eating poorly and just got run down. We had this double deadline and we were falling behind, and I just overextended myself.

T: So, it is interesting that there are three people in this room and only one seems unconcerned about being rushed to the ER. The one who seems unconcerned is the person who thought he was having a heart attack.

M: He told me to up his life insurance. That really scared me.

C: Just being practical.

T: Okay, let's be practical. When was your last physical?

M: Oh, you are going to love this answer.

C: I don't know, maybe 10 years.

T: Okay, we are going to be practical. You schedule a physical exam this week. Let's confirm that you are right about this being something minor. Do you have a physician or do you need a referral?

M: They gave me a follow-up name for him at the ER. They also said soon.

T: This week! Before we meet on Friday.

Fortunately, Cedric and Merily were frightened enough by the therapist's concerns that he had a complete physical in the ensuing week. As it turned out, there were some physical reasons for concern and proper medication was prescribed.

The Use of Language and Metaphors

One of the ways to approach gender and language issues in couple work is to use sensitive language and metaphors that are relevant and familiar to clients. In short, talk to men and women in their own language, rather than the potentially alienating jargon of therapy. This usually involves talking somewhat differently to each partner in a heterosexual relationship.

Manny was a Gulf War veteran. Both he and Sonia reported that he was unable to express the more tender emotions and was, in her words, "quick to anger when he got frustrated." The precipitating event for the therapy was his being accosted by a security guard for parking close to the door of their children's preschool and waiting for them to come out.

M: I almost lost it, man. I just kept asking him to ease off because I was waiting for my kids. He just kept yelling at me to move, because my bumper was about 3 inches over the white line. I was thinking that other cars with moms were also parked that way, and he just picked on the brown-skinned guy. When he took out his pad to give me a ticket, I almost lost it totally and got out of the car, but then the kids came out and I got them into the car and drove away.

Sonia was not happy with his anger and requested that the therapist teach her husband to respond less vehemently.

Shortly after, as they spoke about their relational conflicts, Sonia began to insist that he respond in a way that she wanted. His reply was to continually repeat what he had said previously, escalating his volume. Neither of them was listening very well to the other. Instead, both focused on making their own point.

The therapist, an African American man, intervened several times at the dyadic level, trying to get them to listen instead of reiterate. At some point, he turned to Manny and asked,

T: Are you getting what you want in this discussion?

M: No. She just won't listen.

T: Tell me what you'd like from Sonia.

M: I'd like her to admit that she was wrong about when she forgot to pay the credit card bill. But she won't listen when I tell her to put the bills in a folder and on the calendar.

T: Sonia, what are you hearing?

S: He always has to be right and ...

T: (Interrupting and holding up his hand to stop Manny from jumping in) What is he saying that you heard?

S: He wants to organize me, so the bills get paid on time. The thing is, I am usually on time.

T: Manny, what would you like from Sonia right now?

M: I just want her to be more organized and do things right, instead of all "half-hazard." In the war, people died when things were disorganized.

T: So, for you this is really serious. Manny, what weapon did you carry in the gulf? M-16?

M: Yeah, one of the variants (looking both quizzically and calmly at the therapist).

T: I never fired one of those, but I did fire a M-1 years ago and you know it was the darnedest thing. I could swear that it was pulling a little up and right all the time.

M: Yeah. It was probably the wood handle. Sometimes the early M-16s had a problem also.

T: So, it wasn't that I was just a bad shot? (as both laughed, Sonia also leaned in attentively). I was thinking that when a rifle pulls like that, the natural tendency is to squeeze off more rounds rapidly, but that actually doesn't solve the problem.

M: Yeah. You have to adjust.

T: Like you have to trick your eyes and aim just a bit low and left of bullseye. So, the answer isn't to repeat what doesn't work, but to find a different solution that actually may seem unnatural.

M: (Smiling) So, if I am telling Sonia (or that stupid security guard) something and it doesn't work, don't just repeat; find something new.

T: What could you say to Sonia that is more likely to be heard?

M: She likes it when I ask for something, not tell her.

S: I want to know what he's feeling.

T: That's a good clue. So, what are you feeling when she doesn't hear what you say?

M: Frustrated … and then I get worried that she will leave me, because of my stubbornness.

T: Is that new information for you? (When she nods, he continues) Respond to his concern.

S: I am not going anywhere! I just want you to let it be when I screw up sometimes.

T: So, you and Manny want the same thing: a trusty teammate who's got your back, rather than a pseudo-parent.

By entering into a very short discussion about rifles, something Manny felt comfortable about, the therapist joined with him and noticed that Manny became more open and attentive. At that point, the therapist was able to discuss the communication/relationship problem through the metaphor of a misfiring rifle. With that indirectness, Manny and Sonia were both able to feel comfortable enough to share what they truly wanted.

Later in therapy, the use of symbols and metaphors with Sonia was equally useful. They were talking about some diminished sexual satisfaction.

S: It's like all he ever wants is sex. Otherwise I don't count.

T: Say more about that.

S: So, last Saturday night we had some wine and a nice dinner, and we were talking and he just reaches across the table and starts stroking my arm.

M: Well, who made you the nice dinner and bought your favorite white wine?

Sonia sighed and slunk down in her seat. When queried, she said,

S: It's just no use!

T: Something just occurred in here that seems to mirror what happened on Saturday. Let's go back to the dinner, and just before he started stroking your arm. What was going on inside?

S: Well, this seems weird, but I was thinking about this song that was streaming in the background. It was played at our wedding, and I was feeling very romantic, but then when he touched me, I lost it.

T: What was the song?

S: No. It seems silly.

T: (Smiling) Music means a lot to you. What song was this?

M: I know, it was "On a Clear Day."

S: It was my mom's favorite song. We actually played it at her funeral shortly before we got married, and I wanted to remember her at the wedding.

T: So, the song brings up a whole mix of emotional memories. It is also very hopeful about the future. What were you feeling?

S: All of those! (crying now)

T: Those feeling are coming back now. What can Manny offer you?

S: I like that he knows the song.

T: Tell him what could make today and even last Saturday night "a clear day."

S: I don't know, I was feeling nice at dinner and then I noticed all the pots in the sink and the dishes, and I remembered that we missed the recycling this week ...

T: You wanted things to be perfect for romance. What would do that?

S: Well, in my head I was thinking that if Manny offered to help me clean up after dinner and then we sat on the sofa and listened to our wedding music ...

M: I was planning on cleaning up after we ate, but I also wanted to connect in bed.

T: How could you let him know how you wanted to be romantic and have the "clear day outshining every star"?

S: I know I have to tell him. He's a lousy mind reader.

T: (Humorously underscoring teamwork) So, something else the two of you share—you both read minds poorly.

A similar example can be found in a couple in which the man was very closely tied to his favorite basketball team. His fiancée was not only uninterested in basketball, but found his "obsession and fanaticism" difficult and annoying. She also believed that he was such a fanatic because it distanced him from her.

Rhys was born in "basketball-mad" Indiana, played for his high school and college teams, and had been in local city leagues for many years. He had tried to find his way onto a college or professional coaching staff twice but was not able to land a position. At the time of therapy, he was a director at a sports media company where he met Xenia, who was in the production department.

During the first session, he spoke extensively about "his Warriors" and how much their recent championship meant to him. At one point, when he spoke about one of the players, Xenia opined that he seemed more passionate about him than her.

X: I just want him to be present for me. The other night, he got out of bed late to check out a box score. Who does that? He easily could have read it in the morning.

R: I have this fantasy team and wanted to see what this one guy did over in a Hawaiian tournament. The draft is next week for the pros and the following week for the fantasy league.

X: (In a sarcastic tone) And this is why he gets out of a warm bed at 2:00 a.m.!

During the first few sessions, he talked about his high school experience of intense teamwork and how much he missed that in his current job.

T: Sounds like you lived in a non-Hollywood version of the film *Hoosiers*.

R: That is my favorite film of all time. It is so real, too.

T: Which character do you most identify with?

R: This will seem funny, but it's Gene Hackman (the coach). I think it used to be Jimmy Chitwood (the fellow who makes the last-second basket), but now it's Coach.

T: So, let's say that the relationship needs a bucket and you need to call a play. What would best serve the needs of team Xenia and Rhys? You have one time out left to plan.

X: Oh, he's good, ha ha!

R: (seriously) I think I'd try to get Xenia to know that the one way I felt like I belonged was through basketball. And it isn't an obsession as much as it's always been my only family.

X: (Moving close and putting her hand on his arm) You know. You told me about being left with relatives by your dad when he went away, but I just didn't know how bad it was. I am your family now.

T: Your dad went away?

R: He went to prison and my mom was an addict, so he was my only parent when I was around 4 ... I grew up with my grandparents and two aunties, and then when I was a teen, my dad came back and wanted into my life. It wasn't pretty.

T: Xenia, your tears are visible, what is that about?

X: When I think of Rhys as a little boy with no place to go, I just want to hug him. Do you mind?

T: Ask Rhys what he'd like.

This broke the pattern of competition to determine who was right, and who was wrong, allowed Rhys to begin to see Xenia as a teammate, and allowed for her to connect with him in a cooperative, understanding way. Again, the metaphor and respect for the client's imagery allowed them to go deeper.

Through these examples of using not only gender, but person-appropriate language, we are carefully tracking not only the content and process, but the mode in which clients typically speak—not in order to mimic them, but to enter their frame of reference and elicit their motivation for change. Listening to their interest in sports, music, movies, travel, hobbies, or other issues, their use of clichés and even slang and curse words, enables us to do this effectively. We also do not want to basically change our own style, but by judiciously using their frame of reference we can heighten their attention and emotional engagement in treatment. We use humor in this manner when appropriate, and even the occasional curse word. An early model of matching client language and style was developed by Erickson (1980) and elucidated by Bandler and Grinder (1975) as *neurolinguistic programming*.

Decision Box 11.1. Using Humor: Many of our colleagues consider humor or cursing by the therapist to be deleterious to therapy and the therapeutic frame. We consider humor at the human condition, or when the therapist is the butt of any jokes, to be not only useful, but also an effective way to connect with clients for whom humor is a way for them to relate. What is your opinion and rationale, here?

Gender-Related Core Anxieties for Men and Women: Abandonment and Suffocation

There is a theme that goes through these vignettes, aside from metaphors about activities common in gender-related issues, involving a fear of abandonment and rejection. For many reasons, this seems to be the cornerstone anxiety for men in North America today (Shapiro, 2016). This is a curious counterpoint to fears of being targeted, blamed, or shamed upon entering therapy. It is a good guideline to keep in mind as a couple therapist that if the therapy or the underlying reasons for some feelings or action are unclear there may be a fear of rejection at the core.

Male-sensitive therapy includes an understanding of a man's need for being part of a team (belonging). It also acknowledges the impact of cultural images such as the "Marlboro man"—the stoic, tough, loners—and how it can interfere with couple relationships. (Englar-Carlson, Evans & Duffy, 2014). It is essential to recall that even emblematic fictional examples of yesteryear, like the "the Lone Ranger," were not alone: He had his companion, "Tonto." Robinson Crusoe had "Friday."

For women, fear of abandonment may arise from parental separation or divorce during childhood or adult experiences with partner abandonment and conflicts strongly with women's inclinations toward affiliation and involvement with other women. Historically also, divorced women have fared far worse financially than men and have ended up with greater frequency on welfare.

Counteracting Fears of Abandonment

If abandonment is indeed the core fear, then acceptance is the prime relief. In working with couples around gender issues, it is essential for both the therapist to demonstrate acceptance for gender-related behaviors and for partners to comprehend how to relate with acceptance in mind. It is important to note that for men the core fear is likely rejection; for women it may be either rejection or suffocation. Thus, true acceptance around gender issues involves each partner's understanding of the other's needs for affiliation and to feel less controlled and have more autonomy.

Counteracting Fears of Suffocation

The fear of being trapped or of losing oneself in a relationship is less common for men than for women. With men, what may appear as a fear of commitment may actually disguise a fear of vulnerability and subsequent rejection, which may result in his leaving prematurely in anticipation of rejection, before such fears can be confirmed. For women however, the fear of loss of self may be a core anxiety. As Ruth, a 60-year-old woman described it, "I went from my father's house to my husband's. I lost my name, my freedom of choice, and 5 decades of my life. I don't really know who I am now that Bruce is retired and home all the time." With help from their therapist, she was ultimately able to face her own fears of the unknown and let go of her tight grasp on security before being able to set off on many adventures, both with Bruce and alone in her later years.

It isn't particularly easy to be empathic with process as well as content, yet it is a primary goal of couple therapy to help partners see the world through each other's eyes and to experience, if only empathically, what the impact of gender roles are on a partner.

These generalizations about men, women, and core fears are most important as interesting areas of investigation when the therapy is stuck. Such explorations may be accurate and lead to meaningful interactions or greater understanding by the members of a couple. However, even if the assumptions are inaccurate for a particular individual, either that individual or their partner will "correct" the "error" and set the therapy on a fruitful path. Thus, it is not about the therapists being right, as much as it is for them to be able to interact effectively with the couple.

The Prime Directive for Men: Protect and Provide

From their earliest days as boys, men grow up with a gender role expectation that they will *protect and provide*. It is expected that a man will provide financially for himself and his family and protect them from harm.

When there is an unusual possibly foreboding noise downstairs in the middle of the night, the man is expected to get up and explore. If there is a physical threat, the man is the member of the couple to confront it. This is quite understandable, given the relative size advantage the male usually has. Although this has been changing in recent years, in the case of war it is men who are expected to be both the fighters and also considered disposable if necessary to protect the homeland.

Farrell (1993) describes another aspect of this when discussing options that prevail, at least for upper-middle-class families, when a child is born. He reports that women are afforded three choices: continue full-time work after a pregnancy leave, work part time, or be a stay-at-home mom. He argues that the three choices for men are work, work or work.[6]

The intersection between failing to uphold the prime directive and fear of rejection is often quite strong. For example, one of the greatest threats to relationships is male unemployment.

Male Unemployment

Because of that prime directive that men must protect and provide, one of the most difficult things for couples to face is prolonged male unemployment. It contrasts with the expectations of both partners and is related to depression and lower relational satisfaction (Luhmann et al., 2014; Vinokur, Price & Caplan, 1996). Female unemployment does not seem to have the same impact, even in the less-common situation[7] where she had the higher income (e.g., Cross & Madson, 1997).

For therapists, addressing directly the unemployment, normalizing the anxiety and reactive depression, and opening the potential discussion of shame (at failure) may be crucial.

A failure to recognize that a man's sense of letting down his partner or his community is related (depending on his cultural context) to guilt, shame, and fear of abandonment and isolation may be paramount to losing the couple from treatment.

This can be especially problematic when working with couples from lower socioeconomic strata where male unemployment—or more typically underemployment—is often common. It also occurs when a man is laid off or "downsized" from a good position later in life.

DeShaun is a well-known professional athlete whose persistent injuries ended his career prematurely. He went from the field to the coaching staff and remained a valuable member of the team until a new general manager was hired. The new administration replaced all the coaches with new staff. DeShaun was out of work for several months before hooking up with another team and then went into broadcasting as a color commentator on the local media. Then, when he was almost 50, three events coincided. The second of his three children went off to college, his wife lost her job and began training for a new career, and the radio station that hired him was sold. When they came into therapy, DeShaun and Alysse had gone from two incomes for five people to no incomes for five people, and two were in expensive colleges.

> D: Well Doc, I don't know if you can help, but what we need is work. Alysse is pursuing a new grad program. We have some savings, but we can't go on like this for too long.

> A: Yeah, and DeShaun is very depressed about the station being gone to a new format and no work in sight.

---

6   This is slowly changing today, with men being afforded parental leave in some settings, albeit rarely with pay. They are also increasingly involved with infants for extended periods of time.
7   The enduring discrepancy in male and female incomes for equivalent work is a major source of inequality that has multiple effects on a relationship.

T: This sounds like you made all the right moves and ran into the perfect storm.

A: Yeah. Maybe I could go back to my old career. I hated it, but I could probably hook on, but Deshaun here is so specialized, there just aren't many things available around here.

D: I could maybe hook on as an assistant coach with my old boss, but it'd mean selling the house, uprooting our son who is a junior in high school, and moving to a place we don't really like.

T: You seem to be doing all the right things now; where do you see the roadblocks to getting another position?

D: My age is working against me and …

T: You are also African American in a field that has what seems like quotas?

D: I'm glad you know that. It's not easy to have to be better to be equal.

A: He has always done it before. Do you know how long unemployment is for guys his age these days?

T: I don't know about sports, but other guys in their 50s in other industries usually are looking for 12–18 months these days. Sorry if that is bad news.

D: Actually, it's a relief. I'm still on my retirement pay for 3 more months. I didn't know that it was normal not to get something right away.

A: He was crying last week when we thought we'd have to take the girls out of the private colleges and go to state schools.

T: Sounds like you are really a good dad. It's interesting that you feel like a failure after so many successes in three careers. Say more about that.

D: As a man and as a dad, I just want the best for my kids.

Dual-Income Couples

When there are two working partners, the "protect and provide" standard may also be disrupted. This is often true with lesbian and gay partners. Friction can develop between the higher-earning and lower-earning partner. For example, the lower-earning individual may believe him- or herself to be in a lower status when it comes to spending, or the higher-income partner over time can come to resent how his or her stay-at-home or lower-income partner spends his or her day or is frivolous with money. Practical arrangements between partners need to be made. In therapy, restoring harmony and minimizing conflict and resentment over finances often requires clear negotiations, compromises, and mutual agreements, such that each person's autonomy will be respected.

Power and Privilege

Earlier in this chapter, we explored the fact that women in our culture are often under-privileged by comparison to men. Many authors have commented that it is important that men, particularly White men, understand and acknowledge their privilege in society. It is important to note that this term may potentially dislodge process in therapy. Although it may be essential for a man to understand his woman partner's deep suffering as "unprivileged," he may not see himself as part of the privileged group. Indeed, he may have suffered his whole childhood and adult life from a sense of non-belonging and inferiority. As Kimbrel (1991) noted, "Most men lead powerless, subservient lives in the factory or office" (p. 70). Thus, when his fears of rejection emerge in couple therapy, it can come as a surprise to his partner.

Why Do Men Not Feel Their Obvious Privilege?

What may be culturally obvious to anyone who is not in a powerful social group, such as minorities, women, and members of a lower socioeconomic status, may not be so to a man. Unless he feels so, he may not consider himself privileged. An individual male client may be running fast just to meet his personal sense of obligation as a protector and provider and to distance himself from the potential of failure (and fantasized, inevitable rejection). He may believe he is unable to take the time for self-care and to pursue personal interests. This will not feel like privilege to him. It will more likely feel like he is constantly running on empty. He may also feel that he is always being evaluated and self-denigrates in anticipation of a negative review. As Jordan, a 34-year-old in his first serious relationship, told his partner Brittany, "I get jealous when you flirt with guys at parties, like last weekend."

> B: I am just being friendly, and you just went off in a corner and almost disappeared.

> J: I can't compete with those guys from your work. I don't have the position, the common experiences, the salary or even the words. So, when you and Chris were laughing and going on, I was really threatened, and so I thought going away and letting you be was better than trying to break in and change the subject to something I know.

> B: Well, why can't you just hang out and be my partner, like I do when you and your friends are going on about some software glitch in a new car?

> T: What do you hear Jordan telling you, Brittany?

> B: That he feels threatened by my relating to other guys, especially Chris.

T: Does that make sense to you?

B: Well, Chris is a big flirt and he is always hitting on everyone at work, but nobody takes him seriously.

T: Is there some way that Jordan could be more involved and you could include him better?

B: I guess I didn't know how much it bothered him. There is nothing serious, just banter. (To Jordan) Why do you feel intimidated by Chris? I am going home with you!

With a lot of encouragement from the therapist, Jordan said,

J: I am shorter than both of you. I am overweight. I am prematurely balding. I make less money as a teacher than you and Chris do. I worry that you may find him more attractive with his fashionable clothes and bearing.

B: That is just silly. I am not into guys like Chris.

T: Respond directly to his concerns.

B: Well, all that stuff doesn't matter to me. I like you, and I am with you. I want you to come to the office parties. I am proud that you are a teacher and money isn't the best measure of who is a good person. I wish I had a calling like you and not just a job that I like and that pays well. Besides, I have more experience than Chris and he makes more just because I am a woman.

This dialogue points out a number of issues. Jordan does not enjoy the sense of privilege that is often part of supposed male experience. Instead, he finds himself competing mentally with a more "alpha" male type and worried that he will lose his relationship. It is important to note that Brittany, a White woman, also feels less privileged when she is subject to gender-based salary discrimination.

By focusing on and underscoring the importance of the relationship between them, the therapist allows both to listen to how Jordan feels like a lesser being, even though his race, gender, job, and economic position all reflect some potential social privilege. Because he doesn't experience it subjectively, he will not be able to relate to having advantages. He will be able to understand how, as a woman, Brittany also feels cheated as a woman in both salary and in how she is considered a sex object by some men in her workplace. It is not necessary to help each of them notice how much better off they are by virtue of social strata. It is far more useful to allow each to connect with the other's pain around how they perceive themselves and to enhance their experience of interpersonal intimacy.

The opposite issue is with women who, despite the current focus on women's empowerment, do not feel respected in their jobs, are often the only woman in their work group, and may be paid less than men doing similar work. A male partner who feels dominated may find it difficult to understand her frustration when he sees the increased attention on women's issues and perceives (perhaps incorrectly) that he is disadvantaged himself.

The bottom line is that therapists can make errors around gender if they assume objective statuses provide certain social benefits. One useful focus is to recognize that as real as male privilege may be in our culture, the unique clients sitting across from the therapist may not experience the potential privilege in positive or negative ways or at all. Men who are poor, unemployed, uneducated, short, physically weak, those for whom English is not a primary language, even some with high status, are often unlikely to see themselves in a privileged position. As in many situations in therapy, this is where the therapist must have a firm grasp on where reality and perception collide and show empathy toward perception and emotion and respectfully question client's views on objective reality.

It is primarily the subjective experiences that require focus in couple therapy. Working with the gendered nature of masculinity or femininity as a couple therapist requires significant cultural competency. Understanding the wide range of a man's relationship with other men is essential, and it is possible for men (and women who are gender fluid) to relate effectively to the feelings of women who have been oppressed and harassed. Just because a person is in a privileged category doesn't necessarily translate to feelings of superiority. Indeed, being in such a category may lead to negative comparisons with others. We all know of clients who have self-tortured themselves because they have not achieved the success of others in their subgroup.

Two Key Issues to Explore With Men

Gender-based explorations with men in couple therapy may well involve their interactions with other men outside of therapy. Shapiro (1993, 2016) reports that two issues that emerge ubiquitously in men's therapy or growth groups are (a) a man's relationship to his father or a significant father figure and (b) his male friends.

Gender socialization encourages adult men to be focused on "protect and provide" and less on the relationship with their children. This may lead to a "father hunger" (Biller, 1971; Herzog, 2001) particularly in boys. Such a deficit leads directly to (additional) fears of abandonment in relationships.

A second gender-related factor is the connection of men to other males as friends. As a society, we have inhibited groups of men from regular connection. Many adult men, when asked about their best friends, will often describe men they knew years ago in school, the military, or their annual holiday phone call, and so on. They are discouraged from making friends later in life because of competition, family and work responsibilities, and so on.

Whatever the reason, when therapists explore these issues, they discover a sense of isolation in clients.

Gender-Oriented Couple Therapy Skills

Couple therapists must be aware of potential issues between partners that relate to inherent characteristics factors of the partner. Several of these are presented in Therapy Box 11.2.

THERAPY BOX 11.2: CULTURAL FACTORS THAT MAY IMPINGE
ON PERSONAL IDENTITY AND COUPLE RELATIONSHIPS

- Ethnicity and culture of origin
- Race
- Socioeconomic status
- Gender
- Sexual orientation
- Age (and age discrepancies)
- Religion
- National or regional identity
- Disability
- Work and family identities
- Immigration status
- Degree of socialization into the dominant culture

Therapists must be able to explore the subjective meaning of these influences on the couple relationship.

Inquiring About Gender Identity in Couple Therapy

Regardless of personal definitions of gender identity and fluidity, the issue of gender bias can be quite problematic in couple therapy for both male and female clients. Focusing on gender roles and gender socialization may be fruitful areas of inquiry for many couples. However, assuming that there are gender problems violates a basic principle of psycho-therapy (Frank, 1961/1993) that we accept our clients where they are and do not try to change them in activist or political ways.

Thus, we cannot assume that gender is a major cause of relational disharmony, but when gender role strain or gender-based restrictiveness seem to be a factor in couple distress, it is useful to inquire about each member's relationship and understanding of gender-related strain. It may offer new insight and connection. In addition to normalizing patterns, some open-ended questions may be useful:

- How do you identify in terms of your gender?
- What does your gender mean to you?
- What is your sense about stress coming from particular automatic or unnegotiated roles you fill in the relationship?
- What kinds of social pressure arise from your gender?
- What are the most important gender rules and roles you feel you have to follow?
- In what ways does your gender impact your primary relationship?
- In what ways does your gender impact your relational stress with family?

- How does your gender identification interact with other identities that influence opportunities and meaning in your life?

Each of these questions is best answered by members of the couple to their partner. Request for reactions and open discussions are important. This process can enhance mutual attunement and vulnerability, promotes a sense of equality, honors differences, opens up discussions of matters that seemed natural but were previously unknown, facilitates greater emotional safety, explores intrusions into the relationships that are conditioned by social contexts, and promotes understanding.

These questions are best considered in the manner in which clients talk about themselves. For example, use of the term *gender* could easily be asked, based on self-definitions, as in "How do you identify as a man/woman?" To get at intersectionalities, such a question might look like this: "How does being a bisexual, Mexican person who grew up in a barrio influence opportunities and meaning in your life?"

It is important that therapists who pursue such lines of inquiry have a deep and comfortable understanding of their own personal gender socialization. This involves questioning how automatic your personal responses to gender-based status are and how aware you are regarding how you experience gender-role demands.

A core aspect of successful counseling and psychotherapy draws from Socrates's dictum "know thyself."

SUMMARY

Exploring gender, gender role socialization, gender stereotypes, and gender identification may well be an important consideration in couple therapy. It is always important to consider how the intersection of multiple factors—which couples may experience as "automatic" or "natural"—can negatively affect the couple relationship. Gender stands out as a major cultural variable, one that is worthy of consideration, especially when clients are unaware of sociocultural pressures that are creating discord and loss of intimacy in their relationship.

12

Reaching Integration: Feuding Cousins or Kindred Spirits?

I n this final chapter, the authors attempt to synthesize into a conceptual whole two
disparate approaches to couple therapy. We examine the basic tenets of cognitive
behavioral couple therapy and existential couple therapy, finding core similarities
where they exist and examining essential differences. We explore these convergences and
divergences through a single case study: the couple Jose and Edna.

Jose and Edna

Edna and Jose are a middle-aged bicultural professional couple who have been married
for 26 years. Both are in their second marriages. They have five children in their blended
family. She has a married daughter from her first marriage. He has a son and daughter
from his first marriage. They have two daughters who currently live with them from their
current marriage. They report that the blended family relationships are "satisfactory,"
and four of the children get along nicely. His son is much more connected to his first wife
and her current family and works with his stepfather in an import business that focuses
on Latin countries.

They both work primarily from home and reportedly have entered therapy because
of frequent, intense arguments and an overall lack of emotional and physical intimacy.

They report that from the outside their relationship appears excellent to their many
friends and the four children with whom they are close. They socialize and travel on
annual vacations and report that they are happy when they are engaged in these activities. The precipitating event for them seeking therapy was a major argument over Jose's
announcement that he plans to travel alone on a 2-week business trip to El Paso, Texas,
Ciudad Juarez, Mexico, and Cali Colombia. His rationale for going without her was that
it might be dangerous for an Anglo woman who spoke no Spanish in those regions.

Edna's response was to become infuriated, accusing him of avoiding her and ultimately
questioning their relationship altogether. She has long complained that living with Jose

was like living alone or with a "roommate." She yearns for more validation as a person, a more active sex life, and quiet, shared moments together.

By contrast, Jose claims that he "just wants to stop the bickering." He expresses little need for more intimacy with Edna. In fact, when pressed, he reiterates that he just wants peace and "to be left alone." He characteristically seeks this by withdrawing to reading, his computer, and long solo hikes.

The disparity in expressed desires (Edna desiring more time together and Jose seeking more alone time) leaves Edna despondent at times, and she expresses hopelessness in regard to achieving her goals of greater intimacy with Jose. The pursuer-distancer pattern seems like a long-term homeostasis that is serving them less as they age and going through a major life transition.

They both reported that they did not want to live the way they are and desired therapy to alleviate the "pain and suffering." Neither was seeking an end to the relationship, citing the good times they had when they were out with friends or traveling together.

There is no history of clinical psychopathology in either partner.

Work Life

Edna works as a medical research scientist and is widely esteemed in her profession. She has managed several grants and has been able to keep soft-money positions for 2 decades. She has twice been offered lucrative executive positions with a start-up company with whom she had been consulting but preferred being a grant writer, researcher, and independent consultant.

Jose purchased and ran a franchise restaurant for several years. Approximately 2 years ago, he sold the business and has "been coasting" for a while. About 6 months ago, he got involved in a software start-up that has yet to pay off but had promise of turning into a successful business with sufficient funding. Because the software focuses on Spanish-speaking populations, his goal for the trip was to try to arrange for funding in Spanish-speaking areas.

Families of Origin and Brief History

Jose (55), the youngest of three, reports being relegated to last place by his parents and two sisters (both of whom married within their Latin culture of origin). His family immigrated to the United States from Mexico when he was 10. He is a naturalized U.S. citizen and describes himself as the most "American" in his family.

In what he described as a "semi-arranged" marriage, he reports that his first wife, a Latina, had very conventional ideas about male and female roles. She viewed him primarily as a "breadwinner" who should fill a traditional role. According to him, although she is bilingual, she preferred not to speak English. Their marriage ended after 6 years, soon after his son was born and he purchased the restaurant.

Edna (56), who is White, tall, has bright red hair, a face full of freckles and a significant upper Midwest accent, was first born in her family of eight. She describes her family as "Scotch-Irish and devout Christians." She was always expected to be a second mother to her younger siblings and a "super achiever." Her first husband was a very dependent man who wanted her to "mother" him and to support him while he tried to create several small new businesses, none of which succeeded. Their marriage lasted for 7 years, during which Edna, feeling a lot of loneliness, sought out other men and had three affairs. The marriage ended when Jose became her lover.

Core Factors in Treatment

Throughout this book, we have employed an integrated approach to couple therapy as much as possible. Where our approaches and theories differ, we provide two alternative approaches. We begin our treatment options with Jose and Edna with a look at what is common across all approaches to couple therapy; we follow this with different therapeutic approaches based on the two theories and conclude with treatment that we would both use.

The field of psychotherapy has throughout its history represented two contrasting trends: a desire to discover and employ the "one true theory" for all clients and a contrasting pluralism with a search for certain core factors that are shared by multiple theoretical methods. Throughout this text, we have supported the latter, more integrative approach respecting the notion that matching client and therapist capabilities was more significant than finding one, core uniform approach. We believe that the essential chemistry and match of therapist and client "theories" of change are the most salient factor.

Core Conditions

As early as 1951, Rogers argued that there were core conditions that were promotive of change in all areas of psychotherapy. Dollard and Miller (1950) translated psychoanalytic constructs into behavioral terms, trying to demonstrate concordance between very different methods. Lazarus and Messer (1991), and Lazarus, Beutler, and Norcross (1992), argued poignantly that counseling and therapy techniques could be applied effectively across theoretical models. Patterson (1997) concurred, delineating the distinction between *theories* and techniques. He detailed how techniques might be applied trans-theoretically with impunity. More recently, Murguia and Davis, (2015) extended this concept further, illustrating how a philosophical approach such as existentialism, as it is applied in existential therapy, is not inherently incompatible with the pragmatism and rationalism that is inherent in CBT. Although, as Shapiro (2016) and Shapiro, Patterson, and Fishman (2019) indicate, they are often approaching the clients from opposite angles.

> Recent work in the field has focused increasingly on whether there are core factors that cross therapeutic models. If there are such common factors across pluralistic theories, they would provide a basis for synchrony in approaching any case in counseling and psychotherapy. Norcross and Goldfried (2005) offer an analysis of a considerable literature that supports such core factors. In addition, compatibility among approaches and identified *common factors* may also be found in ongoing research into evidence-based practice (EBP), which led to the identification of effective psychotherapy. Grencavage and Norcross (1990) found that the majority of metanalyses indicate that one factor (the therapist-client relationship) is the essential factor. Frank (1961/1993) and Wampold

(2001) linked common factors directly to EBP. By combining the work on common elements for successful therapy, we have distilled the following:

- An emotionally charged bond between the therapist and patient (positive therapeutic alliance)
- Providing the opportunity for expression
- Instilling hope or positive client expectations
- A confiding healing setting in which therapy takes place
- A therapist who provides a psychologically derived and culturally embedded explanation for emotional distress
- An explanation that is adaptive (i.e., provides viable and believable options for overcoming specific difficulties) and is accepted by the patient
- A set of procedures or rituals engaged by the patient and therapist that leads the patient to enact something that is positive, helpful, or adaptive (Laska, Gurman, & Wampold, 2014)
- An opportunity for learning and practicing new behaviors
- Exploring the important security benefits of the current status quo and supporting the implications of facing the fears of the unknown and of making changes

Of course, any therapist will emphasize or downplay some of these factors over others depending on the client's presenting issues, context, culture, and both therapist and client theories of change (Shapiro & Bohart, 2014).[1]

Core Factors in Couple Therapy

All of these points relate to all forms of counseling and psychotherapy. It is difficult enough to evaluate and compare specific techniques and models in individual therapy because of the great variability of therapists and their chemistry with specific clients. With couple therapy, those "nonspecific" variables are far more complex and defy effective empirical evaluation, at least by the standard outcome measurements. In fact, the evidence base for success seems particularly elusive for laboratory researchers employing random controlled studies, such as those used in drug trials (Luborsky et al., 1986; Orlinsky & Howard, 1987; Shapiro, 2016).

Are There Particular Common Factors That Distinguish *Couple Therapy?*

Sprenkle, Davis, and Lebow (2009) name four distinct common factors in couple therapy:

1. Couple difficulties are conceptualized in relational—rather than individual pathology—terms
2. A goal of couple therapy is to first comprehend a couple's dysfunctional relational patterns and then to disrupt the ongoing homeostatic balance

---

1 The notion that clients have theories about how change occurs has been largely ignored by the field of psychology. Yet, it seems essential to map therapist and client belief systems to improve the results of therapy.

3. Therapeutic approaches focus more directly on the here-and-now system in treatment
4. A therapeutic alliance must be created with each partner and with the couple relationship as an entity

To Sprenkle, Davis, and Lebow (2009),

> The therapeutic alliance underlies all change occurring in psychotherapy and impacts on treatment in numerous ways. It is the key ingredient for most clients in successful (or unsuccessful) engagement, setting the stage for intervention. Basically, it is the sine qua non of couple treatment. (p. 87)

We agree with their ordering of what is powerful in treatment. In short, the couple therapist is characteristically more active than her or his individual therapist counterpart, and the relationship between the therapist and the clients generally supersedes the techniques used. The relationship is characteristically considered a real—rather than a projected or transferential—one.

A common factors approach may account for different models' locus of change: Does it reside primarily in the therapist or in the client? And, in fact, we differ on that, with CBT placing far more responsibility on the therapist to recommend and initiate change. Existential approaches, by contrast, focus more on eliciting change that originates in the clients.

Applying a CBT Approach to Edna and Jose

Theory

The basic premise behind cognitive-behavioral couple therapy is to assess the contingencies surrounding behavior, such as the antecedents and consequences of both desired and undesired behaviors in the relationship, and to activate behaviors that enable each partner to be willing to reciprocate sufficiently in order to make the relationship work. The primary therapeutic goal is to increase the functional, and to decrease the dysfunctional, dynamics between partners. In behavioral parlance, this is not considered a theory per se, but a functional approach to achieve the outcomes the couple desires.

Although there are many forms of CBT, including behavior therapy (BT), cognitive therapy (CT), rational emotive behavior therapy (REBT), integrative couple behavior therapy (ICBT), dialectical behavior therapy (DBT), and so on, the core assessment paradigm is *functional analysis* in order to determine the circumstances leading to a particular outcome. Targeted interventions, devised by the therapist, are then designed to *change behavior*. The addition of a cognitive element involves identifying thoughts, whether intrusive or automatic notions or persistent beliefs that lead to emotions and behaviors. The addition of emotions (as in REBT or DBT) examines the interstices between thoughts and behaviors (or between emotions and behaviors, whichever comes first). Pure CBT, to the extent that it actually exists in clinical practice, affords equal weight to thoughts, emotions, and behavioral activation in affecting change, while CT places primacy on the role of modifying cognitions in changing behavior. Radical behaviorism does not recognize the validity of thoughts and emotions but views them as private behaviors that cannot be observed or measured. The difference, when any of these are practiced in their true form, is in the degree of *emphasis* placed on thoughts, emotions, and behaviors as pathways to change.

Assessment

The Dyadic Adjustment scale (Spanier, 1976) described earlier, is a standard in the field and the most frequently used inventory. Many others, such as the Marital Satisfaction Inventory, the Areas of Change Questionnaire, the Conflict Tactics scale, and others are documented by Patterson and McClanahan (1999) and elsewhere, including Chapter 6 of this text.. The most widely known tool that is useful in tracing intergenerational patterns is the genogram (McGoldrick & Gerson, 2008). For clients who desire a more extensive probe of their dynamics and are willing to take the time, the therapist may ask the couple to complete the CPCI (Stuart, 1987), which covers 13 critical aspects of functioning. The inventory is completed by each to indicate his or her personal views and his or her perception of how his or her partner would rate the same issues.

Using some form of systematic assessment is more crucial than the particular tools used. These inventories are derived primarily from CBT research and practice and used infrequently by other models. Other assessment modes can include personal and couple developmental histories, records from previous therapy, structured exercises, and guided interviews and observations. With more sophisticated equipment, sessions can be recorded and played back in segments to clients to provide more objective observation of their interaction. The recordings may also be "scored" by independent raters, especially when the therapy process is being examined. Biofeedback equipment has also been used to measure emotional arousal states.

Goals

To begin, Jose and Edna have disparate goals regarding behavior change. Jose reportedly "wants peace," while Edna is distraught about the overall deterioration of their intimacy at nearly all levels. Based on their responses on the Dyadic Adjustment scale (Spanier, 1976), neither has one foot out the door and they are invested in continuing their long marriage. Thus, the first step in assessment is to explore their separate goals while seeking some common ground. Assuming they can agree on a focus, and they can realistically explore possibilities and the logistics of scheduling regular therapy sessions, a useful approach is to ask them each to describe the foundations of their relationship regarding values, common interests, respect, and so on. Drawing from positive psychology (Seligman, Rashid & Parks, 2006), they are asked to state what they most enjoy about each other, how they met, and what they admire about each other. This sets the tone that not all is lost and that they can build on the positive experiences they have had and perhaps establish new patterns.

The next phase involves introducing the opposite: the conflicts that brought them to therapy and the ability to listen to one another. By dint of the therapist's acceptance (but not necessarily agreement) with the other's feelings and perceptions, the couple may become more open to productive communication.

While it may be necessary for the therapist to set ground rules and intervene when the discussion becomes defensive or escalates out of control, success at this task softens the tone and provides relief in the realization that they are truly being heard and accepted for who they are, perhaps for the first time. Methods from emotion-focused therapy (EFT) (Greenberg & Goldman, 2018; Johnson, 2019) can also be useful in lowering the emotional climate between them. A frequent EFT technique is to encourage a client with heated emotions to take a break, breathe deeply, and to reframe (reconceptualize) anger as "irritation" and blaming as "disappointment."

For example, the approach would involve identifying and labeling "cooler emotions" for anger such as *fear, sadness, and disappointment,* which shifts the tone from accusation to self-disclosure and encourages each partner to empathize rather than become defensive and retaliate, thus setting the potential for greater intimacy.

When both Jose and Edna are able to express their differences and desires and be heard and accepted, they are then asked to prioritize those changes that would make the most difference to them, both short term and in the distant future. They may run through a long list of both trivial and critical issues, and along with examining their basic values, they may be asked to order the top three they want to address in therapy. This often takes a number of sessions in order to agree on what can actually be accomplished within the agreed-on time frame they have allocated to therapy. The therapist guides them in each session to become more specific and refined on desires and willingness to change, specifically in the following ways:

- By having Edna and Jose practice communication skills through active listening and *I messages*
- By having them practice de-escalation methods during an argument
- By having them commit to reinstate *quality time on a weekly basis* such as a date night

In this manner the global frustration and seemingly overwhelming need for the other to change become delineated and tangible tasks for them to prioritize between sessions and are discussed.

Each session typically reveals issues that are essential to what each partner can do and also what they need to stop doing, like stopping verbal or physical abuse, name-calling, demeaning each other, or slamming doors while dramatically leaving the room during an argument. Beginning with the initial session, it is useful to establish what to recommend they actively do, or avoid doing, between sessions. It may be advisable to request that they text the therapist a brief comment on whether they accomplished that task during the next week. A typical text might be the following:

CASE BOX 12.1

Homework

Edna was out of town and we hardly saw each other; looking forward to practicing the technique as needed.

Or,

Jose and I used the de-escalation technique we practiced in session and managed to take a time out and come back later to resolve a dispute,

---

In this way there is a direct focus on both their desired goals and on actions that are impeding achieving those goals. Their success also reinforces their hope that further change can occur and a new era of mutual goodwill can develop.

Small improvements serve two purposes: as a major goal, per se, and as a test of their desire and ability to change. However, the therapist must keep aware of any major hindrances to their success, such as an enduring *resentment,* borne of past transgressions one or both are keeping alive, regardless of a partner's improvement. Thus, Edna is urged to journal about this, commend Jose for small acts of support, and work on her lingering resentment in personal therapy, if needed.

For his part, Jose is asked to remain engaged in conversations with Edna by using the communication methods learned in therapy and to examine ways in which he might actually be inadvertently fostering (reinforcing) the bickering he complains about with Edna. These efforts would be encouraged as early as possible in the therapy so as to generate good will and apply skills in other areas as therapy progresses. For instance, Gottman (2006) and Zenger and Folkman (2013) describe an ideal praise-to-criticism ratio, which in Gottman's formulation, is four positive comments to each critical one.

It is essential to identify intransigent cognitions and emotions if mutual effort is to occur. One key to this is the notion of *negative sentiment override* (Weiss, 1980), which involves generalization of negative affect to the point where even behaviors with positive intentions are viewed by the partner as inconsiderate, selfish, or otherwise negative. An example is Edna's belief that Jose's wanting to go to South America without her is a sign of his not caring about their intimacy and basic connection, even though his motivation is presumably to keep her safe. These types of attributions must be identified and modified in order for progress to occur.

Whatever forays are taken into such underlying thoughts and feelings are neither the goal, nor the essence of CBT. However, overriding them is important in activating the desired behavior as efficiently as possible. Through the assessment, goal setting, and beginning intervention phase, the following is an example of how this could play out with Jose and Edna:

J: I'm so tired of the bickering and Edna always asking me to tell her my feelings. I just want peace and quiet.

E: I hate it too, but I really feel I don't know you much after 26 years, and just having peace feels like we're roommates.

T: You seem to have different needs and goals for what you want to accomplish in therapy.

J: I like being close to Edna too, but we've had a lot of struggles, and isn't it normal for things to seem routine in a long marriage?

T: Yes, interest and excitement waxes and wanes, but boredom and bickering push each other further and further apart. What would be one improvement you would like to see now in order to feel better about your relationship?

J: If she'd not push me to tell her how I feel and let me show her by surprising her with some things I'd like us to do together.

T: Jose, you're saying if Edna does not keep asking you to open up, you would feel freer to initiate activities together; is that correct?

J: Yes, if only she'd give me a chance to surprise her instead of pushing me.

T: Edna, do you get what Jose is saying and would you be willing to give that a try?

E: Yes, I do, and I can try, but I have such resentment over Jose avoiding me and playing the "end game" like "our marriage is over."

T: Jose, can you tell Edna now that you will refrain from saying "Our marriage is over" and similar statements that close off communication?

J: Yes. I can stop myself from saying that again. I don't really mean the marriage is over. I just want the *conversation* to be done with.

T: Next session I would like to first see you each separately to see how that resentment can be overcome and how you can take beginning steps toward each other. I'll then see you together for the last half hour.

It would be naïve to assume that lingering resentment should be glossed over, as it may be the key to motivating each partner to open up and be receptive to one another's efforts. In a more process-based (e.g., psychodynamic) approach, this issue would likely be addressed at length until it is resolved. Under a CBT model we can address it through brief individual sessions, outside individual therapy, journaling, reading, and ultimately through direct conjoint communication at home and briefly in therapy. This approach allows the couple to act first before having insight into the ways that they are carrying excess baggage from the past. It also highlights the need to address it both individually and together for progress to be made. Jose's agreement can initiate the process, allowing Edna to begin letting go of her resentment and be more open to Jose. The assumption is that the resentment does not necessarily require extensive exploration in conjoint sessions and that each individual can make efforts in the present to overcome blocks to intimacy and patterns of avoidance and bickering that resentment engenders.

A Setback

During individual interviews preceding the next conjoint session, an apparent setback occurred. A key to exploring such events is to uncover the *resentment* that each partner is carrying from being "nagged" (Jose) and from not getting results from frequent prodding (Edna). In therapy, Patterson may describe this resentment as "a gunny sack of heavy rocks that one uses to pull out one-at-a-time to sling at the other." He then invites each partner to leave the sack in the office. The dialogue reveals this resentment:

T: Edna, how are you doing with prioritizing your requests of Jose and waiting for a good time to discuss them with him?

E: I'm just so over telling Jose to do things he should do without my asking; I've just given up.

T: What would it take to get past your resentment?

E: If he would start doing things on his own without my asking.

T: I often find that a stalemate can be broken if one partner is willing to take a risk and do his or her part without waiting for the other—would you be willing to try that?

E: I would, and I'll see how it goes.

T: Good! I'd like you to imagine you're leaving all those feelings you've carried around as a burden for so long in the office and start fresh when you leave today.

A similar dialogue ensues with Jose:

T: How are you doing with taking on some of the things you know are needed but have resisted because of Edna's nagging and staying in an argument rather than walking away?

J: I've had it with her telling me what to do; it makes me feel like a kid when my dad would always be on my case. I'm doing better with hanging in there when we argue though, and I've stopped playing the "end game" when I'm frustrated with her.

T: Good that you're doing that, though you've acknowledged that you're neglecting things you know need to be done. Are you willing to begin doing some of those for yourself, rather than because Edna is asking you to do them?

J: Yes, that seems like the right thing to do.

T: Great, and each time remind yourself that you're fulfilling your responsibility, and you might notice Edna's reaction.

Individual Change Leads to Interaction and Couple Change

There is a related factor operating with resistance and resentment in that partners get into a *quid pro quo* mind-set; that is, they won't do what is needed because the other won't do what they want them to do, and a distorted chess game takes place, with each waiting for his or her partner to make the first move. A key element in CBT couple therapy involves *individual self-change, leading to a cycle of awareness and subsequent changes.* Halford (2003) guides us on this issue, in that *individual self-change,* or assumption of individual responsibility, is the essential key to breaking logjams in couples. An exchange in the middle and later phases of therapy when individuals assumed responsibility for their role in negative patterns might look like the following:

T: Edna, you've noted recently that your "nagging," as you've put it for Jose to express his feelings and show more interest in your relationship, was actually pushing him away.

E: Yes, I'm embarrassed to know I was doing that, but I was so frustrated, and in the past weeks I feel I've gotten to know Jose better, and we've started to enjoy things together that Jose has taken the initiative to plan for us.

J: I've become aware that my avoiding and withdrawing from conflict comes from the arguments I hated that were a constant in my parents relationship when I was growing up. If we don't walk away from arguments, we can work out our differences and feel closer.

E: I've noticed that our kids seem more relaxed and open with us too.

T: I want to commend each of you for showing your commitment to each other and taking the initiative to do your part, without knowing whether the other would do so; that shows trust and love and goes a long way to restore good will.

As termination approaches and Edna and Jose have successfully adopted the concepts and methods during the intervention phase of therapy, their dialogue might look like this:

J: I feel much better when I hang in there when an argument comes up with Edna, but I have to catch myself each time because of my tendency to withdraw.

E: My nagging of Jose has stopped, and I realize the difference when I don't repeatedly say the same things that bother me to him, and it goes nowhere. I'm more able to let minor things go and pick a place and time when Jose is receptive to discuss more important things.

T: Are you also finding that you hold onto things less and as a result feel less resentful?

E: Definitely. I really feel that Jose and I are more "up to date" with each other and enjoy time together more.

Applying an Existential Therapy Approach to Edna and Jose

Theory

Let's begin by exploring briefly some basic tenets of existential work with couples.

THERAPY BOX 12.1: A BRIEF SUMMARY OF TENETS OF EXISTENTIAL COUPLE THERAPY

1. It is *rooted in philosophy* and focused phenomenologically, primarily on clients' subjective experience.
2. Unlike most natural science theories that highlight discovery and decoding of real-world phenomena, existentialism is an *encoding theory.* It begins with observable (often subjective) data and builds very individualized client-based theories.
3. The actual relationship between the therapist and clients (including the couple unit) is the active ingredient for healing and change. In short, *intimacy is considered the antidote to normal feelings of alienation, meaningless, and fears of mortality.*
4. There is a primary value in making explicit what was previously implicit (saying the unsayable) particularly in the here-and-now relationship.
5. Therapy is process centered, and all content is viewed in its unique context.
6. Parallel process, in which the client enacts with the therapist with the same dynamic as in outside life, is particularly valuable for both understanding and treatment.
7. Existential therapy works in both affective (feelings in the moment) and cognitive (insight) realms.
8. Clients' present awareness is viewed as both goal and method for clients to live more deliberately, more authentically, and more purposefully. When in their relationship and in therapy meetings is there sadness, anger, or relief with fighting? What ensues when the fight is over or subsides? More distance? If so, what advantage does that have?
9. Focus of awareness on the ongoing tension between the push toward freedom and the often unconscious pull of security—this central tension and its relationship to fear (of the unknown) and guilt (of the stagnation of the status quo) are viewed at both macro and micro (here and now) levels.
10. Exploration in therapy is *less on what objectively occurred than on what meaning the event is given by individuals.*
11. Anxiety is seen as the engine for change and is welcomed as part of the therapy. What does this couple do to alleviate sharing potentially positive anxiety?
12. Often, clients report confusion around their sense that they are doing everything right but feeling unhappy or empty.

Assessment (Anamnesis)

Jose and Edna, a middle-aged, bicultural professional couple who have been married for 26 years, are both in their second marriage. Some of the questions on basic intake forms involve information about children, ages, life situation, education, marriages, and so on. There are also questions about drug (medication), alcohol, and caffeine use; financial and legal difficulties; in-laws; prior therapy experiences as individuals and as a couple, and so on.[2] Depending on their answers, especially about who else is at home or involved in their relationship, the therapy might have different foci.

For Edna and Jose, there was no particular mention of problem drinking, financial or legal difficulties, or excessive medication. She was taking a hormone supplement under her doctor's care to help with menopausal difficulties, and recently a low dose antidepressant. He had been on an antianxiety medication to help deal with stress for the past 4 years. They both reported that they were social drinkers (a couple of drinks) at parties with friends and that seemed to "loosen them up" and allow them to have a good time. Jose was a bit excessive in his use of caffeine (four cups of coffee a day). There were no family problems, except for the distance between Jose and his son, and some lingering financial disputes from his ex-wife and her family. They dated the current discord to approximately 6 months after he sold his business and began spending more time at home.

Assessment: Process

In the current case context, one issue that will get played out in therapy is the felt helplessness that results from Jose and Edna's perceived inability to change relational patterns. How, for example, will Jose and Edna individually play out their relational dynamic with the therapist, and how will the couple unit present what seems like a locked system?

To what extent do Edna and Jose present their problem as unsolvable and one in which the therapist cannot have any effect in changing?

E: You know, Jose has been like this for years, I don't think he even wants closeness with me. Every time I get close, he calls me a "nag."

J: She does nag and criticize and then expects me to be warm and loving toward her. Nobody could do that.

T: So you both would like it to be more warm and loving, but you each seem to have methods to make that particularly hard.

E: Yes. He just won't change.

T: (Very aware of what he did say) Edna, I'm interested in what you just heard me say.

E: That it's hopeless.

---

2   Model intake forms may be found in Chapter 6.

T: (Deciding not to correct her or clarify at this point) What if it was unchangeable?

E: Then we are stuck.

T: Jose, is that what you heard me say also?

J: Pretty much.

T: So, that's a place where you both agree (underscoring how they are together on something)

Note that the therapist actually focused on their relationship becoming more intimate, but they had blocks. They both heard that there was no chance of a better outcome. From an assessment standpoint, their process is to reinforce the notion that the status quo is both inevitable and somehow preferable. Nonverbally, neither of them seemed particularly upset as they recounted the hopelessness they interpreted from what the therapist said.

This leads to some testing by the therapist. First, he or she acknowledges that they agree on the interpretation. Second, he or she will press the matter to explore the depth of their need to keep the current homeostasis.

T: I am curious about what you would have to deal with, if it did not change?

E: Disappointment. This is pretty intolerable.

T: Then, what would you have to deal with if it did change and you got closer (like when you are traveling or with other people)? (Noticing some nonverbal anxiety, he continued) What just happened inside Jose?

J: Not much.

T: You looked like you experienced a shift in emotion. It may not make sense, but were you aware of anything shifting inside?

J: I guess I felt uncomfortable thinking of it?

T: Somehow, a change seems to bring up more anxiety, either at what kind of demands might be made of you and/or what you'd have to face if you were more open to Edna.

E: Well, we have been like this for a long time.

T: You have. So, letting go of it may require you each to face some hard decisions and changes.

J: What do you mean?

T: Well, I wonder if we could engage in a little experiment for just a few minutes. I'd like Edna to ask you for more closeness in her usual way, and instead of retreating and looking for peace, I'd like to ask you, Jose, to tell her what it feels like when she does that in here.

Although this may take several "takes," this allows the therapist to assess process in real time and to give the couple a sense of how they collude to maintain the homeostasis, even if it is painful.

A significant question is how does the couple system impact the therapist? Does he or she get put off or feel hopeless in the face of their stagnant process?

Assessment: Behavior

When in their relationship and in therapy meetings is there sadness, anger, or relief with fighting? What ensues when the fight is over or subsides? More distance? If so, what advantage does that have? What does this couple do to alleviate sharing potentially positive anxiety? What is it that Jose and Edna expect, and what is the discrepancy between that and what they experience (e.g., Weissberg, Kumpfer, & Seligman, 2003)?

In existential work, part of early assessment is to explore, at both the macro and micro levels, the ongoing process tension between a push for freedom and variety and a counteracting, pulling for security, and familiarity. One goal of this analysis is to quickly assess their strengths. Later in the therapy phase of treatment, the therapist can bring those skills to bear on the issues of concern. We begin by exploring together what is going well in the relationship (Carlson, 2007), including their story of their courtship and early relationship, and the extent to which the current concerns are painting an inordinately, over-generalized, negative picture of the entire relationship. In addition to the exploration of their successes, we would help them describe any relevant personal and couple developmental histories, any prior therapy, and the results.

Beginning the Therapeutic Alliance: Start With the Obvious

With Jose and Edna, it is important to quickly note the cross-cultural nature of the relationship and to explore with them what aspects of the current concerns stem from cultural differences. This is far less intrusive than other openings. They already know about the cultural differences and have discussed them previously. It is also an early indication that the *context* of their relationship will be of interest. Often discussing such "external" characteristics is less threatening than focusing early on intrapsychic or interpersonal problems.

One set of hypotheses the therapist may have with this couple involve stereotypical assumptions about culture and gender. For example, it may be assumed that as a Latino, Jose may be less culturally conditioned to play a secondary role to women. Yet, in his family of origin, he was secondary to his sisters in the eyes of his parents, and that may now be replicated by his being between jobs and with his wife, who is asking for something that he is unable or unwilling to deliver. The big therapeutic questions here are, "How comfortable is that familiar process?" and "How does that serve him?"

T: You seem to have come from different backgrounds; how does that impact the relationship and the problems you came here to work on?

A: I am Mexican American, but am now here decades. I think I am a fairly normal, assimilated, naturalized American.

T: How about for you Edna?

E: Well we both have stuff in our background that isn't always easy to understand.

T: Such as?

E: Well, Jose goes quiet and I don't know what's going on and then there is a major explosion.

J: She grew up in a house where nobody raised their voices, so when we disagree she thinks it's a major argument.

T: So that's one difference; what are some others?

This is primarily designed to gain a sense of what occurs and how culturally related it may be, especially if they characteristically discount culture as an issue. Early in cross-cultural relationships, those who look different have less intra-couple conflict (attributing a lot to the cultural differences, not personal issues). Later, such couples seem to ignore the cultural differences and over-personalize difficulties.

This also is a lead-in to the question of how they met and their choreographed description of their early history. Frequently, there are some significant clues in that history about the more appealing aspects of each other, and also a point from which the question can be posed about when and how things changed for the worse.

The second aspect of assessment is the present situation: the precipitating event or situation that pushed them to seek help. What is it about the current dilemma that was "over the self-help edge?"

Finally, through careful clinical interviewing, it is important to discern whether any individual pathology exists in either person. There was none of note with Edna or Jose.

Goals

For any therapy, the client couple goals for outcome are a primary consideration. In existential therapy, attention is paid to what each wants from the therapy. The therapist then holds up the places where their desires are consistent and where they are contrasting.

T: I am interested in what you each would consider a favorable outcome from our meetings.

E: I want us to be closer and feel like we do when we are on vacation or with our friends.

J: I want the fighting to stop, and I want more peace.

T: What does peace mean to you?

J: No bickering, feeling good. Just feeling like I am safe from criticism, in my own home.

T: So, Edna wants more connection and Jose wants a different kind of connection, one that is more loving and less stressful. You both seem to agree that when you are away, like on vacation, it goes well. How can we get those vacation-like feelings more present in day-to-day living?

E: That would be good, but he is different at home and away.

J: You are really different. You mellow out and even though we are together 24/7, you don't make a lot of demands.

E: That's because you pay attention to me.

T: Should we set that as a major goal: less stress, fewer demands, and less withdrawal? Let me ask you a question (*miracle question*). If tonight, when you go to sleep a miracle occurs and you wake up at home with that vacation feeling, what would that be like?

E: Well, it all sounds good, but impossible. There are chores to be done. There is the house to take care of. There is work. Not so simple.

J: Yeah. When we are on vacation, there are no stresses or demands. The girls don't need anything.

T: (Seeding an interpretation that will be used later) Interesting that you both agree that in the face of an imaginary miracle, you find the negatives. No question that they are real, but it's curious that's where you went.

Approach

The first intervention was to get Edna and Jose to enact the usual at-home argument. This serves both diagnostic (where and how their interaction escalates) and therapeutic goals (working together on a solution).

T: Talk to each other; I will listen in. Start with what you have tried already that didn't work and where there might be some openings to reach the goals you desired.

What followed was an attempt by each to prove the other wrong and to try to convince each other to change, without a commensurate personal shift. This is where the therapist can intervene, help them communicate more effectively, note that one will not change without the other, and encourage their working as a team. The therapist can also illuminate aspects of their process and ability to maintain the current homeostasis, rather than face fears of changing.

As Edna encourages Jose to be more available to her, "especially when [she is] upset and hurting," he tends to withdraw more. The therapist may intervene here.

T: Jose. This seems to be a dilemma for you. There is a pattern where Edna asks for something, perhaps in a stressed voice, and you naturally pull back. That pushes her to come on stronger.

J: Yeah. But sometimes I need peace and quiet.

T: Well, how is that working out?

J: Not so hot.

T: So, you want peace and you try to avoid conflict as best as you can. It makes sense as a tactic. It's too bad it works in reverse. What do you make of that?

J: Well, it's because she is relentless. She doesn't take no for an answer.

T: (Not letting Edna react here) Given that you cannot change the situation external to yourself, what can you do to better understand what is occurring inside each of you, and what is something that has at least a low probability of being successful? I wonder what would work in this situation?

J: I don't know.

T: Why don't you check with Edna? (Promoting enactment and hopefully an intimate conversation; focusing on process)

Similarly with Edna, the therapist worked to influence her interactive style.

T: Edna, I have the sense that you want something and then wait too long to try to get it, and in the meantime, you get irritated that Jose isn't reading your mind, and by the time you ask him for something, it comes across as criticism to him.

E: He hears everything I say as criticism.

T: I am suggesting that you ask for what you want, but do it before you get upset.

E: But what if I ask nicely and he ignores me?

T: Nothing lost there. You get the reaction you expected in the first place. It seems like there is little risk, at least on the surface.

E: What do you mean?

T: Let me be you and talk with Jose. Jose, I am Edna now. Let's imagine it is during dinnertime and I say to you, "I am a little stressed out from work today. Could we sit down and talk about it after dinner?" How would that be for you?

J: That isn't what she does!

T: Respond as if she said it the way I just did.

J: I guess I'd be curious and ask if she wanted to talk during dinner.

T: How would that be for you, Edna?

E: He never ...

T: He just did, so how would that be?

E: I'd like that.

The Middle Stage of Therapy

As the communication between Edna and Jose improved, two separate reactions occurred. First, they were getting along much better and at the very least were responding to what their partner actually said, rather than their assumptions (negative override). For some couples, that is all that is necessary for success.

At some point though, as Edna and Jose communicated more effectively, they began to get more stressed and the new interaction stagnated. This was a point in therapy where the therapist had to hypothesize that the earlier poor communication was obfuscating some other (structural) problem. For Edna and Jose, it was the problem that as they communicated more effectively, they began to become more intimate. This unbalanced the distance status quo and led to additional anxiety.

During the fifth week of therapy, this interaction occurred.

E: We had a fight this week. Things were going well, and we were getting close, and it all fell apart.

J: We were cuddling and I became aroused, so I began touching her and then all of a sudden, she wanted to quit.

E: I have had trouble with "dryness" since I began menopause, and I didn't want to feel pain if we had intercourse.

T: Is that new information for you, Jose?

J: She never said anything, just stopped and broke off our connection.

T: So, you wanted to take it further and proceeded in a way that was scary for Edna.

For the therapist, there are two issues to address here: The first is how to help Jose and Edna talk about intimate desires more effectively, and the second is how to help them overcome the fear of intimacy and regression to unsuccessful patterns that came about with their increased closeness and improved communication.

> T: It sounds like it all began quite nicely, and then anxiety popped up about closeness, per se, and potential pain for you, Edna, and the way you dealt with the anxiety together was to create distance.

For the next few weeks, they focused on their fear of vulnerability in intimacy and how fighting and distance was unpleasant but less fearful than experiencing that level of openness. Jose was able to tell Edna that he wished she could come with him on his business trip, but that he would worry too much about her safety to effectively carry out his fundraising work. He added that he wanted to keep in close touch, because she was so good at fundraising and that he would miss her.

Her reaction was to say that she did wish she could go, but if he maintained close contact, she would understand. Then she suggested that when he returned the two of them take a vacation trip together. To her surprise, he had already booked a surprise trip to Hawaii and worked it out with their daughters.

The Setback

Often in couple therapy there is a regression or setback in treatment. The couple returns to old, less effective behavior. They move away from their stated goals. They report to the therapist that the work isn't effective, and so on.

Every theoretical approach explains the setback differently. For existential work, one of the most important is the developing intimacy moving too quickly and throwing them into greater fears of the unknown. The key to therapy is to support the status quo while encouraging them to take the next step toward greater ability to experience what Buber (1937/1970) referred to as "I-thou" moments.

> T: This is an impasse you are experiencing, and it may be a message to pull back to some aspects of the way it was before. It can be scary to give up the old balance. Those methods are safe, albeit at a price.

> E: Well, I don't want to go back to the frustration, but I also want some more security!

> T: How about you, Jose?

> J: Yes. I agree. What we have been doing lately is trying a lot of new things, and that may cause problems.

> T: Let's talk about the risks of the new unknowns.

J: For me, I don't know any more what Edna will do or say.

T: What's the worst fantasy you have?

J: That she will leave me.

E: I have no interest in leaving. I just want some more predictability.

T: So, you both are committed to being in the relationship but want less uncertainty. How may we work toward that? Is there something I can do to offer more security?

The second issue that emerged was related to Edna's increasing anxiety about Jose's business prospects. She wanted him to be more active in his attempts to pull together the new business. He was feeling pressure and withdrawing. As this was being discussed, the therapist intervened:

T: Edna, could you tell Jose about your anxiety regarding his currently being without a salary from work?

E: Yes. That's it. I think I will have to support us forever.

J: I have always been a major contributor. I have worked since I was 14 years old, and I am being criticized for a short break between jobs.

T: Edna, it seems like this is a déjà vu experience from your first marriage. Unlike Jose, your first husband did leave the bulk of the financial stress on you.

E: (Looking a bit shaken) You know, I have been thinking about him a lot lately and have some left-over anger from the settlement.

J: We didn't need that money. I made enough to cover it, and we were fine.

T: Do you believe that Jose will continue to be successful?

E: Yes. (Reaching for his hand and addressing him directly) You have a great track record.

T: Tell him that you are having flashbacks and that it is not about your relationship, but about your anxiety about having to be the only breadwinner.

Termination

There are two essential goals in termination:

- Saying goodbye and extricating the therapist from the primary relationship
- Transfer of training

Goodbyes are never easy in a meaningful relationship. For Edna and Jose, their new-found intimacy was still a little precarious. How might they grow it without help from the therapist? Will they unconsciously create crises to come back into therapy? Must the goodbye be permanent?

They partially resolved these questions by spreading out the last few sessions to include gaps of 3 to 4 weeks. They also scheduled a "check-up" appointment 6 months in the future. When he scheduled that appointment, the therapist said, "It is in my calendar, but please know, if things are going well as we expect, you may feel free to cancel it ahead of time. Of course, in the unlikely event that you need to come in again, either sooner or later, just call."

It is not unusual for couples to check back in from time-to-time after therapy has officially terminated. They do so more frequently than individual clients. Edna and Jose did make two more appointments some months later. At the time, his new business was still not generating much income, and he felt it necessary to do a disproportionate share of the family tasks because Edna contributed most of their working income. Because of this, he felt secondary and inferior (a throwback to his feelings as a child).

At this point, the therapist opened up the issue of Jose's role in his family of origin. Since he came from a traditional (characteristically patriarchal) Latino family and he was the only son, there were naturally some expectations that he would become a family leader. As the youngest child, however, he reported being relegated to last place by his parents in his family of two sisters. Similarly, in his first marriage, his wife saw him only as a breadwinner who should fill a traditional role. Now faced with depending more on Edna's income, at least in the foreseeable future, he was feeling "dissed" again.

The therapeutic work was fairly short. Edna was encouraged to support his feelings and to understand what he was experiencing from his perspective. Because of their improved relationship (and her caretaker role as the eldest of eight in her family of origin), she was able to show considerable support for his struggle and encourage his future prospects.

CBT and Existential Couple Therapy

Throughout this text we have explored similarities and differences in the two theoretical methodologies. Although the two approaches begin with different assumptions and different understanding and interventions, they both work effectively, sharing some common factors.

To the extent possible, we have tried to examine the convergences, divergences, and integration of the two methods.

Similarities Between CBT and Existential Couple Therapy

1. Both explore *consequences* versus motivation of current behavior.
2. Both focus on *relationship* rather than individuals within the relationship.
3. Both require the development of *strong therapeutic alliance*.
4. *Both interrupt dysfunctional relational patterns* (costly homeostasis).

5. Both use *homework/experiments* to try out new behaviors.
6. Both primarily employ an *ahistorical focus* for change (present, future).

Differences Between CBT and Existential Couple Therapy

1. Existential approaches are born in philosophy; CBT in experimental psychology.
2. Existential therapists understand the person from internal subjective experiences (inside-out); CBT approaches from the outside-in, focusing on behavior and thoughts.
3. Existential uses inductive logic; CBT uses deductive logic.
4. Existential embraces deep, complex, emotional experience that is difficult to operationalize; CBT focuses more on observables.
5. In existential, clients are the locus of change; in CBT, the therapist is the locus of change.
6. In existential, the relationship is intimate with active sharing between therapist and clients; in CBT the relationship is more professionally distant.
7. In existential, the data are subjective experiences; in CBT the data are observables and objective reality.

CBT	Existential Therapy
Cognition	Meaning
Functional therapy relationship	**Intimate** functional therapy relationship
Learn/practice new behaviors	Help them find meaning through interaction and in tension berween pull of security (Status quo) and freedom (Facing fear of unknown)

FIGURE 12.1 **Theoretical differences**

Bottom Line

The methods presented here represent basic couple therapy. We have chosen to do so from two apparently opposing perspectives, but in the process have explored a great deal of overlap that is useful with all couples. Readers are encouraged to use the material in two ways:

1. To employ the approach that fits better with therapist personal value systems
2. To employ approaches that fit better with client couples' personal value systems

Fishman (2019) recommends an assimilative integration, in which both novice and advanced therapists take concepts, strategies, and techniques from one theory and adapt them to the different epistemological environment of the other theory. This is particularly true in viewing the importance and nature of the therapeutic relationship, the centrality of emotion in couple therapy, and the importance of attending to behavioral patterns in therapy (whether they are the core of therapy or an indication of some deeper elements).

We share this perception and believe that this text has provided a step toward such integration in treating couples.

Appendix A

Bibliotherapy

Recommended Reading for Couples

Bach,G. and Wyden, P. *The Intimate Enemy: How to Fight Fair in Love and Marriage.* New York: Avon Books.

Carlson, J., & Dinkmeyer, D. C. (2003). *Time for a better marriage.* Atascadero, CA: Impact Publishers.

Chapman, G *The 5 Love Languages: The secret to Love that Lasts.* Chicago, IL: Northfield Publishing.

Christensen, A., Doss et al *Reconcilable differences: Rebuild Your Relationship by Rediscovering the Partner You Love – Without Losing Yourself.* New York: Guilford.

Fruzzetti, A. (2006). *The high-conflict couple: A dialectical behavior therapy guide to finding peace, intimacy, and validation.* Oakland, CA: New Harbinger Publications.

Goldsmith, B. (2011). *Emotional Fitness for Couples.* Read HowYouWant. com.

Gottman, J. & Silver, N. The Seven Principles for Making Marriage Work: A Practical Guide from the Country's Foremost Relationship Expert. New York: Harmony

Heitler, S. (1997). *The Power of Two.* Oakland, CA: New Harbinger Publications

Marcus, E. (1999). *The male couple's guide: Finding a man, making a home, building a life.* Harper/Perennial.

Marston, A. A. (1997). *Planning for love: the politics of prenuptial agreements. Stanford Law Review,* 887–916.

Redfield, K. *An Unquiet Mind: A Memoir of Moods and Madness.* New York: Knopf.

Rich, J. (2003). *The Couple's Guide to Love and Money.* Oakland, CA: New Harbinger.

Rodman, S (2016). 52 E-mails to Transform Your Marriage. Oakland, CA: New Harbinger Publications

Shapiro, J. *Finding Meaning, Facing Fears in the autumn of your years: 45–65.* Oakland, CA: New Harbinger Publications.

Skeen, M. (2011). *The critical partner: how to end the cycle of criticism and get the love you want.* Oakland, CA: New Harbinger Publications.

Spring, J. After the Affair: *Healing the Pain and Rebuilding Trust When a Partner Has Been Unfaithful.* New York: William Morrow.

Stone, D., Patton, B. & Heen, S. *Difficult Conversations: How to Discuss What Matters Most.* London: Penguin Books.

Tatkin, S. (2012). *Wired for Love: How Understanding Your Partner's Brain and Attachment Style Can Help You Defuse Conflict and Build a Secure Relationship.* Oakland, CA:New Harbinger Publications.

Whiffen, V. E. (2009). *A secret sadness: The hidden relationship patterns that make women depressed.* Oakland, CA: New Harbinger Publications.

References

Ables, B. S., & Brandsma, J. (1991). *Therapy for couples.* San Francisco, CA: Jossey Bass.

Acevedo, B. P., & Aron, A. (2009). Does a long-term relationship kill romantic love? *Review of General Psychology, 13*(1), 59–65.

Acevedo, B. P., Aron, A., Fisher, H. E., & Brown, L. (2011). Neural correlates of long-term intense romantic love. *Social Cognitive and Affective Neuroscience, 7*(2), 145–159.

Ackerman, N.W. (1970) *Family process.* New York, NY: Basic Books.

Albee, E. (2001). *Who's afraid of Virginia Woolf?* New York, NY: Signet.

Allen, E. S., & Atkins, D. C. (2012). The association of divorce and extramarital sex in a representative US sample. *Journal of Family Issues, 33*(11), 1477–1493.

Allgood, S. M., & Crane, D. R. (1991). Predicting marital therapy dropouts. *Journal of Marital and Family Therapy, 17*(1), 73–79.

Amato, P. R., & Rogers, S. J. (1997). A longitudinal study of marital problems and subsequent divorce. *Journal of Marriage and the Family, 59*(3), 612–624.

American Association of Marriage and Family Therapy (AAMFT). (2015). *AAMFT code of ethics.* Alexandria, VA: Author.

American Psychiatric Association. (2013). Diagnostic and statistical manual of mental disorders (5th ed.) (DSM-5) Arlington, VA: Author.

American Psychological Association. (2002). Ethical principles of psychologists and code of conduct. *American Psychologist, 57,* 1060–1073.

American Psychological Association. (2016). *Demographics of the U.S. psychology workforce.* Retrieved from www.apa.org/workforce/publications/13-demographics/index

American Psychological Association. (2017). *Ethical principles of psychologists and code of conduct.* Retrieved from https://www.apa.org/ethics/code/index

American Psychological Association. (2018). *APA guidelines on boys and men.* Retrieved from https://www.apa.org/about/policy/boys-men-practice-guidelines.pdf

American Psychological Association. (2019). APA guidelines on boys and men launch important—and fiery—national conversation. *Monitor on Psychology, 50*(2). Retrieved from https://www.apa.org/monitor/2019/02/male-guidelines

Bach, G. R., & Wyden, P. (1970). *The intimate enemy: How to fight fair in love and marriage.* New York, NY: Avon.

Bachelor, A., Laverdière, O., Gamache, D., & Bordeleau, V. (2007). Clients' collaboration in therapy: Self-perceptions and relationships with client psychological functioning, interpersonal relations, and motivation. *Psychotherapy, 44*(2), 175–192.

Bader, E., & Pearson, P. (1988). *In quest of the mythical mate: A developmental approach to diagnosis and treatment in couples therapy.* New York, NY: Routledge.

Bader, E., & Pearson, P. (2016). *Couples therapy in action: 4 techniques for rapid and lasting change with Drs. Ellyn Bader and Peter Pearson* [DVD]. Eau Claire, WI: PESI.

Baer, D. (2016). Turns out that the husband's job is probably the best predictor of divorce. *The Cut.* Retrieved from https://www.thecut.com/2016/07/husbands-job-predicts-divorce.html

Bagarozzi, D. A., & Sperry, L. (Eds.) (2012). *Family assessment: Contemporary and cutting-edge strategies.* New York, NY: Routledge.

Balderrama-Durbin, C., Snyder, D. K., & Balsis, S. (2015). Tailoring assessment of relationship distress using the Marital Satisfaction Inventory—brief form. *Couple and Family Psychology: Research and Practice, 4*(3), 127–135.

Bandler, R., & Grinder, J. (1975). *The structure of magic I: A book about language and therapy.* Palo Alto, CA: Science and Behavior Books.

Bandura, A., & Walters, R. H. (1970). *Social learning and personality development.* New York, NY: Hold, Rinehart and Winston.

Banmen, J. (2002). The Satir model: Yesterday and today. *Contemporary Family Therapy, 24*(1), 7–22.

Barlow, D. H., Allen, L. B., & Choate, M. L. (2004). Toward a unified treatment for emotional disorders. *Behavior Therapy, 47*(6), 838–853.

Barnett, J. E., Behnke, S. H., Rosenthal, S. L., & Koocher, G. P. (2007). In case of ethical dilemma, break glass: Commentary on ethical decision making in practice. *Professional Psychology: Research and Practice, 38*(1), 7a.

Bateson, G. (1972). *Steps to an ecology of mind: Collected essays in anthropology, psychiatry, evolution, and epistemology.* Chicago, IL: University of Chicago Press.

Baucom, D. H. (1982). A comparison of behavioral contracting and problem-solving/communications training in behavioral marital therapy. *Behavior Therapy, 13*(2), 162–174.

Baucom, D. H., Sayers, S. L., & Sher, T. G. (1990). Supplementing behavioral marital therapy with cognitive restructuring and emotional expressiveness training: An outcome investigation. *Journal of Consulting and Clinical Psychology, 58*(5), 636–644.

Baucom, D., Shoham, V., Mueser, K., Daiuto, A., & Stickle, T. (1998). Empirically supported couple and family interventions for marital distress and mental health problems. *Journal of Consulting and Clinical Psychology, 66*(1), 53–88.

Beall, A. E., & Sternberg, R. J. (1995). The social construction of love. *Journal of Social and Personal Relationships, 12*(3), 417–438.

Beaton, A., Cook, M., Kavanagh, M., & Herrington, C. (2000). The psychological impact of burglary. *Psychology, Crime & Law, 6*(1), 33–43.

Beaton, J. M., Norris, J. E., & Pratt, M. W. (2003). Unresolved issues in adult children's marital relationships involving intergenerational problems. *Family Relations: An Interdisciplinary Journal of Applied Family Studies, 52*(2), 143–153.

Beck, G. A. (2016). Surviving involuntary unemployment together: The role of resilience-promoting communication in familial and committed relationships. *Journal of Family Communication, 16*(4), 369–385.

Beier, E. G., & Young, D. M. (1984). *The silent language of psychotherapy,* (2nd ed.). New York, NY: Aldine.

Benson, L. A., McGinn, M. M., & Christensen, A. (2012). Common principles of couple therapy. *Behavior Therapy, 43*(1), 25–35.

Berdondini, L., Elliott, R., & Shearer, J. (2012). Collaboration in experiential therapy. *Journal of Clinical Psychology, 68*(2), 159–167.

Berk, A., & Shapiro, J. L. (1984). Some considerations of infertility: Psycho-therapeutic Implications and a Case Study. *Family Therapy, 11*(1), 37–48.

Bertolino, B., & O'Hanlon, B. (2002). *Collaborative, competency-based counseling and therapy.* Needham Heights, MA: Allyn & Bacon.

Biernat, M., & Wortman, C. B. (1991). Sharing of home responsibilities between professionally employed women and their husbands. *Journal of Personality and Social Psychology, 60*(6), 844–860.

Biller, H. (1971). Father, child, and sex role: Paternal determinants of personality development. New York, NY: Lexington.

Blanchflower, D., & Oswald, A. (2004). Money, sex and happiness. An empirical study. *Scandinavian Journal of Economics, 106*(3), 393–415.

Blank, R. (1985). The infertility epidemic. *Futurist, 19*(17), 177–180.

Blum, H. P. (1989). The concept of termination and the evolution of psychoanalytic thought. *Journal of the American Psychoanalytic Association, 37*(2), 275–295.

Bono, G., McCullough, M. E., & Root, L. M. (2008). Forgiveness, feeling connected to others, and well-being: Two longitudinal studies. *Personality and Social Psychology Bulletin, 34*(2), 182–195.

Boswell, J. (1791/1986). *Life of Samuel Johnson.* In C. Hibbert (Ed.) New York, NY: Penguin Classics.

Boszormenyi-Nagy, I., & Spark, G. (1973/1984). Invisible loyalties: Reciprocity in intergenerational family therapy. New York, NY: Harper and Row.

Boudreaux, E., Kilpatrick, D. G., Resnick, H. S., Best, C. L., & Saunders, B. E. (1998). Criminal victimization, posttraumatic stress disorder, and co-morbid psychopathology among a community sample of women. *Journal of Traumatic Stress, 11*(4), 665–678.

Bowen, M. (1966). *Family theory in clinical practice.* Lanham, MD: Rowman & Littlefield.

Bowen, M. (1974/2004). Toward the differentiation of self in one's family of origin. In M. Bowen (Ed.) *Family therapy in clinical practice* (reprint ed.) (pp. 529–547). Lanham, MD: Rowman & Littlefield.

Boyd-Franklin, N. (2003). Race, class, and poverty. In F. Walsh (Ed.), *Normal family processes: Growing diversity and complexity* (3rd ed.) (pp. 261–279). New York, NY: Guilford.

Bradford, L., Gibb, I., & Benne, K. D. (1964). *T-group theory and laboratory method in re-education.* Hoboken, NJ: Wiley.

Brase, G, L., Adair, L., & Monk, K. (2014). Explaining sex differences in reactions to relationship infidelities: Comparisons of roles of sex, gender, beliefs, attachment, and sociosexual orientation. *Evolutionary Psychology, 12*(1), 73–96.

Breunlin, D. C., Pinsof, W., Russell, W. P., & Lebow, J. (2011). Integrative problem-centered metaframeworks therapy I: Core concepts and hypothesizing. *Family Process, 50*(3), 29–313.

Britt, S. L., Huston, S., & Durband, D. B. (2010). The determinants of money arguments between spouses. *Journal of Financial Therapy, 1*(1), 43–60.

Bronfenbrenner, U. (2006). The bioecological model of human development. In R. M. Lerner & W. Damon (Eds.), *Handbook of child psychology: Theoretical models of human development.* Hoboken, NJ: Wiley.

Brown, J. H., & Brown, C. S. (2002). *Marital therapy: Concepts and skills for effective practice.* Belmont, CA: Brooks/Cole.

Brown, M. W. (1942). *The runaway bunny.* New York, NY: Harper and Row.

Brown, S., & Lewis, V. (1999). *The alcoholic family in recovery: A developmental model of recovery.* New York, NY: Guilford.

Buber, M. (1937/1970). *I and thou* (W. Kaufmann, Trans.). New York, NY: Scribner.

Busby, D. M., Crane, D. R., Larson, J. H., & Christensen, C. (1995). A revision of the Dyadic Adjustment scale for use with distressed and nondistressed couples: Construct hierarchy and multidimensional scales. *Journal of Marital & Family Therapy, 21*(3), 289–308.

Buss, D. (2018). Sexual and emotional infidelity: Evolved gender differences in jealousy prove robust and replicable. *Perspectives on Psychological Science, 13*(2), 155–160.

Butler, M. H., Hall, L. G. & Yogason, J. B. (2013). The paradoxical relation of the expression of offense to forgiving: A survey of therapists' conceptualizations. *American Journal of Family Therapy, 41*(5), 415–436.

Butler, M. H., Seedall, R. B., & Harper, J. M. (2008). Facilitated disclosure versus clinical accommodation of infidelity secrets: An early pivot point in couple therapy. Part 2: Therapy ethics, pragmatics, and protocol. *American Journal of Family Therapy, 36*(4), 265–283.

Cachia, P., & Scharff, J. S. (2018). The ending of couple therapy with a couple who recovered joy. In D. E. Scharff (Ed.), *Psychoanalytic couple therapy: Foundations of theory and practice* (pp. 201–214). New York, NY: Routledge.

Campbell, S. (1980). *The couples journey: Intimacy as a path to wholeness.* Atascadero, CA: Impact.

Carlson, J. (2007). *Couples at an impasse* [Video file]. Washington, DC: American Psychological Association.

Carter, E. A., & McGoldrick, M.. (1988). Changing family life cycle: Individual, family, and social perspectives. Boston, MA: Allyn and Bacon.

Casares, R. D., Jr. & White C. C. (2018). The phenomenological experience of parents who live with a boomerang child. *American Journal of Family Therapy, 46*(3), 227–243.

Chapin, T. M., & Aldao, A. (2013). Gender differences in emotional expression in children: A meta-analytic view. *Psychological Bulletin, 139*(4), 735–765.

Chapman, G. (2015). *The 5 love languages: The secret to love that lasts.* Chicago, IL: Northfield.

ChenFeng, J. L., & Galick, A. (2015). How gender discourses hijack couple therapy—and how to avoid it. In C. Knudson-Martin, M. A. Wells, & S. K. Samman (Eds.), Socio-emotional relationship therapy: Bridging emotion, societal context, and couple interaction (pp. 41–52). New York, NY: Springer.

Christensen, A., Atkins, D. C., Berns, S., Wheeler, J., Baucom, D. H., & Simpson, l. E. (2004). Traditional versus integrative behavioral couple therapy for significantly and chronically distressed married couples. *Journal of Consulting and Clinical Psychology, 72*(2), 176–191.

Claiborne, C. D., Goodyear, R. K., & Horner, P. A. (2001). Feedback. *Psychotherapy 38*(4), 401–405.

Clay, R. A. (2015). Competence vs. conscience. *APA Monitor on Psychology, 46*(4), 64.

Coche, J. M. (2011). *Couples group therapy: A clinical treatment model.* New York, NY: Routledge.

Coche, J., & Coche, E. (1990). *Couples group psychotherapy.* New York, NY: Brunner/Mazel.

Conger, R. D., Conger, K. J., & Martin, M. J. (2010). Socioeconomic status, family processes, and individual development. *Journal of Marriage and Family, 72*(3), 685–704.

Coontz, S. (2005). *Marriage, a history: From obedience to intimacy or how love conquered marriage.* New York, NY: Viking.

Cooper, A. (1998). Sexuality and the Internet: Surfing into the new millennium. *Cyberpsychology and Behavior, 1*(2), 181–187.

Cordova, J. V., & Mirgain, S. A. (2004). Problem-solving training for couples. In E. C. Chang, T. J. D'Zurilla, & L. J. Sanna (Eds.), *Social problem solving: Theory, research, and training* (pp. 193–208), Washington, DC: American Psychological Association.

Corsini, R. (1957). *Methods of group psychotherapy.* New York, NY: McGraw Hill.

Cowan, C. P., & Cowan, P. A. (1992). *When partners become parents: The big life change for couples.* New York, NY: Basic Books.

Cowan, C. P., & Cowan, P. A. (2012). Prevention: Intervening with couples at challenging family transition points. In C.P. Cowan & P. A. Cowan, *How couple relationships shape our world: Clinical practice, research, and policy perspectives* (pp. 1–14). London, UK: Karnac Books.

Crampton, G., & Gergely, T. (1945). *Tootle.* New York, NY: Random House.

Cross, S. E., & Madson, L. (1997). Models of the self: Self-construals and gender. *Psychological Bulletin, 122*(1), 5–37.

Crowe, M. (1997). Intimacy in relation to couple therapy, *Sexual and Marital Therapy, 12*(3), 225–236.

Crowe, M., & Ridley, J. (1990). *Therapy with couples: A behavioural-systems approach.* Oxford, UK: Blackwell Scientific.

Cudmore, L. (2012). Commentary on chapter three. In A. Balfour, M. Morgan, & C. Vincent (Eds.), *How couple relationships shape our world: Clinical practice, research, and policy perspectives* (pp. 85–90). London, UK: Karnac Books.

Cummings, e. e. (1926/1972). She being brand new. In *Complete Poems 1914–1962.* New York, NY: Harcourt.

Daniluk, J. C., Leader, A., & Taylor, P. J. (1987). Psychological and relationship changes of couples undergoing an infertility investigation: Some implications for counsellors. *British Journal of Guidance and Counseling, 15*(1), 29–35.

Dattilio, F. M., & Hanna, M. A. (2012). Collaboration in cognitive-behavioral therapy. *Journal of Clinical Psychology, 68*(2), 146–158.

Davidson, G. N. S., & Horvath, A. O. (1997). Three sessions of brief couple therapy: A clinical trial. *Journal of Family Therapy, 11*(4), 422–435.

Deaux, K. (1984). From individual differences to social categories: Analysis of a decade's research on gender. *American Psychologist, 39*(2), 105–116.

De Jong, P., & Berg, I. K. (2002). *Interviewing for solutions.* (2nd ed.) Pacific Grove, CA: Wadsworth.

de Shazer, S., & Berg, I. K. (1997). "What works?": Remarks on research aspects of solution-focused brief therapy. *Journal of Family Therapy, 19*(2), 121–124.

DeWall, C. N., & Richman, S. B. (2011). Social exclusion and the desire to reconnect. *Social and Personality Psychology Compass, 5*(11), 919–932.

Diamond, J. (2016). *The enlightened marriage: The 5 transformative stages of relationships and why the best is still to come.* Wayne, NJ: New Page.

Diamond, M. J. (2010). The impact of the mind of the analyst: From unconscious process to intrapsychic change. In M. J. Diamond & C. Christian (Eds.), *The second century of psychoanalysis: Evolving perspectives on therapeutic action* (pp. 205–237). London, UK: Karnac.

Diamond, M. J., & Shapiro, J. L. (1983). *Introduction and the paradoxes of intimacy* [Audiotape]. San Francisco, CA: Proseminar.

Dickson, P. (2011) *Baseball is...: Defining the national pastime.* Mineola, NY: Dover Publications.

Dienhart, A. (2001). Engaging men in family therapy: Does the gender of the therapist make a difference? *Journal of Family Therapy, 23*(1), 21–45.

Doherty, W. J. (2013). *Take back your marriage: Sticking together in a world that pulls us apart* (2nd ed.). New York, NY: Guilford.

Doherty, W. J., & Harris, S. M. (2017). *Helping couples on the brink of divorce: Discernment counseling for troubled relationships.* Washington, DC: American Psychological Association.

Dollard, J., & Miller, N. E. (1950). *Personality and psychotherapy: An analysis in terms of learning, thinking, and culture.* New York, NY: McGraw Hill.

Domar, A. D., Smith, K., Conboy, L., Iannone, M., & Alper, M. (2010). A prospective investigation into the reasons why insured United States patients drop out of in vitro fertilization treatment. *Fertility and Sterility, 94*(4), 1457–1459.

Donovan, S., & Emmers-Sommer, T. M. (2012). Attachment style and gender as predictors of communicative responses to infidelity. *Marriage & Family Review, 48*(2), 125–149.

Doss, B. D., Atkins, D. C., & Christensen, A. (2003). Who's dragging their feet? Husbands and wives seeking marital therapy. *Journal of Marital and Family Therapy, 29*(2), 165–177.

Doss, B. D., Simpson, L. E., Morrison, K. R., Libet, J., Birchler, G. R., Madsen, J. W., & McQuaid, J. R. (2012). Couple therapy for military veterans: Overall effectiveness and predictors of response. *Behavior Therapy, 43*(1), 216–227.

Doull, M., Oliffe, J., Knight, R., & Shoveller, J. A. (2013). Sex and straight young men: Challenging and endorsing hegemonic masculinities and gender regimes. *Men and Masculinities, 16*(3), 329–346.

Douthit, R. (2019, January 19). In search of non-toxic manhood. *New York Times.* Retrieved from https://www.nytimes.com/2019/01/19/opinion/sunday/toxic-masculinity.html?searchResultPosition=1

Dunn, R., & Schwebel, A. (1995). Meta-analytic review of marital therapy outcome research. *Journal of Family Psychology, 9*(1), 58–68.

Durband, D. B., Britt, S. L., & Grable, J. E. (2010). Personal and family finance in the marriage and family therapy domain. *Journal of Financial Therapy, 1*(1), 7–22.

Dyregrov, A., & Dyregrov, K (2017). Parents' perception of their relationship following the loss of a child. *Omega: Journal of Death and Dying, 76*(1), 35–52.

Eamon, M. K., & Venkataraman, M. (2003). Implementing parent management training in the context of poverty. *American Journal of Family Therapy, 31*(4), 281–293.

Ehrensaft, M. K., & Vivian, D. (1996). Spouses' reasons for not reporting existing marital aggression as a marital problem. *Journal of Family Psychology, 10*(4), 443–453.

Englar-Carlson, M., Evans, M. P., & Duffey, T. (2014). *A counselor's guide to working with men.* Alexandria, VA: American Counseling Association.

Englar-Carlson, M., & Shepard, D. S. (2005). Engaging men in couples counseling: Strategies for overcoming ambivalence and inexpressiveness. *The Family Journal, 13*(4), 383–391.

Englar-Carlson, M. & Stevens, M. (2006). *In the room with men: Casebook of therapeutic change.* Washington, DC: American Psychological Association.

Epstein, N., & Baucom, D. H. (2002). *Enhanced cognitive-behavioral therapy for couples: A contextual approach.* Washington, DC: American Psychological Association.

Erickson, B. A., & Keener, B. (2006). *Milton H. Erickson, MD: An American healer.* Sedona, AZ: Ringing Rocks Books.

Erickson, M. (1965). The use of symptoms as an integral part of hypnotherapy. *American Journal of Clinical Hypnosis, 8*(3), 57–65.

Erickson, M. (1980). The collected papers of Milton H. Erickson on hypnosis. New York, NY: Irvington.

Falconnier L. (2009). Socioeconomic status in the treatment of depression. *American Journal of Orthopsychiatry, 79*(2), 148–158.

Fals-Stewart, W., Schafer, J., & Birchler, G. R. (1993). An empirical typology of distressed couples that is based on the areas of change questionnaire. *Journal of Family Psychology, 7*(3), 307–321.

Farrell, W. (1993). *The myth of male power.* New York, NY: Simon and Schuster.

Fast, J. A. & Preston, J.D. (2012) *Loving someone with bipolar disorder.* Oakland, CA: New Harbinger.

Feldman, D. B., & Kravetz, L. D. (2015). *Supersurvivors: The surprising link between suffering and success.* New York, NY: HarperCollins.

Fergusson, D. M., Boden, J. M., & Horwood, L. J. (2007). Unemployment and suicidal behavior in a New Zealand birth cohort. *Crisis, 28*(2), 95–101.

Fincham, F. D., & Beach, S. R. H. (2007). Forgiveness and marital quality: Precursor or consequence in well-established relationships? *Journal of Positive Psychology, 2*(4), 260–268.

Fisch, R., & Weakland, J., & Segal, L. (1982). *The tactics of change: Doing therapy briefly.* San Francisco, CA: Jossey Bass.

Fisher, H. E. (2004). *Why we love: The nature and chemistry of romantic love.* New York, NY: Henry Holt.

Fisher, H. E., Aron, A., & Brown, L. L. (2006). Romantic love: An fMRI study of a neural mechanism for mate choice. *Journal of Comparative Neurology 493*(1), 58–62.

Fisher, H. E., Xu, Aron, A., & Brown, L. L. (2016). Intense, passionate, romantic love: A natural addiction? How the fields that investigate romance and substance abuse can inform each other. *Frontiers in Psychology, 7,* 687.

Fishman, D. (2019, June 6). CBT and existential/humanistic approaches to couple therapy: Convergence, divergence and integration: Commentary. Annual meeting of the Society for Exploration of Psychotherapy Integration. Lisbon, Portugal.

Fitzgerald, F. S. (1926). The rich boy. In *All the sad young men* (pp. 1–9). New York, NY: Scribners.

Flamez, B., Hicks, J. F., & Clark, A. (2015). Effectively using research and assessment in couples and family therapy. In D. Capuzzi & M. D. Stauffer (Eds), *Foundations of couples, marriage, and family counseling* (pp. 71–100). Hoboken, NJ: Wiley.

Floyd, K. (2006). *Communicating affection: Interpersonal behavior and social context (advances in personal relationships).* New York, NY: Cambridge University Press.

Follette, W. C., & Callaghan, G. M. (2008). Behavior therapy: Functional-contextual approaches. In S. B. Messer & A. S. Gurman (Eds.), *Essential psychotherapies: Theory and practice* (3rd ed.) (pp. 184–222). New York, NY: Guilford.

Forbes, S. & Fikretoglu, D. (2018). Building resilience: The conceptual basis and research evidence for resilience training programs. *Review of General Psychology, 22*(4), 452–468.

Formica, M. (2009, January 8). Gender differences, sexuality and emotional infidelity. *Psychology Today.* Retrieved from http://www.psychologytoday.com/blog/enlightened-living/200901/gender-differences-sexuality-and-emotional-infidelity

Framo, J. L. (1992). *Family-of-origin therapy: An intergenerational approach.* New York, NY: Brunner/Mazel.

Frank J. D. (1961/1993). *Persuasion and healing: A comparative study of psychotherapy,* Baltimore, MD: Johns Hopkins University Press.

Frank, J. D. (1974). Psychotherapy, the restoration of morale. *American Journal of Psychiatry, 131*(3), 271–274.

Frankl, V. E. (1959). *Man's search for meaning: An introduction to logotherapy.* New York, NY: Washington Square Press.

Freud, S. (1937). Analysis terminable and interminable. *International Journal of Psycho-Analysis, 18,* 373–405.

Fruzzetti, A. (2006). *The high-conflict couple.* Oakland, CA: New Harbinger.

Furstenberg, F. J. (2010). On a new schedule: Transitions to adulthood and family change. *The Future of Children, 20*(1), 67–87.

Gabriel, L. (2005). *Speaking the unspeakable: The ethics of dual relationships in counselling and psychotherapy.* London, UK: Routledge.

Gallardo, M. E., Johnson, J., Parham, T. A., & Carter, J. A. (2009). Ethics and multiculturalism: Advancing cultural and clinical responsiveness. *Professional Psychology: Research and Practice, 40*(5), 425–424.

Galst, J. P. (2018). The elusive connection between stress and infertility: A research review with clinical implications. *Journal of Psychotherapy Integration, 28*(1), 1–13.

Garcia, M., & McDowell, T. (2010) Mapping social capital: A critical contextual approach for working with low-status families. *Journal of Marital and Family Therapy, 36*(1), 96–107.

Glass, S. P. (2002). Couple therapy after the trauma of infidelity. In A. S. Gurman & N. S. Jacobson (Eds.), *Clinical handbook of couple therapy* (3rd ed.) (pp. 488–507). New York, NY: Guilford.

Glass, T. A. (1997). Ethical issues in group therapy. In R. Anderson, T. Needles & H. Hall (Eds.), *A practitioner's guide to ethical issues in psychology specialty areas* (pp. 95–126). Springfield, IL: Charles Thomas.

Goldfried, M. R., & Norcross, J. C. (1995). Integrative and eclectic therapies in historical perspective. In B. M. Bongar & L. E. Beutler (Eds), *Comprehensive textbook of psychotherapy: Theory and practice* (pp. 254–273). New York, NY: Oxford University Press.

Goldman, A., & Greenberg, L. (1992). Comparison of integrated systemic and emotionally focused approaches to couple therapy. *Journal of Consulting and Clinical Psychology, 60*(6), 962–969.

Goldman, J. D. G. (2008). Responding to parental objections to school sexuality education: A selection of 12 objections. *Sex Education, 8*(4), 415–438.

Goldman, R. N., & Greenberg, L. S. (2007). Integrating love and power in emotion-focused couple therapy. *European Psychotherapy, 7*(1), 117–135.

Goldsmith, A. H., Veum, J. R., & Darity, W., Jr. (1997). Unemployment, joblessness, psychological well-being and self-esteem: Theory and evidence. *Journal of Socio-Economics, 26*(2), 133–158.

Golladay, K., & Holtfreter, K. (2017). The consequences of identity theft victimization: An examination of emotional and physical health outcomes. *Victims & Offenders, 12*(5), 741–760.

Goode, J., Park, J., Parkin, S., Tomkins, K. A., & Swift, J. K. (2017). A collaborative approach to psychotherapy termination. *Psychotherapy, 54*(1), 10–14.

Goodrich, T. J., Rampage, C., Ellman, B., & Halstead, K. (1988). *Feminist family therapy: A casebook.* New York, NY: Norton.

Gordon, K. C., Baucom, D. H., & Snyder, D. K. (2004). An integrative intervention for promoting recovery from extramarital affairs. *Journal of Marital and Family Therapy, 30*(2), 213–231.

Gordon, K. C., Khaddouma, A., Baucom, D. H., & Snyder, D. K. (2015). Couple therapy and the treatment of affairs. In A. S. Gordon, J. L. Lebow & D. K. Snyder (Eds.), *Clinical handbook of couple therapy* (5th ed.) New York: Guilford (pp. 412–444).

Gordon, T. (1970). *PET: Parent effectiveness training: the tested new way to raise responsible children.* New York, NY: PH Wyden.

Gottlieb, M. C. (1993). Co-mingling of patient records: What's a family psychologist to do? *Family Psychologist*, 19–20.

Gottlieb, M. C. (1995). Ethical dilemmas in change of format and live supervision. In R. H. Mikesell, D. Lusterman, & S. H. McDaniel (Eds.), *Integrating family therapy: Handbook of family psychology and systems therapy* (pp. 561–570). Washington, DC: American Psychological Association.

Gottlieb, M. C., Lasser, J., & Simpson, G. L. (2008). Legal and ethical issues in couple therapy. *Clinical Handbook of Couple Therapy*, 698–717.

Gottman, J. M. (1994). *What predicts divorce?* Hillsdale, NJ: Erlbaum.

Gottman, J. M. (1998). *Clinical manual for marital therapy: A scientifically-based marital therapy.* Seattle, WA: Seattle Marital and Family Institute.

Gottman, J. M., & Gottman, J. S. (2006). *Ten lessons to transform your marriage* New York, NY: Crown.

Gottman, J. M., & Silver, N. (1999). *The seven principles for making marriage work: A practical guide from the country's foremost relationship expert.* New York, NY: Harmony

Gottman, J. S., & Gottman, J. M. (2015). *10 principles for doing effective couples therapy.* New York, NY: Norton.

Grant-Jacobs, J. A. (2016). Love at first sight. *Frontiers in Psychology, 7*, 1113.

Gray, J. (1992). *Men are from Mars, women are from Venus: A practical guide for improving communication and getting what you want in your relationships.* New York, NY: HarperCollins.

Green, L.W. (2008). Making research relevant: If it is an evidence-based practice, where's the practice-based evidence? *Family Practice, 25*(1), 20–24.

Greenberg, L.S. (2002) *Emotion-focus therapy: Coaching clients to work through their feelings.* Washington, DC: American Psychological Association

Greenberg, L. S., Ford, C. L., Alden, L. S., & Johnson, S. M. (1993). In-session change in emotionally focused therapy. *Journal of Consulting and Clinical Psychology, 61*(1), 78–84.

Greenberg, L. S. & Goldman, R. N. (2008). *Emotion-focused couples therapy: The dynamics of emption, love and power.* Washington, DC: American Psychological Association.

Greenberg, L. S. & Goldman, R. N. (2018). *Clinical handbook of emotion-focused therapy.* Washington, DC: American Psychological Association.

Grencavage, L. M., & Norcross, J. C. (1990). Where are the commonalities among the therapeutic common factors? *Professional Psychology: Research and Practice, 21*(5), 372–378.

Grigoriadis, V. (2011) A major league divorce. *Vanity Fair.* Retrieved from https://www.vanityfair.com/news/2011/08/mccourt-divorce-201108

Grimes, M. E., & McElwain, A. D. (2008). Marriage and family therapy with low-income clients: Professional, ethical, and clinical Issues. *Contemporary Family Therapy, 30,* 220–232.

Gurman, A. (1988). Issues in the specification of family therapy interventions. In L. Wynne (Ed.), *The state of the art in family therapy process research: Controversies and recommendations* (pp. 125–138). New York, NY: Family Process Press.

Gurman, A. S. (2008). *Clinical handbook of couple therapy* (4th ed.). New York, NY: Guilford.

Gurman, A. S. (2010). *Clinical casebook of couple therapy.* New York, NY: Guilford.

Gurman, A. S. (2013a). Behavioral couple therapy: Building a secure base for therapeutic integration. *Family Process, 52*(1), 115–138.

Gurman, A. S. (2013b). Functions and factions: A reflection on possibilities for couple therapy integration. *Journal of Marital and Family Therapy, 39*(4), 424–426.

Gurman, A.S., Lebow, J.L. & Snyder, D.L. (2015) *Clinical Handbook of Couple Therapy.* New York: Guilford.

Haddock, S., & Lyness, K. P. (2002). Three aspects of the therapeutic conversation in couples therapy: Does gender make a difference? *Journal of Couple and Relationship, 7,* 5–24.

Haley, J. (1963). *Strategies of psychotherapy.* New York, NY: Grune and Stratton.

Haley, J. (1973). *Techniques of family therapy.* New York, NY: Basic Books.

Haley, J. (1973/1993). *Uncommon therapy: The psychiatric techniques of Milton H. Erickson,* MD. New York, NY: Norton.

Haley, J. (1976). *Problem solving therapy.* San Francisco, CA: Jossey-Bass

Haley, J. (1990). Interminable therapy. In J. Zeig & S. Gilligan (Eds.), *Brief therapy: Myths, methods, and metaphors* (pp. 3–17). New York, NY: Brunner/Mazel.

Halford, W. K. (2003). *Brief therapy for couples.* New York, NY: Guilford.

Hanisch, C. (2006). *The personal is political.* Retrieved from http://www.carolhanisch.org/CHwritings/PIP.html

Hare-Mustin, R. T. (1978). A feminist approach to family therapy. *Family Process, 17*(2), 181–194.

Hare-Mustin, R. T. (1983). An appraisal of the relationship between women and psychotherapy: 80 years after the case of Dora. *American Psychologist, 38*(5), 593–601.

Hare-Mustin, R. T. (2017). Those were the best of times, and then … *Women & Therapy, 40*(3–4), 346–357.

Harris, S. M., & Hays, K. W. (2008). Family therapist comfort with and willingness to discuss client sexuality. *Journal of Marital and Family Therapy, 34*(2), 239–250.

Hatfield, E., & Rapson, R. L. (1993). *Love, sex and intimacy: Their psychology, biology and history.* New York, NY: Harper Collins.

Hatfield, E. & Sprecher, S. (1985). *Mirror, mirror: The importance of looks in everyday life.* New York, NY: SUNY.

Hatfield, E., & Walster, G. W. (1978) *A new look at love.* Reading, MA: Addison Wesley.

Hawkins, M. W., Carrère, S., & Gottman, J. M. (2002). Marital sentiment override: Does it influence couples' perceptions? *Journal of Marriage and Family, 64*(1), 193–201.

Hayes, S. C., Strosahl, K. D., & Wilson, K. G. (2009). *Acceptance and commitment therapy.* Washington, DC: American Psychological Association.

Herzog, J. (2001). *Father hunger: Explorations with adults and children*. Hillsdale, NJ: Analytic Press.

Hewison, D., Casey, P., & Mwamba, N. (2016). The effectiveness of couple therapy: Clinical outcomes in a naturalistic United Kingdom setting. *Psychotherapy, 53*(4), 377–387.

Hill, M., Glaser, K., & Harden, J. (1998). A feminist model for ethical decision making. *Women & Therapy, 21*(3), 101–121.

Hirschmann, M. J., & Sprenkle, D. H. (1989). The use of therapeutic paradox among members of the American Association for Marriage and Family Therapy. *American Journal of Family Therapy, 17*(4), 340–358.

Hochschild, A. (1989). *The second shift*. New York, NY: Viking.

Holland, K. (2015). Division of labor: Same sex couples likely to share chores, study says. *NBC News*. Retrieved from https://www.nbcnews.com/business/consumer/division-labor-same-sex-couples-more-likely-share-chores-study-n369921

Hollander, C. E. (2002). Psychodrama, skill training, and role playing. *International Journal of Action Methods, 54*(4), 147–157.

Holmes, E. K., Sasaki, T., & Hazen, N. L. (2013). Smooth versus rocky transitions to parenthood: Family systems in developmental context. *Family Relations, 62*(5), 824–837.

Holtzworth-Munroe, A., Marshall, M. A., Meehan, J. C., & Rehman, U. (2003). Physical aggression. In D. K. Snyder & M. A. Whisman (Eds.), *Treating difficult couples: Helping clients with coexisting mental and relationship disorders* (pp. 201–230). New York, NY: Guilford Press.

Holzworth-Munroe, A., & Stuart, G. L. (1994). Typologies of male batterers: Three subtypes and the differences among them. *Psychological Bulletin, 116*(3), 476–497.

Hooghe, A., Neimeyer, R. A., & Rober, P. (2011). The complexity of couple communication in bereavement: An illustrative case study. *Death Studies, 35*(10), 905–924.

Horsley, G. C. (1997). In-laws extended family therapy. *American Journal of Family Therapy, 25*(1), 18–27.

Howard, J. (1984). *Margaret Mead: A life*. New York, NY: Simon and Schuster.

Howe, G. W., Levy, M. L., & Caplan, R. D. (2004). Job loss and depressive symptoms in couples, common stressors, stress transmission, or relationship disruption? *Journal of Family Psychology, 18*(4), 639–650.

Hoyt, M. F. (2015). Solution focused couple therapy. In A. S. Gurman, J. L. Lebow & D. K. Snyder (Eds.), *Clinical handbook of couple therapy* (5th ed.) (pp. 300–332). New York, NY: Guilford.

Humphreys, F.G. (1983). *Marital therapy*. Englewood Cliffs, NJ: Prentice Hall.

Hyde J. S. (2005). The gender similarities hypothesis. *American Psychologist, 60*(6), 581–592.

Hyde, J. S. (2014). Gender similarities and differences. *Annual Review of Psychology, 65*, 373–398.

Hyde, J. S. (2018). Gender similarities. In C. B. Travis, J. W. White, A. Rutherford, W. S. Williams, S. L. Cook, & K. F. Wyche (Eds.), *APA handbook of the psychology of women: History, theory, and battlegrounds, Vol. 1* (pp. 129–143). Washington, DC: American Psychological Association.

Inclan, J. (2001). Steps toward a culture and migration dialogue: Developing a framework for therapy with immigrant families. In S. H. McDaniel, D. D. Lusterman, & C. L. Philpot (Eds.), *Casebook for integrating family therapy: An ecosystemic approach*. Washington, DC: American Psychological Association.

Ingraham, L. (2019, January 14). Interview with Ed. Adams. *Laura Ingraham Show/Fox News*. Retrieved from https://www.youtube.com/watch?v=9QEDyRKTexl

Jacobs, E. E., Schimmel, C. J., Masson, R. L., & Harvill, R. L. (2016). *Group counseling: Strategies and skills* (8th ed.). Boston, MA: Cengage.

Jacobson, N. S., & Addis, M. E. (1993). Research on couple therapy: What do we know? Where are we going? *Journal of Consulting and Clinical Psychology, 61*(1), 85–93.

Jacobson, N. S., Christensen, A., Prince, S. E., Cordova, J., & Eldridge, K. (2000). Integrative behavioral couple therapy: An acceptance-based, promising new treatment for couple discord. *Journal of consulting and clinical psychology, 68*(2), 351–355.

Jacobson, N. S., Gottman, J. M., & Shortt, J. W. (1995). The distinction between type 1 and type 2 batterers—further considerations: Reply to Ornduff et al. (1995), Margolin et al. (1995), and Walker (1995). *Journal of Family Psychology, 9*(3), 272–279.

Jacobson, N. S., Gottman, J. M., Waltz, J., Rushe, R., Babcock, J., & Holtzworth-Munroe, A. (1994). Affect, verbal content, and psychophysiology in the arguments of couples with a violent husband. *Journal of Consulting and Clinical Psychology, 62*(5), 982–988.

Jacobson, N. S., & Margolin, G. (1979). *Marital therapy: Strategies based on social learning and behavior exchange principles.* New York, NY: Brunner/Mazel.

Jamison, K.R. (1996) *An unquiet mind: A memoir of moods and madness.* New York: Vintage Books.

Jankowiak, W. R. (Ed.). (2008). *Intimacies: Love and sex across cultures.* New York, NY: Columbia University Press.

Jankowski, P. J., & Hooper, L. M. (2012). Differentiation of self: A validation study of the Bowen theory construct. *Couple and Family Psychology: Research and Practice, 1*(3), 226–234.

Johnson, S. M. (2003). The revolution in couple therapy: A practitioner-scientist perspective. *Journal of Marital and Family Therapy, 29*(3), 365–384.

Johnson, S. M. (2019). *Attachment theory in practice: Emotionally focused therapy (EFT) with individuals, couples, and families.* New York, NY: Guilford.

Johnson, V. (1996). The parenting couple. In H. Kessler (Ed.), *Treating couples* (pp. 229–256). San Francisco, CA: Jossey-Bass.

Jong, E. M. (1975). *Fear of flying.* New York, NY: Penguin.

Jordan, J. V. (2017). *Relational-cultural therapy* (2nd ed.). Washington, DC: American Psychological Association.

Julian, K. (2018). The sex recession. *The Atlantic.* Retrieved from https://www.theatlantic.com/magazine/archive/2018/12/the-sex-recession/573949/

Jurek, J., Janusz, B., Chwal, N., & de Barbaro, B. (2014). Premature termination in couple therapy as a part of therapeutic process: Cross case analysis. *Archives of Psychiatry and Psychotherapy, 16*(2), 51–59.

Kaplan, H. S. (1979). *Disorders of sexual desire and other new concepts and techniques in sex therapy.* New York, NY: Brunner/Mazel.

Kaslow, F. W. (2005). Treating couples across the socioeconomic spectrum. In M. Harway (Ed.), *Handbook of couples therapy* (pp. 386–404). Hoboken: NJ: Wiley.

Kaslow, N. J., Rubin, N. J., Forrest, L., Elman, N. S., Van Horne, B. A., Jacobs, S. C., ... & Grus, C. L. (2007). Recognizing, assessing, and intervening with problems of professional competence. *Professional Psychology: Research and Practice, 38*(5), 479–485.

Kelly, S. (2017). *Diversity in couple and family therapy: Ethnicities, sexualities, and socioeconomics.* Santa Barbara, CA: Praeger.

Kerig, P. K., & Swanson, J. A. (2010). Ties that bind: Triangulation, boundary dissolution, and the effects of interparental conflicts on child development. In M. S. Schulz, M. K. Pruett, P. K. Kerig, & R. D. Parke (Eds.), *Strengthening couple relationships for optimal child development: Lessons from research and intervention* (pp. 59–76). Washington, DC: American Psychological Assn.

Kershaw, C. J. (1992). *The couple's hypnotic dance: Creating Ericksonian strategies in couple therapy.* New York, NY: Brunner/Mazel.

Kimbrell, A. (1991) A time for men to pull together. *Utne Reader,* 66–71.

Knapp, S., Handelsman, M. M., Gottlieb, M., & VandeCreek, L. D. (2013). The dark side of professional ethics. *Professional Psychology Research and Practice, 44*(6), 371–377.

Knapp, S., Vandecreek, L. D., Handelsman, M. M., & Gottlieb, M. (2013). Professional decisions and behaviors on the ethical rim. *Professional Psychology: Research and Practice, 44*(6), 378–383.

Knudson-Martin, C. (2013). Why power matters: Creating a foundation of mutual support in couple relationships. *Family Process, 52*(1), 5–18

Knudson-Martin, C., & Huenergardt, D. (2015). Bridging emotion, societal discourse and couple interaction in clinical practice. In C. Knudson-Martin, M. A. Wells, & S. K. Samman (Eds.), *Socio-emotional relationship therapy: Bridging emotion, societal context, and couple interaction* (pp. 1–13). New York, NY: Springer.

Knudson-Martin, C., Huenergardt, D., Lafontant, K., Bishop, L., Schaepper, J., & Wells, M. (2015). Competencies for addressing gender and power in couple therapy: A socio-emotional approach. *Journal of Marital & Family Therapy, 41*(2), 205–220.

Koivula, K., Kokki, H., Korhonen, M., Laitila, A., & Honkalampi, K. (2019). Experienced dyadic emotion regulation and coping of parents with a seriously ill child. *Couple and Family Psychology: Research and Practice, 8*(1), 45–61.

Krantzler, M. (1974). *Creative divorce: A new opportunity for growth.* Guilford, CT: M. Evans and Co.

Krantzler, M. (2014). *Creative divorce: A new opportunity for growth* [E-book]. New York, NY: Open Road Integrated Media.

Kuo, F. C. (2009). Secrets or no secrets: Confidentiality in couple therapy. *The American Journal of Family Therapy, 37*(5), 351–354.

Kurri, K., & Wahlström, J. (2005). Placement of responsibility and moral reasoning in couple therapy. *Journal of Family Therapy, 27*(4), 352–369.

Kwan, K. (2013). *Crazy rich Asians*. New York, NY: Anchor Books.

Kwee, A. W., & Hoover, D. C. (2008). Theologically informed education about masturbation: A male sexual health perspective. *Journal of Psychology and Theology, 36*(4), 258–269.

Lachance-Grzela, M., & Bouchard, G. (2010). Why do women do the lion's share of housework? A decade of research. *Sex Roles, 63*(11–12), 767–780.

Lambert, M. J. (2010). "Yes, it is time for clinicians to routinely monitor treatment outcome." In B. L. Duncan, S. D. Miller, B. E. Wampold, & M. A. Hubble (Eds.), *The heart and soul of change: Delivering what works in therapy* (2nd ed.) (pp. 239–266). Washington, DC: American Psychological Association.

Lambert, M. J. (2015). Progress feedback and the OQ-system: The past and the future. *Psychotherapy, 52*, 381–390.

Langs, R. (1981). *The technique of psychoanalytic psychotherapy*. Lanham, MD: Roman and Littlefield.

Larson, J. H. (1984). The effect of husband's unemployment on marital and family relations in blue-collar families. *Family Relations, 33*(4), 503–511.

Laska, K. M., Gurman, A. S., & Wampold, B. E. (2014). Expanding the lens of evidence-based practice in psychotherapy: A common factors perspective. *Psychotherapy, 51*(4), 467–481.

Laumann, E. O., Nicolosi, A., Glasser, D. B., Patik, A., Gingell, C., Moreira, E., & Wang, T. (2005). Sexual problems among women and men aged 40-80 y: Prevalence and correlates identified in the Global Study of Sexual Attitudes and Behaviors. *International Journal of Impotence Research, 17*(1), 39–57.

Lazarus, A. A. (2008). Multimodal therapy. In R. J. Corsini & D. Wedding (Eds.), *Current psychotherapies* (8th ed.) (pp. 368–401). Belmont, CA: Thompson.

Lazarus, A. A., Beutler, L. E., & Norcross, J. C. (1992). The future of technical eclecticism. *Psychotherapy: Theory, Research, Practice, Training, 29*(1), 11–20.

Lazarus, A. A., & Messer, S. B. (1991). Does chaos prevail? An exchange on technical eclecticism and assimilative integration. *Journal of Psychotherapy Integration, 1*(2), 143–158.

Lebow, J. (1997). The integrative revolution in couple and family therapy. *Family Process, 36*(1), 1–17.

Lebow, J. L. (2008). Twenty-first century psychotherapies: Couple and family therapy. In J. Lebow (Ed.), *Contemporary approaches to theory and practice* (pp. 307–346). Hoboken, NJ: Wiley.

Lebow, J. L. (2014). *Couple and family therapy: An integrative map*. Washington, DC: American Psychological Association.

Lebow, J. L., Chambers, A. L., Christensen, A., & Johnson, S. M. (2012). Research on the treatment of couple distress. *Journal of Marital and Family Therapy, 38*(1), 145–168.

Lebow, J. L. & Rekart, K. N. (2008). *Integrative couple and family therapy*. In K. Jordan (Ed), *The quick theory reference guide: A resource for expert and novice mental health professionals* (pp. 461–467). Hauppage, NY: Nova Science.

Lederer, W. J. & Jackson, D. D. (1968). *Mirages of marriage*. New York, NY: Norton.

Leslie, L. A., & Southard, A. L. (2009). Thirty years of feminist family therapy: Moving into the mainstream. In S. A. Lloyd, A. L. Few, & K. R. Allen (Eds.), *Handbook of feminist family studies* (pp. 328–337). Thousand Oaks, CA: SAGE.

Levant, R. F. (1995). *Masculinity reconstructed: Changing the rules of manhood-At work, in relationships, and in family life*. New York, NY: Dutton.

Levant, R. F. (2011). Research in the psychology of men and masculinity using the gender role strain paradigm as a framework. *American Psychologist, 66*(8), 765–776.

Levant, R. F., & Pollack, W. S. (Eds.). (1995). *A new psychology of men*. New York, NY: Basic Books.

Levant, R. L. & Richmond, K. (2016). The gender role strain paradigm and masculinity ideologies. In Y. J. Wong & S. R. Wester (Eds.), *APA handbook of men and masculinities* (pp. 23–49). Washington, DC, American Psychological Association.

Levy L. B. & O'Hara, M. W. (2010). Psychotherapeutic interventions for depressed, low-income women: A review of the literature. *Clinical Psychology Review, 30*(8), 934–950.

Lindblad-Goldberg, M., Dore, M., & Stern, L. (1998). *Creating competence from chaos: A comprehensive guide to home-based services*. New York, NY: Norton.

Livingston, G., & Brown, A. (2017, May 18). Intermarriage in the U.S.: 50 years after *Loving v. Virginia. Pew Research Center*. Retrieved from http://www.pewsocialtrends.org/2017/05/18/intermarriage-in-the-u-s-50-years-after-loving-v-virginia/

Lloyd, A., & Hansen J. (2003). The philosophical foundations of professional ethics. In W. O'Donohue & K. E. Ferguson (Eds.), *Handbook of professional ethics for psychologists: Issues, questions, and controversies* (pp. 17-33). Thousand Oaks, CA: SAGE.

Lloyd, S. A. (1987). Conflict in premarital relationships: Differential perceptions of males and females. *Family Relations, 36*(3), 290–294.

Locke, H. J., & Wallace, K. M. (1959). Short marital adjustment and prediction tests: Their reliability and validity. *Marriage and Family Living, 21*(3), 251–255.

Lucas, R. E., Clark, A. E., Georgellis, Y., & Diener, E. (2004). Unemployment alters the set point for life satisfaction. *Psychological Science, 15*(1), 8–13.

Luhmann, M., Weiss, P., Hosoya, G., & Eid, M. (2014). Honey, I got fired! A longitudinal dyadic analysis of the effect of unemployment on life satisfaction in couples. *Journal of Personality and Social Psychology, 107*(1) 163–180.

Mackrill, T. (2010). Goal consensus and collaboration in psychotherapy: An existential rationale. *Journal of Humanistic Psychology, 50*(1), 96 –107.

MacNeil, S., & Byers, E. S. (2009). Role of sexual self-disclosure in the sexual satisfaction of long-term heterosexual couples. *Journal of Sex Research, 46*(1), 3–14.

Madsen, W. C. (2011). Collaborative helping maps: A tool to guide thinking and action in family-centered services. *Family Process, 50*(4), 529–543.

Mahalik, J. R., Good, G. E., & Englar-Carlson, M. (2003). Masculinity scripts, presenting concerns and help-seeking: Implications for practice and training. *Professional Psychology: Research & Practice, 34*(2), 123–131.

Mahlstedt, P. P. (1985). The psychological component of infertility. *Fertility and Sterility, 43*(3), 335–346.

Malcolm, J. (1981). *The impossible profession*. New York, NY: Knopf.

Mark, K. P., Janssen, E., & Milhausen, R. R. (2011). Infidelity in heterosexual couples: Demographic, interpersonal, and personality-related predictors of extradyadic sex. *Archives of Sexual Behavior, 40*(5), 971–982.

Mashkin, K. (1983). Beginning couple therapy. [Unpublished paper]. California Graduate School of Family Therapy, San Rafael, CA.

Mattinson, J. (1988). *Work, love and marriage*. London, UK: Duckworth.

McCarthy, B., & Wald, L. M. (2013). New strategies in assessing, treating, and relapse prevention of extramarital affairs. *Journal of Sex & Marital Therapy, 39*(6), 493–509.

McGoldrick, M., & Carter, B. (2003). Family. In F. Walsh, (Ed), *Normal family processes: Growing diversity and complexity* (pp. 375-398). New York, NY: Guilford.

McGoldrick, M. & Gerson, R. (2008). *Genograms: Assessment and intervention* (3rd ed.). New York, NY: Norton.

McGoldrick, M., Gerson, R., & Shellenberger, S. (1999). *Genograms: Assessment and intervention*. New York, NY: Norton.

McGoldrick, M., Preto, N. A. G., & Carter, B. A. (2015). *The expanding family life cycle: Individual, family, and social perspectives*. Boston, MA: Pearson.

McNulty, J. K., & Russell, V. M. (2016). Forgive and forget, or forgive and regret? Whether forgiveness leads to less or more offending depends on offender agreeableness. *Personality and Social Psychology Bulletin, 42*(5), 616– 631.

Messer, S. B. (Ed.) (2001). Special issue on assimilative integration. *Journal of Psychotherapy Integration, 11*(1), 1–154.

Miller, C. C. (2018, May 5). How same-sex couples divide chores, and what it reveals about modern parenting. *New York Times*. Retrieved from https://www.nytimes.com/2018/05/16/upshot/same-sex-couples-divide-chores-much-more-evenly-until-they-become-parents.html

Miller, R. B., Yorgason, J. B., Sandberg, J. G., & White, M. B. (2003). Problems that couples bring to therapy: A view across the family life cycle. *American Journal of Family Therapy, 31*(5), 395–407.

Miller, S. A., & Byers, E. S. (2008). An exploratory examination of the sexual intervention self-efficacy of clinical psychology graduate students. *Training and Education in Professional Psychology, 2*(3), 137–144.

Miller, W. R., & Rollnick, S. (2013). *Motivational interviewing: Helping people change* (3rd ed.). New York, NY: Guilford.

Minuchin, P., Colapinto, J., & Minuchin, S. (2007). *Working with families of the poor.* New York, NY: Guilford.

Minuchin, S. (1974). *Families and family therapy.* Cambridge, MA: Harvard University Press.

Minuchin, S., & Fishman, N.C. (1981). *Family therapy techniques.* Cambridge, MA: Harvard University Press.

Moller, N. P., & Vossler, A. (2015). Defining infidelity in research and couple counseling: A qualitative study. *Journal of Sex & Marital Therapy, 41*(5), 487–497.

Mollon, P. (2005). The inherent shame of sexuality. *British Journal of Psychotherapy, 22*(2), 167–177.

Moreno, J. L., & Fox, J. (1987). *The essential Moreno: Writings on psychodrama, group method and spontaneity.* New York, NY: Springer.

Moreno, J. L., & Moreno, Z. T. (2011). *Psychodrama* (Vol. 2). London, UK: Northwest Drama Association.

Morgan, M. (2012). How couple therapists work with parenting issues. In A. Balfour, M. Morgan, & C. Vincent (Eds.), *How couple relationships shape our world: Clinical practice, research, and policy Perspectives* (pp. 71–83). London, UK: Karnac Books.

Morgan, R. F. (2006). *The iatrogenic handbook.* Toronto, Canada: IPI.

Morrissette, P. J. (2012). Infidelity and revenge fantasies: An integrative couple therapy approach. *Journal of Couple & Relationship Therapy, 11*(2), 149–164.

Murguia, E., & Díaz, K. (2015). The philosophical foundations of cognitive behavioral therapy: Stoicism, Buddhism, Taoism and existentialism. *Journal of Evidence-Based Psychotherapies, 15*(1), 37–50.

Murphy, C. (2015, June 2). Interfaith marriage. *Pew Research Center.* Retrieved from http://www.pewresearch.org/fact-tank/2015/06/02/interfaith-marriage/

Murphy, M. J. (2017). Feminist couple therapy. In M. D. Reiter & R. J. Chenail (Eds.), *Constructivist, critical, and integrative approaches to couples counseling* (pp. 46–75). New York, NY: Routledge.

Napier, A. (1991). Heroism, men and marriage. *Journal of Marital and Family Therapy, 17*(l), 9–16.

Navarra, R. J. (2018). Systematic addiction treatment in couple and family therapy. In J. Lebow, A. Chambers & D. C. Breunlin (Eds.), *Encyclopedia of couple and family therapy.* San Francisco, CA: Springer Nature.

Neill J.R. & Kniskern, D.P. (1989) *From psyche to system:The evolving therapy if Carl Whitaker.* New York: Guilford.

Nichols, D. (1945). The bells of St. Mary's. *Wikipedia.* https://en.wikipedia.org/wiki/TheBellsof_St._Mary%27s

Nichols, W. C. (1988). *Marital therapy: An alternative approach.* New York, NY: Guilford.

Noah, T. (2016). *Born a crime.* New York, NY: Spiegel and Grau.

Norcross, J. C., & Goldfried, M. R. (Eds.). (2005). *Handbook of psychotherapy integration.* New York, NY: Oxford University Press.

Norsigian, J. and Boston Women's Health Care Collective (2011) *Our Bodies, ourselves.* New York: Atria Books.

Nutt, R. L. (2005). Feminist and contextual work. In M. Harway (Ed.), *Handbook of couples therapy* (pp. 228–249). Hoboken, NJ: Wiley.

Nutt, R. L. (2012). Couples counseling. In H. Sweet & S. Barlow (Eds.), *Gender in the therapy hour: Voices of female clinicians working with men* (pp. 91–102). New York, NY: Routledge.

Nutt, R. L. (2013). In multiple contexts. In C. Z. Enns & E. N. Williams (Eds.), *The Oxford handbook of feminist multicultural counseling psychology* (pp. 358–372). New York, NY: Oxford University Press.

Olson, D. (2011). Faces IV and the circumplex model: Validation study. *Journal of Marital and Family Therapy, 37*(1), 64–80.

O'Neil, J. M. (2008). Summarizing 25 years of research on men's gender role conflict using the Gender Role Conflict scale. *Counseling Psychologist, 36*(3), 358–445.

O'Neil, J. M., Fishman, D. M., & Kinsella-Shaw, M. (1987). Dual-career couples' career transitions and normative dilemmas: A preliminary assessment model. *The Counseling Psychologist, 15*(1), 50–96.

Orlinsky, D.E. & Howard, K.l. (1987) A generic model of psychotherapy. *Journal of Integrative and Eclectic Psychotherapy.6*, 6–26.

Osofsky, H. J., & Osofsky, J. D. (2013). Hurricane Katrina and the Gulf oil spill: Lessons learned. In A.C. McDonald (Ed.), *Child and family advocacy: Bridging the gaps between research, practice, and policy* (pp. 91–105). New York, NY: Springer.

Palazoli, M. S., Boscolo, L., Chechin, G., & Prata, G. (1985). *Paradox and counterparadox: A new model in the therapy of the family in schizophrenic transaction.* Lanham, MD.: Roman and Littlefield.

Palmer, P., Gillette, G. & Shaw,S. (2007) *The ESPN Baseball encyclopedia.* New York: Sterling Publishing.

Papaharitou, S., Nakopoulou, E., Moraitou, M., Tsimtsiou, Z., Konstantinidou, E., & Hatzichristou, D. (2008). Exploring sexual attitudes of students in health professions. *Journal of Sexual Medicine, 5*(6), 1308–1316.

Pappas, S. (2019). APA issues first-ever guidelines for practice with men and boys. *Monitor on Psychology, 50*(1), 34–40.

Park, J., Goode, J., Tompkins, K. A., & Swift, J. K. (2016). Clinical errors that can occur in the treatment decision-making process in psychotherapy. *Psychotherapy, 53*(3), 257–261.

Parker, K. (2012, March 15). *The boomerang generation: Feeling ok about living with mom and dad.* Washington, DC: Pew Research Center.

Parker, L. (1999). Bridging gender issues in couples work. *Journal of Family Psychotherapy, 10*(2), 1–15.

Parker, K., & Wang, W. (2013, March 13). Roles of moms and dads converge as they balance work and family. *The Atlantic.* Retrieved from https://genderedinnovations.stanford.edu/institutions/Modern%20 Parenthood%20%7C%20Pew%20Social%20&%20Demographic%20Trends.pdf

Parton, D. (1974) *Jolene.* https://www.youtube.com/watch?v=1W25foOMkwl

Patterson, C. (1995). Families of the lesbian Baby Boom: Parents' division of labor and children's adjustment. *Developmental Psychology, 31*(1), 115–123.

Patterson, C. J., Sutfin, E. L., & Fulcher, M. (2004). Division of labor among lesbian and heterosexual parenting couples: Correlates of specialized versus shared patterns. *Journal of Adult Development, 11*(3), 179–189.

Patterson, J., Williams, L., Edwards, T. M., Chamow, L., & Grauf-Grounds, C. (2018). *Essential skills in family therapy: From the first interview to termination* (3rd ed.). New York, NY: Guilford.

Patterson, T. (1997). Theoretical unity and technical eclecticism: Pathways to coherence in family therapy. *American Journal of Family Therapy, 25*(2), 97–109.

Patterson, T. & McClanahan, T.M. (1999) *The couple and family clinical documentation sourcebook.* Hoboken, NJ: Wiley.

Patterson, T., & Sexton, T. (2013). Bridging conceptual frameworks: A systemic heuristic for understanding family diversity. *Couple and Family Psychology: Research and Practice, 2*(4), 237–245.

Patterson, T., Shapiro, J. L., & Kelly, S. (2018, August 9). What do clinicians need to know about couple therapy? Teaching beginning courses effectively [Symposium]. Annual Convention of the American Psychological Association, San Francisco, CA.

Pederson, P. B., Lonner, W. J., Draguns, J. G. & Trimble, J. E. (2007). *Counseling across cultures* (6th eed.) Thousand Oaks, CA: SAGE.

Perel, E. (2018). *My story, background and inspirations.* Retrieved from https://www.estherperel.com/my-story

Perls, F. S., Hefferline, R., & Goodman, P. (1951). *Gestalt therapy: Excitement and growth in the human personality.* Gouldsboro, ME: Gestalt Journal Press.

Philpot, C. J., Brooks, G. R., Lusterman, D., & Nutt, R. L. (1997). Women's gender-role stress and changing status. In *Bridging separate gender worlds: Why men and women clash and how therapists can bring them together* (pp. 67–86). Washington, DC: American Psychological Association.

Piaget, J. (1967) *Six psychological studies by Jean Piaget.* New York, NY: Random House.

Pinsof, W. M. (2002). The death of "till death us do part": The transformation of pair-bonding in the 20th century. *Family Process, 41*(2), 135–157.

Piper, W. (1930). *The little engine that Could*. New York, NY: Platt & Munk.

Pittman, F. (1985). Gender myths: When does gender become pathology? *Family Therapy Networker, 9*(6), 25–33.

Pomus, D. & Shulman, M. (1960) *Save the last dance for me* [Video file]. Retrieved from Pomus, D. & Shulman, M. (1960) *Save the last dance for me*. New York: Atlantic records https://www.youtube.com/watch?v=n-XQ26KePUQ.

Pope, K. S., & Keith-Spiegel, P. (2008). A practical approach to boundaries in psychotherapy: Making decisions, bypassing blunders, and mending fences. *Journal of clinical psychology, 64*(5), 638–652.

Price, J. E., & Jones, A. M. (2015). Living through the life-altering loss of a child: A narrative review. *Issues in Comprehensive Pediatric Nursing, 38*(3), 222–240.

Quatman, T. (2015). *An acquired art: Psychodynamic psychotherapy from classroom to clinic*. London, UK: Routledge.

Rappleyea, D. L., Jorgensen, B. L., Taylor, A. C., & Butler, J. L., IV. (2014). Training considerations for MFTs in couple and financial counseling. *American Journal of Family Therapy, 42*(4), 282–292.

Reese-Weber, M. (2015). Intimacy, communication, and aggressive behaviors: Variations by phases of romantic relationship development. *Personal Relationships, 22*(2), 204–215.

Reissing, E. D., & Di Giulio, G. D. (2010). Practicing clinical psychologists' provision of sexual health care services. *Professional Psychology: Research and Practice, 41*(1), 57–63.

Richardson, J. P. (1959) *Running Bear*. Retrieved from https://www.songfacts.com/lyrics/johnny-preston/running-bear

Richardson, M. O. (2008) *The relationship seasons: Navigating the 5 stages of relationships*. Brigham City, UT: Brigham Distributing.

Rider, K. V. (2011). Using a metaphor to help couples rebuild trust after an affair. *Journal of Family Psychotherapy, 22*(4), 344–348.

Rober, P. (2015). The challenge of creating dialogical space for both partners in couple therapy. *Australian and New Zealand Journal of Family Therapy, 36*(1), 105–121.

Roberts, L. J., & Prager, K. J. (2004). Deep intimate connection: Self and intimacy in couple relationships. In D. J. Mashek & A. Aron (Eds.), *Handbook of closeness and intimacy* (pp. 43–61). New York, NY: Routledge.

Rogers, C. R. (1951). *Client-centered therapy: Its current practice, implications, and theory*. Boston, MA: Houghton Mifflin.

Rogers, C. R. (1986). Person-centered Rogers on the development of the person-centered approach. *Person-Centered Review, 1*(3), 257–259.

Rogers, R., & Hammerstein, O. (1949) *Some enchanted evening*. Retrieved from https://www.stlyrics.com/lyrics/southpacific/someenchantedevening.htm

Rojano, R. (2004). The practice of community family therapy. *Family Process, 43*(1), 59–77.

Rollie, S. S., & Duck, S. (2006). Divorce and dissolution of romantic relationships: Stage models and their limitations. In M. A. Fine & J. H. Harvey (Eds.), *Handbook of divorce and relationship dissolution* (pp. 223–241). Mawhah, NJ: Lawrence Erlbaum.

Rovers, M., Kocum, L., Briscoe-Dimock, S., Myers, P. C., Cotnam, S., Henry, T., ... & Sheppard, D. (2011). Choosing a partner of equal differentiation: A new paradigm utilizing similarity and complementarity measures. *Journal of Couple & Relationship Therapy, 6*(3), 1–23.

Russell, V.M., Baker, L.R.,McNulty, J.K. & Overall, N.C. (2018) 'You're forgiven, but don't do it again!' Direct partner regulation buffers the costs of forgiveness. *Journal of Family Psychology, 32*(4), 435–444.

Sarmiento, I. A., & Cardemil, E. V. (2009). Family functioning and depression in low-income Latino couples. *Journal of Marital and Family Therapy, 35*(4), 432–445.

Satir, V. (1967). *Conjoint family therapy* (rev. ed.). Palo Alto, CA: Science and Behavior Books.

Scharff, D. E., & Scharff, J. S. (2004). *Object relations couple therapy*. Lanham, MD: Rowman & Littlefield.

Scharff, D. E., & Scharff, J. S. (Eds.) (2014). *An overview of psychodynamic couple therapy*. London, UK: Karnac.

Scheinkman, M. (2005). Beyond the trauma of betrayal: Reconsidering affairs in couples therapy. *Family Process, 44,* 227–244.

Scher, M. (1990). Effects of gender role incongruities on men's experience as clients in psychotherapy. *Psychotherapy, 27*(3), 322–326.

Schnarch, D. M. (1997/2009). Passionate marriage: Keeping love and intimacy alive in committed relationships. New York, NY: Norton.

Seligman, M.E.P., Rashid,T. & Parks, A.C. (2006) Positive psychotherapy. *American Psychologist, 61,* 774–788.

Seligman, M.E.P., Steen, T.A., Park, N. & Peterson, C. (2005) Positive psychology progress: Empirical validation of interventions. *American Psychologist, 60,* 410–421.

Selvini Palazzoli, M., Boscolo, L., Cecchin, G., & Prata, G. (1978). *Paradox and counterparadox.* New York, NY: Jason Aronson.

Sexton, T. L., Weeks, G. R., & Robbins, M. S. (2003). The future of couple and family therapy. In T. L Sexton, G. R. Weeks & M. S. Robbins (Eds.), *Handbook of family therapy: The science and practice of working with families and couples* (pp. 515–534). New York, NY: Brunner-Routledge.

Shadbolt, C. (2009). Sexuality and shame. *Transactional Analysis Journal, 39*(2), 163–172.

Shapiro, J. L. (1984). A brief outline of a chronological divorce sequence. *Family Therapy, 11*(3), 269–278.

Shapiro, J. L. (1993). *The measure of a man: Becoming the father you wish your father had been.* New York, NY: Delacorte.

Shapiro, J. L. (2010). At the risk of losing our misery. In A. S. Gurman (Ed.), *Clinical casebook of couple therapy* (pp. 300–426). New York, NY: Guilford.

Shapiro, J. L. (2012). *Finding meaning, facing fears: In the autumn of your years.* Berkeley, CA: New Harbinger.

Shapiro, J. L. (2013, February 13). A curmudgeon's valentine's day primer for guys. *Huffington Post.* Retrieved from http://www.huffingtonpost.com/jerrold-shapiro/valentines-day-mens-advice_b_2658191.html

Shapiro, J.L. (2015) Male-bashing in prime time advertising: Implications for understanding the paradox of male empowerment and second class status in certain media. Unpublished paper. Santa Clara University.

Shapiro, J. L. (2016). *Pragmatic existential counseling and psychotherapy: Intimacy, intuition and the search for meaning.* Thousand Oaks, CA: SAGE.

Shapiro, J. L. & Bohart, A. (2014, August 7). How existential and humanistic therapies overlap and differ and some thoughts on proper approaches to a viable evidence base. Paper presentation at annual meeting of the American Psychological Association Washington, DC.

Shapiro, J. L. & Diamond, M. J. (1982). *The psychology of intimacy* (revised ed.). San Francisco, CA: Proseminar.

Shapiro, J. L., Patterson, T., & Fishman, D. (2019, June 6). CBT and existential/humanistic approaches to couple therapy: Convergence, divergence and integration. Presentation at the annual meeting of the Society for Exploration of Psychotherapy Integration. Lisbon, Portugal.

Shapiro, J. L., Peltz, L. S. & Bernadett-Shapiro, S. T. (2019). *Basics of group counseling and psychotherapy: An introductory guide.* San Diego, CA: Cognella.

Shatel, T. (1986, December 14). The unknown Barry Switzer - poverty, tragedy build Oklahoma coach into a winner. *Chicago Tribune.* Retrieved from https://www.chicagotribune.com/news/ct-xpm-1986-12-14-8604030680-story.html

Shepard, D. S., & Harway, M. (2012). Engaging men in couple therapy. New York, NY: Routledge.

Shifren, J. L., Brigitta, U. M., Russo, P. A., Segreti, A., & Johannes, C. B. (2008). Sexual problems and distress in United States women. *Obstetrics & Gynecology, 112*(5), 970–978.

Shostrom, E. L. (1976). *Actualizing therapy: Foundations for a scientific ethic.* San Diego, CA: Edits.

Siegel, J. P. (2010). Good enough therapy: An object relations approach. In A. S. Gurman (Ed.), *Clinical casebook of couple therapy* (pp. 134–152). New York, NY: Guilford.

Siegel, J. P. (2015). Object relations couple therapy. In A. S. Gurman, J. L. Lebow & D. K. Snyder (Eds.), *Clinical handbook of couple therapy* (pp. 224–246). New York, NY: Guilford.

Silverstein, J. L. (1998). Countertransference in marital therapy for infidelity. *Journal of Sex & Marital Therapy, 24*(4), 293–301.

Silverstein, L.B. (2003) Classic texts and early critiques. In: L. B. Silverstein & T. J. Goodrich (Eds); *Feminist family therapy: Empowerment in social context*. American Psychological Association; 2003, 17–35.

Silverstein, L. B., & Brooks, G. (2010). Gender issues in family therapy and couples counseling. In J. C. Chrisler & D. R. McCreary (Eds.), *Handbook of gender research in social and applied psychology* (Vol. 2) (pp. 253–277). New York, NY: Springer.

Slater, S., & Mencher, J. (1991). The lesbian family life cycle: A contextual approach. *American Journal of Orthopsychiatry, 61*(3), 372–375.

Smith-Lovin, L., & Brody, C. (1989). Interruptions in group discussions: The effects of gender and group composition. *American Sociological Review, 54*(3), 424–435.

Smock, P. J. (2004). The wax and wane of marriage: Prospects for marriage in the 21st century. *Journal of Marriage and Family, 66*(4), 966–973.

Snyder, D. A. (2005). *Treating difficult couples* [Video file]. Washington, DC: American Psychological Association.

Snyder, D. K., Heyman, R. E., & Haynes, S. N. (2009). Assessing couples. In J. N. Butcher (Ed.), *Oxford handbook of personality assessment* (pp. 457–485). New York, NY: Oxford University Press.

Snyder, D. K., & Mitchell, A. E. (2008). Affective-reconstructive couple therapy: A pluralistic developmental approach. In A.S. Gurman (Ed.), *Clinical handbook of couple therapy* (4th ed.) (pp. 353–382). New York, NY: Guilford.

Snyder, D. K., Simpson, J., & Hughes, J. N. (2006). *Emotion regulation in couples and families: Pathways to dysfunction and health.* Washington, DC: American Psychological Association.

Snyder, D. K., & Wills, R. M. (1989). Behavioral versus insight-oriented marital therapy: Effects on individual and interspousal functioning. *Journal of Consulting and Clinical Psychology, 57*(1), 39–46.

Spanier, G. B. (1976). Measuring dyadic adjustment: New scales for assessing the quality of marriage and similar dyads. *Journal of Marriage and Family, 38*(1), 15–28.

Sperry, L., Carlson, J., & Peluso, P. R. (2006). *Couples therapy: Integrating theory and technique* (2nd ed.). Denver, CO: Love Publishing.

Sprenkle, D. H., Davis, S. D., & Lebow, J. L. (2009). *Common factors in couple and family therapy.* New York, NY: Guilford.

Spring, J. A., & Spring, M. (1996). *After the affair.* New York, NY: Harper Collins.

Stanton, M., & Welsh, R. K. (2011). *Specialty competencies in couple and family psychology.* London: Oxford University Press.

Stefano, J. D., & Oala, M. (2008). Extramarital affairs: Basic considerations and essential tasks in clinical work. *The Family Journal, 16*(1), 13–19.

Stratton, P., Silver, E., Nascimento, N., McDonnell, Powell, G. & Nowotny, E. (2015) Couple and Family Therapy Outcome Research in the Previous Decade: What Does the Evidence Tell Us? Contemporary Family Therapy.37(1), 1–12.

Stuart, R. B. (1980). *Helping couples change: A social learning approach to marital therapy.* New York, NY: Guilford.

Stuart, R, B. (1987) *Couple's Precounseling Inventory CPCI.* Champaign, IL:Research Press

Stuart, R. B., & Jacobson, B. (1987). *Couple›s pre-counseling inventory: Counselor›s guide; CPCI.* Champaign, IL: Research Associates.

Subotnik, R. (2007). Cyber-infidelity. In P. Peluso (Ed.), *Infidelity: A practitioner's guide to working with couples in crisis* (pp. 169–190). New York, NY: Taylor & Francis.

Sue, D. W., & Sue, D. (2012.) *Counseling the culturally diverse: Theory and practice* (6th ed.). Hoboken, NJ: Wiley.

Sutherland, O., LaMarre, A., Rice, C., Hardt, L., & Le Couteur, A. (2017). New sexism in couple therapy: A discursive analysis. *Family Process, 56*(3), 686–700.

Swift, J. K., Callahan, J. L., & Vollmer, B. M. (2011). Preferences. *Journal of Clinical Psychology, 67*(2), 155–165.

Swift, J. K., & Derthick, A. O. (2013). Increasing hope by addressing clients' outcome expectations. *Psychotherapy, 50*(3), 284–287.

Takefman, J. E., Brender, W., Boivin, J., & Tulandi, T. (1990). Sexual and emotional adjustment of couples undergoing infertility investigation and the effectiveness of preparatory information. *Journal of Psychosomatic Obstetrics and Gynecology, 11*(4), 275–290.

Tannen, D. (1991). *You just don't understand: Women and men in conversation.* New York, NY: Ballantine.

Tillich, P. (1952). *The courage to be.* New Haven, CT: Yale University Press.

Tillich, S. R. (2016, April 22). Practicing peace at home [Video interview]. Retrieved from https://www.youtube.com/watch?v=2zzlmRz1s80

Titelman, P. (2012). *Triangles: Bowen family systems theory perspectives.* New York, NY: Routledge.

Tompkins, K. A., Swift, J. K., & Callahan, J. L. (2013). Working with clients by incorporating their preferences. *Psychotherapy, 50*(3), 279–283.

Tryon, G. S., & Winograd, G. (2011). Goal consensus and collaboration. *Psychotherapy, 48*(1), 50–57.

Tucker, P., & Aron, A. (1993). Passionate love and marital satisfaction at key transition points in the family life cycle. *Journal of Social and Clinical Psychology, 12*(2), 135–147.

United Jewish Committee. (2004). *The national Jewish population survey 2000–2001: Strength, challenge and diversity in the American Jewish population.* New York, NY: Author.

Unger, R. K. (1979). Toward a redefinition of sex and gender. *American Psychologist, 34*(11), 1085–1094.

Ungureanu, I. (2017). Death of a child: Impact on the parents' couple relationship. In J. Fitzgerald (Ed.), *Foundations for couples' therapy: Research for the real world* (pp. 103–111). New York, NY: Routledge.

Vasquez, M. J., Bingham, R. P., & Barnett, J. E. (2008). Psychotherapy termination: Clinical and ethical responsibilities. *Journal of Clinical Psychology, 64,* 653– 665.

Vespa, J. (2017, August 9). A third of young adults live with their parents. *U.S. Census Bureau.* Retrieved from https://www.census.gov/library/stories/2017/08/young-adults.html

Vinokur, A. D., Price, R. H., & Caplan, R. D. (1996). Hard times and hurtful partners: How financial strain affects depression and relationship satisfaction of unemployed persons and their spouses. *Journal of Personality and Social Psychology, 71*(1), 166–179.

Vontress, C. E., & Epp, L. R. (2015). Existential cross-cultural counseling: The courage to be an existential counselor. In K. J. Schneider, J. F. Pierson & J. F. T. Bugental (Eds.), *The handbook of humanistic psychology: Theory, research and practice* (2nd ed.) (pp. 473–491). Thousand Oaks, CA: SAGE.

Vossler, A., & Moller, N. P. (2014). "The relationship past can't be the future": Couple counsellors' experiences of working with infidelity. *Sexual and Relationship Therapy, 29*(4), 424–435.

Wachtel, E. F. (2017) *The heart of couple therapy: Knowing what to do and how to do it.* New York, NY: Guilford.

Wallerstein, J. (2000). *The unexpected legacy of divorce: A 25-year landmark study.* New York, NY: Hyperion.

Walsh, E., & Scheinkman, M. (1989). (Fe)male: The hidden gender dimension in models of family therapy. In M. McGoldrick, C. M. Anderson, & F. Walsh (Eds.), *Women in families: A framework for family therapy* (pp. 16–41). New York, NY: Norton.

Walsh, F. (1982) *Normal Family Process: Growing diversity and complexity.* New York: Guilford.

Walsh, F. (2009). Religion and spirituality in couple and family relations. In J. H. Bray & M. Stanton (Eds.), *Wiley-Blackwell handbook of family psychology* (pp. 600–612). Hoboken, NJ: Wiley.

Walters, M., Carter, B., Papp, P., & Silverstein, O. (1991). *The invisible web: Gender patterns in family relationships.* New York, NY: Guilford.

Wampold, B. E. (2001). The great psychotherapy debate: Models, methods, and findings. Mahwah, NJ: Erlbaum.

Wampold, B. E., Mondin, G. W., Moody, M., Stich, F., Benson, K., & Ahn, H. (1997). A meta-analysis of outcome studies comparing bona fide psychotherapies: Empirically, "all must have prizes." *Psychological Bulletin, 122*(3), 203–215.

Wang, W. (2015, June 12). Interracial marriage: Who is "marrying out"?. *Pew Research Center.* Retrieved from http://www.pewresearch.org/fact-tank/2015/06/12/interracial-marriage-who-is-marrying-out/

Ward, R., & Spitze, G. (2007). Nest-leaving and co-residence by young adult children: The role of family relations. *Research on Aging, 29*(3), 257–277.

Watzlawick, P., Bevelas, J. H., & Jackson, D. D. (1967). Pragmatics of human communication: A study of interactional patterns, pathologies, and paradoxes. New York, NY: Norton.

Watzlawick, P., Weakland, J. H., & Fisch, R. (1974). *Change: Principles of problem formation and problem resolution.* New York, NY: Norton.

Weakland, J. (1990). Myths about brief therapy: Myths of brief therapy. In J. Zeig & S. Gilligan (Eds.), *Brief therapy: Myths, methods, and metaphors* (pp. 100–107). New York, NY: Brunner/Mazel.

Weeks, G. R., & L'Abate, L. (1982). *Paradoxical psychotherapy: Theory and practice with individuals, couples, and families.* New York, NY: Brunner/ Mazel.

Weeks, G. R., Odell, M., & Methven, S. (2005) *If only I had known: Avoiding common mistakes in couple therapy.* New York, NY: Norton.

Weil, E. (2012, March 2). Does couple therapy work? *New York Times.* Retrieved from https://www.nytimes.com/2012/03/04/fashion/couples-therapists-confront-the-stresses-of-their-field.html

Weingarten, K. (1990). A systemic perspective on the opening of a therapeutic encounter. In R. Chasin, H. Grunebaum, & M. Herzig (Eds.), *One couple: Four realities: Multiple perspectives on couple therapy* (pp. 145–170). New York, NY: Guilford.

Weiss, R. (1980). Strategic behavioral marital therapy: Toward a model for assessment and intervention. In J. P. Vincent (Ed.), *Advances in family assessment and theory, Vol. 1* (pp. 229–271). Greenwich, CT: JAI Press.

Weissberg, R. P., Kumpfer, K. L., & Seligman, M. E. P. (2003). Prevention that works for children and youth: An introduction. *American Psychologist, 58*(6–7), 425–432.

Werner, P. D., Green, R. J., Greenberg, J., Browne, T. L., & McKenna, T. E. (2001). Beyond enmeshment: Evidence for the independence of intrusiveness and closeness—caregiving in married couples. *Journal of Marital and Family Therapy, 27*(4), 459–471.

Werner-Wilson, R. J., Price, S. J., Zimmerman, T. S., & Murphy, M. J. (1997). Client gender as a process variable in marriage and family therapy: Are women clients interrupted more than men clients? *Journal of Family Psychology, 11*(3), 373–377.

West, C., & Zimmerman, D. H. (1983). Small insults: A study of interruptions in cross-sex conversations between unacquainted persons. In B. Thome, C. Kramarae, & N. Henley (Eds.), *Language, gender and society* (pp. 103–117). Rowley, MA: Newbury House.

Whipple, V. (1996). Developing and identity as a feminist family therapist: Implications for training. *Journal of Marital and Family Therapy, 22*(3), 381–396.

Whisman, M. A., Dixon, A. E., & Johnson, B. (1997). Therapists' perspectives of couple problem and treatment issues in couple therapy. *Journal of Family Psychology, 11*(3), 361–366.

Whitaker, C. (1988, April 5). Meeting with the couple [Invited address]. Santa Clara University. Santa Clara, CA.

Whitaker, C. (1989). *Midnight musings of a family therapist.* New York, NY: Norton.

Whitaker, C. A., & Bumberry, W. A. (1988). *Dancing with the family: A symbolic-experiential approach.* Levitown, PA: Brunner/Mazel.

Whitaker, C. A., & Keith, D.V. (1981). Symbolic-experiential family therapy. In A. S Gurman & D. P. Kniskern, *Handbook of family therapy* (pp. 188–225). New York, NY: Brunner/Mazel.

Whitbourne, S. K. (2012). 5 principles of effective couples therapy. *Psychology Today.* Retrieved from https://www.psychologytoday.com/us/blog/fulfillment-any-age/201203/5-principles-effective-couples-therapy

Wile, D. B. (1992). *Couple therapy: A nontraditional approach.* Hoboken, NJ: Wiley.

Wile, D. B. (2006). *Psychotherapy live: Session 9—Dan Wile, couples.* San Francisco, CA: CIIS.

Winters, J., Fals-Stewart, W., O'Farrell, T. J., Birchler, G. R. & Kelley, M. L. (2002). Behavioral couples therapy for female substance-abusing patients: Effects on substance use and relationship adjustment. *Journal of Consulting and Clinical Psychology, 70*(2), 344–355.

Wiseman, H., Tishby, O., & Barber, J. P. (2012). Collaboration in psychodynamic psychotherapy. *Journal of Clinical Psychology, 68*(2), 136–145.

Witte, T. H., & Mulla, M. M. (2012). Social norms for intimate partner violence in situations involving victim infidelity. *Journal of Interpersonal Violence, 27*(17), 3389–3404.

Wood, N. D., & Crawford, C. B. (2012). A visual method for couple assessment, therapy progress, and identifying clinically significant change. *Journal of Couple & Relationship Therapy, 11*(2), 165–180.

Worthington, E. L., Jr. (1993). Psychotherapy and religious values: An update. In E. L. Worthington, Jr. (Ed.), *Psychotherapy and religious values* (pp. 127–144). Grand Rapids, MI: Baker Book House.

Wright, J. P. (2019, February 4). Twelve scholars respond to the APA's Guidance for Treating Men and Boys. *Quillette Magazine*. Retrieved from https://quillette.com/2019/02/04/psychologists-respond-to-the-apas-guidance-for-treating-men-and-boys/

Zell, E., Krizen, Z., & Teeter, S. R. (2015). Evaluating gender similarities and differences using metasynthesis. *American Psychologist, 70*(1), 10–20.

Zenger, J. & Folkman, J. (2013). The ideal praise-to-criticism ratio. *Gottman Institute.* Retrieved from https://www.gottman.com/blog/the-workplace-the-ideal-praise-to-criticism-ratio/

Zuckerman, E. L., & Kolmes, K. (2017). *The paper office for the digital age.* New York, NY: Guilford.

Zunin, L., & Zunin, N. (1972). *Contact: The first four sessions.* New York, NY: Ballentine.

Index

male unemployment, 313–314
Marital Satisfaction Inventory, 325
marital therapy, 78. *See also* couple therapy
match, 148–149
meeting. *See* initial meeting
men, 297–298, 317
mental health ethics, 20–21
metaphors, 268–270, 306–312
middle stage of family transition, 97
minimal personal experience, 253–254
miracle question, 167–168
miscommunication, 6–7. *See also* communication
money, 256–257
motivational interviewing, 57
multicultural complications, 258–259
multiple relationships, 86–87. *See also* relationships
myths, intimacy, 42–49
  all-or-none myth, 45–46
  beauty, 46
  case study, 44–45
  differences in intimacy, 48–49
  enchanting fairytale, 43–44
  finding and beginning, 44–46
  intimate paradox, 47–48
  intimate partner, 44
  maintenance and development of, 48–49
  nature of intimacy, 43–44
  responsibility, freedom and security, 46–47
  sexual, 43
  soul mate, 44
  strife, 43

N
negentropy, 54
neurolinguistic programming, 311
new start, 86–89
nights. *See* date nights
nonlinear (intuitive) sources of data, 262–271
  auditory imagery, 267–268
  feelings (kinesthetic imagery), 263–266
  metaphors, 268–270
  stories, 270–271
  symbols, 268
  therapeutic intuition, 262–263
  visual imagery, 266–267
normalizing, 181–183
nurturance and assertiveness, 286–287

O
one-night stand(s), 107
one subject at a time, 298
open expectations, 299
orchestrator, 159
orchestrator skills, 159
outside relationship, 74–75

P
pacing skills, 163
pair bonding, 58
paradoxical interventions, 217–220
parallel development, myth, 48–49
parenting, 178, 181–182
perception, 57
personality, 50
personal relationship, 252–259
pitfalls and errors, 34–35
positive psychology, 304
power differentials and gender, 287–290
pragmatism and rationalism, 322
pregnancy. *See* unwanted pregnancy
premature terminations, 244–246. *See also* dissolution and divorce; termination
pre-treatment
  overview, 122
pre-treatment phase, 122–154. *See also* treatment goals and process
  after the session, 153
  appointment-making, 123–126
  assessment tools, 141
  building rapport, 137–139
  clarifying goals, 139–140
  emotional assessment, 146–147
  history, 144–145
  initial meeting, 127–151
  match, 148–149
  referrals, 123, 149–150
  relationship history, 147–148
  shared plan of action, 152
  structure, 149–151
  treatment planning, 153–154
preventative guidelines and behaviors, 230–231
preventative rituals, 228–232
privacy, 31
privilege, 31
problems, 9–10, 223–226
problem-solving, 7, 56–57, 220, 233
processing systems, 261–271
prognosis after affairs, 80–81

programming, 311
promoting couple strengths, 9
property losses, 114–115
protect and provide, 312–315
psychoeducation, 176–184
  arguing, 176–177
  bibliotherapy, 180–181
  expectations and actual experience, 177
  extended family, 178
  family-of-origin, 178
  infertility, 179
  in-law, 178
  normalizing, 181–183
  parenting, 178
  reframing, 183–184
  transition to parenthood, 178–179
  unwanted pregnancy, 179
psychology. *See* positive psychology
psychopathology, 35

Q
quid pro quo, 57

R
racism, 201–202
rational emotive behavior therapy (REBT), 324
rationale to be apart, 75–76
rationalism and pragmatism, 322
readjustments, 92–93
reassurance, 243
record keeping, 35
referrals, 123, 149–150, 246–248
reframing, 183–184
relational aspect, 5–6
relationships, 64–90
  altering views of, 8
  committed, 59–60
  cycles, 66–71
  dissolution, 72–90
  divorce, 72–90
  fiduciary, 30
  history, 147–148
  inappropriate dual, 35
  intimacy committed in, 59–60
  love, 66
  overview, 64–65
  personal, 252–259
  primacy, 76–81
  stability in, 54–59
  structural problems in, 187–189
  trajectory, 93–100
relationships cycles, 66–71
  communication breaks, 69–71
  emotional attraction and desire, 68–69